PENNSYLVANIA'S DELAWARE DIVISION CANAL

Sixty Miles of Euphoria and Frustration

Albright G. Zimmerman

Published by Canal History and Technology Press
National Canal Museum
Hugh Moore Historical Park and Museums, Inc.
30 Centre Square
Easton PA 18042-7743

Except where otherwise credited, the illustrations in this book came from the archives of the National Canal Museum. Most of them are from the Pennsylvania Canal Society collection, which is held by the National Canal Museum.

ISBN 0-930973-26-7

Library of Congress Control Number: 2002113780

Publication of Pennsylvania's Delaware Division Canal: Sixty Miles of Euphoria and Frustration has been supported by a donation from Friends of the Delaware Canal.

Cover photographs: Front: Family on a canal boat passing south through New Hope in about 1895. Back: Francis Palmer photograph of Lock 14 below Point Pleasant in 1930; a group at Uhlerstown on a Sunday (Raymond E. Holland Regional and Industrial History Collection).

Canal History and Technology Press

National Canal Museum
Hugh Moore Historical Park and Museums, Inc.
30 Centre Square, Easton, PA 18042-7743

$\backsim$ CONTENTS $\backsim$

∼ FOREWORD ∼

I have known the Delaware Canal for over four decades. It has been my hobby and my passion for as long as I have lived along its banks. In the years I spent researching state and company records, reading old newspapers and other journals, and of personal involvement in organizations devoted to this waterway, I have compiled and distilled vast amounts of material related to the Delaware Canal. This has been the basis for several academic papers and now, at the urging of my wife and others who recognize the value of these many years of research, I have put much of it into this book so others can share my knowledge.

Academic historians may call this work pedestrian because of its many-faceted approach that attempts to show the whole picture, while they may prefer the deductive use of selected aspects of the canal's history in order to develop an ideological or methodological approach. My publisher and I, on the other hand, hope that this work will give the broadest picture of the history of the canal—political, economic, and technological—while at the same time exploring the social environment and the human element. Unfortunately it won't satisfy the methodological demands of too many in the historical fraternity who want to find an exploited class or sociologically or psychologically deprived or traumatized elements of a population. Of course, historians are limited by their sources and can in actuality only make conjectures as to motives and values based on circumstantial evidence. These conjectures, from my viewpoint, can best be judged if the author is unencumbered with ideological preconceptions.

I have sought to see the canal, particularly life on the canal, through the eyes of, and using the values of, those involved at all levels of its operations. I am particularly fortunate that there are still alive a fast-diminishing few who worked on and who lived along the canal prior to its closing in 1931. Their recollections, and the oral history tapes made by others recently deceased, have helped to obtain a feel of the positives and negatives of what was, in our terms, "child labor."

What follows will, I hope, give the reader a total picture of the canal, as close to the realities of the canal and its life styles as the number of pages and the supply of sources permit.

Albright "Zip" Zimmerman
Yardley, Pennsylvania, 2000

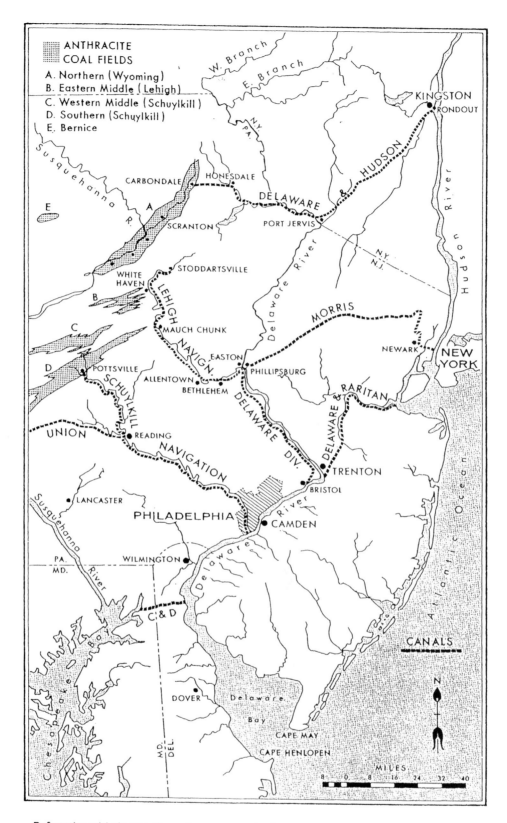

ANTHRACITE
COAL FIELDS
A. Northern (Wyoming)
B. Eastern Middle (Lehigh)
C. Western Middle (Schuylkill)
D. Southern (Schuylkill)
E. Bernice

Before the mid-nineteenth century a network of canals had been dug to carry anthracite from Pennsylvania's anthracite regions to markets. Anthracite became a vitally important fuel for the industrial revolution; it was used not only to power steam engines in factories and on farms, it was also used by families to heat homes throughout the northeastern United States. The Delaware Canal remained in operation as a towpath canal longer than others because no rail line was constructed along the Pennsylvania side of the Delaware River that could serve coal dealers in towns from Easton to Bristol.

∼ PROLOGUE ∼

In the beginning was the River Delaware, one of Nature's pathways into the interior where the Appalachian region of northeastern Pennsylvania was endowed with extensive beds of anthracite coal, one of the finest combustible materials ever created in nature. Together, river and coal constituted the two aspects of an enigma awaiting a fortuitous union.

The anthracite was found in the hills near the banks of the upper reaches of the Delaware's two major tributaries, the Lehigh and the Schuylkill. These rivers flowed through vast forests of white pine, spruce, and hemlock that were being harvested long before exploitation of the anthracite deposits began.

In historic times, a one-way transportation pattern of lumber rafts and coal arks slowly developed on the river and its tributaries. By the 1750s it was not uncommon for rafts of cut timber to pass down these rivers, following the current to Philadelphia. Ingenious Durham boats that would float downstream and could then, with several tons of cargo, be laboriously poled back upstream, plied the river at the same time.

The beds of "stone-coal" in the upper Lehigh and Schuylkill valleys lay untouched until their discovery in the late years of the eighteenth century. Moravian missionaries as early as the 1750s knew of the coal, but there was little need to experiment with this mineral fuel until the 1790s, when the increasing shortage of available wood resources encouraged Philadelphia merchants and manufacturers to look for alternative fuels. It was not until the period after the War of 1812 that experimenters discovered how to burn anthracite in stoves and furnaces. Following marketing strategies that convinced a doubting public of its utility, a demand was created. And then came the challenge, how to get the "black diamonds" cheaply and efficiently and in sufficient quantity to market to solve America's "First Energy Crisis", the result of the fast-growing urban centers that taxed the existing timber stands as a source of fuel.[1]

In 1825, New York completed its Erie Canal, which reached out to the growing regions beyond the Appalachians and appeared to threaten the economic viability of the other eastern cities as now they had less accessibility to growing western markets and resources. Pennsylvania responded in 1824, 1825 and 1826 when its appointed commissioners made surveys that would finally result in a hybrid system of state-owned canals and railroads. This was the so-called "Mainline" from Philadelphia to Pittsburgh.

Internal improvements were expensive, and regional interests politicized the state's legislators for and against the works.[2] In response, and to obtain votes and gather support from the citizenry of other regions, promoters of internal improvements designed the so-called "lateral" canals, those north from Pittsburgh to Lake Erie, north up the Susquehanna to the New York border, and also north up the Delaware.

In the meantime, thanks to entrepreneurs Josiah White and Erskine Hazard, the anthracite mines above Mauch Chunk (today's Jim Thorpe) had been opened and the Lehigh and Delaware rivers provided the avenue to market. As early as 1814, arks—flat-bottomed plank boats—were constructed by the Lehigh Coal Mine Company, loaded with coal, and dispatched south on the spring freshet.[3] Upon reaching their markets the arks were broken up and sold, the crew gathering up the metal hardware and hiking back by land. In 1819, White and Hazard started to improve the Lehigh with a series of "bear trap" locks that enhanced one-way passage of the coal arks. In 1827, they constructed the famous switchback, a gravity railroad from Summit Hill. It ran nine miles from the mines at Summit Hill to the loading docks on the Lehigh River at Mauch Chunk. During that same year they began the conversion of their navigation system to its ultimate configuration, which combined slackwater pools with canal sections.[4]

Prologue

The Commonwealth of Pennsylvania was not so unconcerned with internal improvements as many accounts would have us believe. As early as 1771, the legislature had declared the rivers Delaware and Lehigh, along with the "Neshemiy" and the "Lechawaxin," to be common highways and named a board of commissioners with the right to apply a "large sume of money" that had been subscribed by many persons for the improvement of navigation on these waterways. The commissioners were empowered to remove obstructions and "make set up ... dams, pens for water-locks" or other improvements.[5]

The river would remain an avenue of trade down into the twentieth century, particularly for lumber. In the spring of 1829 it was estimated that a thousand lumber rafts descended the Delaware. This equated to "fifty millions of feet of lumber," not an inconsiderable vested interest.[6]

An agreement with the State of New Jersey negotiated in 1783 guaranteed that the Delaware would be kept free for navigation wherever that river was the common boundary between the two states.[7] An act of 1789 called for an appropriation of £5,000 annually to improve navigation across the state. The Delaware was specifically included in this act, which called for the appointment of commissioners who were charged with, among other things, "marking places where locks and canals are necessary."[8] In 1790, a Society for Promoting the Improvement of Roads and Inland Navigation was founded with Robert Morris, financier of the Revolution, as president. At least partially as a result of their efforts an act of 1791 provided monies, including £3,500 specifically for the Delaware north of the falls at Trenton, for the improvement of navigation on certain rivers.[9] A less-than-exhaustive examination of the minutes of the assembly and the senate reveals that an act was passed and signed by Governor Snyder on March 13, 1817, "To improve the navigation of the river Delaware." Ten thousand dollars was appropriated for the purpose; one of the three commissioners appointed was Lewis S. Coryell.[10]

In 1825, several petitions were received in the Pennsylvania legislature on behalf of the plan of Edward Clarke of Philadelphia to "improve the navigation of the river Delaware from tide water upwards." A company to improve navigation on the Lehigh was chartered in 1814, and the act was passed again in 1816. According to an 1822 senate report of Mr. Raguet, "Nothing was ever done by this company."[11]

On March 20, 1818, an act was passed authorizing "Messers. White and Co." to improve the navigation of the river Lehigh. On August 10 of the same year, with the required amount of stock subscribed, the unincorporated Lehigh Navigation Company was organized. On February 13, 1822, the navigation company was combined with the Lehigh Coal Company and the now-incorporated Lehigh Coal and Navigation Company came into existence.[12] During 1823 and 1824 the company, henceforth to be referred to as the LC&N, petitioned the state with a plan, which, according to Josiah White, was not to create a canal but rather "to make a channel and slack-water navigation."

Over the next several years petitions were submitted to the legislature on behalf of White and Hazard's proposals to improve the navigation of the Delaware. Their plan did not draw universal support, however, and there were petitions from inhabitants of Stroudsburg and Lower Mount Bethel townships "against any interference of the Lehigh Coal and Navigation company in the navigation of the said river Delaware."[13] White later speculated that the

> Law for Improving the Delaware by Canal, was brought by Col¹ Erie of Easton, who was then a Senator. We believed brought about to oppose our Cº procuring the Law for makᵍ the River a Slackwater navigation, as that Borough was allways opposed to us.[14]

Even earlier, according to Josiah White, during the years 1822–1823 the LC&N had contributed some $4,000 or $5,000 to improve the Delaware. Actually, the LC&N had supplemented state appropriations that had been exhausted.[15]

By the middle of the decade of the 1820s, statewide interest in a cross-state navigation system took center stage. The Delaware was of secondary importance as a major transportation route, except when it was considered as a portion of a possible route to the west. Interest in the Delaware was revived only when a political plum was needed to seduce the needed votes from the eastern part of the state to support the proposed main line system across the state.

DELAWARE NAVIGATION

THE above is a sketch of the plan proposed for the improvement of the river Delaware, by the Lehigh Coal and Navigation Company.

No. 1 represents the kind of improvement to be adopted at all the falls where the water can be made three feet deep by means of wing dams (or by sinking the bottom of the river), to confine it in an open channel, without making it too rapid for a boat to ascend by the power of a steam-engine,—all such channels to be improved by the company and kept in repair at their expense, and to be used by the public *free of toll*.

No. 2 is an example of the improvement of a fall, where the water would be too rapid for the ascent of a steamboat by the power of her engines. In all such cases, a lock, thirty feet wide and one hundred and thirty feet long, would be made at one of the shores, and all boats, etc., *using the lock*, either in ascending or descending, would be subject to toll. But at these places the present channels would be left uninterrupted and free for the passage of boats without toll. The work to be conducted in such a manner that the use of the river by boats and rafts, on the present plan, shall not be interrupted during any stage of its progress. Openings can be left in the wings near the shore to admit the upward passage of the Durham boats.

NOTE:—The above plan guarantees the continuance forever of a free open channel, improved and kept in repair at the expense of the company, except the channels in the same fall with the lock, which will be left open as they now are. No part of the improvement overflows or injures private property. The mills at present erected on the river will be secured in their titles, and finally, the river will be made capable of transporting a greater amount of tonnage than any canal now in existence.

From the inspection of the map of Pennsylvania, it will be evident that the improvement of the Delaware must be a matter of deep interest to nearly one-half of the population of this State and of New York, as canals to connect it with the Susquehanna and with the New York Grand Canal at the Seneca River are quite practicable, and this route would have the advantage of being the shortest, and of affording, upon arrival in Easton, the choice of the two best markets in the country,—that of Philadelphia, by the Delaware, and that of New York, by the Jersey Canal.

The Lehigh Coal and Navigation Company have proposed this plan, and are desirous it should be adopted, either by the State on its own account, or by the borough of Easton, or by a new incorporation; or if none of these are willing to undertake the task, they ask the liberty of doing it themselves. If the State would undertake it, and make the *locks free*, the Lehigh Company would contribute handsomely to the work.

Drawing and description of White and Hazard's proposal to improve the Delaware River from Richard Richardson's 1873 Memoir of Josiah White, pages 131–133.

PART ONE
1824–1931

~ CHAPTER I ~

First Years of the Delaware Canal

BEGINNINGS

As early as 1824 the state of Pennsylvania had appointed canal commissioners. Over the next several years they initiated a series of surveys to locate a satisfactory route for an east-west artificial waterway. Their surveys included both the Susquehanna Valley and the routes from Pittsburgh north to Lake Erie.

Construction on the so-called "Main Line" started in 1826. However, on March 17, 1827, *Niles Register* reported that on March 2, a Mr. Lehman had offered a report in the state assembly, accompanied by a bill that called for the construction of most of the so-called lateral canals, including one up the Delaware.[1]

William Lehman and other supporters of the costly canal movement wanted the support of the representatives from northeastern Pennsylvania.[2] The Delaware Division Canal first appears in the official records in Section 8 of the Act of April 9, 1827, which called for an examination to be made "during the insuing summer" of the Delaware valley from "Philadelphia, or Bristol, or any intermediate point between Bristol and the height of navigation [Morrisville/Trenton] to Carpenter's Point [just north of Port Jervis, NY]."[3] The proposed Delaware Division Canal would be a separate entity that would not connect with any other part of the state canal system.

Three surveys were conducted in 1827. A party was assembled under the direction of Henry Sargent, one of the many engineers the state would recruit out of New York.[4] The survey from Easton to Bristol commenced on July 9 and was "run on account of accuracy and dispatch with two levels." The survey was accepted, and almost immediately a more detailed examination commenced on September 13 from Bristol to Taylor's Ferry (Washington Crossing).

On the first survey T.G. Kennedy was listed as an "assistant engineer and draftsman." By the second survey he had been appointed superintendent for the Delaware Division, a position he would hold until the end of 1830. A third survey commenced on September 13, when Sargent apparently left Kennedy in charge as he led his survey team north to examine the route from Easton north to Carpenter's Point on the Delaware and Hudson Canal, a short distance upstream of today's Port Jervis.[5]

In 1828, Colonel D.B. Douglass, who "stands second to no one as an Engineer in the U.S. West Point Institution," contracted to make a second survey north from Easton to Carpenter's Point, a survey that was included in the Canal Commissioners' Report for 1828–1829.[6] Subsequently, there is no evidence of any continued interest in this canal segment, possibly because there was little interest in providing an avenue whereby Pennsylvania anthracite could be siphoned north, away from Philadelphia, to add to the stream that was already flowing eastward from the coal fields to New York's Hudson River via the Delaware and Hudson Canal.

Sargent's report, based on his first survey, called for a 56-mile canal south from Easton through Morrisville to Tullytown or for a 60-mile canal terminating at Bristol. He estimated that a canal ending in Tullytown would cost $669,898, or $11,962 per mile. The Bristol option would cost $686,596, or $11,443 per mile.

Before any contracts could be let, the route had to be determined. The record seems to indicate that the greatest issue was the location of the southern terminus for the canal. Van Hart's Creek near Tullytown had its supporters—but their arguments were challenged by proponents of a terminus in Bristol Borough.

The right to petition was certainly much used in that day and the canal commissioners' records contain many petitions as well as supporting depositions taken from various commanders of river sloops and other watermen. Presumably these were convincing, as they pointed out the hazards of navigation north of Bristol. According to 57-year-old sloop Captain John Johnson—who had navigated the river for upwards of 30 years—there were few sloop captains who would hazard to navigate these waters. He noted that the "Hollow-bar … has increased within 6 or 7 years both in extent across the River and in highth." In addition, a "large body of Flats puts out from Burlington-island opposite the Hollow-Bar making the channel only 100 or 120 yards wide." From here north he listed various additional obstructions. He had even known of "two Durham boats" running up on Kirk's bar. It was also pointed out that the state would have to compensate a Mr. Headley for the destruction of his saw mill on Van Hart's Creek, compensation that was estimated to be "not less than 5000 dollars."

On September 3 the citizenry of Easton submitted their petition, which called for "a continuation of the Canal to the City of Philadelphia … But if it should not be so extended we are of the opinion that it ought to terminate at Bristol."[7]

Another proposal came from the citizens of Newtown, Pennsylvania, calling for a route that would leave the Delaware River three miles south of New Hope by Knowles (?) Creek, then across country to follow Newtown Creek to its junction with the Neshaminy and from there on to the Delaware. The route would, its supporters pointed out, go through the most populous portions of Bucks County, through Newtown, Bridgetown, Attlesborough (Langhorne), Hulmeville, and Newport. Other advantages would be that the terminus was closer to Philadelphia and that the route was adjacent to the stone quarries and mills along the Neshaminy. It seems that this option was related to the Neshaminy Lock Navigation Company, originally incorporated in 1814 but reincorporated in 1832 with Thomas G. Kennedy as one of the principal incorporators.[8]

These efforts were ineffectual, for the canal would terminate at Mill Creek in Bristol rather than at Van Hart's Creek or Newtown. The hazards referred to north of Bristol are the reasons one finds references to a New Jersey group that was seeking to construct a canal across Pennsbury Manor. These were the supporters of the various Delaware and Raritan Canal proposals, who were seeking to avoid some of the obstacles in the river between their Bordentown terminus and more open water at Bristol. An informal proposal had been made in 1827 by J.N. Simpson of New Jersey on behalf of the Delaware and Raritan Canal. Presumably, he was proposing an outlet into the river and entry into the projected D&R feeder for passage on the Jersey side, down the Delaware from a spot near Easton to Trenton or Bordentown. He then proposed a Pennsylvania canal across "Pennsborough Manor" which would be desirable "were it only to obviate the obstructions in the Delaware" between Trenton and Bordentown. He seems to document that there was some opposition to the canal as planned, created by a "Legislature, influenced by the selfish views of the Philadelphia Merchants." Easton, he proposed, would be very happy with a connection with New York. Pennsylvania, he noted, had been less than fair in its treatment of New Jersey.[9]

Sargent spelled out the details. First, he noted, "it was most important to determine the most eligible mode of crossing the Lehigh, and making use of that stream as a feeder."

It must be remembered that the Lehigh Coal and Navigation Company was just commencing construction of its canal. Sargent's greater concern was connecting with the Delaware and Hudson Canal—then under construction—north up the Delaware from Easton, not in a connection with a Lehigh River canal. He anticipated problems in the future for this route:

> [the] most important difficulty is in passing bluff rocky hills, which in many places form the shore of the river: making it necessary to raise embankments from the water's edge, which must be protected by a wall, varying in height from fifteen to twenty feet.

Sargent also called for locks to be constructed "100 feet clear in length and 14 feet width." [10] Locks of this size would allow the passage of boats carrying approximately one hundred tons of anthracite. They would, however, be smaller than those being built on the Lehigh Navigation, which were larger and designed to allow the passage of boats that could carry up to two hundred tons of anthracite.

Surveys, Designs and Start of Construction

Each member of the Pennsylvania Board of Canal Commissioners served as an acting superintendent on one of the divisions of the state works, and the board held its meetings at different locations across the state. When the board found their manpower was too thin, acting superintendents were named. Usually the major concern of business at a commissioners' meeting would be the nearby works.

The concerns for the Delaware Division of the Pennsylvania Canal were most often addressed when the board was meeting in Bristol or in Philadelphia where, for example, the members assembled on September 10, 1827. The minutes of that session reveal that the board, using language almost identical to that of the enabling law, called for the letting of contracts if "after a suitable examination by competent Engineers" the canal appeared to be feasible between "a point at Bristol and a point at or near the borough of Easton." The commissioners estimated that the canal to Easton could be completed at a cost of $12,000 per mile and that the first 18 miles of canal "beginning at or near the mouth of Mill Creek in the said borough of Bristol, and extending thence" to Taylorsville (today's Washington Crossing) could be completed for under $100,000. They also directed that the dimensions of the canal prism should be

> Forty feet on the water line; twenty-five feet at bottom, and with five feet depth of water; that the locks shall be eleven feet in width and one hundred feet within the chamber. [11]

The next day, Thomas G. Kennedy, [12] one-time sheriff of Pennsylvania's Bucks County, was appointed a "Superintendent for the Delaware Division … with the same powers, duties and responsibilities as an acting commissioner." [13]

Superintendent Kennedy, in his report to the board, announced that he had placed advertisements in six newspapers, two each in Philadelphia, Easton, and Doylestown, calling for bids on the first 18 miles or on 35 sections of one-half mile each. He appended a chart indicating the details and noted that by November 5, the date of his report, many of the contractors were already at work. The 60-mile canal was divided for purposes of letting contracts into 118 half-mile sections, starting with section No. 1 at Bristol and ending with No. 118 at Williamstown (sometimes called Williams Port) or South Easton. [14]

On September 10, 1827, engineer Sargent submitted estimates for an extension south from Bristol to Kensington (in Philadelphia). The 17½-mile canal, including four aqueducts and a basin at the southern terminus, was estimated at $200,799, or $11,474 per mile. [15] In 1832, J. Edgar Thompson, at the time an assistant engineer on the Delaware Division, submitted a map and a survey that detailed a canal south from Bristol to Kensington in Philadelphia. [16]

Locks on the Delaware Division Canal

Long-term negative economic effects resulted from the dimensions of locks on the Delaware Division Canal. The Lehigh Coal and Navigation Company had started constructing its canal about the same time as the state started constructing its Delaware Division, yet despite appeals from the Lehigh company the dimensions on the Delaware Canal were determined independently. The influence of William Strickland, engineer and architect on the early planning of Pennsylvania's internal improvements, cannot be overemphasized. In 1825 Strickland, along with apprentice engineer Samuel Kneass, was sent to England by the Pennsylvania Society for the Promotion of Internal Improvements. As per his instructions, he reported back on canals, tunnels, railroads, and iron manufacture. His reports, which included 75 beautiful engineering drawings, were published in a superb example of the bookmaker's art in 1826. In this volume he wrote:

The locks constructed on the Delaware Division were 11 feet wide and 95 feet in length. These dimensions forever imposed a serious constraint on the Lehigh Navigation, as the Lehigh Coal and Navigation Company operated the Lehigh Navigation and the Delaware Division Canal as one entity, carrying anthracite from the coal fields of the upper Lehigh River valley. Other operators of canal boats paid tolls to use the Lehigh-Delaware canal system. In this photograph of Lock 12 at Lumberville, one of the other problems in the design of the canal is evident: here and at other sections where there was little separation between the canal and the river, both the canal and the locks would be subject to damage whenever the Delaware River was in flood. Photos of flood damage in this section of the canal may be seen on pages 32 and 133.

the lock chambers of many of the most profitable canals are narrow and long … These are seventy-five feet long and eight feet wide.

… After a careful examination … I am induced to draw a conclusion unfavorable to the construction of wide locks…. Narrow lock chambers are expeditiously and conveniently filled; they are less expensive; they require but little water; they save time; and in this country [England], where they have been practically improved and tested, they are now approved and adopted.[17]

On May 30, 1827, Jon Fell of the LC&N wrote to Joseph McIlvaine, secretary of the Board of Canal Commissioners. He called attention to the dimensions of the Lehigh Canal, then under construction, and, in a very real sense, lectured the state on the optimum dimensions for a canal. There were advantages, he insisted, "passing heavy Cargoes [a principle] pretty well settled that economy in Transportation by water is more certainly attained by carrying large quantities and moving slow, [rather] than by greater speeds with lesser burdens." The Lehigh Canal, he wrote, would be capable of carrying boats of 150-tons burden and would be 45 feet wide and 5 feet deep with locks 22 feet wide and 100 feet in length. If the commissioners could not see these dimensions, the size should be as large as practicable "with locks not less than 11 feet wide and with 5 feet depth of water."[18]

On January 4, 1828, James Clarke, then president of the Board of Canal Commissioners, offered his views on lock sizes. Presumably in response to the desires of the Lehigh Canal people, he wrote:

> A decision so unexpected, and contrary to Science and engineers—to please a company, however meritorious, is I apprehend, an oversite [*sic*] that will be hencefore regretted. I really believe that no <u>honest</u>, disinterested and capable Engineer in the U.S. will say "Upon his [illegible]" that a canal of forty feet wide should have locks seventeen feet wide.[19]

He favored, he said, the 11-foot locks of the Delaware Canal, as "The 14 – 14½ & 15 feet locks on the New York Canals are said to be generally condemned amongst intelligent men in that state."

Originally, the locks were to be constructed out of wood but, in the spring of 1828, the Board of Canal Commissioners received a petition from members of the legislature representing the region touched by the Delaware Canal. They proposed that a new survey might be made concerning the availability of stone for lock construction. On May 25, engineer Sargent communicated to the board that stone was available and that the first difference in cost would be offset by reduced maintenance costs. So the locks were built with stone.[20]

Easton and its Dam

On July 31, 1828, engineer Henry Sargent summarized the options that had been considered for watering the Delaware Division Canal from its northern terminus. The first proposal, the one ultimately selected, called for a dam across the Lehigh "at its confluence with the Delaware, ten feet above common Low water." The second proposed "the Erection of a dam across the Delaware about one and a half miles below Easton." The second choice, he admitted, would save the Commonwealth money and was probably the better choice if it were not for the problems of dealing with New Jersey as to the maintenance of free passage down the Delaware.[21]

The decision was still unsettled when, in June of 1829, three representatives of the Lehigh Coal and Navigation Company met with Pennsylvania's Board of Canal Commissioners.[22] Their purpose was to reach an agreement whereby the state canal would obtain sufficient Lehigh River water to supply the new Delaware Division of the Pennsylvania Canal. The company representatives, Messrs Joseph Watson, Erskine Hazard, and James Schotte, were ready with their proposal.

First, they proposed that "the waters of the Lehigh shall be thrown into the Penn^a Canal at the point where a straight line would bisect the angle formed by the junction of the rivers Lehigh and Delaware, and on the same level as the Penn^a Canal at that point."

Second, the LC&N would provide sufficient quantity of water "excepting only the detentions necesary [*sic*] for the repair and construction of their works, and the failure of a sufficient quantity of water in the river Lehigh."

Third, the LC&N would elect their own plan and would have jurisdiction over the constructed works.

Fourth, the company should be entitled to any damages incurred from supplying the water, less the costs of construction for which they would be compensated.

Fifth, the Lehigh Coal and Navigation Company should receive from the state, as a compensation for works constructed, a remission of tolls on the Delaware Canal to the amount of $15,000.

Sixth, if the company should elect to extend a feeder canal to supply the state improvement, the state should be permitted at any future date to build its own dam across the Lehigh.

And finally, if the foregoing proposals were rejected, the Lehigh company proposed to build a dam across the Lehigh River "with the necessary lift and guard lock for the Penn^a Canal," as approved by a "substantial and trust worthy contractor." The delegation from the LC&N withdrew and the proposal was "Laid on the table" by the Board of Canal Commissioners.[23]

Four days later, Canal Commissioner David Scott reported to the board. After pointing out obvious mutual benefits for both parties, he pointedly noted that any arrangement must not subject the state and its operations to the control of the Lehigh company. No permanent arrangements should be made, he warned, for any such might imply a right for the company "to interfere with or to limit, direct or otherwise affect the active operations" of the state canal. Even the "right to transportation" on the state waterway should be left totally at the discretion of the state. The dam was necessary as the state saw completion for the Delaware Division during the coming year (1831), but all that was actually needed was the dam. The negotiating committee representing the board saw no reason to pay the Lehigh company for the water or to give them any special privileges on the Delaware Canal.[24]

The agreement, finally entered into on June 29, 1829, was concerned only with a dam across the mouth of the Lehigh, which would be constructed by the LC&N for a sum of $16,000. The approval of the design was the responsibility of the state engineer.[25] On December 29, 1830, Thomas G. Kennedy, superintendent of the Delaware Division, accepted the receipt from the LC&N for the final payment of $16,000 by the state. There would subsequently be other contracts for embankment and masonry work to be performed by the Lehigh company.[26]

In November of 1830, the Board of Canal Commissioners considered a memorial from the LC&N. It called for recognition of their rights, which, according to prior agreement, entitled them to free passage from the pool behind the Lehigh Dam into the Delaware River through an outlet lock. The board by resolution confirmed the right.[27] This right was important because it would enable canal boats to cross over to Phillipsburg. There they could enter the Morris Canal, which was then being constructed across New Jersey to Newark Bay.

In 1829, as they completed their Lehigh canal, the LC&N sold industrial waterpower sites along the last section of their canal between the Chain Dam and the pool behind the prospective dam at the mouth of the Lehigh at Easton. The ten-foot height of the Easton dam took that amount of fall away from the waterpower available to the industries, something they already knew when they contracted for their sites. In 1840, high water took out the abutments of the dam; it was rebuilt, presumably at the same height. However, the water users insisted that their usable fall of water was decreased. In 1840, and again in 1856 at which time the state was negotiating the sale of the Delaware Division Canal, they sought restitution. Finally, Edward F. Gay, state engineer, did a survey in which he included the history of the dam and concluded that there had been no reduction in the useful drop of the water.[28]

1843 lithograph of Easton from the south side of the Lehigh River. The water-powered industrial park developed by the Lehigh Coal and Navigation Company is just upstream, to the left of this view. In the center foreground is the outlet lock of the Lehigh Canal, where boats entered the pool behind the dam that LC&N constructed to let water into the Delaware Division Canal. Both the dam and the entrance to the Delaware Canal are downstream, off the picture to the right.

Industries (Mill Houses) in Williamstown (South Easton) contracting waterpower from the Lehigh Canal.

McKeen & Quinns Cotton Factory take 400 Cubic inches of water at $3.– per inch per annum amounting to $1200.– per year or equal to a capital of $20,000.

Wells & Kidds Iron Foundry formerly Charles Swifts Merchant and Grist Mill. They have 150 inches of water at the same rate. Amounting to $450.– per annum equal to a capital of $1500.

John Maxwells Flour Mill 100 inches at the same rate amounting to $300 equal to a capital of $5000.

James McKeens saw mill 200 inches of water at the same rate amounting to $600 per annum equal to a capital of $10,000.

McKeen & Quinns Weaving Mill formerly Edwards and Cos Rifle Factory, 250 inches of water at the same rate amounting to $750 per year equal to a capital of $12,000.

Charles Jackson & Company Anthracite Furnace in the village of South Easton 700 inches at the same rate amounting to $2100 per annum equal to a Capital of $35,000.

Stewart & Company Wire Factory & Rolling Mill 850 inches of water at the same rate amounting to $2550 per annum equal to a Capital of $42,500.

The Glendon Iron works near the line of the Borough of South Easton in Williams Township 1600 inches at $2 per inch amounting to $3200 per annum equal to a capital of $53,333 33/100.

Source: "To the Canal Commissioners of Pennsylvania. The Case of the Mill owners in South Easton respectfully Submitted." October 22, 1856.

Construction — Progress and Problems

Groundbreaking for the Delaware Division Canal was marked with great ceremony. The excavations were begun on October 27, 1827, with imposing civic and military demonstrations. At eleven o'clock in the morning a procession numbering several hundred marched from Bristol to the present location of lock number three, under the direction of Chief Marshall William F. Swift. The exercises began at high noon with prayer by the Episcopal rector, after which Colonel Peter A. Browne of the Philadelphia bar gave the major address.

Then came the ground breaking, performed by George Harrison of Hulmeville, and State Senator Peter Ihrie, Jr., of Easton. Harrison appeared with a wheelbarrow and Ihrie with a pick and shovel, with which he dug a wheelbarrow load of earth, which Harrison then wheeled a short distance and dumped. Marshall Swift delivered an oration "replete with congratulations to the people of the county upon the beginning of what was described as one of the grandest enterprises of the age." The band played "Hail Columbia," the people gave three cheers, and they then adjourned to the Delaware House, kept by Mr. Bessonet, where several hundred people " 'dined and wined,' made speeches, and got happy under the music of the popping corks." Lewis S. Coryell here made a glowing tribute to "Michael Fackenthal, the Revolutionary companion of Morgan, now our venerable guest." Fackenthal was an ardent champion of the canal.[29]

Contracts for construction of the first parts of the canal had been let in October of 1827, and work began on the 36 lower half-mile sections, or the 18 miles of canal north from Bristol. This work, engineer Sargent reported, would cost $97,121.[30]

Completion of the canal would be years away. Frequent personnel changes and alterations in plans occurred during the next six years. Accidents, high waters, and breaches in canal walls would occur again and again. It would not be until 1833 that the canal would stay open continuously throughout its whole length and even that year its performance was more a promise than a reality. In 1828, the canal board pressed forward. By May of that year they had an additional seven miles under contract from Taylorsville

(Washington Crossing) to New Hope. At the same time they directed Mr. Sargent to make location adjustments so as to guarantee an adequate supply of water.

At that time, it was still to be determined whether the canal would be watered totally from the Lehigh River at Easton or whether it would draw its water from both the Lehigh and the Delaware Rivers. Kennedy had originally specified that a guard lock should be constructed at New Hope "18 feet wide and of similar length with lift locks." It should be capable of securing the canal against any freshet or rise of the river of 14 feet above the "low water mark on the Delaware which was ascertained during the lowest stage of water in the present season to be 2.17 feet above the bottom of the canal in the guard lock."[31]

Sargent, anticipating that feeding the canal below New Hope would still present a challenge, and the engineer, inexperienced in hydraulics, addressed the following problem to Secretary Joseph McIlvaine of the board on April 18: What would be, if any, "[t]he superior advantages of using force pumps and the difficulties to be encountered by dipping into the river," they wanted to know. Not being "practically acquainted" with such devices, would Mr. McIlvaine discuss their importance with the board and obtain the answers to two questions:

> 1st. What quantity of water with 5 ft. head would be required to give a velocity equal to 15 revolutions per minute to a wheel of 6 ft. radius, and what quantity of water could be raised 18 ft. high by said wheel per minute?
>
> 2d, What would be the probable expense of all the machinery necessary for raising water 18 ft. high, and to the extent of the wheel above described?[32]

Answers were not immediately forthcoming, but the germ of an idea had been planted. The board, as inexperienced in canal-watering problems as was Mr. Sargent, continued to let contracts. As already noted, a section 18 miles north from Bristol had been brought under contract in September of 1827. On May 20, 1828, the 10½ miles from Taylorsville to New Hope were let, and on September 19, bids for the 18½ miles from New Hope north to Tinicum were let at New Hope. Between 200 and 300 persons were reported to have been in attendance, most of whom offered bids. This left ten miles to be let later during 1828, carrying the work to today's Raubsville, six miles below Easton. The last six-mile section was scheduled for bids early the following year.

Bidding was for "excavation and canal formation." The mechanical work, locks, aqueducts, culverts, waste weirs, and bridges would call for subsequent contracts. Eleven miles above Taylor's Ferry were reported to have their "excavation and canal formation completed," while other sections were "actively advancing."[33] However, superintendent Kennedy's report at the end of November made it clear that none of the "mechanical work" on the Delaware Division beyond six waste weirs and some work on culverts and bridge abutments had been rendered and paid for in 1828.[34]

Considerably more progress was achieved during the next year, 1829. The annual report of the superintendent, made in November, revealed expenditures of $617,692.03 and the Commonwealth still owed $141,353.11 for additional work already completed. The engineer's report revealed that, out of the "mechanical work" listed in the report, almost all of the masonry on 19 locks was finished; the dam, outlet lock and guard lock at Easton were nearing completion; and most of the masonry on all nine aqueducts and the wooden trunks of three was finished.[35] According to a testimony furnished by Kennedy and Sargent, they had "examined King Livingston's Patent Cast Iron Paddle Gates for Canal Locks, and have adopted them on the Delaware Division." The manufacturers described them as follows:

> The Gate, together with the gudgeons on which it turns is of one entire piece of cast metal, and is secured to its place by a movable key, by which means, if required, without drawing off the water, the Gate can be taken out and replaced in five minutes. It is less than half as expensive as any other paddle gate now approved of, and is believed to be the least liable to get out of order of any thing of the kind now in use. One of the gates two feet square, under ten feet head, is easily opened by a child ten years of age.[36]

In 1835, patent rights for the "Patent Valve gate invented by John F. King and patented 29th Nov 1828" were offered to the state for the duration of the patent, until 1842, for a sum of $3,000. In 1835, the "Report of Simpson Torbert, late Superintendent" included a payment of $350 out of the "old work fund" to King and Livingston "for cast iron paddle gates.[37]

Work on road bridges had not been pushed as much as Mr. Sargent had desired, and unforeseen difficulties had presented themselves in the excavation of hard pan and rock. Despite that, the engineer projected that, if the dam at Wells Falls (New Hope), which was designed to supply water through a guard lock to the lower canal, were completed, the whole line would be ready by July of 1830 "to receive the water for navigable purposes."[38]

The commissioners of Pennsylvania and New Jersey had signed an inter-state agreement on December 5, 1829, that permitted each state to construct the dams necessary to feed canals. Neither state should at any time draw more than one-quarter of the water in the current between the two riverbanks. One article of the agreement permitted Pennsylvania to erect a dam at the head of Wells Falls to water the canal below New Hope, while another provision permitted New Jersey to erect a dam "at the head of Warford's Falls, at Eagle Island, or at Bull's Island" to supply a feeder for the contemplated Delaware and Raritan Canal. The other provisions of the agreement either implemented or restricted other uses of the river.[39]

The year 1829 saw many changes. This was the year during which the money supply dried up. Early in the summer the necessary subscribers failed to come forward to cover a state loan offering. By July however, a compulsory loan exacted from the banks of the state covered the shortfall and work on the public improvements resumed.[40]

Elections were in the air, with the prospect of changes in leadership and personnel. In December of 1829 George Wolf would replace Governor J. Andrew Schulze and the membership of the Board of Canal Commissioners would change. Early in the summer, Lewis S. Coryell, who resided below New Hope, had written David Scott, president of the canal board, that "Mr. Kennedy was too important to the well being of this Division of the Canal to be dispensed with." He hoped there were no moves to remove him.[41]

On December 21, Canvass White, principal engineer of the Lehigh Coal and Navigation Company, wrote to Mr. Kennedy on the subject of changes contemplated in the engineering staff of the Delaware Canal. White remarked that since the managers of the Lehigh company had a deep interest in the completion of the state work, he regarded it as only proper for him to recommend a man out of his own corps, John Hopkins, to the

Governor J. Andrew Schulze 1823-1829

Governor George Wolf 1829-1835

superintendent. His only misgivings were that Mr. Hopkins, as a Commonwealth servant, might not have the privilege of choosing the staff to serve under his direction, and that the young engineer would confront the kind of obstacles faced by everyone who attempted to complete a task that others had begun.[42] Due to the political changes, Henry G. Sargent submitted his resignation on December 26 and was replaced by White's nominee, John Hopkins.[43]

The next year, 1830, was approached with confidence. Josiah White wrote in the LC&N Annual Report on January 7:

> It is expected the Delaware division of the Pennsylvania Canal and the Morris Canal will both be ready for use by midsummer of the present year.[44]

When construction resumed, the principal engineer under superintendent Kennedy was John Hopkins; among his assistants were Colonel Simpson Torbert and Lewis S. Coryell, the latter designated as "Inspector or Supervisor of mechanical work.[45]

Six and one-half months later, on November 1, the superintendent reported that the canal was on the verge of completion. On October 11 the dam across the mouth of the Lehigh was completed and water was directed into the canal. There now existed a system that included twenty-three lift locks, a guard lock

Canal historian C.P. "Bill" Yoder painted this view of the dam at the mouth of the Lehigh River (on the far right), and the entrance to the Delaware Division Canal. The level of the Lehigh was raised so water would flow into the Delaware Canal and provide its source of water. The painting also shows a hypothetical view of the cable crossing across the Delaware River to New Jersey's Morris Canal.

at Easton, a dam and outlet lock at Easton, and a basin, pier, and tide lock at Bristol. There were nine aqueducts, twenty culverts, nineteen waste weirs, eight turnpike bridges, forty-seven common road bridges, forty-nine farm bridges, and eight foot bridges, along with some 16,599 rods of fencing and sixteen lock houses. Kennedy admitted there was still uncompleted but contracted-for work to be done on the pier, basin, and tide lock at Bristol, on 4,000 rods of fencing, and on one or two lock houses. In his report, he ignored the fact that the dam at Wells Falls needed to supply water to the lower canal was still to be constructed and he made no specific note that the $1,195,558.92 already spent on the canal was far in excess of Engineer Sargent's earlier estimate of under $700,000. No tolls had been collected on the canal in 1830.[46]

Josiah White, then "acting Manager" for the LC&N, reported at the end of 1830 that

[The Delaware Division] has had water in about half its length, and all the contracts along it were considered as completed, but a few of the sections proved to have been badly constructed, and require heavy repairs.[47]

The canal created near euphoria. One narrator tells us that on July 31, 1830, with the stretch of twenty-five miles between Bristol and New Hope completed and water admitted to it, presumably from the guard lock at New Hope, a party of forty persons made an excursion four miles down from New Hope and four miles back, their boat horse-drawn and in two and a half feet of water. One week later, amidst the excitement created by the first outing, some seventy or eighty inhabitants of Upper Makefield boarded the *Governor Wolf*, which was fitted up in style, awnings overhead, and sides, stern and bow decorated with laurel and pine and drawn by two horses. They departed from Aqueduct No. 3 (Jericho Creek or Stony Run) and cruised north between throngs of spectators who lined both banks.[48]

On December 27, 1830, John Barber replaced Kennedy, adding the title of Acting Superintendent of the Delaware Division to his designation as Superintendent of the Columbia and Philadelphia Railroad.[49] On April 9, 1832, William B. Mitchell was designated by the board to replace Barber in both superintendencies.[50] It would still be three years before the canal became fully operational. The year 1831 was basically a disaster: $97,339.51 had to be expended on repairs and new water sources. The twenty-four miles between New Hope and Bristol had been opened for navigation in March and continued in good order throughout the season. But tolls for these first few months totaled only $899.43.[51]

Accounts in old family letters are revealing. A quote from December 12, 1831 reads: "Our Easton-Bristol canal has never been in operation throughout. A Durham boat was changed into a canal boat, neat little cabin and so on and made a few trips between New Hope and Bristol."[52]

The canal between Easton and New Hope remained idle, the water from the Lehigh seeping through the porous bottom of the ditch and emptying the canal before it reached New Hope. The limestone structure of section No. 108, just north of locks 22 and 23 near Daniel Raub's tavern, collapsed at four different times when water was admitted to it. Other sections created almost as much difficulty.[53] The individuals who tackled the problems, and who would ultimately find solutions, were Lewis S. Coryell, supervisor of mechanical work under engineer John Hopkins, and Josiah White, founder and member of the board of managers of the Lehigh Coal and Navigation Company.

Coryell was a man well acquainted with the Delaware River who had recently become involved with the canal being constructed along that waterway. From a family that had, as far back as the Revolutionary War, operated a ferry from the Jersey side of the river at Lambertville, Lewis S. Coryell had become a landowner on the Pennsylvania side of the river south of New Hope. He was also a part owner of the Union Mills at New Hope. During the years 1818, 1819, and 1822, he had served as a Delaware River Commissioner in the employ of the State of Pennsylvania, charged with improvement of navigation north of the Falls of the Delaware at Trenton. In this role he had learned about men, water, and contracts. This served as an apprenticeship when he transferred his efforts towards the canal.[54] On March 10, 1829, superintendent Kennedy appointed Lewis S. Coryell as "Superintendent of Stone and Woodwork," On January 10, 1831 he was appointed a principal assistant engineer.[55]

On December 31, 1830, the board considered a communication from superintendent Kennedy "relative to the boundaries of a basin at the borough of Bristol." They unanimously endorsed the suggested boundaries as drawn on Kennedy's map, which enclosed an area extending from Lock #1 to the point of the future tidal lock, incorporating the area of today's Mill Street parking lot. The tidal basin covered five and one-half acres and was "enclosed on two sides by a pier faced with timber and filled with earth." One pier was 500 feet long and 40 feet wide while the other "including the length of the tide lock, and extending to the foot of lift lock No. 1 is 1089 feet long."[56]

Water Supply, Wells Falls Dam and New Jersey

It had not taken long for those responsible for the construction of the Delaware Division Canal to discover that there were problems in maintaining water throughout the whole canal. Originally it was expected that the water admitted at Easton and supplemented by feeders from several watercourses such as Durham Creek would direct sufficient flow into the canal. However, almost from the beginning, it was assumed that additional water could be obtained from an outlet or guard lock at New Hope that would also permit boats to pass in and out from the Delaware River. As summarized in a report to the New Jersey Senate in 1835, two plans were being considered for the wing dam at Wells Falls (New Hope). The options were a feeder extended up the Delaware above the falls a sufficient distance to raise the water level, which was estimated at $70,000, or deepening the level of the canal below the falls 2½ feet for 8½ miles, estimated at $170,000. Pennsylvania selected the option of a wing dam at Wells Falls that would raise the level of the river sufficiently to guarantee a flow of water from the river into the lower portion of the canal.[57]

The hydraulic problems of getting river water into the canal were being discussed. Seemingly, it was not until the end of 1831 that the decision for a supplementary water wheel to pump water was reached. Lewis Coryell was relieved of responsibilities on other parts of the works, so that he would be able to devote his efforts to the construction of the needed dam and "erect[ing] a water wheel with such other fixtures" as might be necessary to supply the canal "from the combined locks [double chambered locks No. 8 and 9] near New Hope to Bristol."[58]

Heavy floods had prevented work during the previous July, and Simpson Torbert, at the time Coryell's aide, suffered a severe illness so Coryell used that time to prepare a one-inch-to-one-foot scale model of the projected wheel. The canal board desired a mechanism that would raise 2,400 cubic feet per minute; the model would raise 7½ feet when 51 cubic feet of water passed beneath it in that amount of time. If the board accepted Coryell's proposal for a "water wheel 15 ft, 3 in in diameter with a 25 foot bucket acting under a head fall of 4 feet," he claimed he could provide the canal with not 2,400 but rather 6,000 cubic feet per minute. This power wheel would be geared into the shaft for the raising wheel by means of cast-iron cog wheels in such manner as to give it a motion of 3⅛ feet per second. These quantities of water were sufficient even if the flow of water from the Lehigh was completely lacking. Enough water could presumably be drawn out of the Delaware to furnish an adequate supply for the lower section of the canal.[59]

Josiah White simplified the model by substituting direct drive for the system of cog wheels and a "self acting gate to supply the proper depth of water in the chamber of the Raising Wheel."[60]

A traveler arriving at New Hope in 1832 was

enlightened with a very simple fixture which had been placed there by Josiah White, Esq. … for supplying the southern part of the Canal … It consists of an undershot water wheel, driven by the power of the river Delaware, having coupled with it, and driving another water wheel, which works in a close chamber, into which the water of the river is admitted. The water thus gets between the bucket boards of this second water wheel, and is raised by them to a height sufficient to allow it to flow from the buckets into a trunk leading to the Canal.— This simple contrivance, without gearing or valves, or anything else liable to get out of order, is more than sufficient to supply the Canal from New Hope downwards. The person who attends it told me that at the lowest water in the Delaware it raised the water eight inches in the upper level of the Canal, which is eight miles in length, and at the same time supplying the Canal from New Hope to Bristol.[61]

The New Hope wheels raised 3,500 cubic feet of water per minute. They remained in operation until 1923. It was the Pennsylvania commissioners who had selected New Hope as the point most favorable to Pennsylvania. Pennsylvania had also, according to the New Jersey legislative committee,

without the consent of New Jersey … constructed a Dam at the mouth of the Lehigh, which almost entirely diverts the waters of that stream (the greatest which rises in the State of Pennsylvania, and runs into the Delaware,) from its natural course, before it reaches its destination in its natural flow and channel.[62]

The Jersey commissioners did admit that the wing dam with its shute for rafts and Durham boats helped descending navigation past what were actually whitewater rapids that "presented more impediments to the natural navigation, than any other portion of the river between Easton and Trenton." In order to aid ascending river traffic, New Jersey called for the construction of two wooden locks "below the falls," at the mouth of Neely's Creek, which would take the traffic into the canal and then return the traffic back into the river above the dam "free of toll".[63] New Jersey's desires would never be implemented.

A major concern developed as a result of the proposals for a Delaware and Raritan canal, for its promoters discovered that the feeder could provide an alternative to the Pennsylvania Delaware Division, then under construction. The river was virtually clear of obstacles between Easton and Warford Falls or Bull's Island, where river traffic might enter the feeder and pass down to a terminus, either at Trenton or at Bordentown. Therefore, the outlet lock at Easton and, even more importantly, the guard locks proposed at various times at Upper Black Eddy, at Smithtown, and at Wells Falls became matters of particular importance to New Jersey and of special concern to Pennsylvania and particularly to the interests of Philadelphia.

Three different engineer's surveys were made during 1833 and 1834, essentially to deal with the problems of watering the lower portion of the Pennsylvania canal. Consideration of the various other guard locks and connections became significantly interrelated with the matter of watering the canal. The first survey was by Pennsylvania engineer Samuel Kneass. The second, also contracted for by Pennsylvania, was by Edward F. Gay, while the third, for New Jersey, was by E.A. Douglas.

All three pointed out a major design error in the Delaware Division; in order to guarantee water from the Delaware River when the water level was low, the level south for nine miles from New Hope to Yardley should have been constructed two and a half feet lower. Remedying this error would involve an expenditure of $170,000 as well as a lengthy shutdown of the canal. Therefore, other avenues were sought. Since all proposed remedies called for taking additional water out of the Delaware, this concerned New Jersey.

Without attempting to catalog in detail the various agreements and negotiations, let it suffice to say that most concerned Wells Falls at New Hope. Engineer Gay in 1834 said that a dam two foot above mean water level would be adequate to supply the Delaware Division through a guard lock. Later the same year, Douglas differed, saying that at least a 3½-foot height would be needed, the guard lock should be altered to a lift lock, and that a guard lock at Upper Black Eddy would be necessary to provide the canal with sufficient water. Both Kneass and Douglas indicated the need for an Upper Black Eddy guard lock that would also permit boats to enter the river to get to the D&R feeder on the New Jersey side. This would cause the State of Pennsylvania to lose a great deal in toll income as a result of the shortened trip on their canal. Article 9 of the 1829 agreement between the two states contained a provision that there should be

> an easy, safe, and direct communication, between the Pennsylvania canal and the pool formed by the feeder dam of the said Delaware and Raritan canal; and the state of New Jersey shall form an easy, safe and direct communication, between the said Delaware and Raritan Canal feeder and the pool formed by the feeder-dam of the Pennsylvania Canal at Well's falls.[64]

It would be 1848 before a connection was made between the two canals.[65]

Contracts, Land Acquisition and Corruption Charges

When we look back to supposedly simpler days, we are usually not aware that canal-building of the 1820s and 1830s constituted a bureaucratic patronage monster. We must stop and realize that the original estimate for a 60-mile canal from Bristol to Easton was $686,596 and that the final finished cost for this canal, one of the lesser elements in the state system of internal improvements, was well over a million dollars.

There is no way of accurately converting these amounts into modern real dollars, but multiplying by ten or even twenty would not be unreasonable. By the time contracts were let for excavation, grubbing, mechanical work on locks, aqueducts, culverts, bridges, waste weirs, and weigh locks along with fencing and the construction of lock tenders' houses, they numbered in the hundreds.

In 1831 the Board of Canal Commissioners designed a printed form of contract that replaced those previously spelled out in longhand. (See Appendix II) The contractor furnished all of his tools as well as his men, and fifteen percent of his compensation was withheld pending approval of his work.[66] Contracts went to the lowest bidder. Josiah White criticized the system: "By over desire to save too much, you use all." For the Delaware Division much could be saved by "the use of better materials, by harrowing and rolling the bed of the canal, and by a dam and other devices."[67]

The contractors were often less than reliable. For example, on February 12, 1828, superintendent Kennedy wrote Joseph McIlvaine, secretary of the Board of Canal Commissioners:

> on my coming here I find something not just as we could be wished. Parson, Contractor on No. 12 has been sold out by the Constable, he is habitually drunk and has been grossly insolent and abusive to the Ass^t Engineers.
> … [I] declared his contract void and refused to let it to a person to whom he had or was about to transfer it. I thought it had to make an example at once.[68]

Another illustration of the problems that could occur was the affair of Barker and Downing. Robert Barker and Joseph M. Downing had contracted for work on a section of the canal, but before final settlement the partners had fallen out and Downing apparently retained the contractual rights. Robert Gue (?), acting for Barker, had gone before "Arbitrators" and had been awarded the sum of $901. Downing appealed the award and the arbitrators "Authorize[d] and require[d] Thomas G. Kennedy, Esq. Superintendent of the Del Div Penn^a Canal to retain in his hands the sum of One thousand Dollars monies due to the said Firm of Barker and Downing and now subject to the Control of said owing." Only then should Kennedy pay the necessary judgement and retain the balance for Downing. Dr. John Phillips posted security for Downing.[69]

On November 5, 1830, James Madison Porter of Easton, attorney for Robert Barker, requested that Kennedy not pay any money to Downing. He caustically commented: "I confess I have long since ceased to have any Confidence in the integrity or fair dealing of Mr. Downing and such I may add is the opinion of people generally down the line." On April 12, 1831, Downing signed a receipt acknowledging $1,000 received from T.G. Kennedy, "late Superintendent." Appended to the receipt was a statement guaranteeing Kennedy against any "risk, suit, claim or responsibility" resulting from the payment. Dr. John Phillips witnessed the transaction that was signed by Downing and Wood with their seal affixed.[70]

Damage claims included the costs of obtaining a right-of-way or supplementary property, and of making settlements for damage to property or for loss of earnings that were the result of constructing the canal. In addition, the state had to replace broken road connections with bridges, and furnish farm bridges where property holdings were divided by the canal. Many property owners simply signed off, giving the right-of-way to the state, but many entered damage claims. On the Delaware Canal these numbered in the thousands. The usual procedure was for canal officials to make an offer that too often turned out to be only a fraction of what the property owner asked for or expected.

After the filing of several initial lawsuits, the state had established a board of appraisers to whom the dissatisfied party could appeal for redress, and legislated that the state could not be sued. The canal officials often claimed, and in some cases the appraisers agreed, that no compensation was in order as the canal had increased rather than diminished the value of the property. However, in 1831, when provisions had finally been made for a board of appraisers, one hundred and seven cases were appealed on the Delaware Division; where the canal commissioners had offered $10,115 compensation, the appraisers made awards amounting to $31,975.[71]

Sooner or later corruption charges would be leveled across the whole state against canal superintendents. On the Delaware Division they appeared in the form of a petition in 1829 charging superintendent Kennedy with committing "great abuses" by "giving contracts to favorites at an advanced price." They accused him of ignoring the commitments made by the engineer. One party, Jacob Stover, Jr., wrote to the canal commissioners asking to have his name removed from the petition as he had signed it only to please the circulator. The board arranged a hearing and testimony was taken but it appears to have been inconclusive.[72]

The Board of Canal Commissioners administered the construction and maintenance of a multimillion-dollar enterprise, and its members were political appointees. Involved were the employment of supervisors, lock tenders, and collectors, the awarding of contracts for repairs and maintenance, the construction of the locktenders' and collectors' houses, and the awarding of permits for applicants to excavate turning basins and slips along the canal, all of which required an incredible commitment of time and effort.[73]

Josiah White to the Rescue

In 1831, the supposedly finished canal was still in a pitiful state. It would not hold water; when it did, a depth of two to three feet was the maximum achievable. Many of the works, underbuilt, were collapsing under the pressure of spring freshets—often just as a result of their inadequacies both as to construction and materials.

The Quaker Josiah White had a noteworthy background. Son of a widowed mother who had apprenticed him to a hardware merchant in Philadelphia, he had learned the trade and become a hardware merchant himself, retiring wealthy before the age of thirty. Dissatisfied with idleness, he decided to apply his "means & talents in a way of singular use to his Fellow being." Sure, in his Quaker way, that Providence was behind him, he bought a waterpower site at the Falls of the Schuylkill from Robert Kennedy. The purchase included the right to construct a lock and make a charge of fifty cents for every vessel navigating the river past the spot. At that date, 1810, no dam and no lock had ever been put into the Schuylkill. For seven years he worked. He had, as he tells us in *Josiah White's History given by himself,*

> [to] leave all my mechanical amusements & strip & turn into the Ruffest & most exposed part of the business, & in cold weather up to my Brest in water, to Raise stone of the channel, & in truth I had to say to my Workmen come boys, in the place of as I had expected after I had made my fortune, to say, go boys.[74]

The next seven years he spent trying to unload his project while he operated a nail manufactory at the Falls in partnership with Erskine Hazard. He was convinced that the Schuylkill could be conquered by a slackwater navigation system but his proposals for the development of navigation and for the development of the coal beds up the river were fruitless, as they failed to obtain any support in the legislature of Pennsylvania. These failures prepared him for his next endeavors.[75]

Josiah White

A few years later, with Hazard and a new colleague, George F.A. Hauto (who turned out to be a charlatan), he accomplished on the Lehigh what he had failed to do on the Schuylkill. Early in 1818, they acquired a twenty-year lease on 10,000 acres of the Lehigh Mine Company's coal lands. They were certain that they would succeed in getting anthracite to market although their lessors had failed twice in their efforts to work the mines and had failed five times in their efforts to improve the river. With Hazard and with borrowed sighting levels, White surveyed the Lehigh River and determined what would become the outlines of a successful development of the Lehigh Valley as an avenue to the anthracite riches.[76]

A decade later, master of men and of a river, inventor-entrepreneur Josiah White was the chief spirit of the successful Lehigh Coal and Navigation Company. "Gravity"-powered cars were loading coal at Summit Hill and discharging it into boats on the Lehigh. The boats and arks descended that river by slack-water pools and passage through the bear-trap locks which the ingenious Quaker inventor had designed "for artificial freshet navigation."[77]

By 1829, the Lehigh Coal and Navigation Company, desperate to find a more efficient means of meeting the growing demand for coal in Philadelphia, had already employed Canvass White to rebuild the Lehigh Navigation and completed a canal-and-slackwater transportation system with true lift locks that permitted upstream as well as downstream traffic. The Morris Canal across New Jersey and the Delaware and Raritan Canal were both still in the future. White and his Lehigh associates eagerly awaited the completion of the Delaware Division of the Pennsylvania State System; its failures were of great concern.

Then, in March of 1831, White, frustrated, moved into action. He came and rode with Lewis Coryell along the Delaware Division. He desired, he said, "to be better acquainted with Lewis' manner of repairing and finishing the defective parts of the Canal—a Canal in which no Company feels an interest in next to our own."[78]

He reiterated some history in the letter which he sent to the president of the Board of Canal Commissioners, James S. Stevenson. His company had begun its canal in 1827; the first boats passed through it on July of 1829. The state had begun its canal in the same year and had led him to believe that it would be completed simultaneously with the Lehigh Coal and Navigation Company's canal, but now, four years later, the state effort was a largely unwatered, useless ditch. For two years, his company had lost the returns they would have gained had the Delaware Canal been in operation. The Commonwealth had also lost projected returns during the same period. The letter continued, addressing what had been a major stumbling block:

> You will please Recollect that the opposition to a Dam is greater in Bucks County and Easton than any where else. Some little from lumber interests above; but this is positively protected by preserving the channel as mentioned: & therefore fully answered: & Just as the Boating interest by connecting the lower level at Wells Falls with the Canal, etc. But let us consider seriously what interest should in equity have the preponderating influence, as to the Dam at Wells Falls. For argument, we will suppose Bucks County was opposed to the canal & dam.[79]

The canal, White wrote, is a highway that helps not just the county, but also the whole state. "It is said these public improvements of Canals etc <u>bring</u> <u>remote</u> parts of the State <u>10 or 15</u> times <u>nearer</u> Market than common roads; consequently all the districts geographically nearer Market, have an increasing rivalship in the Market." Therefore it is the back country that contributes to the growth of the cities and in turn the back country prospers if canals, as avenues of trade, are supported.[80]

The activities of Coryell and White, supplemented by White's letter, bore fruit. Less than five weeks later the Board of Canal Commissioners acknowledged a subsequent communication from the Lehigh Coal and Navigation Company that offered, because of its interest in getting the Delaware Canal into operational condition, to have Josiah White "undertake the duty of Superintendent and of Engineer on that part of the Division above Wells Falls for the present season or until the canal should be completed." They offered this "free of charge or compensation."[81]

On August 1, 1831, the canal board resolved unanimously to appoint Josiah White engineer on the Delaware Canal at a salary of four dollars a day and to place all the supervisors of canal construction subject to his instructions. In addition, they placed the construction of the wing dam at Wells Falls and of the water wheels that would feed the lower twenty-five miles of the canal under the direction of Lewis S. Coryell.[82]

It was too late in the season to finish the tasks, but a team was assembled that would finish the job. Engineer Hopkins was relieved. Superintendents Torbert and Carey remained under the direction of Josiah White.

Late 1831 saw many problems. There was a scarcity of labor "caused by the general prosperity of the country, and the great amount of work in market in Pennsylvania, and throughout the United States." High waters continued during the late summer, retarding work on the dam. In July, Lewis Coryell reported Simpson Torbert was sick and his affliction was life threatening. Torbert recovered but Coryell, his wife and his children suffered illness during the month of September as did almost every family in the village of New Hope and its vicinity.[83]

Erection of the great lifting wheels was not able to start until 1832. By April they had the necessary white oak timber for the wheels and their frames, and engineer White was awaiting instructions to go ahead with the work. June, when the water would be at a low level, was deemed a proper month to begin installation. Even without the wheels, the twenty-four miles of canal below New Hope were opened in March. As spring advanced, however, breaches occurred again and again and it was not until June that the entire length of canal could be watered. Continuing breaches kept it from assuming "an active business until about the middle of October," too late to retrieve much from the season.[84]

Meantime, Josiah White labored to master the continuing problems of seepage through the alluvial matter along many of the sections of the upper part of the canal. The innovative engineer developed techniques based on the study of his predecessors' work and of the terrain through which they had built. Earlier construction had been pursued with little foresight. Cuts had been made through rock. The canal prism had been formed with both berm-bank and towing-path embankments on either side simply being created from excavated materials and the bottom filled with loose sand. Resistance to water was negligible.

It seemed to White that such methods were akin to an old woman who carried a willow basket to a store to be filled with molasses. It irked him that at hand was finer used rubble stone produced by the cuttings and at many points along the canal were great deposits of gravel that no one had thought to employ. He turned to the rubble stone and the gravel, and poured these in determined proportions on porous bottoms and embankments and then permitted the rain to wash them in and compact them as fill rather than merely to try to fill crevices. It was a slow process, but as the wall of moist earth compacted and became increasingly resistant to the passage of water, success was achieved.[85]

Along with solving the seepage problems, White applied his engineering knowledge to the construction of aqueducts, locks, feeders, waste weirs, and other necessary fixtures. By the end of 1832, many of the solutions and devices he had proposed to the canal board had been implemented. The 1832 year-end Annual Report of the Canal Commissioners could accurately report the canal as completed. Tolls to the extent of $8,043.00 had been collected during 1832, while expenditures were $76,524.88. On November 30, Francis R. Shunk, secretary of the Board of Canal Commissioners, had a receipt from Josiah White for $730, his salary for 182½ days of work.[86]

Not the least of the concerns was the irresponsibility of personnel. Josiah White, for example, was particularly perturbed with John Carey, supervisor for the Upper Division. His management was slipshod. White wrote to the board on September 3, 1832. During the week before, he had hoped to

> see all that unfortunate Canal full of boats but we are doomed to another break at the head of Rocky falls in the sand Bank & where it ought not to have broke & would not if the Water <u>had not Run</u> <u>over</u> <u>the Bank</u> owing to not drawing off the Water as usual into the lower levels.[87]

This could have been remedied "by finishing the feeders Round the Locks" and making sufficient "overfalls." Every problem was an accident, according to Carey. White then noted, "I have recently been inform[d] from various Respectable sources that our Supervisor ... is in the practice of getting Drunk." Cary was, White later reported, drunk when he was informed of a shortage of funds. About the same time White found a "Company of 15 or more men" trimming up banks that were 5 or 6 feet above water while the threatened bank was a mere 6 to 10 inches above water level. "It won't look like good stewardship to trim in one place while the bank is so near to breaking in another." In the politically charged arena of canal appointments, White consulted various persons around Easton and found support from everyone except attorney J.M. Porter, a politician who would one day be Secretary of War under President John Tylor—and even "Porter don't object to it." White proposed John Forsman as a replacement. Forsman was a longtime LC&N employee who the previous year had been in charge of the Mauch Chunk Gravity Railroad.[88]

James Madison Porter

The minutes of Pennsylvania's Board of Canal Commissioners for October 25, 1832, noted the resignation of John Carey and the nomination of both John Forsman and Joshua Colvin as replacements for the post of "supervisor upon the Delaware division, from the first bridge over the canal north of Tohickon creek, to Easton." White, now one of the canal commissioners, cast his vote for Forsman.[89]

In his letter of September 21, White reported that water had again been let into the canal and estimated that possibly one hundred craft of thirty tons each had departed down the canal. "We can barely supply the lower level [near New Hope] with water."[90]

There were more disappointments ahead in 1833. After a propitious beginning in the spring, there were three extraordinary floods on the Delaware and some of its tributaries in May, in June, and in October.[91] The canal was breached in many spots and repairs were expensive. After each disaster, there was difficulty in refilling the thirty-five miles above New Hope. Serious consideration was given to a new waterwheel feeder at Upper Black Eddy. However, other effective modifications were made. Crib work strengthened the Lehigh Dam. New work was introduced around the guard lock. Additional waste weirs and stop gates were installed. Boats moved over the whole canal during the year. Tolls of $41,825.14 were collected. Lewis S. Coryell had the satisfaction of knowing his lifting wheels were firmly in place and supplying adequate water for the lower section.[92]

Completion, Projections and Prospects

Additions and improvements would be made over the years. In April of 1833, a contract was let "to Messrs. Land and Law" for a weigh lock capable of handling 100 tons. John Cole constructed the "weighing apparatus" with a "capacity sufficient to weigh 100 tons." It was completed and in working order by November of the same year when superintendent Simpson Torbert made his annual report.[93]

The canal commissioners, who now numbered Josiah White among their members, were convinced that the Delaware Division Canal would become one of the most profitable in the state system, particularly "on account of the mineral coal which must pass through it to market." The officials of the Lehigh Coal and Navigation Company likewise looked with optimism toward increased profits. The next six years would indicate a bright and profitable future for the canal.[94]

On December 6, 1832, State Treasurer A. Mahon noted that "The Delaware Division of the Pennsylvania canal, is the only canal completed in the state ..." While it was not until October of that year that it was "fit for active operation, the tolls collected in one month give promise for the whole state system."[95] On November 8 of 1833, the *Easton Whig* reported, "The Delaware Canal is in the full tide of successful experiment and the Lehigh Canal is stout and strong."[96]

The Delaware Division, despite its problems of narrow locks, occasional bouts with flood and rain, breaches in lock walls and, later, competition from the railroads, would still prove to be, during the years of its operation by the Commonwealth of Pennsylvania, the most profitable of all the state-built works.

∿ CHAPTER II ∿

J. Edgar Thomson
and the Proposed Extension of the
Delaware Division Canal to Philadelphia

In 1832, the Commonwealth of Pennsylvania was in the midst of a massive program of canal and railroad building. The Delaware Division of the Pennsylvania Canal, soon to become the most profitable unit of the whole state system of internal improvements, was approaching completion.[1]

Although the fall line of the Delaware River lies some ten miles north of Bristol, the canal would be constructed along that portion of the river, providing easy navigation for that stretch; the proposed extension would do the same for the much longer portion of the lower river above tidewater.

The real rationale for the construction of a canal along an apparently navigable stream had to do with the state of technology. The use of steam-powered vessels was still in its infancy and navigation on rivers, particularly where channels were narrow or subjected to sand bars and snags, was difficult and hazardous for sailing vessels. Therefore, canals were viewed by many as universal cure-alls.

Illustrative were the numerous petitions received by both the houses of the legislature and by the canal commissioners, "praying" for the extension of the canal, then under construction, at least to Bristol rather than to a more northerly Tullytown terminus or, better yet, to Philadelphia.[2]

The promoters of a Delaware and Raritan Canal in New Jersey were also concerned with navigational difficulties on those portions of the navigable river from their Bordentown terminus to Bristol. These concerns resulted in two feelers that never really reached the formal proposal stage. One was to carry the Delaware and Raritan Canal by aqueduct across the river at Trenton, whence it would continue south to a terminus over Pennsylvania's Delaware Division Canal, which the Jersey interests hoped would be enlarged. The other informal proposal had been made in 1827 by J.N. Simpson of New Jersey on behalf of the Delaware and Raritan Canal. Presumably he was proposing an outlet into the Delaware River not too far below Easton, and entry into the projected D & R feeder for passage on the Jersey side down along the Delaware to Trenton. He also proposed a Pennsylvania canal across "Pennsborough Manor" which would be desirable "were it only to obviate the obstructions in the Delaware" between Trenton and Burlington. He seems to document that there was some opposition to the canal as planned, created by a "[Pennsylvania] Legislature, influenced by the selfish views of the Philadelphia Merchants." Easton, he observed, would be very happy with a connection with New York. Pennsylvania, Simpson noted, had been less than fair in its treatment of New Jersey.[3]

In 1832, the Pennsylvania Canal Commissioners had a survey run for a prospective Bristol-to-Philadelphia extension. The immediate justification was the fact that construction was starting on the Trenton and Philadelphia Railroad, whose charter called for its route to avoid that of the potential canal extension. Thomas G. Kennedy, who in 1827 was appointed the first superintendent of the Delaware Division Canal, resigned his state post in 1832 and became the major entrepreneur and promoter of the Trenton and Philadelphia Railroad.[4]

The engineer commissioned to make the survey was John Edgar Thomson. Young Thomson, to be known to posterity as J. Edgar Thomson, came from a Delaware County family with Quaker antecedents but Presbyterian adherence. His father, John, worked a farm that had been in the family since an ancestor had come to Pennsylvania with William Penn. The elder Thomson had gained renown as a surveyor and engineer. He had worked for the Holland Land Company in northwestern Pennsylvania in 1795 and with Benjamin Henry Latrobe on the first attempt at a Chesapeake and Delaware Canal. He had been employed in 1809 by Thomas Leiper to construct a wooden-railed, three-quarter-mile-long railway connecting Leiper's quarry with Crum Creek in Delaware County, Pennsylvania.[5] Undoubtedly the elder Thomson provided young J. Edgar's basic engineering education. For reasons that Thomson's biographer, James A. Ward, is unable to explain, young J. Edgar, contrary to what was reported to have been his strong desire, did not attend the United States Military Academy. Rather than attending what at the time was probably the nation's best training institution for engineering skills, he obtained his education through the on-the-job apprenticeship route.[6]

In 1827, at nineteen years of age, Thomson worked as a $30-per-month rodman on the survey for the as-yet-to-be state-constructed Columbia and Philadelphia Railroad. The 1827 survey season was suspended when virtually all of the survey team came down with malaria, but Thomson was out in the field again in 1828, participating in a more detailed pre-construction survey. He drew the attention of Major John Wilson, engineer in charge of building the Columbia and Philadelphia; in 1829 Thomson was appointed principal assistant engineer and was put in charge of constructing the first twenty miles out of Philadelphia. This section included the 984-foot-long Columbia Avenue Bridge and the 187-foot-high, 2,805-foot-long Schuylkill inclined plane.

Pennsylvania was experiencing financial problems at the time, resulting from a failure to find the necessary subscriptions for projected state loans. This, along with the decease of Major Wilson, terminated Thomson's employment by the state in the spring of 1830. During 1830 and 1831, Thomson worked on the Camden & Amboy Railroad in New Jersey and also for the Oxford Railroad Company.[7]

Biographer James A. Ward cannot account for Thomson's activities during the years from June 1831, when he left the employ of the Oxford Railroad, to 1834. He notes that most traditional accounts suggest that he may have made a trip to England and Scotland during that period, an excursion taken by many prospective engineers to expand their engineering horizons. However that may be, J. Edgar Thomson, now apparently a recognized engineer, undertook in 1832 the state commission to do the survey for a southern extension of the Delaware Division Canal.[8] He would later recall that in 1832, "I was as much respected at twenty-four as I ever was at the height of my reputation."[9] The next year, 1833, he did a survey for a downstream extension of the Schuylkill Navigation to the junction of the Schuylkill and the Delaware. Concerning the latter, there exists only a copy of his plan but no additional information.[10]

According to W.B. Mitchell, superintendent of the Delaware Canal, there was some delay in commencing the survey due "to the prevalence of disease in the city and vicinity of Philadelphia." The survey, but not the report, was finished by the end of November, 1832, when Mitchell made his annual report and Thomson's report for the Delaware Canal extension was finished by February of 1833.[11]

In the introductory remarks that preceded his survey, Thomson noted that the valley of the Delaware was characterized by "gentle rising ground, receding from the river in successive and uniform slopes." Thus, a long level could be achieved on a line varying in distance of from one-half to three miles from the river. The route would cross four streams, the "Neshamony," "Poquesson," "Pennepack," and the Frankford. They should be crossed on the same level, Thomson noted, as the tide on several of the streams crossed which reached above the line of the canal could not feasibly be incorporated in the canal.

Thomson started his survey from what he called the "Two Mile Reach," just above what he referred to as lock No. 4; actually it was lock No. 3 of the Delaware Division Canal.[12] This point was some 14½ feet above "ordinary high tide," an elevation that he believed would place the line above danger of freshets. The entire extension would run at that level until it reached Kensington, where it would descend to the river by two locks of 7½-foot lift each. It would cross the Neshaminy with an aqueduct of "three spans, one of ninety feet and two of seventy feet each." It would have rubble masonry and a wooden superstructure. The engineer noted that solid rock could be reached at a depth of no more than seven feet at low tide. Over the Poquessing, he proposed

> a stone aqueduct, of two arches, each thirty-three feet span. The foundation is solid rock, and bare at low water; materials for the construction of most of the work can be obtained on the ground.[13]

The Pennypack Creek would be crossed with a single wooden span of seventy-five feet, supported by masonry abutments. Frankford Creek would be bridged with two wooden spans of sixty-six feet each. Here he observed that "the depth to rock foundation ... would be considerable."

The crossing of the lesser streams would be accomplished by culverts. These were included in the estimates, which also provided for road and farm bridges. The latter were to be constructed north of the city with wooden superstructures and stone piers, while brick arches would be the design followed within the incorporated limits of the city of Philadelphia. The other consideration of note was the need for a swing bridge where the canal passed the Philadelphia and Trenton Turnpike near the Neshaminy crossing.

The last hundred "chains," presumably 6,600 feet, were estimated to consume about 25 percent of the $361,042 estimated as the total cost for the construction of the extension. Within this distance would be two locks of 7½ feet lift each,

> to be placed one hundred yards apart, in the vicinity of Harrisons laboratory.[14] These locks are estimated to be executed of cut stone, laid in the best manner, one hundred and twenty feet long, by twenty-two feet in the chamber. Between Marsh and Beach streets, is thought to be the best position, of the out let locks, one of five feet lift; the other, the tide lock, six feet. These are to be combined and executed in a like manner with the others.[15]

There would be two basins, one between Front Street and the river and one above Front Street, the latter to "be surrounded on the inner side by a wharf," while the former would permit "the ground to take its natural slope." The basins each contained "eight feet depth of water."

The extension would "have a capacity sufficient for the passage of sloops." Its total length would be 19 miles and 40 perches at an average cost of $18,878; 25 percent of the total cost was for the last portion in Kensington, the portions from there north to Bristol would average only $14,480 per mile. The one additional concern that Thomson had not figured into the cost was guaranteeing adequate water into this lower portion. The problem of supplying adequate water to the lower portions of the canal, then being built, were still being addressed and the best Thomson could do was to suggest that the cost of "extending the works at New Hope, which would be rendered necessary in the event of the completion of this line," should be factored into the cost estimates.[16]

A statement by William B. Mitchell, briefly superintendent of the Delaware Division Canal in 1832 following Kennedy's resignation, endorsed the Thomson route:

> The passage of the canal through the city can be effected without interfering with any improvement of much value; the valley of the Cohocksink [Creek] forming a natural and capacious basin.[15]

Appended to Thomson's initial report was a supplement, produced after his "location of the canal down the valley of the Delaware" in response to a request that he "ascertain the practicability of extending a branch from it to the Schuylkill river." It is interesting and instructive to note that the estimate for construction of two miles and 290 perches of canal through the northern sections of the city are roughly three-quarters of the estimate to build nearly twenty miles through the less-settled route paralleling the Delaware River. This Schuylkill extension would leave the Delaware portion just above Harrison's laboratories above the locks, thus maintaining the Bristol-to-Philadelphia level. A dam would be constructed on the main branch of the Cohocksink Creek, which would create a basin. The canal moved roughly to the westward until it reached a spot near Broad and Spring Garden streets. Just prior to that spot,

J. Edgar Thomson, 1808–1874, was one of America's most noted engineers and managers. After his work on the Delaware Division, he served as chief engineer of the Georgia Railroad and is renowned for having given its terminus the name "Atlanta." He joined the newly incorporated Pennsylvania Railroad as its chief engineer in 1847, for which his first responsibility was to establish a route through the Alleghenies. His design for Horseshoe Curve remains an engineering marvel. Thomson became the president of the PRR in 1852, serving until 1874. During his time as president, the PRR purchased large sections of the state canal system. Thomson's tenure was marked by the introduction of steel rails, the expansion of the PRR system from 250 to over 6,000 miles, an increase in company profits from $617,000 to $8.6 million, measures that cut costs over 9 cents per ton-mile, and the introduction in 1857 of a new system of organization designed to make the increasing complexity of an enormous railroad network manageable. His "line-and-staff" organizational structure was adopted by other large railroad companies and was followed into the twentieth century.

Thomson proposed that the canal would enter a 1,225-yard-long tunnel. The tunnelling would not be approached in the usual manner; therefore, Thomson noted, its cost would not be too difficult to estimate. Rather than pushing underground, the tunnel would be achieved in the manner of creating big "common suers [sic]."

The earth will be first removed, then the arch turned, and the earth replaced …

The dimensions proposed for the tunnel, are fifteen rise of arch and twenty four feet in width, four feet of this width to be occupied for a towing path. These dimensions will fully suffice to pass one Schuylkill canal boat at time. The dimensions of the Delaware canal are continued to the Germantown rail road; thence it is narrowed to twenty five feet bottom and slope one and a half to one.[18]

From the tunnel the line would continue just south of due west until it crossed Vine Street and then it would run parallel to Vine Street to the Schuylkill River, where the canal would be locked down twenty-five feet to river level, the last five feet of which would be accomplished by a tide lock. Testimony as to the rapid rate of growth of the city was Thomson's assertion that despite the fact that a Callowhill Street terminus might be superior, the improvements already made along this line made the adoption of one at Vine Street necessary.[19]

On February 7, 1833, Thomas Kennedy wrote to the canal commissioners, appending a map showing the canal route surveyed by Thomson along with the proposed route for the railroad. After noting the provisions of the original act of the legislature concerning the route of the railroad, he requested of the commissioners that "Should you be of [the] opinion … that the Route of the Rail Road will not interfere with that of a Canal, you will oblige the Company by giving a Certificate to that effect." The railroad was built and ultimately became an important segment in the Pennsylvania Railroad.[20]

Over the next several years the minutes of the state assembly and senate as well as those of the canal commissioners are interspersed with petitions advocating that the canal extension be implemented. Additionally there was pressure on the same political bodies to implement the transit of canal boats on the Delaware River from Bristol to Philadelphia. In this instance what was sought were steam-powered towing boats.

In 1834, apparently in response to petitions, the Pennsylvania Assembly passed a resolution directing their committee on inland navigation and internal improvement

> to enquire into the expediency of authorizing the canal commissioners to procure a steam towing boat, to ply between Bristol and Philadelphia, in order to accommodate the trade of the Delaware division of the Pennsylvania canal, until such time as the said canal shall be extended to the city of Philadelphia.[21]

The committee responded that it was not expedient for the state to get into "the business of transportation" and recommended that nothing be done "awaiting the convenience of the steam tow boats owned by the Lehigh Coal and Transportation."[22]

The towing boat remained a matter of continuing concern. On April 1, 1836, a law was passed appropriating $8,000 for such a steam tow boat.[23] Apparently the state House of Representatives had also passed resolutions to the same effect on April 1 and June 16 of 1836. A letter dated March 28, 1838, from Moses Sullivan addressed to Lewis Dewart, Speaker of the Pennsylvania House of Representatives, reported that there was no tow boat available for hire and that the appropriated sum was inadequate to pay for the construction of a new boat.[24]

On January 14, 1836, "the Committee on Inland navigation relative to the extension of the Delaware Division of the Pennsylvania Canal from Bristol to Philadelphia" had submitted their report. While endorsing the project in spirit, they abstained from calling for any present implementation "in view of [the] embarrassed finances" of the state. They did suggest a favorable consideration "If a company could be organized to construct this work with a provision for the sale of it to the commonwealth on the ordinary terms." A bill entitled "An act to incorporate the Bristol and Philadelphia canal company" was introduced into the legislature on January 24, 1838. The proposal appears to have died.[25]

It is impossible to say when the Lehigh Coal and Navigation Company first placed a towing boat in the Bristol-to-Philadelphia traffic, but the annual report of that company for 1838 noted:

> The Company's tow-boat Pennsylvania, employed on the Delaware, was fitted up last spring with tubular boilers like those of the locomotives, and has in consequence burnt less than two-thirds of the fuel used in 1836. She has towed upwards of one thousand tons of coal in twenty boats, all attached to her at the same time.[26]

The *Pennsylvania* had been in the LC&N's service for seven years but apparently not all of these were on the Delaware.

In 1838 alone, the Pennsylvania House of Representatives received eleven petitions plus a number of resolutions calling for the canal extension. This apparently generated a committee in each house for the purpose of re-examining the proposed canal.[27] A report from Mr. Mich. Snyder, chairman of the "Committee of the Senate Appointed to View the Contemplated Line of Canal from Bristol to Philadelphia" was submitted to the State Senate on February 26, 1838. The committee reported that its members had made a physical survey of the canal starting from the mouth of the Cohocksink and proceeding north to Bristol. They were accompanied by members of an ad hoc committee made up of representatives of the inhabitants of Bristol and Philadelphia, whose recommendations were appended to the report. They noted that close to the river, near the mouth of Cohocksink Creek, was a "depression of the earth's surface" which was often flooded; the local inhabitants were desirous that what they considered a nuisance— "a loathsome morass" —might be converted into "a beautiful sheet of pure water, covered at times with canal boats." As they proceeded north they noted extensive recent building, often mills and industrial buildings, that would be vulnerable to the construction of the canal. At Bristol, in particular, many improvements had been made, the canal basin had been constructed along with state wharves, creating a body of water that was already supporting an extensive passage of coal boats into the southern terminus of the Delaware and Raritan Canal, some eight miles to the north at Bordentown.[28]

The citizens' committee estimated that a canal extension would now cost more than a million dollars to construct. In addition, the canal would "destroy a very large number of water powers of great value," and would as well "put a stop to the navigation of several creeks, which now admit sloops of the largest class." The additional costs that would be incurred by the payment for damages would "in all probability, exceed the cost of the work." They pointed out that the Delaware River was navigable as far up as Bristol for vessels of from "<u>one</u> to <u>three</u> hundred tons burthen," and suggested that, except during a severe gale, little use would be made of the canal.[29]

Both the senate committee and the citizens' committee recommended against the construction of the canal extension, and the citizens' committee recommended that the state pass the enabling legislation for the creation of "a Steam Tow Boat Company." They also argued against the construction of an outlet lock at Upper Black Eddy, a short distance below Easton, which would create a route that would enable the Lehigh Coal and Navigation Company to bypass the lower sections of the canal as they shipped coal to the New York market.[30]

Isaac Van Horn, the toll collector at Bristol in 1846, described the tasks of the locktender under his supervision at that location as "more arduous and responsible than [at] any Lock on the line owing to the Tide supplying the Basin." Among his duties was the "opening the gates night & day when the gates needs attention and deciding disputes that occur at the arrival and departure of the Tow boats which is 4 times in 24 hours."[31] The gate could be left open when the river and basin were at the same level, but had to be opened and closed when the rising and falling of the tides in the river made the levels unequal.

The fate of the proposal in which Thomson played the catalyst by making the survey illustrates how, in an incredibly short period of time, technological advances in ship construction and in applications of steam power had a spectacular impact on the economic realities of canal extensions. The episode is an informative illustration of the interrelationships between the dynamic urban growth that was taking place at the time and rapidly changing political and technological options.

∼ CHAPTER III ∼

Problems of Operating a Canal:
Floods, Politics, and Manipulations

The year 1834 saw the canal finished and ready for a full year's operation. In November, engineer Edward Gay reported that the line of the canal had "continued in good navigable order through the past season" and that there had been no interruptions on it "worthy of notice." The canal was blessed with "an abundance of excellent materials" obtainable along the way and constantly used for repairs, a situation "well calculated to render it in a few years (the mechanical work excepted) one of the most permanent canals in the state." A new breast had been constructed on the dam at Easton, and the only concern for the future was the barely sufficient water supply below New Hope, furnished both from Easton and the water wheels at New Hope. He noted that many of the farm and road bridges were already in a "ruinous condition …, two have already fallen, and with each a team of horses with driver, wagon and load, all precipitated into the canal together, doing considerable damage in both instances."[1]

There were still other concerns to be dealt with. It appears that during the first few years of full operation there was much adjusting as various parties attempted to throw their weight around and gain advantages. Such was the situation in 1839 that Martin Coryell, assistant engineer on the Delaware Division Canal, brought to the attention of James Clark, president of the Board of Canal Commissioners. It seemed that Supervisor Harmon had directed the locktenders to give preference at the locks to those boats that were paying the most toll. Coryell was "unable to ascertain whither this order emanated," whether from the board or from "interested persons," but was concerned that the way in which it was being implemented could prove "injurious & detrimental as I [Coryell] will endeavor to show."

During the previous season there had been two or three "companies owning Freight boats" that intended to carry all the country produce along the canal and also to "take back-freight." They had since united into one company with 19 boats and more being built, and intended to monopolize all the non-coal freight. They now went on the canal in "companies from five to ten and carry more freight either way than the coal boats & of course pay more toll & under present regulations pass the locks before the coal boats." This caused accumulations of coal boats at the locks, many delays and much expense and, incidentally, damage to the canal. For, as Coryell noted, "Boats locking thru to [sic] near each other interfered with the level and damaged them in some degree, causing the lower level to get too full & the water wasted whilst the upper level is too much reduced." As a final postscript, the "men carrying coal have but a small capital, they generally own the boat, horses &ct that they use." They had previously participated in the back freight but the monopoly had now shut them out of it.[2]

And in March of 1834, the Board of Canal Commissioners passed a motion applicable to lock tenders across the Commonwealth:

> in addition to the general duties of lock keepers in attending to the locks under their charge, they are also required under the direction of the supervisor of the line to do such repairs about the locks, lock houses and lock house lots, as can conveniently be done by a common laborer; but for which they shall not be allowed any pay except their monthly wages.

Additionally, they must assist the supervisors

when called upon to repair breaches in the canal. For which service they shall be paid a sum not exceeding fifty cents per day in addition to their monthly wages in full for labor and boarding.[3]

In 1835 proposals were made to increase the capacity of the canal by deepening it, but these efforts were premature and only limited repairs were done during that year. And in 1836, to quote the canal commissioners' annual report:

Navigation was obstructed on this [the Delaware] division during nearly the whole month of April; a great freshet occurred on the tenth of that month; the waters rose to a height sufficient to overflow the canal banks; the current swept away whole sections of the outer bank, a distance of several hundred yards. The water was re-admitted about the 25th, from which time the navigation was interrupted but little.[4]

In many ways, 1837 was another year of great promise: receipts totaled some $90,000 while expenses were about $28,500. But, as the commissioners noted in their annual report, the canal, new though it might seem, was constructed with "perishable" materials and many structures needed refurbishing. During 1837 a number of lock gates had been renewed and the superstructures of twenty bridges reconstructed. They were learning from experience that a large portion of the wooden structures connected with the canal required renewing every seven or eight years. The division was already "undergoing the first general renervation of this kind." With the repairs contemplated for the following year, the board expected these expenses in the future would be somewhat reduced.[5]

Even so, despite occasional floods, breaches, and mechanical failures, the future could be viewed with optimism. Receipts increased almost yearly, the Lehigh Coal and Navigation Company and other coal producers were expanding their output, and markets appeared limitless.

Passenger Traffic

During the first years of the operation of the canal there had been some formal passenger traffic. Bits of documentation still exist, such as the 1836 notice of J.H. Hellings and Company advertising the "Union Line for Philadelphia by Canal Freight and Packet Boat 'Gazel'—Fare, through, $2.50." The *Gazel* would "leave Easton at 4 o'clock a.m. on Mondays, Wednesdays and Fridays for Morrisville; from thence passengers will take the cars to Bristol and the steamboat from Bristol arriving in Philadelphia at 5:30 p.m." The returning passenger would leave Philadelphia at 6:00 a.m. by steamboat or 6:30 by railroad on Tuesday, Thursday or Saturday and reach Easton again by the packet boat from Morrisville early in the afternoon.[6]

A minuscule amount of passenger traffic continued. In the annual report of the canal commissioners for the year 1846, at the end of the report of articles shipped, the figure 1,340 is listed under "Passengers, miles traveled," south from Easton; and 2,543 is listed for passenger miles traveled to "Easton by the Canal from the South." The figure for "sent Southward by the Canal from New Hope" is 3,906, and 3,231 for northward miles. For Bristol, the figures recorded are 7,785 to the north and 3,119 from the north. Any further detail that would explain this passenger traffic seems to be unavailable. The numbers may seem significant, but if these figures for passenger miles are divided by 60 (the length of the canal) or by 30 (the approximate distance from Bristol to New Hope), the totals become far less impressive.[7]

By the middle of the nineteenth century, the vestigial formal passenger traffic appears to have ended for all practical purposes. Anything later was at best informal. Yet there are numerous remembrances of oldsters who can still recall persons, often youngsters, taken for a trip on the canal. The typical boatman, it appears, was often hospitable enough to offer, even to a stranger, a ride or lift on his boat. In 1891 a Pinkerton agent, charged with trying to discover dishonesty in the canal operations, was able (at least, according to his report) to "hitch" several rides of a few miles duration along the canal.[8]

Personnel problems

The first years of the canal's operation were replete with politics, bitter rivalries, and problems. Seemingly, charges and countercharges were made against individuals in what appears to have been a highly politicized situation, marked by extreme bitterness.

In 1834, John Kain appeared before John Solliday, Justice of the Peace in Tinicum Township, to make a negative deposition, affixing his mark to his statement relating that he had been hired to quarry stone "for the waterway around Lock N° 12," and that when he had quarried a quantity "Anthony Fly told me to lay the good stone aside for his new house which he was about building." He and others also directed gravel and state planking be used for scaffolding in the Fly house construction and then, even though he knew it was "at the xpense [*sic*] of the Commonwealth," he signed the check roll for the work that had been done.

William Fritz, who had worked as a common laborer on the canal during the years 1832 and 1833, essentially supported the allegations in Kain's deposition. From the testimony of Reuben Simson, one of three "under bosses" in 1832 and part of 1833 under Anthony Fly, one gets a different picture. (The other "under bosses" were George M. Twining and John D. Cass; according to several of the depositions, George M. Twining "did not like to work.") According to Simson, and John Wood's deposition taken in 1834 before Joseph Hough, Jr., a political opponent of Solliday, Anthony Fly never used state materials on his house. Wood testified that "I believe Fly never used a Stone for his own use that was quarried by Kain or at the expense of the State." He did operate a tavern, however, which he left under the supervision of his wife and wife's sister to free him for the daily supervision of the canal. According to Wood, "all the time I worked on the Canal Anthony Fly was daily superintending the hands." As for John Kain, Wood testified that his character "was generally and universally bad on the canal among the workmen." He had proposed to various hands—including Wood himself—that "they should join and make holes in the canal so that a breach would take place that would make better times for them." According to Wood, it was he who let out the "secret" and Fly subsequently discharged Kain.[9]

Isaac Van Horn, former contractor, wrote to canal superintendent Simpson Torbert endorsing Fly and condemning his critics. In the summer of 1832 Fly had been foreman working on some feeders around locks under Van Horn's supervision. Van Horn asserted that "some of the same persons that were still at enmity with him were so base as to open gates on his new made work and raise the water to the height of 6 feet to destroy it while others would write to the canal Commissioners that he knew nothing about such business and earnestly requested that some of their favourites might be appointed in his Stead."

The resulting investigation by the canal commissioners revealed the "base deeds" of the supervisors, according to Van Horn, and established Mr. Fly as "a person who was both well qualified and by his strict attention was an efficient superintendent." There is no evidence of any additional action.[10]

The supervisors continuously discovered that there were always some employees who left something to be desired. Examples were three of the four locktenders appointed by Robert P. Lovett, supervisor of the southern half of the canal, in April of 1836. One was Joel Cheston at Locks Nos. 2 and 3, whom he had to replace a year later "for frequent intoxication and gross neglect of duty." The other two, likewise appointed in 1836 and removed for the 1837 season, were David McCracken at Lock No. 4 and Job Winner at Lock No. 6, "each removed for receiving and secreting Coal, from off the boats on the canal, & selling the same." James Linton at Locks Nos. 8 and 9 and the guard lock at New Hope, was "removed of his own accord."[11]

In the fall of 1837, Lovett reported replacing John Quick as locktender at Lock No. 20 whom he had in September "discharged for manifest neglect of duty, leaving the Lock for more than a week at a time, hence the boatmen proffered heavy complaints against him and there was frequently great detention of boats in consequence." Quick was replaced on October 1 by Samuel Fox.[12]

Mortality and human physical weaknesses also had to be overcome. In the nineteenth century the Delaware Valley was malarial and at times was victimized by epidemics of cholera and other maladies. The pathetic introductory note to a letter written to the board by William Rogers, collector at Bristol, about tolls, deductions, and overpayments, described how

> I arrived home on Saturday morning at half past 10 o'clock and found my youngest child in convulsive fits. [The seizures continued until] quarter past three on Sunday morning when he terminated his earthly existence. … [It] cast a gloom on my family and more particularly when it is the fourth child out of six that we have followed to the grave.[13]

Less than two months later, William Muirhead, clerk, wrote to James Clark, president of the Board of Canal Commissioners, that "It becomes my duty to inform you of the decease of Mr. Dusenbury which took place this morning." Clark endorsed Muirhead's action of assuming Caleb Dusenbury's duties until a successor could be named. According to Muirhead, Dusenbury's widow was "destitute" except for accumulated salary due from the state. Muirhead continued his duties for some months.[14] Torbert himself was struck down with illness and for a period of time in 1831 was unable to fulfil his duties.[15]

Joseph Hough of Point Pleasant, appointed by Governor Ritner as supervisor of the northern segment of the canal in 1836, assumed office, presenting reports of his detailed surveys of the canal and of how he was attacking all the problems of the canal.[16] His degree of application and competence were called to question by five petitioners from Easton who wrote in a June 28, 1837, missive that they felt "compelled to represent" that he "has for some time past shown himself unworthy of the Trust confided in him." He had shown "intemperance" and they predicted problems for the state because of "the negligence of her public agent."[17] It is possible that some but not all of his problems may have been the result of an antagonistic Democratic legislature which may have deprived him of funds. His replacement, Robert P. Lovett, spelled out some of the problems and questioned the validity of many of the bills presented and of entries on Hough's check rolls. Lovett wrote:

> Excuse me in giving this statement of facts, I merely do it to give some idea of how things have been managed, and the consequent difficulty in adjusting such accounts.
>
> I expect not to escape censure in endeavouring to cleanse this truly Augean Stable, amongst other matters.[18]

Political Climate

In 1835, Joseph Ritner, an Anti-Masonic Whig, was elected to the governorship in a contest where his plurality was to a large degree the result of divisions in the Democratic ranks.[19] Governor Ritner proceeded to appoint a new board of canal commissioners: Moses Sullivan, John Dickey, and Joseph Smith.[20] This board, which controlled the greatest body of patronage in the state, proceeded with wholesale firings and hirings. On the Delaware Division they replaced supervisor Simpson Torbert, who was in charge of the southern section of the canal from Bristol to Point Pleasant, with Robert P. Lovett, and replaced supervisor Joshua B. Calvin, who controlled the portion north to Easton, with Joseph Hough.[21] The patronage appointments worked down to the weighmaster at Easton as well as to collectors, foremen, locktenders—even laborers.[22]

During the Ritner administration, the makeup of the board changed four times. In May of 1838, he named Elijah F. Pennypacker, John Dickey, and Thaddeus Stevens. Stevens was elected chairman of the board.[23]

During 1838, an election year, according to all accounts Stevens mobilized the board for political purposes. The Democrats charged that all bidders on state contracts were investigated for their "moral character or religious principles." A "missionary fund for the purpose of diffusing useful knowledge among the people" was instituted, and workers were organized for the purpose of mobilizing votes.[24]

Young William C. McPherson, a medical doctor and secretary to the commission, described the commissioners' activities in letters to his father. Two days after Stevens' appointment, the commissioners began a "grand tour" over the public works of the state. They went first to Bristol and then "had a delightful trip up the Delaware" to Easton. McPherson reported that "Dickey … took occasion to introduce politics with other matters and always with management. The face of things in that region wears a pleasing aspect. We rode the canal in an open skiff and stopped often. Pennypacker acted as steersman, I as bowsman. The folks thought us real democrats."[25] The commissioners then proceeded across the state.

Governor Joseph Ritner
1835-1839

The period of Ritner's administration was marked by increasing economic uncertainty. The antimonopoly policy pursued by the administration of President Jackson included a successful effort to prevent the rechartering of the Second Bank of the United States. The cumulative effects of this resulted in an orgy of financial speculation that collapsed in the Panic of 1837, which spawned the worst economic depression in early American history. The Commonwealth of Pennsylvania, then in the midst of its great scheme of public improvements, found its ability to raise money greatly reduced. The depression would eventually lead to international embarassment, discussed in the following chapter, when the Commonwealth was unable to meet interest payments on its bond debt.

The state election was held on October 9, 1838, and the Democrats led by David Rittenhouse Porter regained the governor's mansion. However, the Ritner forces were still not prepared to surrender control of the legislature. The result was the notorious Buckshot War that saw contested Democrats, backed by gangs of Philadelphia toughs, seated in the legislature while Stevens and other Whig leaders, fearing for their lives, left the Senate chambers through a rear window. The militia was called out but the legislature remained Democratic.[26]

Porter was inaugurated on January 15, 1839. Thaddeus Stevens resigned on January 23, 1839, and was replaced by Democrat James Clarke, who had earlier served a number of years as a commissioner. The "Old Board" was still in place when the Great Freshet of 1839 struck, but was out of office by the time most of the cleanup and repair took place. The same pattern existed for the supervisors, all political appointees, along the line—they assumed their responsibilities in the midst of disaster.

As soon as Porter assumed office in 1839, James Clarke, William F. Packer, and Edward Hubley were appointed as the new board of canal commissioners.[27] The newly organized board proved no less able than had been its predecessor in installing its members' supporters up and down the canal. On Thursday February 13, 1840, they replaced the two Whig-appointed supervisors with three good Democrats as follows: David Connor, Joshua D. Calvin, and D.Y. Harmon.[28]

Governor David Rittenhouse Porter
1839-1845

The Democratic legislature instituted an extensive investigation into the record of the Whig board of canal commissioners. The majority and minority reports, along with transcripts of testimony, fill hundreds of pages.[29] One of the more persistent charges was that favored contractors were permitted to throw off their contracts and were then permitted, without bidding, to renegotiate on much more favorable terms.[30] There were only one or two such cases along the Delaware Division, but partisan recriminations would continue over the years. Letters exist such as that penned by supervisor David Connor on behalf of a seeker of a position as assistant weighmaster who "had always been a consistent democrat, as well as all his familey [sic], at least ten in number who were among the most active of our party at the last election."[31]

Supervisor Joshua Calvin in 1840 complained to the auditor general about the practices on the canal "when the Administration fell in to the hands of Joseph Rittner."[32]

The senate committee from the now-Democratic legislature that visited most of the state works during the spring of 1839 opined:

> Your committee regrets the necessity of adverting to these things. They deprecate the introduction of anything like political or party in the prosecution or management of our internal improvement system; but the inference was too glaring to escape observation, and too palpable to be permitted to pass unrebuked.[33]

They could, however, find no fault with the present supervisors across the state.[34]

The Flood of 1839

The Philadelphia *Public Ledger* of Monday, January 28, published a story headed "GREAT STORM AND FRESHET." It was given an unprecedented two and one-half columns and the paper continued to detail the story during the balance of that week. The *Ledger* reported that the storm, "the most destructive storm known in this vicinity for forty years," struck at 9 o'clock P.M.

> with a violent westerly wind and a deluge of rain which continued with unmitigated violence until near 5 o'clock on Saturday afternoon, when a strong wind from the northwest suddenly sprang up, the rain ceased, and the atmosphere, under the influence of the northwester, assumed a feeling of frigidity which soon lowered the thermometer some dozen degrees nearer to zero.[35]

Over the next three days the *Ledger* reported the extent of the storm. "The gale at New York city … blew a perfect hurricane." Damage and flooding spread across New Jersey and up the Delaware and Schuylkill valleys.[36] Dams and canals seemed to be particularly vulnerable. The Schuylkill Canal was breached and damaged in various spots, with some buildings and properties completely carried away. At Jersey City "the roof of the Morris Canal Banking house was blown off" while "the Morris canal had broke."[37] However, the "Lehigh Company's Works, on the Lehigh river, have not sustained any serious injury from the late storm." It was estimated that repairs on the Lehigh would not exceed one thousand dollars.

The 1839 annual report of the canal commissioners prefaced its section on the Delaware Division as follows:

> This division of the public works has been peculiarly unfortunate during the present season. A freshet on January 27th reached 22 feet above the low-water mark at Easton, overflowing all the low levels of the Canal, sweeping off aqueducts, destroying the banks and in many cases filling the canal with earth. At the same time, the swollen Lehigh, higher than it had ever been known, overflowing the guard banks of the dam at Easton—swept entirely away the southern abutment.[38]

Josiah White of the Lehigh Coal and Navigation Company penned an undated letter at the end of January with his prediction:

> And as the Delaware goes down the Rapidity of the water through the Breach will be increased, & consequently if the Embankment will continue being washed away, until it be [illegible] by filling in with stone etc. Fortunately for the State, the Citizens of Easton felt more interest in the work than the <u>Old</u> officers whose duty it is to attend to the work. They have had a Town Meeting & expressed a willingness to Repair the Breach as promptly as possible. Know that by doing so the whole of the Breaches can be Repaired and the canal put in complete order by the usual time of opening the navigation and trust in the Faith of the state for repaying them.
>
> They however desire the Sanction of their Labors by the Canal Commissioners as well as their directions in the business.

As Josiah White wrote on February 2:

> The main Damage is the Easton Dam. The South Abutment appears all fell down, but being well Cemented, it lays in such masses at end of the Dam as to have preserved the Dam which is not materially injured. …
>
> The Embankment next the South Abutment of Dam has gone about 30 ft further since my Last letter. and moved a great body of earth and masonry in a solid mass, creating a vast outlet into the Delaware.[39]

Engineer William K. Huffnagle in his annual report recalled:

> The dam, deprived of its protection by the loss of an abutment, was in a most precarious situation, leaving its safety entirely dependent upon the most energetic measures.[40]

The resultant crises were met with vigor. It is impossible to improve on the language of engineer Huffnagle:

> The patriotic spirit of the inhabitants of Easton, did not long remain inactive. The destruction of an important portion of the public works, was rapidly progressing and each individual felt interested in its preservation. A public meeting was immediately held, and the work undertaken by the guarantee of individuals; arrangements being made with the Easton bank, and having secured the valuable services of Mr. S. Chapin,[41] a heavy force was instantly raised, and the breach attacked with a vigor, and under circumstances, which, must be fully known, to be properly appreciated.

In the wet and frigid weather, this "heavy force" commenced casting mass after mass of stone into the raging current. On February 16 the Governor's brother, Easton resident James Madison Porter,[42] reported: "The work at the Dam is going on rapidly under Mr. Chapin's direction and this Evening the breach is within 15 feet of being closed."

Porter noted that a Colonel McKean had advanced money, to date to the total of $11,150, guaranteeing that the hands could be paid every Saturday evening. Otherwise, he observed, "they could not be got to work." He added that the supervisor needed funds to meet the payroll.[43]

The April 9, 1839, minutes of the Lehigh Coal and Navigation Company contain a resolution enabling the executive committee "to pay the wages of the hands employed in repairing the Delaware Canal for this month, to be refunded out of the first money appropriated by the legislature."

On February 28, the Easton *Democrat and Argus* could report that the repairs on the dam were being carried on with "unusual spirit…. The breach that looked so formidable at first has been entirely closed, and the water again runs over the dam."[44] At the end of six weeks of incessant labor, the workers had brought the Lehigh again under control by filling and finally gravelling the breach. So effective were their efforts that when another freshet struck on April 8, the barrier held.[45]

Downstream, all along the canal, there was additional damage. Robert P. Lovett, the out-going supervisor of the lower section of the canal, wrote on January 28 that "The heavy rain of Saturday last has done immense injury to the canal." The aqueduct at Point Pleasant (Tohickon) had suffered substantial damage, "one pier entirely gone, one other so mutilated that it must be taken down. One span of the superstructure also gone, but is lodged in the trees a short distance from the canal and can be recovered."

Additionally, Lovett noted two breaches "of considerable extent" along with undetermined damage to waste weirs, while the "canal embankments and the towing path [were] partially destroyed in several places." What additional damage there was could not "be perceived owing to the immense quantities of heavy ice that remains piled up in the canal and on the embankments mountain high." As he had heard that the dam at Easton had failed, he predicted that navigation would be delayed "to the serious disadvantage of many."[46]

The canal continued to be plagued by high waters during the whole season. On Thursday April 11, according to the *Mauch Chunk Courier*, it started raining, which contributed to

> one of the greatest freshets; raising the water to 8 feet above the combs of the Lehigh dams and carrying away lumber and other property but doing little damage to the Lehigh Canal. The work on the Delaware Canal was halted as the basin at Easton was again flooded.
>
> The water rose to 23 feet above the high water mark at the Easton Bridge.[47]

There were many minor problems that could, at least on occasions, be handled with surprising speed. Assistant engineer Martin Coryell reported that "a small breach occurred in our Canal Bank above Lock 19" at night on July 2. A passing boat brought the information and a report that the water was shut off from above, and the "water weir gates raised." The breach was apparently in a gravel bank well away from the river; the assumption was that it was caused by muskrats. When Coryell arrived on the scene at 3 o'clock

A severe freshet would not only damage the locks, gates, and banks of the canal, but would also strand canal boats. Sometimes the damage was so severe the canal was closed for months for repairs. This is at Lumberville, an especially vulnerable section since the canal and river were so close to each other.

the next day, he found that supervisor Calvin and his foreman had already repaired the break. Traffic was held up in all less than 30 hours.[48]

There was a much more serious crisis about August 16, 1839, when a 200-foot breach developed in the towpath some three and one-half miles below Easton. Philadelphia's *Public Ledger* reported that muskrats were the cause. Engineer Huffnagle's opinion differed. His report said that the break was caused by "the original malformation of the canal at that point."

> … An exposed side hill, and the water deep, a foundation was raised of rough material, composed of stumps and rocks, through which a light coating of good lining gradually filtrated, and undermining the entire bank.
>
> [A slight leak was discovered and then a] sudden irruption took place, carrying the repair boat into the breach, and crushing it to pieces. This point having been properly sheet-piled, and a dam thrown across the canal above, gravel was boated and the whole effectually repaired.

The canal did not reopen until early September, releasing "the hundreds of boatmen who for several weeks were obliged to lie idle."[49]

The saving of the Lehigh Dam was the big event of the year, but engineer William K. Huffnagle, appointee of a new canal board, could record in his annual report many lesser repair and reconstruction efforts. During the season, the stream carried under the canal by the culvert at Raub's (now Raubsville) rose and destroyed the culvert, which was replaced by an aqueduct (now known as Fry's Run or Kleinhaus Creek) with a 12-foot span.

The aqueduct at Durham failed and was replaced with a new single span of 50 feet with an arch and truss superstructure. The aqueduct at Gallow's Run required a new pier, replacement of its trunk, and a crib on the upper side to protect an abutment. A new buttress was needed at the Tinicum Aqueduct; the Tohichon Aqueduct needed one new pier, strengthening the underpinning of another pier, two spans of new trunk plus reinforcing; the aqueduct at New Hope over Ingham's Creek needed its trunk replaced.

For the first time the lifting wheels at Wells Falls (New Hope) needed repairs, the force of the freshet having "unshipped" them, carried away their guards and fractured the connection between their chambers and the sluice that carried the raised water away from the canal. Mr. Huffnagle's efforts were equal to the tasks and on March 24, the wheels started again. Four days later navigation was resumed from New Hope to Bristol while the portion of the canal north of New Hope went into service before May 13.[50] William Innis, collector at Easton, could report that "navigation commenced this season on the 14th of May 1839."[51]

(Left) The great lifting wheels south of New Hope, first built in 1832 and rebuilt in 1880, that lifted river water into the canal. The feeder dam or wing dam that directed water to the wheels can be seen in the company map below.

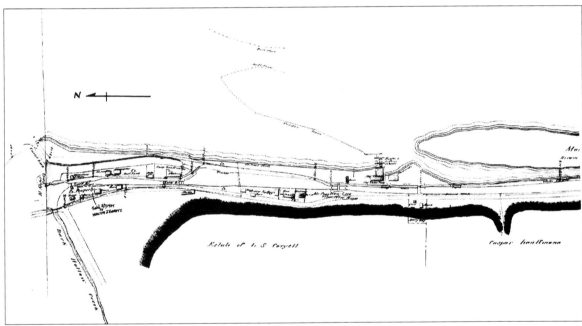

The repairs had been aided by two coal companies anxious to resume shipping. The Lehigh Coal and Navigation Company had sent some one hundred and thirty men, and the Beaver Meadow Company, which shipped coal from docks above Mauch Chunk, had sent eighty of their employees to help restore the damaged canal. Additionally, Joshua Calvin, supervisor of the middle section of the canal, had dispatched many of his hands to aid in meeting the more critical problems in the northern section of the canal.[52]

Tolls that year, despite the belated opening, rose to a figure some $26,000 above what had been received the previous year. The canal was now carrying a new commodity, limestone, and the completion of a slackwater system by the Lehigh Navigation 26 miles north from Mauch Chunk to Whitehaven promised additional traffic in coal and lumber.[53] Huffnagle estimated that repairs and refurbishing for the year 1839 would be $122,128.36, including 10 percent for "contingencies and supervision."[54]

The aforementioned senate committee of 1839 listed what they saw as the needs of the Delaware Division and its locks, aqueducts, and bridges, many of which were already under repair either as a result of the floods or—and this was certainly a concern of the Democrats—a lack of proper maintenance by their predecessors. Additionally, the committee noted:

The locks on this canal are but eleven feet wide, and the canal in many places too narrow for the accommodation of the increased trade, which the extensive coal fields, to which it constitutes a principal outlet, will eventually throw upon this line of improvements. Your committee are of the opinion that whenever it becomes necessary to rebuild locks, the dimensions thereof should be increased to fifteen or sixteen feet, so that, in time, the capacity of the whole line may be made commensurate with the business that may be offered … The towing path, in many places, is too low, and subject to be overflown during high freshets; this cannot be obviated without incurring enormous expense.

The committee made their own estimates of prospective costs, which they found to be far less than those of the engineers. Their estimate for the Delaware Division was only $40,000. The lack of proper maintenance was not wholly the fault of previous officialdom, the committee noted: much of the blame would seem to rest on "the Legislature, who had neglected to make the necessary provisions for making repairs."[55]

While the dam was under reconstruction and the canal closed, many boatmen from Easton took it upon themselves to descend by way of the river. Those who made it then petitioned the Board of Canal Commissioners for permission to return by way of the re-opened canal without having to pay the penalty for one-way use.[56] Their petition was granted, but the efforts to use the river were not without pitfalls as Captain Allen Hice of the "decked boat, Ohio" learned when he apparently "miscalculated the draught of water on the dam" as he "attempted to cross too near it" and instead of exiting through the outlet lock "went over the dam stern foremost." The boat, which belonged to a Mr. Kugler, was valued at $750 while the cargo of flour and cornmeal, which was partially recovered, sustained a $650 loss. Most of the boats of the "Millers, Distillers and Others" that originated at Easton made the dangerous passage down the river without incident.[57]

Financial Considerations

On February 20, 1839, the Board of Canal Commissioners by resolution ordered Solon Chapin to prepare check rolls to facilitate payment of the personnel he had recruited to meet the January 1839 emergency, and ordered David Connor, supervisor of the northern section of the Delaware Division to pay the individuals.[58]

The procedures for compensating the laborers, who were paid by the day and not by salary, was for the appropriate foreman to enter the names and the number of days on the check roll. This was a large monthly chart that listed the names of the individual laborers down the left margin and the days across the top of the chart. In the right columns, in addition to totaling the days, it listed the rate of compensation and the total compensation for the month, leaving a far right-hand margin in which the laborer signed his name or his witnessed mark when he received his pay, thus verifying what compensation he was entitled to.[59]

The appropriate supervisor would physically go up or down his division and pay the workers who signed both the check roll and a small receipt. Properly authenticated by the foreman and a justice of the peace, the receipts were then approved by the appropriate supervisor and dispatched to the auditor general in Harrisburg for approval. When approved by this functionary, they were sent to the canal commissioners, who then ordered warrants to be sent to the state treasurer, who released the warranted funds for the next round of payments. These documents—the check rolls, vouchers, and receipts along with the documentation for purchases and for payment of contracts—were filed in the board room of the canal commissioners at Harrisburg.[60]

It is impossible to determine whether the bureaucratic hang-ups that occurred were the result of greater diligence on the part of a new auditor general, whether it had something to do with the bitter charges and recriminations of the party change in Harrisburg, or whether it had something to do with the growing financial problems of the state, now in debt for some $40,000,000 as a result of its expenditures on internal improvements.

All would have worked fine had the supervisors received their funds on schedule but such was not the case in the troubled Commonwealth. As the pay ran sometimes a month in arrears—and often much longer—complications developed. Amidst the mass of receipts and check rolls to be found among the papers of the Board of Canal Commissioners in Harrisburg are dozens of slips of paper, usually about 3" by 8", each addressed to a supervisor, often David Connor at Easton, authorizing him to pay the wages due a worker to another party, who had in many cases already advanced the money to the worker. Many were for as little as two or three days' employment. For example, one group consisting of several dozen, all dated May 1, 1839, were concerned with wages earned several weeks earlier in the month of April.[61]

Solon Chapin, the hero of the struggle to save the Easton dam, fell afoul of the system. An examination of the correspondence during the month of April, 1839, between supervisor David Connor and Solon Chapin on the one hand and Mr. N.P. Horton, auditor general of the Commonwealth of Pennsylvania, is enlightening. Chapin wrote on April 22 that upon receipt of the previous letter from the auditor general, both Connor and he "supposed … that the rolls were all right except so far as they wanted authority from me to him to receive the money disbursed to the hands." However, he noted, he discovered with the return of the rolls that "there are other difficulties which either did not strike you before or which you have since discovered." For example:

> one George Vogel is put down as George Baughman on the roll. This occurred in this way. He is the putative [supposed] son of George Vogel. His mother's name is Baughman & he is so generally called by the public although he himself signs his name Vogel.

In another case, two boys who were not present to sign their names when the rolls were paid off were each owed 50 cents. The money was left with a Mr. Opdyke. Chapin continued listing his examples and then confessed:

> I was a volunteer supervisor created for the occasion and I may not have understood … as well as one more versant in this sort of business. But I can vouch for the accuracy of everything about them. For when the Easton Bank advanced the funds I procured Mr Forman & Mr. Opdyke two of the most competent as well respectable of our citizens to witness the disbursement of the money and the taking of the receipts.[62]

Chapin had been instrumental in getting funds to meet the emergency, and the check rolls were the documentation required normally to get reimbursement. As Connor protested:

> The amount of these check Rolls was advanced by the Easton Bank, and a part of it paid out before I received my appointment and I thought as he had commenced paying that he might continue until the whole of it was paid out. The Bank does not want the amount due knowing that if they took theirs, that the laborers would quit work, on account of their having to wait so much longer for their pay. The Bank is yet willing to wait until all the hands are paid off, and if needs be, they would furnish more money to do so. Everyone is anxious to see the canal in navigable order, and if we can only keep the hands to work which we have now, and pay them off in a short time, they shall be gratified pretty soon.[63]

The problems are further illustrated in the correspondence dispatched by David Connor to George R. Espy, auditor general of Pennsylvania, on October 23 of 1839. After explaining a difference of one dollar in the accounts, Connor said the error had occurred in transcription, that the duplicate was in fact the original, and the correction had been made. However, his explanation for another variance, this one of nine dollars, was circumstances that had caused the names of Jacob Donaldson, Jonathan Warner & Charles Reeder to have

> been written by the same hand. At the time the Check Roll was sent you it was neglected to have sent on the authority, which authorized Mr [Martin] Coryell, the assistant Engineer to draw their pay, and witnessed by Mr. Calvin, the Sup^r on the middle section of the Canal. They being Masons who reside between 30 & 40 miles from here, and sent here by the Engineer, in consequence of the scarcity of hands at that time. When they left we had no money to pay them and when we got money they did not appear after which Mr. Donaldson, the Master Mason gave Mr. Coryell the accompanying order to receive the pay for him and this hands. …

The reason the marks of others were not witnessed was that Geo. Sigman who attended to the Rolls when they were paid off left it until we got through with the whole, on account of the throng, which is attendant upon such occasions. He wrote all their names which you may discover by reference—and has now witnessed them all.

Another problem was the rate to which wages had risen during the spring of 1839. On April 12, 1839, David Connor, supervisor at Easton, wrote the auditor general noting that much damage had been done to private property as well as to the state works. He pointed to the heavy work and the necessity of paying "the highest price for labor done on the canal." Laborers "can get employment anywhere, and it is with difficulty that we can get as many as we require." Wages in arrears did not help the situation.[64]

The Commonwealth was facing a growing revenue shortfall as the effects of the depression that followed the Panic of 1837 began to limit its ability to raise funds. On May 22, Connor wrote the canal commissioners protesting that the auditor general of the financially troubled Commonwealth had returned his check rolls "stating that One dollar was the highest wages that could be allowed for labor on the Canal."[65]

I was obliged to give $1.12½ per day in order to get hands, and could not get even at that price as many as we required. At the commencement of the work early in the Spring we paid one dollar for common hands but as soon as the farmers commenced their own work, a majority of whom worked on the canal, they left it and employed all the hands they could get to assist them in their business. The Morris Canal Co. at the same time was employing a great many hands at the same price and paying them off every week which we were not able to do, and in consequence of which I was induced to raise the wages as above mentioned, or else we could not have continued the work.

There were, Connor told the commissioners, many lime kilns also competing for laborers and "indeed in the whole of this section of country there is plenty of work occasioned by the late freshet injuring private property as well as the public works."

Other employers all paid a dollar a day and paid by the day. Further, echoing the oft-repeated protest of the state officials, "they would not work for us and wait a month or so for the money."[66] The only salvation had been the Lehigh Coal and Navigation Company:

[The Mauch Chunk Company] assisted us by sending between one and two hundred men on and furnished money to carry on the work without which we would have been compelled to linger on this work for at least a month and a half to bring it where it now is.[67]

As late as July of 1840, James Madison Porter wrote protesting the auditor general's disallowance of an item for $74 for blankets that had been furnished the workers from Mauch Chunk the previous April. Porter added that if funds could be advanced to David Connor, who had many repairs to accomplish during the "Coming Season" —during the winter months when the canal would be closed down— "It will have a decidedly beneficial Effect on this vicinity".[68]

The financial problems would not go away. Supervisor Harmon complained on July 9, 1840, about failures to honor his draft: "It is Certainly a very unpleasant business to Disappoint the Laborers who have been waiting for their money since September last."[69]

One can sympathize with supervisor David Connor, writing on July 19, 1839, to protest he had received no advance of funds whereas Joshua Calvin, whose section butted against Connor's, had received funds and was able "to pay off all his bills for materials and labor performed and that I do not pay." His creditors did not understand that Calvin's obligations were smaller or that Connor's problems were complicated by the rejection of his check rolls by the auditor general. It was particularly difficult for individuals who had delivered materials to Connor rather than to others: they "were anxious to see the canal in order" but were still awaiting the pay that they had expected to receive far sooner. If there are any funds, protested Connor, please make them available so "that I may be placed on an equal footing with the Rest of the Supervisors."[70] Supervisor Harmon in July opined:

It will take longer to pay the Laborers now than it would if they were paid every month because they are not working on the Land at this time and are squandered all over the Country and [it] takes great trouble to find them.[71]

The Commonwealth at this time was in a state of near financial disaster. It had survived the Panic of 1837, but two state loans, each authorized to raise the funds to continue work on the still-unfinished state system of internal improvements, failed to be taken up by potential lenders. The first loan was under Governor Ritner while the second was under the administration of Democratic Governor Porter. Compulsory loans exacted from state-chartered banks induced bank failures. The Commonwealth of Pennsylvania would fail to make interest payments on its debt from 1842 to 1845, a period of severe financial stringency.[72]

Repairs were usually contracted for at the end of the season, but across the state the call was for economy and cut-backs of everything above the minimum necessities.

The Flood of 1841

January of 1841 saw "unpremeditated high freshets" in the two rivers (the Lehigh and the Delaware) that brought destruction on the Delaware for a distance of 37 miles. The canal basin was carried out at Easton, the abutment for the still-unfinished new dam, the locks (guard lock and outlet lock), and the partially completed weigh lock were materially damaged and the toll collector's office was carried away.

The *American Railroad Journal and Mechanics' Magazine* in February 1841 used the destruction caused by "the late severe freshet" as a rationale to recommend construction of wire suspension bridges which offered, among their other attractions, no obstruction to a flood. Bridges without number had been destroyed by a disaster that had spread destruction "over a greater extent of country than any like disaster for many years … and several canals have suffered severely, but none so much as the Lehigh canal."[73]

During the evening of January 7, 1841, James Madison Porter, brother of the Governor and one of Easton's most influential citizens, excitedly wrote:

> The rains of yesterday and to-day have melted nearly all the snow in our country and the result is a freshet in both our rivers of an unprecedented character. The water in the Lehigh was as high as in January 1839, and it is feared has carried away the gravel bank of the basin from near the abutment of the new dam around to near the Outlet Lock. The nature and extent of the injury cannot even be guessed at, as the water is still high and the rain continuing. … The injury will be twice as great as that of the winter of 1839.

In a postscript he added, "10 o'clock at night—The Lehigh still rising and the breach increasing." On the next morning, January 8, with the flood waters still raging, he continued his letter to E.B. Stuckey:

> I wrote you last night expecting that the mail would leave this place for Philadelphia this morning, but before the time for starting the bridge over the Lehigh was carried away by the freshet. The damage done is almost incalculable. The Lock house and the Engineers Office at the basin are gone. The basin as I stated cut out. The stone house belonging to Mr Chapin and myself is capsized against the Tavern House of Mr. Diehl opposite the Guard Lock. The whole canal I expect is overflowed for miles and I presume the aqueducts at Frey's run, Durham creek and Gallows run are gone. If they are not it is almost a miracle. … The freshet is at least ten feet higher than that of January 1839.[74]

The base mark used for measuring floods by engineer Huffnagle in his 1841 annual report was "low water" at Easton and he recorded that on the "8th and 9th of January of this year" a freshet occurred,

> unknown in extent, to the oldest inhabitants of that section of the country. The Delaware at Easton, rose to the unprecedented height of thirty-five feet above low water mark, being four feet higher than the great freshet of 1783. Seven feet above that of 1804, and ten feet greater than that of 1839.[75]

The damage on the Lehigh River, "one of the most unruly and turbulent of streams," and to the Lehigh Canal were devastating. The Lehigh Coal and Navigation Company had to resort to heroic measures and great expenditures before their works could be reopened. According to one account:

> The bridges at Stoddartsville, Lehighton, Siegfried's, Biery's, Allentown, Bethlehem, Freeman's, Easton—all of them swept clean away. The beautiful bridge at our borough [Easton], went about four

o'clock in the morning of the 8th. It brested the flood most gallantly for hours, but at last was obliged to yield, and gracefully parting, floated off upon the angry waters that destroyed.[76]

Three days later, while reports of the damages were still being collected and evaluated, Porter listed many for the Board of Canal Commissioners:

The entire berm is swept away from the southern abutment of the Lehigh dam to the outlet lock. The weigh Lock is much injured, so is the Guard Lock and the Collector's Office turned about and much damaged. So far as heard the damage on the canal will be fully equal to those of the winter of 1839. I am glad to say that the aqueduct at Frey's run and at Durham creek are both uninjured.

He added in a postscript that "The Dam at Easton is not much injured, but each of the embankments is injured."[77]

Downstream, supervisor Daniel Y. Harman reported on January 8 that at Tinicum Creek the piers of the aqueduct were undermined, for miles along the bluff sections the towing path was cut down, and extensive areas of the prism was filled with debris.

I hasten to inform you that we have one of the most awful rivers that has been known by our oldest residents. It is now 5 feet higher than it has ever been. It has swept all before it. All the bridges from Easton to Trenton are swept clear. Houses and barns and even men were swept down the furious element.

One man who was on the centre bridge at the time it moved off went with the same and was carried with the current 17 miles before he could be taken off, which fortunately was effected. It is impossible to give you any description of the damage done to the State works, but it will be very great. The wheels, Breast Work etc. at Wells Falls is all gone. The water is still raising rapidly and to what extent it will go is not known.

At Wells Falls (New Hope) the lifting wheels were not merely unshipped, they were swept away. Little wonder that costs soared during the year. Other breaches occurred during June, July, and August. It was not until August 21 that the interrupted navigation was restored. The promise of the previous several years was reversed as tolls fell to only $64,974.93 while expenditures climbed to $109,338.81.[78]

On January 12, 1841, the Lehigh Coal and Navigation Company's board of directors dispatched Josiah White, now 61 years of age,[79] and engineer E.A. Douglas to examine the company's navigation and "to ascertain and report to the Board as soon as practicable, the entire damage sustained by the recent unprecedented freshet."[80]

The damage was immense. On January 19, even before its engineer could come up with a firm estimate, the LC&N board authorized the immediate repairs that were necessary for "the preservation of the works of the Company from further serious injury."[81]

To meet the emergency, the board authorized its finance committee to "defer the present payment of the principal of any Certificate which may be presented." These expenses would tax the resources of what was possibly America's largest corporation at the time to such a degree that its very integrity was threatened. In February a memorial was dispatched to the legislature of Pennsylvania noting that the damage had been so extensive that additional public borrowing would be necessary. Despite the company's investment of $5,500,000, the board pointed out, its capital stock was limited to $1,600,000, a situation that made further fundraising difficult.[82]

E.A. Douglas

The Lehigh Coal and Navigation Company had been engaged in a running battle of words and, sometimes, harassing charges with the Board of Canal Commissioners and the city of Philadelphia. Most commonly these concerned the LC&N's complaints about the inadequate size of the Delaware Division Canal, challenges to the toll charges on the Delaware Division, and the oft-repeated petition of the LC&N for an outlet lock at Upper Black Eddy, some twelve miles below Easton. Philadelphia interests charged conspiracy with New York and claimed that the proposed outlet lock would divert the coal trade that rightfully belonged to Pennsylvania. The LC&N responded with statistics about how much business would be generated, and the potential losses to the state if they diverted coal for the New York market over a proposed enlarged Morris Canal, completely bypassing the Delaware Division Canal.[83]

The appeal for expansion of the capital stock elicited an attack in Philadelphia's *Public Ledger* on Thursday, February 23, 1841. A correspondent using the pseudonym "ANTHRAX" titled his letter "SIX MILLION MONSTER" and warned that a company with liabilities of $1,600,000 in capital and $3,900,000 in loans should be watched: "We repeat our caution to the widow and orphan loan holders, to examine narrowly into every movement of the monster which may impair their security ..."

Two days later, on Saturday, the same newspaper printed a much longer response over the signature of Joseph Watson, president of the company, refuting ANTHRAX's innuendoes.[84]

Possibly the best picture of the extent of the damages to the Delaware Division of the Pennsylvania Canal and the amount of extraordinary expense can best be ascertained by an examination of the annual reports of David Connor, supervisor of the canal from Easton to Tohickon Creek, and of W.J. Rogers, supervisor from Bristol to Point Pleasant. Supervisor Connor in his December 1, 1841, report listed a total of $30,981.91 in expenses, broken down into some $10,000 in ordinary expenses and more than $20,000 in extraordinary expenses, largely as a result of flood damage. "The Freshet of January, 1841, did very serious injury to the whole of the canal under my charge, leaving the greater portion of it in ruins."[85] There were expenditures necessary all along his section:

> Of the Mechanical Work, the following are of the most consequence.
> Basin at Easton — still in progress — cost not ascertained
> Repair of Outlet, Guard & Weigh Locks at Easton — The repair is thorough
> & extensive — cost $10,871.27 —
> Tinicum Aqueduct — Rebuilt — cost $10,248.23

Connor noted that, because of the expenditures, most of the canal was in good condition; only Lock No. 18 needed rebuilding. He recommended that the towing path be raised for the length of the canal. In response to a question from the canal commissioners, he could see no way to reduce his ordinary expenses for the coming year. Instead of having opened on April 1, the normal date, the canal had admitted water on July 15 and the first boat had not passed until July 27. The canal closed on December 18, a better performance than the normally projected December 1 to 15 closing date.[86]

On December 1, supervisor Rogers reported expenditures totaling some $50,000 for the previous year, from November 1840 to November 1841. Some $10,000 were for ordinary expenses, while he listed more than $40,000 in extraordinary expenses, largely flood-generated.[87] Repairs had been necessary as follows: the tide lock at Bristol; guard gates below Neely's Creek; locks 8, 9, 10, 11, 12, and 13; the aqueducts at Knowles' Creek, Hough's Creek and Lumberville; the waste weirs above and below Blacks Eddy, at Johnson's, and above and below New Hope, along with numerous bridges. In addition, the towing path had been raised, walls had been reinforced, excavation had taken place while the water wheels at New Hope were being rebuilt and shanties, tool houses, and other small buildings had been replaced along the canal.

The disastrous flood of January had been followed by floods in June, July and August, which caused

> several breaches in the Canal at and near Naylor's overflow, distant about a half a mile above the
> mouth of the creek [Neelys] carrying away the slope wall & the entire tow path ...

Rogers estimated that more than $15,000 worth of work was still needed:

I would most earnestly recommend to the Board the immediate construction of guard gates above the entrance of Neely's creek into the canal, the expense of which I have estimated at $2,000. The breaches in June, July and August and numerous other breaches might have been prevented, if Guard gates had been erected at this point, as they would have thrown the great body of water from this rapid stream from its entrance in the canal, directly into the river, and entirely protected the navigation from this fruitful and inevitable source of destruction.[88]

One especial problem area revealed by the floods was at Neely's Creek, some two miles below New Hope.[89] It was one of the few waterways along the canal that drained directly into it, entering the canal at a right angle. Engineer Huffnagle echoed the concerns: "This stream has never yet been brought into proper subjection." As can be seen from the rough diagram that resides in the state archives, one proposal was for three "safety gates," one above and one below the creek plus another down the canal below a waste gate. The towpath bank along the canal would be lowered for a distance of about 200 feet to water level, providing an overflow that could be drained into the river. These plans would eventually be implemented.[90]

Rogers also noted the growing obstruction in the basin at Bristol, caused by "a large and constant deposit of saw dust, from the tail race of a mill, which empties into the basin at Lock No. 1." On the positive side, however,

> The trade on the Canal, since the repairs caused by the January freshet, which were nearly completed on the first of August, has been much greater than at any subsequent period.

The water was adequate, he added, for boats carrying "sixty tons and upwards."[91]

Reflections

These years that were punctuated by floods brought on by wind, storm, and weather offer mute testimony to the extraordinary and awesome forces of nature as well as to the vulnerability of man-made structures. They illustrate the seemingly eternal problems of governmental inefficiency and uncompromising political partisanship, and proclaim the technical abilities and inabilities of those who were responsible for nineteenth-century infrastructure. In the process they make the reader aware that even modern technological man is still not immune from the mighty devastations of flood waters.

∽ CHAPTER IV ∽

Governments and Transportation Systems:
Pennsylvania as a Case Study

In 1843, the great Commonwealth of Pennsylvania was subjected to a barrage of demeaning publicity, coming particularly from England. The reason: the failure of the Keystone State to meet its interest payments on the accumulated debts of some forty million dollars. British investors had eagerly purchased bonds issued by American states because they had a much higher rate of return than did safer but lower-paying European bonds. In their haste to secure higher interest rates, these investors chose to ignore the often-precarious nature of the credit and financial stability of the American states.

Seventy-three-year-old English essayist the very irate Reverend Sydney Smith, his pen dripping acid, received great notoriety as he addressed the American Congress:

> Your Petitioner sincerely prays that the great and good men still existing among you, may, by teaching to the United States the deep disgrace they have incurred to the whole world, restore them to moral health …[1]

He was one of the numerous Britons who had invested in American securities.

> The State of Pennsylvania cheats me this year out of £50. There is nothing in the crimes of kings worse than this villainy of democracy. The mob positively refuse all taxation for the payment of State debts.[2]

On December 18, 1843, in a personal letter he gloated:

> I hope you were amused with my attack on the Americans … It is a monstrous and increasing villainy. Fancy a meeting in Philadelphia, convened by public announcement, where they came to resolutions that the debt was too great for the people to pay, that the people could not pay it, and ought not to pay it! I have not a conception that the creditors will ever have a single shilling.[3]

A somewhat more restrained, yet still bitter, account comes from the pen of English geologist Charles Lyell, who was traveling in America during 1842 when Pennsylvania was faced with a state of emergency as a result of the "stoppage of one of the banks … in which were lodged the funds intended for the payment of dividends on state bonds, due in a few days." Failing to obtain loans to cover the shortage, the state announced "a delay in Payment." The bank alluded to was the Bank of Pennsylvania, which closed its doors in April of 1843 after having been subjected to the pressure of having to satisfy a series of legally required state demand loans. Other attacks by the pro-Jackson state government in Harrisburg threatened its specie holdings and even its existence. The state, which held three-fifths of the stock of the bank, had earlier failed in the courts to achieve a takeover of the bank.[4]

Lyell summarized the problem from the viewpoint of the worried American bond holders who argued that

> the resources of the state, if well managed, were ample; and that, if it depended on the more affluent merchants of Philadelphia, and the richer portion of the middle class generally, to impose and pay the taxes, the honor of Pennsylvania would not be compromised.

Offering an oft-repeated lament, Lyell called attention to the retirees who

[were left] destitute; many widows and single women have lost their all, and great numbers of the poorer class are deprived of their savings. An erroneous notion prevails in England that the misery created by these bankruptcies is confined chiefly to foreigners, but in fact, many of the poorest citizens of Pennsylvania and of other States, have invested money in these securities.

British investors, who held more than of two-thirds of the $40,000,000 debt, suffered a double disappointment, losing both their money and their faith in the "private worth of the people and their capacity for self-government.[5]

The English periodical *Punch* used ironic derision to impugn the integrity of Pennsylvania. In just one of a number of such items, it reported the anniversary of William Penn as having been celebrated with "appropriate exercises," one of which was "the exciting and national sport of 'Beggar my Neighbour'." Another game played was a version of

Backgammon, played between a Philadelphian and an European in which the latter was invariably gammoned …

"Forfeits" were also largely played by men in drab* and aliens, the latter forfeiting whatever they intrusted to the former.

The populace, in the meantime, loudly exercised their lungs, bawling continually— "Non-Payment!" "No Surrender!" One Quaker, amid much applause, propounded the following sentiment: "Philadelphia! herself independent, can never be depended upon."[6]

The state was even the butt of a sonnet by seventy-five-year old poet William Wordsworth who questioned Pennsylvania's integrity on behalf of an elderly friend, Miss Isabella Fenwick, and his brother, a Cambridge Don, both of whom had invested sizeable portions of their savings in Pennsylvania securities. The mockery read as follows:

TO THE PENNSYLVANIANS
1845

Days undefiled by luxury or sloth,
Firm self-denial, manners grave and staid,
Rights equal, laws with cheerfulness obeyed,
Words that require no sanction from an oath
And simple honesty a common growth—
This high repute, with bounteous Nature's aid,
Won confidence, now ruthlessly betrayed
At will, your power the measure of your troth!—
All who revere the memory of Penn
Grieve for the land on whose wild woods his name
Was fondly grafted with a virtuous aim,
Renounced, abandoned by degenerate Men
For state-dishonour black as ever came
To upper air from Mammon's loathsome den.[7]

Unlike several other states, Pennsylvania never repudiated its debt. The state authorities missed five interest payments during the years 1842, 1843, and 1844, issuing interest-accruing certificates for the amount of the interest, and resumed payments in February of 1845. The quality of the interest payment was becoming suspect, as security values had already fallen on the London market following Andrew Jack-

---

* a derisive reference to Quaker humility

son's Specie Circular of 1837. The subsequent failure of the banks to redeem in specie debased the interest payments to European security holders as they only too often took the form of depreciated instruments of exchange. American securities continued their fall following the 1840 resolution passed by the United States Senate disclaiming any responsibility for state debts.[8]

After 1845 the worst had passed, as the state met its obligations and even achieved some slight reductions in the state debt total although the state works were to struggle until finally, in 1857, they were sold for a fraction of their original cost.[9]

The crisis of the 1840s was the nadir reached by the state in its effort to be the agent for construction of a massive transportation system. It is worth the effort to consider the advantages and the problems inherent in such state activity and to suggest some judgments that could be made concerning the efforts. This fiasco was just another happening in a long historical sequence of events. In many ways, Pennsylvania had led in the area of internal infrastructure improvements. Earlier projects had their beginnings in the eighteenth century, when appropriations had been made for canal surveys and abortive attempts to start construction, and for improvements of river navigation. These were followed by extensive state purchases of turnpike, bridge, bank and canal stocks during the first decades of the nineteenth century. The activities of the Pennsylvania Society for the Promotion of Internal Improvements were spurred by the opening of New York's Erie Canal in 1825. The initial propaganda promoted canals, but by the end of the decade of the 1820s the newly developed railroad was among the society's concerns:

> It has become one of the fondest sources of honourable pride among the citizens of Pennsylvania, that her internal improvements, although not always of the most judicious and profitable kind, are more extensive than those of any of her sister states … accomplished by the joint and concurrent contributions of her liberal legislatures, and her public citizens.[10]

Only one additional great work was still necessary to "make Pennsylvania as great a state as any in the confederacy." That was to achieve the "junction of Lake Erie, the Ohio, the Alleghany, the Susquehanna, and the Delaware" by cheap and accessible transportation facilities.[11]

By 1825, the state had named a board of canal commissioners; by 1828, with new legislation and a newly restructured board of commissioners, contracts were being let for canals and surveys were being made for railroads, all to be constructed by the state. The arguments for construction by the state were basically that only the state had the resources necessary, and that private capital would build only those portions that promised to be profitable, leaving the system less than what was desired. The Jeffersonian fear of monopolies and great wealth intensified under the Jacksonians, until it became a phobia—the maintenance of the freedom of the population made public control of such a system essential.[12]

The cost of construction was to be borne by loans, the first, in 1823, preceded the actual commitment to state-constructed internal improvements. In April of 1826, the Internal Improvement Fund Act was passed. The secretary of the treasury, the auditor general, and the state treasurer were the fund commissioners. Into the Internal Improvement Fund went the various assessments and taxes designated for the works system, along with the dividends from the state-owned securities and appropriations from the legislature. The fund was also empowered to contract loans, pay interest on the debts, make reimbursements on principal, and dispense funds to the canal commissioners to meet the expenses of construction and maintenance. By 1840, the total accumulated state debt had reached more than $34,000,000; with continuing loans plus accruing interest, by the end of Governor Porter's administration in January of 1845, it totaled more than $40,000,000.[13]

Governors, Democratic and Anti-Masonic Whig, warned against expenditures without taxes, but each was swept along by a legislature enamored with the promise of highly remunerative internal improvements. Newly initiated public works were funded by loans based on the consensus belief that the returns from the state works would retire the debts and that these receipts would, in addition, eliminate the need for taxes in the state.

The November 17, 1829, special session of the legislature called by outgoing Governor Shulze passed an act authorizing a loan for $1,000,000 at 5 percent to meet the demands of the system of internal improvements, then under construction. Because of the questionable credit of the state, it was necessary on December 7 for the state to obtain a "compulsory" loan from the banks of the Commonwealth, a requirement written into the charters of the banks. Despite this, Shulze offered his judgment that, with the system of internal improvements already partly in place,

> we have much cause to be proud of the public spirited exertions of our constituted authorities and fellow citizens, and to hope that prosperity and wealth will flow in upon us abundantly, to stimulate our industry to the utmost, and bring to market the mineral and metallic treasures which are now buried and useless.[14]

When Governor George Wolf rode into office on a sizeable majority at the end of December, 1829, he called for the vigorous prosecution of the system of public works, already commenced, despite the doubts of many of "the most zealous friends of the improvement system" as to the future of the system. At the same time he recommended an adequate system of taxation.[15] His efforts achieved a modest level of taxation and revived the credit of the state, whose securities had been in demand for a period of years. Greed, both at home and abroad, kept them trading above face at premiums of sometimes up to fourteen or fifteen percent. The premiums actually covered most of the interest expense and put the Commonwealth into a state of euphoria.[16]

Wolf was originally a friend of Nicholas Biddle's Second Bank of the United States. In his 1832 annual message he called, among other things, for Pennsylvania's congressional delegation to support the recharter of Biddle's bank:

> It has established a circulating medium in which the people have confidence ... [It would be] a subject for regret [if] a too strict adherence to a literal construction of the Constitution ... or a too critical analysis of its expediency in a moral or political point of view [should prevent the renewal of its charter.][17]

Following the 1832 veto of the recharter act, President Jackson easily won reelection.[18]

The bubble started to burst when the bidders for the portions of Pennsylvania's 1833 loan failed to honor their obligation. Much of the debt, even with no premiums, still remained to be assumed, a situation caused not by any financial inadequacies on the part of the state but rather as a result of the Jackson administration's withdrawal of its deposits as part of its continuing attack on the Bank of the United States.

But the tone was changing; rather than oppose the popular president of his own party, Wolf accused the bank of "bringing indiscriminate ruin and distress upon an unoffending community." For the next year (1834), there were no premiums except for the forced loan from the Bank of Pennsylvania. And the governor now vigorously joined the national party in the attacks on the banks, corporations, and private capital. In this 1834 message he stated the bizarre economic judgment that

> By causing bank paper of a description under the sum mentioned, to be gradually withdrawn from circulation, the introduction of gold and silver coins in sufficient quantities to supply the vacuum thus produced, would immediately follow.[19]

In 1832, Wolf bragged that

> [when] the whole of the works authorized, and under contract, shall have been completed, this state will have in her own right, constructed in a period of about seven years, five hundred and ninety three miles ... of artificial improvement by canal and slackwater navigation; and one hundred and eighteen miles ... of railroads, which in magnificence of design, solidity and neatness in execution, and for splendid prospects of future productiveness and usefulness, will stand unrivalled, and will place our state upon a proud eminence ... A work upon a scale so magnificent could not fail to involve, in its construction the expenditure of much treasure and to cause the state to incur heavy liabilities; but I am bold to say, that independent of the future value of these improvements to the commonwealth, the state has been the gainer already, in the resultant prosperity.[20]

In 1834, the main line from Philadelphia to Pittsburgh was completed. Some of the so-called lateral canals that were initiated under legislative pressure, against Governor Wolf's better judgment, were, unlike the Delaware Division, still unfinished and their completion would drag on for years. During this period, the state of Pennsylvania so dulled its sense of financial reality as to oppose taxes, despite the advice of Governor Wolf, who advised in his 1831 annual message

> that this mode of supplying the interest fund by premiums upon loans cannot be expected to continue, and should under any circumstances be too capricious and unsafe to be relied upon.[21]

In 1835, Joseph Ritner, at the head of an Anti-Masonic, Whig, pro-bank Democratic coalition, finally succeeded in his third try for the governor's mansion. His administration was pro-bank and he came into office pro-main line canal but anti-lateral canal so far as internal improvements were concerned. Before he left office, however, he had surrendered to legislative pressure and supported the statewide works.

The political infighting, particularly over the vast spoils system created by the system of internal improvements, was a major divisive issue. It spawned many legislative investigations; some of the most bitter were aimed by the Democratic-controlled assembly at Anti-Masonic, Whig Governor Ritner. The 1836–1837 assembly created an investigating committee that returned a report finding wholesale displacement of employees on the state works as Governor Ritner took advantage of the extensive patronage available to the governor. It was matched by a minority report finding improvement in the workings of the system and accusing the majority of a ruthless lack of integrity. The 1838–1839 assembly conducted another investigation, as did its successor, the 1839–1840 assembly. The report of the latter, aimed at James Cameron, Superintendent of Motive Power on the Columbia and Philadelphia, contained 139 pages of bitter invective and selective testimony. Governors criticized the legislature for the endless politically inspired investigations that interfered with the efficient administration of the works.[22]

In his 1835 inaugural address, Ritner, the new governor, spoke of the great promise offered by the system of internal improvements but went on to note how it had

> encumbered the resources and deranged the finances of the commonwealth [and] produced new but as yet nearly untried channels for business and springs to private enterprise, and materially affected the occupations and interests of the people.[23]

He criticized the derelictions of his predecessors—cost over-runs, payment of workers and contractors in unauthorized script, and the event, faced only too often, of the failure of the legislature to make appropriations.[24]

Ritner's December 1836 annual message was full of optimism. There was a treasury balance; more than a million dollars was due in the form of bonuses paid by banks for the privilege of recharter; over a million dollars was optimistically expected in receipts from the public works; and the real windfall, an estimated three and one half million dollar payment, was to come from the federal government as a surplus distribution based on receipts, primarily from land sales that went into the debt-free treasury. Despite the fact that the modest taxes of the Wolf administration had been permitted to expire, a surplus was projected in the budget, offering the first promise of possible debt reduction.[25]

On the national scene, the Jacksonian Democrats were hard-money, anti-credit, and anti-bank. Many of the Jacksonians, however, particularly the followers of Martin Van Buren and Amos Kendall, were representatives of what historical revisionists call the entrepreneurial group who supported state banks and a different basis for bank credits, and exhibited enmity to Biddle's Second Bank. Most Whigs favored banking institutions that would create stable, expandable national currency and business credit along with adequate instruments for supporting foreign trade.[26]

A majority of the Pennsylvania debt was held abroad, mostly in England. Almost the total debt had been created to pay for the canals and railroads. And such canal and railroad manias were found not just in Pennsylvania, despite the fact that the Commonwealth had created both the nation's greatest mileage of internal improvements and the greatest debt, whether measured in aggregate or per capita. These aberrations were world-wide: in England, on the continent, in India, and in South America, a mania for canals and the Iron Horse ebbed and waned, and Pennsylvania imported millions of dollars worth of railroad iron to implement its program of internal improvements.[27]

This trade, along with America's export of securities and cotton, were facilitated by Nicholas Biddle's Bank of the United States. The structure "created" by Biddle facilitated the easy movement of merchandise based on credit and credit instruments both at home and abroad, and oversaw a stable and flexible circulating medium at home. In 1832, President Jackson vetoed the bill to recharter the second Bank of the United States, an event that was simply the first of what became a continuing attack on the bank.

During February of 1836, a bill, curiously titled "An Act to repeal the state tax on real and personal property, and to continue and extend the improvements of the state by railroads and canals, and to charter a state bank, to be called the United States Bank," ws signed into law by Pennsylvania's Governor Ritner. The legislative architect of the bill was Thaddeus Stevens. The battle in an assembly dominated by a badly divided Democratic majority was bitter. The political log-rolling that took place is obvious in the title of the bill. The bank's books showed $79,052 at this time for expenses, a sizeable portion of which was suspect as lobbying costs.[28] The title of the bill as originally introduced ended with no reference to the bank. It ended simply "and other purposes"; the bank purpose was later interjected as part of a planned strategy. The next several years would see continuing charges of bribery.[29]

On March 2, 1836, one day before its federal charter expired, the United States Bank accepted its charter from the Commonwealth of Pennsylvania.[30] The bank had survived, but the cost was great. It paid the state a $2,000,000 immediate bonus for the privilege of the state charter, committed itself to a yearly payment of $400,000 to the state, and made itself liable to loans upon request by the state to the extent of $6,000,000 in long-term loans and up to $1,000,000 per year in temporary loans. In addition, the agreement committed the bank to another $675,000, to be divided among a number of causes, education, and the stock of various private internal improvement companies as well as a yearly subsidy to education.[31]

Governor David Rittenhouse Porter, a Jacksonian Democrat who defeated Ritner by a paper-thin plurality, revealed at least part of the dilemma. At the same time he was calling for fiscal responsibility and taxes along with the need for responsible banking, he directed the efforts of the state to further attacks on what was now the United States Bank of Pennsylvania. This caused the British financial observer Alexander Trotter, writing for the edification of English security holders, to warn that:

> The strong manner in which the present governor [Porter] shows his opposition to the acts of his predecessor seems very prejudicial to the interests of the state; he opposed, for example, the renewal of the bank charter, and denied its validity; and, acting on this opinion, instead of having recourse to the bank for loans raised this year—which he might have obtained under the terms of its charter at 4 per cent. — he preferred borrowing at a higher rate of interest, rather than do what might be construed into any recognition of its authority.[32]

Trotter was prophetic. The 1843 fiasco faced by Porter was brought about by a combination of Democratic state and national policies. The failure to recharter, the removal of deposits, the Specie Circular of 1837 that required all land sales to be paid for in specie—all drained the country's gold and silver and caused the nation's banks to suspend specie redemption. This increased the difficulty of making interest payments, particularly to foreign holders of securities. With the March 6, 1840, senatorial disclaimer of any federal responsibility for state debts, American securities lost their previous "blue-chip" status. This situation, plus some questionable moves by Biddle's successors at the helm of the bank caused it to close its doors on February 4, 1841, depriving the country of many of its means for conducting foreign trade. Loans could not be placed except at heavy discounts, and the state was faced with the obligation of meeting nearly $2,000,000 in interest expense on its debt that by 1846 totaled $40,986.393.32. The Girard Bank and the Bank of Pennsylvania (as noted above) failed in 1842, so embarrassing the state that it missed its next five interest payments.[33]

There was some pressure to sell the public works during the Porter administration in the 1840s. When the legislature forced the works to be offered at prices that reflected their original cost—against the opposition of the Democratic governor, who looked with suspicion at private capital as a threat to public freedom—the only bids were for the Columbia and Philadelphia Railroad and one canal lock, both at very modest prices. However, by the 1850s, the works, long a financial millstone for the state, were again considered for sale. The Democrats opposed the sale when it was discovered that the sale price must be just a fraction of original cost. However, a public referendum in 1844 produced a majority of more than 20,000 on the side of "sell."[34]

A number of historians have documented the fact that, where the public works were concerned, geography was a more potent determinant than was party affiliation in the votes in the legislature. To put it another way, region and its potential for benefit or lack of benefit from the state works was the overriding factor, at least where the works themselves and their financing were concerned.[35]

This does not mean that the ferocity of party fighting was diminished as they faced off one against another. Patronage meant power, and whoever controlled the Board of Canal Commissioners exercised that power. The make-up of the board was changed, sometimes annually, until it became elective in 1843. The board was further subjected to almost yearly investigations by legislative committees, where dozens, sometimes hundreds of witnesses were interviewed across the state. Local politicians tried to abide by the platforms of the national parties, but the Pennsylvania democracy in particular was shattered on occasions by its stands on the national bank, for a majority initially supported the recharter of the bank—at least until Jackson successfully rejected the recharter—and after the bank, now chartered in Pennsylvania, became vulnerable as a result of Biddle's politicized and inept successors.

Around the state, no politician in the areas that benefited could oppose the state works. This did not mean, however, that he would not complain incessantly about the quality of the work and of the corruption of the administration, particularly when it was in the hands of the opposition party. If, however, his party controlled the legislature and his party's candidate had been elected governor (who appointed his own Board of Canal Commissioners), one party had control over a massive arena of political patronage. This pattern became further complicated after 1843, when the board became elective.[36]

Despite their control of the public works, the governor and/or the Board of Canal Commissioners were subject to the embarrassment of having the needed appropriations withheld by the legislative opposition, wrecking efficient operation of the public works.[37] A reading of the political record would indicate a system that had sunk into the morass of corruption and inefficiency, a record that stands in essential contradiction to the judgments of the engineers who worked on the construction and operation of the works. The historical blackening of the record was supplemented by aggressive attacks made on the system, particularly on the Columbia and Philadelphia Railroad portion of the works, by the Pennsylvania Railroad. The management of the Pennsylvania Railroad had been making criticisms almost from the time the PRR had been chartered in 1846, and continued doing so until long after the sale of the public works in 1857. Even before the sale, the PRR had resorted to the courts, unsuccessfully trying to impose their conditions on the state railroad, and had lobbied continuously against the state-levied tonnage tax and other terms of the sale—a sale that was opposed by the Board of Canal Commissioners and looked upon by many as a "Sweetheart Deal."[38]

The state system, originally planned as an east-west system to compete with New York's Erie Canal, grew as the need for political support brought additions to the works as votes were sought from additional regions of the state. Several of the so-called "lateral" canals were long unfinished and the state attempted to spin off the Erie Extension and the North Branch Extension to private corporations to complete them. The Erie Extension, on which the state had invested in excess of a million dollars, was given to a private corporation who completed the work for a pittance. The North Branch, an almost totally unprofitable part of the system, was not so fortunate: private investors did not purchase stock in the North Branch Canal Company and it was returned, still unfinished, to be completed by the state.[39]

The Gettysburg Railroad, derisively called the Tapeworm Railroad because of its vested-interest-inspired windings, was one of the legacies of possibly the most political of all the chairmen of the Board of Canal Commissioners, the Anti-Masonic Whig, Thaddeus Stevens, appointed during the last few months of the term of Whig Governor Joseph Ritner. This unfinished road was dropped from the state's plans by Ritner's Democratic successor.[40] Ironically, the Delaware Division Canal from Easton to Bristol, which had been added to the state's public works to gain votes from the eastern portions of the state, fitted well into the system of anthracite coal canals needed to supply the growing urban centers of the east coast and proved to be economically the most successful portion of the whole state system.[41]

The legislature, particularly when dealing with railroads, pushed to upgrade the systems, supporting them with appropriations (at least, if the loans were successful), to a degree well beyond the recommendations of the governors, the canal commissioners, and the engineers. At the same time they underbuilt the canals, patterning them after the English system and its dimensions. For example, the Delaware Division was built with locks half the size of its privately built feeder, the Lehigh Canal or Lehigh Navigation. Lehigh Navigation entrepreneur Josiah White never forgave the state for making this a canal that paralleled the Delaware River, a narrow earthen-banked channel rather than, like the Lehigh Navigation, a more versatile slackwater-and-canal system based on dams, sections of slackwater, and locks around the dams. Of course, the fact that Pennsylvania shared jurisdiction of the Delaware River with the state of New Jersey, as well as the fact that the open river was used by the fishing and lumber industries, must have been determining factors. It is a fact that most canals of the period, even New York's Erie, were undersized and had to be rebuilt during the next several decades.

The railroads, the Columbia and Philadelphia along with the spectacular Allegheny Portage Railroad, had many problems, some of which were not eliminated during the whole period of state ownership. The early 1830s had been characterized by debates between the proponents of locomotives on the Portage and the proponents of stationary engines that would pull vehicles over the tracks by rope, at least on grades, along with the possible use of horses or mules on levels. The Portage, ultimately composed of ten inclined planes along with intervening levels, provided an exciting but soon-to-be-proved-inefficient system across the mountains.[42]

The state-owned railroads suffered financial debilitation because they were run like canals rather than as railroads. At least during certain hours private parties were permitted to pay a toll and place their own horse-powered cars on the right of way. That this right continued down to 1845 is indicative of the political clout of the farmers in adjacent counties. The Columbia and Philadelphia never contracted to carry passengers or freight, providing only the trackway and the steam motive power for the passenger and freight carriers who put their own cars on the roadway. Even the sectional canal boats, still operated by private carriers although carried on state rail cars, did not help. Attempts to transfer the profitable carriage of passengers to the canal commissioners was opposed by lobbyists of the politically powerful transportation companies as well as by the political "outs," fearful of the additional political patronage that would be exercised by the Board of Canal Commissioners.[43]

The makeup of the Board of Canal Commissioners over the years did not necessarily lead to maximum efficiency in operation or to desired economy in financial operations. Until 1843, the commissioners were appointed by the governor, but under Governor Porter, Jacksonian principles triumphed and the board became elective.[44] Despite the 1837 claims of Governor Joseph Ritner that the management of the Columbia and Philadelphia was "not exceeded, if it is equalled, any where," the political reality is a story of legislatively imposed interferences with authority, legislative emasculation of the board as a result of unpredictable appropriations, and sometimes ruthless and corrupt exercise of power by the board members themselves.[45]

One must be careful not to submit to the temptation of blanketing the whole system with generalized charges. Selective documentation from highly politicized legislative committee reports by Alvard L. Bishop, the first historian of the state works, along with the unrestrained attacks made by the Pennsylvania Railroad, have created a less-than-accurate picture.[46] Engineers such as W. Hansell Wilson were somewhat critical of the administrative structure and political interference, but they were high in their praises of the engineers employed on the various Pennsylvania works, both canal and railroad, which proved to be a training school for the engineers and administrators who went on to make names for themselves, particularly on private railroads.[47] Among the most notable of these men were John A. Roebling, who would develop wire rope and suspension bridge technology, and John Edgar Thomson, who would eventually become president of the Pennsylvania Railroad.

The happy state of affairs in which America found itself at the beginning of the Jackson administration was enhanced as income, largely from the sale of public land, created a treasury surplus. As Andrew Jackson opposed any federal commitment to internal improvements, the solution promised was to be the distribution of this surplus to the coffers of the states, which created a wave of optimism that triggered a sometimes irresponsible race on the part of the states to expand programs of internal improvements. The inflationary spiral that resulted quickly wiped out the surplus, further muddling the situation.[48]

American cotton went to Europe and paid for American imports—or at least for the interest on imports such as railroad iron that was initially financed by the sale of securities, both public and private, in Europe. The bank provided the channels and the instruments of credit whereby the level of trade and the favorable status of American securities was maintained.[49]

To historian Thomas Govan, the unjustified attacks on the bank and the innuendoes of self-gain, irresponsible speculation, and other *ad hominem* attacks on Biddle himself were unjustified. The Specie Circular, the removal of deposits and the sale of the federally held stock of the Second Bank, undercut its policies for sustaining public credit and healthy trade, policies that Biddle fruitlessly endeavored to continue even after the loss of the bank's national charter and its rechartering by the state of Pennsylvania. The drying up of credit and the nonexistence of the anticipated federal surplus distribution played havoc with state plans and state finances.[50]

If one believes the detractors, both Biddle's contemporaries and our own, the banker is castigated as a monopolist driven to peddling political influence and to speculation. This author accepts the apparent truth of the cogent observation of Joseph Schumpeter that most Americans actually wanted inflation, and finds it difficult to sustain the validity of the hard-money doctrines of the Jacksonians. One can actually find a contradiction in terms—some of the anti-bank Jacksonians proposed that a hard money currency would actually raise prices, an economic heresy that was believed at the time.[51] The Delaware Division Canal suffered, as did all of the state works, from the financial constraints that resulted from the Jacksonians' attacks on Biddle's bank and the related financial structure.

The entrepreneurial thesis of many of today's economic historians may be somewhat more valid, but it would seem to be an oversimplification. The level of enmity and the virulence of the attack on the part of Albert Gallatin and the New York bankers on Biddle's bank appears to have developed principally after the political attack on the bank, which placed it, after the expiration of its charter, in a vulnerable condition. This was in sharp contrast to the prior situation when the Bank of the United States offered benefits of trade and credit that meant profitable opportunities for the international trader. It seems that one must equate the speculator with the entrepreneur, enamored by the economic success of the Erie Canal, to sustain such a proposition.[52]

It is impossible to evaluate in any specific quantitative manner the impact of the social investment of the Commonwealth of Pennsylvania in the area of the state's internal improvements. Using strict fiscal accounting, the state had been engaged in an expensive boondoggle. A balance must be weighed when considering political entrepreneurship and administration, which on the one hand provided adequate funding but at the same time incurred the extra expense of a degree of corruption, inefficiency, and log-rolling. There are also pros and cons in the realm of private investment, a system that only too often resulted in expensive bankruptcies that were often underwritten by the public since it was necessary, in order to get a project initiated, to guarantee funding for the private entrepreneur or speculator. It was argued at the time that had the state not initiated the works, private investors would have implemented only the profitable portions, thus contributing to the inefficiency of a piecemeal system.

The Pennsylvania legislature, particularly in relation to the railroads, upgraded the specifications of the engineers and the Board of Canal Commissioners and state created a railroad, particularly the Columbia and Philadelphia, that would compare favorably with any in the world at that time. The Columbia and Philadelphia was extensively utilized immediately upon its opening in 1834. Its continuing problem of satisfying what appears to have been a pre-existing demand indicates that the state commitment for the railroad did not come prior to the need for it, a fact testified to by the already overtaxed Philadelphia to Lancaster Turnpike.

The main goal of the public works was to provide an east-west route. The Columbia and Philadelphia Railroad constituted only the eastern end and was conceived and implemented as only part of that system, not as an entity. The Board of Canal Commissioners at the time of construction publicly stated their preference for canals; their commitment to the Columbia and Philadelphia and the Allegheny Portage railroads was only grudgingly made when the engineers demonstrated the insurmountable obstacles to watering canals in the particular regions. Pennsylvania's most profitable transportation systems were the privately constructed anthracite canals; only the Delaware Division of the state system was directly involved in this activity and proved to be by far the most profitable of the whole state-built system.[53]

We might use the opinions of "Publius," who, in 1844, at the fiscal nadir of the period, wrote in favor of taxes to enable the embattled state to resume debt payments:

> [When] we look at the vast capital which has been invested in these works by the State, and compare with it the inconsiderable amount of direct income derived from them, we are not to regard this capital as thrown away, or as lost to the people of the state. They are incidentally every day reaping a benefit from it, in the promotion of their personal convenience, in the increased income of their farms, in the enhanced profits of their industry, and in the increased wealth, enterprise, and prosperity of the whole state. Every [user of the] … public improvements, derives from these works a personal benefit, in the saving of time, labor and expense more than equivalent to the amount of his tax.[54]

The Commonwealth was finally able to reestablish its credit by resuming interest payments on its capital debt in 1845. However, the shock of the depression caused by the Panic of 1837 engendered a general change in the prevailing attitude toward state involvement in the construction of transportation facilities. Growing recognition that the Commonwealth should divest itself of its public works was based, first, on the belief that private enterprise should undertake and manage such improvements, and, secondly, on concern about the continuing and costly problems of canal maintenance. Regardless of the long-term decisions on disposition of the canal system, Pennsylvania officials were faced with recurring maintenance problems on the Delaware Division Canal as well as pressure for improvements to be made.

∾ CHAPTER V ∾

Problems of a State-owned
Delaware Division Canal

The Delaware Division was the only unit in the whole state system of internal improvements that produced sufficient revenue to cover not only expenses but also the interest on funds expended on its construction—in its case, $1,454,936.63. This revenue would in most years cover the costs of maintenance and repair plus furnish some additional "profit." Many of the other segments of the state system had been conceived with no realistic sense of economic need but rather had been instituted primarily to get the votes and satisfy the sensibilities of politicians from the various areas of the state. The Delaware Division, on the other hand, was an outlet for the Lehigh Navigation and its coal shipments from Mauch Chunk to Philadelphia and New York.[1]

Outlet Lock

In its 1840 company history, the Lehigh Coal and Navigation Company recalled that in 1827 engineer Canvass White had been overruled when he proposed small locks capable of handling only twenty-five-ton boats. The state had accepted similar arguments, which were based on European experience, and had constructed locks half the width but the same length as those on the Lehigh.[2] The limitation imposed by the narrowness of its locks greatly reduced the usefulness of the Delaware Canal. As the importance of the New York market grew and the dilatoriness of the Morris Canal and Banking Company in enlarging the locks on their canal became apparent, the managers of the LC&N sought an easier access to the Delaware and Raritan Canal. Over the years Josiah White and Erskine Hazard, the major entrepreneurs of the Lehigh Coal and Navigation Company, would keep up a paper barrage in the legislature and to the canal commissioners, cajoling, praying, and threatening, as they sought an outlet from the Delaware Division Canal into the river. Once there was an outlet, they could cross the river to enter the feeder of the Delaware and Raritan Canal, the obviously more direct path to the profitable New York market. Philadelphia capitalists, who were opposed to diverting coal from their city to New York, waged a simultaneous campaign, using their political influence in every way possible to thwart White and Hazard's plans.

On April 19, 1833, the Board of Canal Commissioners received a communication from the Lehigh Coal and Navigation Company "praying for permission to construct a basin on the Delaware Division at Black's Eddy [modern Point Pleasant], and also for the construction of an outlet lock at that point by the Canal Commissioners." The appeal was tabled and apparently never acted upon.[3] A few days later, inhabitants of New Hope petitioned for an outlet Lock from the canal into the Delaware River at the head of Wells Falls. This petition was rejected unanimously.[4]

During January of 1835, Caleb Dusenbery, toll collector at Easton, wrote to James Clark, president of the Board of Canal Commissioners, reporting on the activities of the Lehigh Coal and Navigation Company. He told Clark that he had answered a set of queries from an agent of that company, and commented:

> It evidently appears that the Lehigh Cº wish to have the impression that the Delaware Division from
> Easton to New Hope cannot be sufficiently supplied from the Lehigh—Consequently that their fa-

vorite project of a feeder and Out-let Lock at Black Eddy ought to prevail. To effect this they have been silently but industriously engaged for more than 18 months past.[5]

Among the suggestions was an ingenious proposal from Josiah White for the construction of a crane at Black's Eddy "to lift boats out of the Delaware canal into the Delaware river," in the language of the minutes of the State Senate.[6] White pointed out:

> The Business of the Lehigh which began in 1820 & stocked the Market, that year with 368 Tons already amounts to exceeding 200,000 tons of Coal, and it is now believed, if we had the advantage of our natural choice of Markets by a choice of ways to Market, ways that is also natural and obvious, that in a very short time, the shipments of Coal from the 3 Coal Regions Mentioned [opened by the navigation extension to White Haven and the Ashley Planes to Wilkesbarre] would exceed 500,000 tons a year in addition to the encouragement of all other minerals.… By looking at the Distance You will perceive that no trade fm Lehigh for New York can Profitably go there via Philada Nor much by Bristol, or not go longer, that way; than time to propose either Black Eddy Outlet Lock, or the Morris Canal, or if you please the Aqueduct at Morrisville.[7]

White stated his preference for Black's Eddy, but an outlet either there or at Morrisville would be acceptable. In order to adequately supply the canal with water, a feeder into the canal must be made at

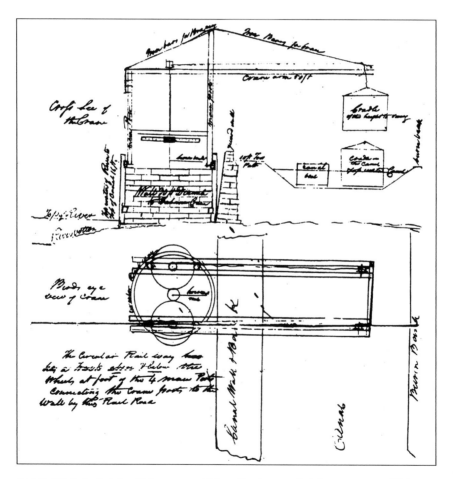

Josiah White's sketch of his proposal (described opposite) for a crane to lift boats from the canal at Black's Eddy into the Delaware River so they could cross over to the Delaware and Raritan Canal and carry coal by a shorter route to the New York market.

the same point 3 miles above Blk Eddy for it is between B Eddy & New Hope where the greatest want of water exists. [An outlet lock is] indispensable all admit or the whole of the Lehigh trade bound to N York goes there by the Morris Canal…

[Would it not promote the interests of the state most to build the lock at Black Eddy and] forever secure 26 miles toll, than not to make it and loose [sic] this, by driving all to the Morris Canal. But the State we all admit, has made her canals for the general benefit of her Citizens; for it is the property of the Citizens, generally, that is accountable for the Payment of her Canals: Now to save this 100,000 Doll[s] annual loss to our Citizens We propose this patronage, a Crane which can be put up in about 3 months, that will suffice the Public purpose until they can determine where the outlet would be made & also to make it. by this course the Public mind can be settled, while the Public interest will not suffer this great Annual Loss ment[d] and the Crane to be taken down when the Lock is made to charge 5 cents a ton on all freight passing either way & 50 cnts for the Boat.

The Arm of the Crane to extend from the Riverside of the Canal Bank at Black Eddy to take a boat out from Berm side of the Canal thence turn it Round to 5 ft Water in River, … to be above the Tow Horse, on tow path & be out of the Way of all Navigation …

I enclose a cross sec. of Canal to show its position.[8]

In a postscript, White refuted the objections that had been raised against an outlet lock at Black's Eddy, namely that there was collusion between the Lehigh Coal and Navigation Company and the Delaware and Raritan

so as to destroy the Provision in Our Law for Constructing a Rail Road to Wilksb[o] which Provides in its 2nd Sec. "That if the Tolls on the Morris Canal the Delaware & Raritan Canal or the Delaware Division of the Penns[a] Canal shall be Raised above their present Rates the Tolls on the Lehigh Canal may be Raised too."[9]

The Lehigh Coal and Navigation Company and Captain Robert Stockton of the Delaware and Raritan had actually made an agreement to maintain present toll rates, White pointed out. The authors of the 1840 history of the Lehigh Coal and Navigation Company, however, noted that

[the canal commissioners] of the present day [1840] have already officially expressed to the Legislature their anticipations that it will soon be necessary to enlarge the whole of the Delaware division, to enable it to pass the immense trade that will undoubtedly be poured into it from the Lehigh.

This enlargement of the Delaware must unquestionably take place soon, or the enlargement of the Morris Canal, by our spirited neighbors of New York, will take off a very large proportion of its trade. The enlargement of twenty-six miles of the Delaware Canal, and of thirteen of its locks below Easton, with an outlet to the river Delaware at Black's Eddy, opposite the feeder of the Delaware and Raritan Canal, would yet admit sea vessels to load or discharge at White Haven.[10]

Apparently the supervisors, engineers, and at least some of the canal commissioners were caught between the desires and interests of the Lehigh Coal and Navigation Company and New York interests on the one hand, and the proprietary interests of the Philadelphians on the other. Engineer William K. Huffnagle included a letter from Josiah White in his 1841 report that spoke to the issue. White argued:

If an outlet lock were made next spring at Black's Eddy or New Hope, it would no doubt, have the advantage of settling completely the unpleasant discussion between Pennsylvania and New York, on another question very interesting to our State, by inducing New York to connect her canals with the North Branch canal, which would thus be in communication with the fertile tier of South-western counties of that State, and open an extensive market for the anthracite coal of Wyoming valley, the returns for which would be made in the plaster,* &c. of New York. This beneficial interchange would be the result of a canal eighteen miles long, from the termination of the North Branch canal to the New York canal at Elmira, crossing the great western railroad; and all purchased at the expense of a single lock from the Delaware canal across its bank into the river Delaware at Black's Eddy or New Hope.

★ "Plaster" or "shin plaster" was a colloquial term meaning paper money.

The city of New York would thus draw a trade from her South-western counties through this channel, and pay to the State of Pennsylvania on one hundred and thirty-six miles of her canals, an amount of tolls far exceeding that which it may be fancied she might lose by the escape through the outlet lock of any freight, which otherwise would be expected to continue on through the remainder of the Delaware canal. The injustice would also be avoided of compelling those citizens, who on their way to N York, now use the Delaware canal, to go double the necessary distance, for no other reason than to pay toll to the State on sixty miles of canal instead of thirty-six.[11]

In a letter inscribed "confidential," canal commissioner J. Miller inquired of David Wagener in 1844 as to the implied threat of an enlargement of the Morris Canal to the state's Delaware Division:

You know the Lehigh Co. have long been asking for an outlet lock at Black's Eddy which has hitherto been refused to them. More recently they have indicated a wish for a connexion near New Hope, and they have expressed a willingness to pay the full am.ᵗ of toll to Bristol … I am apprehensive that if some accommodation is not offered that the Lehigh Co. may make some bargain or arrangements with the Morris Co by which the coal trade may be diverted from our State Canal to the Morris Canal.[12]

On September 2, 1844, Erskine Hazard, acting manager of the Lehigh Coal and Navigation Company, wrote James Clark, president of the Board of Canal Commissioners:

As it is now ascertained that the Delaware division will not be sold, it becomes necessary to see what arrangements can be made to facilitate the Lehigh Coal operations. You are aware that in the original plan of the Delaware division it was contemplated to feed the lower levels by an inlet from the river just above Well's falls. This inlet was constructed, But it was soon discovered that, by some mismanagement, the first level to be supplied was so located that, at extremely low water, the water in the canal had not the required depth by 2 feet 6 or 9 inches.

This difficulty was remedied by closing the inlet and relying upon water wheels to supply the canal from New Hope to Bristol, and by this reason the connection of the navigation of the Canal & river was cut off. To restore this connection, and at the same time to secure to the canal, at all times, a full supply of water independently of the wheel, is now very important and I believe it can be accomplished under existing laws, without injury to any one and with mutual benefit to the interest of the Commonwealth and to all the transporters upon the Canal.[13]

Hazard proposed raising the wing dam at New Hope to a height where, "except possibly for a fortnight of the very driest seasons," it would provide a direct flow into the Delaware Division and, at the same time, provide an outlet into the river. He listed the series of laws and agreements between the states of Pennsylvania and New Jersey and illustrated, at least to *his* satisfaction, that there were no real obstacles to his proposal.

Hazard's correspondence mixed proposals with veiled threats. In November, he reiterated his proposal for a raised wing dam and a direct inlet into the canal, and followed it with a bit of news. "The late sale of the Morris Canal," he wrote, was a subject that should raise Pennsylvania's interest in the outlet:

That canal, we are credibly informed, was sold by the sheriff under a mortgage to the Dutch Bond holders, and that being the first claim, under the division of the Chancellor of New Jersey, clears the canal of all other claims upon it. The Canal is now in the hands of some of the leading Capitalists of New York....

This state of things renders it certain they will make the canal what they promise Viz, capable of passing freely the boats adapted to the Delaware division.

The distance from Easton to New York by that route being 101 miles, it is needless to say to you that without the proposed connection with the Del & Rar feeder, the Delaware div will be a much more expensive route to that city, & can only be expected to be used for any surplus which the Morris Canal could not accommodate.[14]

Hazard's letter listed the capitalists, remarking that they had paid $380,000 for the canal.

Josiah White, on January 31, 1845, wrote Clark a message in which he reiterated his constant call for an outlet lock:

But the State having been beguiled out of her great property by her Route — I see no necessity, of her continuing to loose [*sic*] her Canal

But to bring her canal into usefulness it is <u>now</u> not only necessary to her to make the Outlet lock; where most convenient to her customers, but also to <u>Double the length of the Locks</u> down to Bristol, or at least down to the Outlet lock, with doubling, I estimate will cost 4 or 5000 Doll[rs] each & I believe this is 24 locks to Bristol 12 to Blk Eddy.[15]

In December of 1845, Isaac Van Horn, toll collector at Bristol, wrote to William B. Foster, Jr., president of the Board of Canal Commissioners, to the effect that

The Feeding Wheels at New Hope must soon be renewed or a better mode of Supplying the canal with water from that place resorted to as the wheels will soon be so decayed that they cannot be relied on. If there was a dam built to raise the water 2½ feet with a Shute to improve the decending [*sic*] channel of the river there would be no opposition to its construction and it would afford a water power at this place that would yield fifteen thous[d] doll[s] per annum without any interference with the navigation …[16]

New Jersey was reaping rewards for the sale of waterpower, Van Horn noted, both by the Water Power Company of Trenton and by the Delaware and Raritan Canal, which that winter (1845-1846)

[are] expending thirty thousand dollars to enlarge their feeder for the purpose of supplying water to heavy manufacturing companies at Trenton and N Brunswick, the fall of our canal at Bristol is 22 feet and the Site for a Manufacturing town is the best in the State with water power.[17]

In a communication dated February 4, 1846, Foster addressed the speaker of the State Senate "relative to the construction of an Out-let Lock on the Delaware Division, Pennsylvania Canal." He was responding to a senate resolution of April 5, 1845, requesting

[a] report upon the expediency of constructing an out-let lock at the most convenient point, to connect the Delaware division of the canal with the feeder of the Delaware and Raritan canal; and to increase the size of the locks to suit the passage of double Lehigh boats, together with the probable amount of the same; and also into the expediency and expense of constructing an aqueduct across the Delaware river, at or near the western termination of the Delaware and Raritan canal; and also to report whether in their opinion the effect of the construction of such out-let lock, will be to diminish the resources of the Commonwealth, arising from tolls on said division.[18]

Foster summarized the judgments of the commissioners: The Delaware canal, whose prime role appeared to be to carry coal as an extension of the Lehigh Canal, passed within one mile of the Delaware and Raritan at Morrisville but coal had to be carried to Bristol and then to Bordentown, making an extra circuit of twenty-six miles. A more northerly connection had been proposed over the years. There were three points that had been prominently suggested, of which the most northerly was Black's Eddy, some twenty-six miles below Easton. Black's Eddy was immediately rejected, for, despite its

natural advantages, … [it] is liable to two prominent objections; first, the heaviest and most valuable trade upon the canal, would be diverted from it before having passed one-half its length; and, secondly, the water necessary to supply the canal below, would be diverted from it by the trade passing into the river at this point.[19]

The site at Morrisville would permit the trade to traverse the greatest distance on the canal but a connection there would probably require an aqueduct over the Delaware plus three lift locks, at a cost of some $123,900. Therefore the choice of the commissioners would be Well's Falls (New Hope). If the existing wing dam were raised to provide a better head of water, an adequate flow of water for the lower portions of the canal would be guaranteed, and only a single outlet lock would be required by Pennsylvania. New Jersey could complete the connection with the construction of a single inlet lock.

The commissioners' cost estimate for the improvements of the Well's Falls dam, along with the necessary sluices for river traffic and for constructing the Pennsylvania inlet and the outlock, was only $29,700.00. They called attention to the ever-increasing stream of coal coming from the Lehigh Canal and endorsed the expediency of enlarging the locks on the Delaware Canal to the dimensions of the Lehigh,

(Above) An LC&N company boat, marked with its prominent bullseye, coming out of lock 8 into the basin at New Hope. The outlet lock to cross the Delaware River by cable ferry to Lambertville, completed in 1848, is to the right of lock 8. From here the boat could swing around in the basin and cross over to the Delaware and Raritan Canal to take its cargo to the New York market, or it could continue south on the Delaware Canal to Bristol, where it would be tied to other boats and towed to Philadelphia on the Delaware River.

(Below) A boat makes the crossing from the Delaware and Raritan Canal at Lambertville to New Hope in 1910.

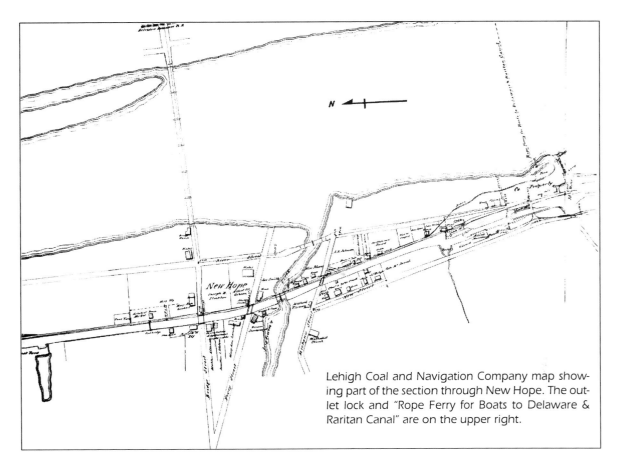

Lehigh Coal and Navigation Company map showing part of the section through New Hope. The outlet lock and "Rope Ferry for Boats to Delaware & Raritan Canal" are on the upper right.

although they believed it would take an additional two years of increase before the trade would "exceed the present capacity of the locks upon the Delaware division."

> [At this time] the works of the Morris canal company are undergoing alterations and improvements, which are expected to be completed by the opening of navigation next spring, and it is believed they may become to a considerable extent, a rival to our state canal.[20]

The commissioners were directly quoted in Foster's concluding comment:

> if such a connection be permitted, that all tonnage passing out of or into the Delaware division at this point, should pay the same tolls as if it passed out or entered at Bristol ... it furnishes no reason why she should lose any of her tolls on a work made purposely for the benefit of such trade.... The Board are further of the opinion ... the State should secure the entire control of the out-let lock at Easton, so that all trade passing through the same be subject to such tolls as she may find it to be her interest to impose.[21]

Such became the practice after the outlet lock was opened two years later, in 1848. In the annual publication of the minutes of the Board of Canal Commissioners from that date on, this was included in the rules, regulations and tolls that were annually enacted. In the section entitled "Delaware Division" in these annual minutes, one finds the toll for coal set "at three mills per 1,000 pounds per mile," and the collectors

> shall charge, collect and pay into the State treasury, the same amount of tolls on all freight passing out of the said division through the out-let lock at Wells' Falls, which would be chargeable on said freights from their place of shipment to Bristol.[22]

The regulations stipulated also that an additional dollar should be charged all boats entering or leaving by the outlet lock.

On July 29, 1846, Erskine Hazard initiated new inquiries of the canal commissioners, suggesting another solution to LC&N's difficulties in conducting a massive coal trade using the less-than-adequate facilities of the state canal. "Looking forward to the increase of the coal business, and the accommodations that will be required for shipping it in the neighborhood of Bristol," the wharf space in the Bristol basin, even though the major wharfage was leased by the LC&N, would not be sufficient for the prospective business. He therefore requested that the commissioners approve the construction of a branch canal "to connect the long level with a basin on the bank of the Delaware, somewhere below the mouth of the Tullytown Creek." He described the details and the benefits, how a lock with a four- to six-foot lift would be necessary to pass the canal under the Trenton and Philadelphia Railroad, and how higher levels would permit screens to be rigged to clean the coal, which would be transferred by gravity from the higher level to river boats.[23] Supervisor John Mathyes described the situation:

> If the business of this Line continues to pass down to Bristol to find its way out into the Delaware or be transshipped, it will be indispensably necessary that some increased facilitys be afforded at that point for the passing of Boats in and out and the Transshipment of Coal; Our Basin at that place is entirely to [sic] small to expedite business with proper dispatch, In case of any interruption to the Tow Boats in the River which is not an infrequent occurrence we find our Basin so much crowded that it is impossible to pass the Boats in and out.[24]

Matheys described the LC&N proposal and its advantages, and offered his views:

> I am of the opinion that a grant of this kind under proper restrictions would operate advantageously to the best interest of the Commonwealth, [for the] success of the Delaware Division depends entirely on the ability of the Lehigh Region to compete with that of the Schuylkill.[25]

The minutes of Monday, December 14, 1847, of the Board of Canal Commissioners reveal that a resolution to implement Hazard's proposals for improvements was voted down 2 to 1 with only board president William Foster voting in favor.[26]

Hazard closed his letter quoted above by asking the board what was the result "of your advertisement for a loan for the construction of the outlet lock at Well's falls. We hope you have the subscription in full from our Del & Raritan Canal friends."[27] The loan had not been taken up; the canal commissioners, in their annual report for 1846, noted that there had not been the necessary subscriptions. Therefore the board found it necessary to postpone "any further steps toward carrying out the object of the enactment." [28]

Sometime in 1847, William K. Huffnagle, now supervisor on the Delaware Division, in correspondence that he titled "Private Communication to the Board," warned board members that they should

reserve their approval of any plan proposed … [for] Mr. [Ashbel] Welch the Engineer & Sup[t] of the Delaware and Raritan Canal is entrusted with the negotiation of the Loan. He is a skilful Engineer & an excellent man fully capable in all respects to undertake the work, if they propose to construct it. However I make the above suggestion of the reservation of our approbation in order that our own works may not be exposed or endangered by any plan they should adopt.[29]

The minutes of the canal commissioners for Saturday, May 15, 1847, contains the acceptance of an offer from a Mr. McAllister to take up the loan for $20,000 to construct the outlet lock, and a resolution to advertise for sealed proposals for the construction of the outlet lock.[30] The commissioners awarded the contract on August 31 to Sumner & Delano, who furnished a bond along with their estimates.[31] Over the next months, the minutes of the commissioners reveal a series of payouts to the contractors based on certifications for work completed.[32] On April 30, 1848, supervisor Huffnagle reported to the commissioners:

Ashbel Welch.
Courtesy of Rev. Joseph DiPaulo

> The Wire Rope has been erected at the Outlet at New Hope & empty boats have been successfully transported between the two Canals no attempt has yet been made to cross the regular coal trade for the Eastern markets.[33]

Coal boats were apparently passed successfully during the season. In September Samuel Ingham, a spokesman for the Beaver Meadow Railroad, which used the Lehigh and Delaware canals to get its coal to markets, wrote questioning a charge of $1.20 for passage through the outlet lock at New Hope: Ingham said he had been informed about the excess toll equal to passage from New Hope to Bristol, but complained that he did not understand the charge for passage through the lock.[34]

In 1848 the outlet lock at New Hope had finally become a reality.

Samuel Ingham.
Courtesy of Rev. Joseph DiPaulo

Enlargement of the Canal

In March of 1851, William B. Foster, the civil engineer who had served as an elected member of the Board of Canal Commissioners, submitted estimates for canal enlargement. It was to be regretted, he opined, that in the original construction the Delaware Division's 11-foot-wide locks had not been built to the 22-foot dimensions of the Lehigh.

Widening the canal was too expensive a project to be undertaken by the state at that time, so Foster suggested that the state, along with the Lehigh Coal and Navigation Company, should increase the depth of their waterways another foot to six feet, which would permit the Delaware Division "to admit the passage of boats carrying ninety tons, while its present limit is about sixty-five tons, or at most seventy tons." Except for the stretch below the dam in Easton, which he recommended deepening, the balance of the canal could attain the additional depth by raising the banks along the canal and the walls at the locks, aqueducts, wasteweirs and bridges. He estimated that this, along with an enlargement of the basin at Easton, the replacing of two locks, one at Uhler's (Raubsville) and one at New Hope, could be achieved for an expenditure of $105,185, exclusive of any injury that might be caused to waterpower above the dam by any raising of the crest of the dam at Easton.[35]

Foster's report marked the beginning of the end of years of agitation for enlarging the Delaware Division.

The rose-colored predictions found in the reports of the Ritner-administration canal commissioners (1835–1839) were soon replaced by prophecies of crisis when the Porter-appointed commission took office. The Ritner optimists had written in their 1838 annual report:

> This division [the Delaware] is destined to become one of the most profitable portions of the public works, owing to its connection with the improvements of the Lehigh company, extending by canal and rail road now nearly completed to the Susquehanna at Wilkesbarre [providing the outlet for a rapidly expanding stream of coal. Thus it would be] necessary at no distant period, to increase the capacity of this division by construction of additional locks along side the present ones, of dimensions corresponding with those of the Lehigh, adapted to boats of 100 tons. The capacity of the canal being thus increased, an additional supply of water may become necessary. This could be obtained by construction of a feeder taken from the Delaware at Catbush island.[36]

Outlet locks at Black's Eddy would render the balance of the Delaware Division useless, the board concluded. It would give advantages only to a rival city (New York), and was a project that "the board deem opposed to the true policy and best interests of the state, and if adopted, would render the enlargement of the canal unnecessary and unprofitable.

As early as November of 1837, engineer John P. Bailey, in response to the resolution of the Board of Canal Commissioners calling for a survey of the canal with the idea of enlarging it, had reported:

> It is intended in the above estimate that the locks should be of solid close-jointed, hammer dressed masonry, through and through ... if well executed, on solid foundations, the locks will be of little expense to keep in repair hereafter, except for renewing of the gates. The present locks are of common rubble masonry, lined with wood and are expensive to keep in repair.... It will be better to construct them on the most permanent and durable plan, in the first instance, which will be the cheapest in the end....

[The Delaware division stands to be] among the most profitable of the State improvements; the coal fields of the Lehigh being inexhaustible, trade for the Delaware division can never stop, but will go on increasing.[37]

Bailey recommended to the board that the canal be enlarged at least as far as Black's Eddy by doubling the size of the locks, and he recommended building the outlet lock at that point. He suggested that boats leaving the canal at that point should pay the same toll as if they travelled through the whole length of the canal, at least until the receipts of the canal covered the cost of construction, after which, he suggested, "allow trade its free course."[38]

Over the years, the minutes of both the State House of Representatives and the Senate are replete with petitions and resolutions calling for the widening of the Delaware Division canal. For example, the house minutes of March 15, 1841, contain the following entries:

> Mr. Dillworth, from the same committee [Inland Navigation and Internal Improvement], to whom was referred the petition of the citizens of Bucks county, praying that the Delaware division of the Pennsylvania canal may be widened so as to admit boats of one hundred and twenty tons burthen to pass through it, made report;
>
> That your committee having duly considered the subject and believe that however advantageous to the transporters and profitable to the State, the widening of the canal may be, it would be inexpedient at the present time to commence such improvement, owing to the embarrassed situation of the Commonwealth.[39]

Similar rejections of proposals for improvements on the internal improvements across the state were the rule of thumb for the financially embarrassed Commonwealth.[40]

A special report produced by William K. Huffnagle, engineer during January of 1841, in response to the flood-caused damage of that year, contained the following suggestion:

> The large amount required for the restoration of navigation, renders the present opportunity the best that may ever be offered for carrying into effect the projected enlargement and improvement in the capacity of this most profitable portion of the public works.[41]

As the water supply for the lower segments of the canal was troublesome and sometimes "barely sufficient, at the low stages of the Delaware, to keep up the requisite supply" of water for the lower sections of the canal, Huffnagle recommended "the extension of the present dam [at New Hope] across the river, leaving a sluice or schute of seventy-five feet in width for descending craft." He listed numerous advantages: adequate water for the lower portion of the canal, a safe connection to New Jersey's Delaware and Raritan canal, easier passage on the river through dangerous Well's Falls, and, finally,

> [the] locks from Easton to this point [New Hope], could then be advantageously widened to a size corresponding with those on the Lehigh, thereby conveying boats of one hundred tons and carrying the entire coal trade.[42]

The necessary agreements with the State of New Jersey should be no problem, according to the report.

The capacity of the canal could be increased in several ways. One, possibly the most simple, was to deepen the canal or in some cases simply to clean bars and litter from the canal bottom to maintain a proper depth. This was highlighted in the canal commissioners' 1841 report:

> The capacity of this line was materially increased during the past season by cleaning out the bars which had formed in the bottom of the canal, and excavating it to its original depth. The engineer reports that boats heretofore carrying only from 45 to 50 tons are now transporting from 55 to 60 tons without difficulty.[43]

The 1845 annual report of the canal commissioners noted the increase in the coal trade

> upon this important and profitable branch of the public improvements ... render[s] it necessary that measures should be taken for enlarging the locks, so as to correspond more nearly with the capacity of those upon the Lehigh navigation. As the distance upon which such enlargement of the locks should

be made, would depend upon whether a connection should be formed with the Delaware and Raritan canal, by an out-let lock at some suitable point, this important subject will be more fully presented to the Legislature in a special report which the Canal Commissioners are required to make, by a resolution of the Senate adopted on the 3d day of April, 1845.[44]

An 1846 report of supervisor John Matheys spelled out many of the problems of maintaining an operating canal, particularly one with the amount of traffic carried on his Delaware Division. The weigh lock at Easton had not been constructed to carry such "increased tonnage"

> In consequence of the Iron not being of as good quality in the Suspension chains and they having been made to[o] light to sustain the weight we frequently pass over them at this time. It will be recollected that the original intention was to carry Fifty-tons of Coal on a Boat over this Line, this season there has been Boats passed with upward of Seventy Tons of Coal and freight of nearly all the Boats exceed Sixty Tons.
>
> We have passed over this line this season much heavier freight Boats than ever passed the line before.[45]

Matheys perceptively warned about possible competitors that might, during the next season, reduce the amount of Lehigh coal carried on the Delaware Division:

> Coal from the Lehigh Region demands at all times in the Eastern market Twenty Five cts. per ton more than that from the Schuylkill.[46]

However, the increased "facility of Transportation" on the Schuylkill posed by the rivalry between the Schuylkill Navigation and the Reading Railroad

> may induce them to put down the price of freight so low as to destroy the advantage of price the Lehigh men have. If this should be the case our line must be affected very materially for a time.[47]

Matheys considered the eternally perplexing question of enlarging the canal. While the "present Financial condition of the Commonwealth" would not justify widening locks and prism of the canal, other feasible methods were still possible. The best immediate expedient was

> the deepening of the channel by increasing the height of the Banks Aqueducts Waste weirs and Locks.
>
> By increasing the height of our dam at Easton Twelve inches and also the wing dam at Wells Falls we might increase the depth of our Canal Twelve inches through out by making the necessary increase to the embankments and Mechanical Structures.[48]

The extra depth would permit the transit of 80 tons on a boat as "easily as we do at the present time carry Sixty Tons." This would permit "us to do one fourth more business with the same number of boats" as were then used.[49]

In 1847 legislation was enacted, apparently in response to the obvious need, calling for the deepening of the canal and the doubling in length of the locks. Petitions continued to flow into the legislature from interested parties who, while they usually agreed with the proposed measures in principle, often disagreed in detail. For example, in January of 1848 a petition from Bucks County called for not only the already legislated increase in depth but also "that the locks may be increased in width and not in length." April petitions from Northampton County called for modification of the 1847 act so as to "increase the depth of said canal six feet, without doubling the length of the locks."[50]

In July of 1847 William Huffnagle, supervisor of the Delaware Division, submitted estimates for the canal improvements. The locks would be

> of the Composite, built during the winter of stone faced with wood. The Towing Path can be best raised by hands in our own Employment commencing about the first of September next.[51]

Huffnagle projected completion between December 10, 1847, when he would draw off the water, and March 10, 1848, when navigation would commence. Contracts for locks would have to be made in sufficient time for the contractors to obtain materials so they could start and complete the work on schedule.

In February of 1848, Huffnagle submitted the more detailed proposal and estimates necessary to increase the canal's capacity as specified by the legislation of the previous year. His first estimate was for the improvement of the canal,

> increasing the length of the Locks already built, thus making a double chamber, & retaining the lower gates in the present structures enable single boats to pass & <u>single</u> lockages be made without waste of water. As this work would necessarily be principally done during the winter and suspension of navigation, a plan avoiding the use of mortar <u>must</u> be adopted in consequence of which <u>dry walls</u> laid up with heavy stone, well bonded, & faced with plank, is the only plan which can be used.[52]

The estimated cost of this was $115,000. His second option was to deepen the canal to give a depth of six feet to the navigation. The advantage of this was that it could be completed,

> affording at a comparatively small expense greatly increased facilities of navigation & could be readily effected during the present season without interruption to the trade. The several foreman of Repairs without additional expense carry out the directions of the Superintendent, keep the time of those hands engaged on the elevation of the Towing path and thus the work conducted with greatest economy.
>
> On some portions of the Canal the banks will require but little additional height to adapt them to six feet water. at others considerable work will be required, & there it is evident that a small gang of hands and an additional scow on each division could economically & rapidly prosecute the work.[53]

The estimated expense would be about $31,000.

Huffnagle's third estimate had to do with the problems at Easton, where raising the height of the dam would threaten the 23-foot fall of water for the "several extensive manufactories of Cotton, Iron, &c." that received their water from the lowest segment of the Lehigh Navigation (see page 7). The fall was from the canal to the Lehigh River, whose level was controlled by the state-built dam across the mouth of the river. Huffnagle proposed that instead of raising the dam, "falling gates" be erected

> in such manner as to be <u>levelled</u> with the comb of the present dam in case of freshet over one foot.— & <u>re</u> erected after it has passed off. The damage consequently created would not be great if the gates at the dam are properly attended to. If not, and a permanent structure should be necessary the damage might be estimated at five thousand dollars.[54]

Another aspect of the proposals for lengthening the locks became apparent when the Lehigh Coal and Navigation Company proposed double boats, that is, two boats in tandem with only a single crew. Erskine Hazard, in Harrisburg on March 1, 1847, communicated a proposal from LC&N to the Board of Canal Commissioners. He had been requested by his company, even without any lengthening of the canal locks, "to call your attention to the subject of Boats navigating the Delaware division coupled together under the charge of a single crew." The rationale for using tandem boats was that only half the usual number of boatmen had appeared at Mauch Chunk to man the coal boats; at the same time there was every expectation of a great increase in traffic. In the face of increased demand, the trade

> on the Lehigh & Delaware division will thus be materially lessened instead of increased unless the expedient of coupling the boats, & letting one await the passage of the other through the locks, be adopted.[55]

If the board found itself incapable of making the decision, Hazard asked if an investigation of the proposal could be referred to the supervisor of the line with the power to make such a decision. The matter was one of some urgency for LC&N: "The near approach of the boating season renders any delay in the decision injurious to such interests." (Tandem boats were in fact never used on the Lehigh or Delaware canals.) Another way to increase the capacity of the canal was to increase the hours of operation. In 1846, supervisor Matheys addressed the Board of Canal Commissioners, telling them that he had

> made arrangements for passing Boats at all hours both day and Knight [*sic*] on our line, last knight we passed at this place Eighteen Boats between 10 oclock in the evening and 5 oclock in the morning that being about the time that operations were suspended under our former regulations. Our Double Lock tenders [who operate two adjacent locks] complain considerable thinking they ought to have had more than an advance of Ten Dollars for the knight work, but I think they will stand it....[56]

Two loaded company boats hitched together traveling south on the 11-mile level above Bristol in 1909. There is a crew on each boat, unlike Erskine Hazard's proposal of 1847, which would have used one crew for two boats.

To Protestant America, Sunday was viewed as a day of rest. The legislature and the Board of Canal Commissioners both received numerous petitions and other communications opposing Sunday business as a desecration of the Lord's Day. But the increasing traffic on the canal made consideration of Sunday business at least a reasonable alternative. In April of 1848, Huffnagle reported:

> The undersigned has suspended the Sunday passage at the Locks on this line. It was found that as the Collectors were unwilling to clear pass the Boats at their offices at Bristol, New Hope & Easton they consequently accumulated in such vast numbers at New Hope particularly as to cause great dissatisfaction among the boatmen & great difficulty in passing them on Monday.[57]

This was a problem that would not go away. On Thursday January 29, 1852, the Board of Canal Commissioners resolved that the locks on all divisions of the Pennsylvania Canal

> shall be closed, on every Saturday night, at 12 Oclock and remain closed until 12 Oclock on Sunday night.... [However,] This Resolution [should] not interfere with the duty of Lock Keepers to keep up their levels during the time the Locks are thus closed.[58]

The minutes of the board for Friday June 10, 1853, indicate the dissatisfaction of the boatmen with the regulation. The following year in a resolution—system-wide and not restricted to the Delaware Division—the board ruled:

> If any person or persons, shall break the Chain Lock of any Lock gate, or in any manner force their way into any Lock after it shall have been closed, in obedience to the Resolution ... authorizing the Locks on the Canals belonging to the Commonwealth, to be closed on the Sabath day. Such person or persons shall for Every such offence be subject to a penalty of twenty five dollars.[59]

The minutes of the Board of Canal Commissioners of April 27, 1847, reiterated the need for expansion:

Whereas the business upon the Delaware Division of the Pennsylvania Canal has increased so as to render it necessary for the convenience of Transporters, and for the increase of the revenue of the Commonwealth, that the navigation should be kept uninterrupted at all hours of the night as well as during the day.[60]

Twenty-four-hour business created extra expense and problems. In August of 1848, William R. Burton, collector at New Hope, wrote the commissioners protesting the rejection of his petition for compensation. Despite the necessity of keeping the collector's office open if the canal were to function around the clock, it was mid-June before he was awarded an assistant, whose salary he paid. There had been no money forthcoming following his first submission: Mr. Hartshorne, then one of the elected canal commissioners, replied upon being queried that it had been overlooked and said he would "endeavour to think of it & bring it before the Board." When he failed to do so prior to the expiration of his term of office, Burton expressed fear that because it had been "so long before it was brought up for action it may have been considered one of those bills which claim payment where services were not rendered & was therefore rejected."[61] The minutes do not record whether the hapless Mr. Burton was ever compensated.

Pennsylvania's auditor general, John Ecky, wrote to A. Gamble, one of the canal commissioners, on July 26, 1850, that the present capacity of the Delaware Division "does not probably exceed the passage of 500,000 annually." He spelled out some problems that must be faced with any enlargement:

It is suggested that the present locks be enlarged to 100 feet by 16 which would allow boats to 15 foot wide carrying 100 tons on the present water. This would increase the capacity of the canal 50 pct. but might not answer the demand for the trade a few years hence and would besides be likely to fail in its object on account of the insufficiency of the breadth of the bottom of the canal which being only 25 feet two loaded boats 15 foot wide could not pass each other without unloading a part of their cargoes & thus producing an obstruction in the canal might reduce the trade to the present extent besides destroying the value of the boats.[62]

Were the locks made 22 feet wide, two Delaware boats could be locked through side by side as was already done on the Lehigh, he wrote. However,

Should the Lehigh C° be disappointed in their expectations of having locks constructed on the del div similar to theirs on the Lehigh they have other resources to look to. They may pass their boats across the delaware river at Easton by Viaduct which is authorized by both the Legislatures of Penns[ia] & N. Jersey. —this would bring them directly on the Trenton & Belved rail road where it is proposed to lay heavy rails between Easton and the entrance of the Delaware & Raritan canal, then the boats of the Lehigh can easily make their trips either to Bristol or New York the advantage to the Lehigh Nav[n] in this case would be that with an expenditure of little over 10,000 Dollars the Lehigh canal could be deepened to 6 feet which would allow a double Lehigh scow to carry a load of 175 tons either to N York or Philad[a]. The boats being divided into sections of 54 tons each they could be drawn down the road to the entrance of the Del & Rar canal, [24 miles below Easton] the grade being easy and descent in the direction of the trade. Nor is it likely the Morris Canal will remain idle observers of the contest between the Lehigh scows and the newly introduced Keel boats on the delaware division. They might easily widen their locks to fit those of the Lehigh. The prise [sic] to be gained is worth an extraordinary exertion.[63]

The same year, Lewis S. Coryell, an engineer back in the days of the construction of the canal, charged that at least part of the canal's problems were the result of mismanagement:

officers are dirilect [sic] in their duties operating serious against the interests of the public at large as well as Penn[a].

[Lock keepers] have no master & have become potent officers—they will create a row & dispute as Idle and in applicable to their duties as the reason why black sheeps wool is warmer than white—and they by litigation detain navigation until their suit is settled before a Justice unless in some cases the boatmen will pay them a fee to make up—then they pass them on—.

It would seem that you are doing all you can, to force the public & Lehigh coal region to unite in creating another facility than yours to get their coal to market.[64]

For most of the length of the canal, when boats passed each other the loaded one would slow down, move close to the berm bank opposite the towpath, drop its tow rope, and let the light boat pass. Here in New Hope, after the canal was widened and deepened, two boats could pass easily without one of them moving over, so long as the one on the berm side dropped its rope. This view is looking south between locks 9 and 10. The two boats in the foreground each have several children on the deck.

In December of 1851, engineer Edward Gay reported on results of his conversations with the executive committee of the Lehigh Coal and Navigation Company. He had received in writing from the LC&N board an expression of preference for lengthening the locks rather than widening them and he indicated that he was in agreement. An underlying reason was that the Delaware Division "has never been, and probably never will be blessed with a superabundant supply of water and this alone should have the most important bearing, in determining the size of the locks." Despite this,

> The President of the Lehigh informed me that the width of the Locks of the Lehigh, was adopted subsequent to the commencement of the work on the Delaware and was made double the size of the Del^e Locks to accommodate <u>two</u> boats, and not with a view to the future enlargement of the boats.
>
> [The] Lehigh Company would not build larger boats, even should all the locks on the Del Div^n be enlarged. but the Company justly apprehend that others might do so in which case, there would be a great loss of waters, and the large boats being unable to pass each other on all parts of the canal, would therefore cause great detention and render the Enlarged Locks of little, or indeed no use, until the whole prism of he canal should be enlarged.... therefore, I would suggest to your Board the propriety of adopting the large Lock at 'Uhlers' and the double longitudinal chamber at all the other Locks, unless where the curvature of the canal would prevent an extension of the Lock, without increased cost.[65]

Gay proposed that funds be made available for widening the lock at Uhlerville (Raubsville) and the two double locks at New Hope, and further widening the aqueduct at New Hope and the canal in that vicinity. According to James Cox, president of LC&N, this should obviate

> [the] delays … [and] the detentions during the past season, from great accumulations of boats at Uhler's & at New Hope, [which] have been the occasion of heavy complaints & much dissatisfaction among those navigating the Canal.— [66]

(Above) A privately owned boat entering the widened Lock 9 at New Hope, circa 1895. Two boats could fit comfortably side by side in the lock, relieving the serious congestion problems that had slowed the passage of boats. On the right is a view of two boats in one of the double locks at New Hope; below is the lock at Lodi, which was not widened.

Cox informed Gay that these improvements, along with increased depth on the Delaware Canal, should,

> at comparatively small cost,— [add] some 33 Per^ct to the present capacity of the Canal, & by improving our position relatively to the other Coal producing regions, [and] would stimulate the augmented production of the Lehigh & swell the revenue to be derived from the State Canal.[67]

It was apparently a year before contracts were let for rebuilding the locks at Uhler's and New Hope. McCulloch & Malone were awarded the contract with the proviso that work must be completed by March 15, 1852, or "The Contractors forfeit $500 per day for each and every day they detain the opening of navigation by the non Completion of their work after the said 15th of March." [68]

On August 25, while the work was underway, the Board of Canal Commissioners found it necessary to pass a resolution declaring "that Boats carrying Materials for the New Locks, & widening the aqueduct, and Prism of the Delaware division, shall have a preference in passing the Locks." [69]

In February of 1851, George W. Closson, supervisor of the Delaware Division, had brought to the board's attention a matter that probably equated to a continuing problem on all public works: "There is a great scarcity of tools and wheelbarrows which ought to be accounted for as they were furnished in great numbers during the repairs of the last season." [70]

On December 13, 1852, Edward F. Gay resigned as engineer for the Delaware Canal. He was replaced by James Worrall, who was appointed "Engineer of the Work, for the Improvement of the Delaware division of the Pennsylvania Canal." [71] Three days later, on December 16, board president John A. Gamble laid before the board the contracts let by Delaware Division supervisor George W. Closson to James Burns for construction of locks at New Hope and "Eulerville," to Bittenger and Greger for an aqueduct and bridge at New Hope, and to Edward Picket for "widening the Canal at New Hope." [72]

In their 1855 annual report, the canal commissioners quoted from their previous annual report:

> it must be apparent that this canal, for all the purposes intended by its construction, has reached its capacity, and that true financial policy requires its immediate enlargement, so as to maintain its present value by a successful competition with the several railroad routes which are penetrating the coal fields from which it draws its present supplies. At present the average tonnage of boats carrying coal is about seventy tons. By adding an additional foot of water, this will be increased to near one hundred tons, equal to an additional tonnage on coal, alone, of two hundred thousand tons per annum beyond its present capacity. This increase, at the present rate of toll, would yield $72,000.00 a year, exclusive of the increase on all other articles shipped over the line—a sum in itself almost sufficient to complete the desired improvement. The Lehigh Coal and Navigation company's canal has six feet water, and is capable of transporting a boat carrying one hundred tons. This canal is the great feeder of the Delaware division. When coal boats from the Lehigh reach the entrance of the State work, if they have one hundred tons, they must unload a portion of their cargo. To obviate this expense and delay, to cheapen transportation, and at the same time add to the public revenues, it is proposed to increase the capacity of the Delaware division to six feet, by cleaning out the bottom and adding one foot to its present depth of water by raising the bank.[73]

In his 1855 report to the canal commissioners, Edward Gay, now a consulting engineer for the state, summarized the details of the canal. The original 25 locks of the canal had been reduced to 24,

> having been reduced by the construction of <u>two</u> Locks at Eulerville [Raubsville] into <u>one</u> of them. The Guard Lock at Easton, Lock at Eulerville, Four Locks at New Hope, and outlet Lock at Bristol, (in all 7 Locks,) are of large size, and capable of passing two boats <u>each</u> at the same time ... leaving 17 locks ... to be enlarged.[74]

Gay opposed enlarging by combining two locks into one at Smithtown and at Black's Eddy. He argued, first, that "<u>large</u> lifts will be more expensive to maintain than the <u>smaller</u> ones." Second,

> When a large number of Boats are waiting, to pass in <u>one</u> direction, or in fact in <u>either</u> they will be passed sooner through the smaller lifts, but the 3^d and most important reason is, that more than double the amount of water will be necessary to pass a boat, or pair of Boats, through the large lifts [than]

would be required for passing them through the small lifts, in other words to pass a boat or two Boats through a Lock of 16 feet or 22 f^t wide would require 15,840 cubic feet <u>more</u> water, than for two 8 f^t lifts!! and as all the water used, must be drawn from the Lehigh, the present strong current in the <u>upper levels</u> (which is now an objectionable feature in its navigation) would be greatly increased, while the Levels adjacent to the large lifts, would be depressed, (especially, when a large number of boats are passing) and thus obstruct, rather than improve the navigation,— [75]

Gay recommended the enlargement of the existing Locks "on their present scites [sic], with the exception of the lower one at Smithtown, which should be removed some 300 feet further down, so as to give a greater space between the Locks." The greatest problem of the canal was a want of "<u>width</u>, (not depth,) both to allow an easier flow to the water and to facilitate the passing of boats." First priority should be the removal of debris from the canal to maintain its depth, and the widening of especially "the hill sections and narrow points." He observed that,

> in its present condition, the Railroad [Belvidere-Delaware] will doubtless prove a successful competitor, for a large share of this valuable [coal] trade, but with enlarged Locks, and its prism widened to fifty feet-water surface, the canal would be secure against rivalry.[76]

On May 17, 1856, Gay assumed a new position, that of state engineer, and made detailed reports on the condition and prospects for the Delaware Division in December of 1856 and again in December of 1857. In 1856, he made a survey of the whole state system and found many undesirable conditions although he admitted that "The mechanical work was found in a tolerable condition on the … Delaware Division."

> [The improvements] were commenced early in June and nineteen miles of the work, extending from Easton to the Frenchtown Lock [today's Uhlertown] was placed under Contract on the 14th of July. This improvement is at present in progress, consists merely in raising the Towing path and Berm banks, Locks, Bridges, Roads, Walls &c. of sufficient height, to admit of increasing the depth of the Canal one foot—this making six foot instead of five.[77]

It would have been better, he believed, had sufficient appropriations been authorized to extend the improvements 25 miles to Point Pleasant rather than just the 19 miles to the "Frenchtown Lock."

There were particular problems, apparently ignored in the past, just below the lock at Eulerville (today's Groundhog or Raubsville Lock). Improvements were, according to Gay "almost, if not absolutely, indispensable."

> [T]he water surface immediately below the Lock … is but 32 feet wide for a distance of 600 feet, most of which is curved. The Lock is one of the largest Lifts on the Line, and when the water is discharged from the Chamber, it rushes with so great velocity through the narrow channel below, as seriously to impede the passage of ascending Boats…. in connexion with this subject, I may say that ever since the completion of this canal, the navigation upon it, has suffered more inconvenience in consequence of the want of a uniform supply of water, than other causes, this defect is attributable mainly to the <u>insufficient</u> width of the upper or Feeder level from Easton to Eulerville, as well as that of the Guard Lock, or Feeder gates at the head of the Canal, which are <u>too</u> small to admit a sufficient supply of water and cannot be enlarged except at great expense, and in such form as would injure the entrance into the Canal.[78]

Gay estimated it would cost $26,535 to increase the "Feeder level to 50 feet water surface." Preferable would be the construction of

> a new Guard Lock, and Feeder Gates about one mile below the present ones … If this improvement is adopted, the use of the present Lock & Gates will be unnecessary except during extraordinary floods…. the canal will be secured, and the mile of canal near Easton (one of the most narrow, and difficult of navigation on the line) will be much improved, both in width and depth, as well as preserved from injury by floods.[79]

Progress on the improvements, he reported, had been slow because of the traffic, the necessity of doing the work in winter after the water was drained, the difficulty of securing the right types of boats, and obtaining sufficient labor, particularly during the autumn. He found further problems:

> The surveys made during the past season, for the extension of the Improvement from Frenchtown to New Hope, and thence to Bristol proves the Towing path to be lower, and the depth of water in the Canal less than had been expected. The former averages but a little over one foot above the water surface, while the latter does not exceed four feet and eight inches in depth on the Lock mitre sills. I have no doubt that all Calculations hertofore made, in reference to this improvement, were based on the supposition that the depth of water was full five feet, and the bank an average of at least eighteen inches above the water surface as on all new Canals, a much larger amount of work will be necessary.[80]

Without the extension of the improvements beyond New Hope and on to Bristol, he argued, it was likely that many owners of enlarged canal boats would be dissatisfied when they were compelled to leave the canal at New Hope. He also argued that an enlarged canal would be a much cheaper carrier and therefore a successful competitor for the railroads.

A few months later, in the spring of 1857, Gay evaluated a proposal to construct "schutes" that would permit the Lehigh Valley Railroad to pass coal from their rail cars into canal boats "at the head of the Delaware Division." He described the site under consideration as "favourable, and if made would doubtless, add to the facilities for trade on the Canal." The facility was never constructed.[81]

In his December 1857 annual report, the last before the sale of the Delaware Division, Gay continued to report on the improvements underway:

> The raising of the Embankments on the entire line from Easton to New Hope [is underway] … the walls, Bridges &c. will be completed during the present month. The Locks are progressing rapidly, and the Aqueducts, waste-weirs &c. will be commenced as soon as the water is withdrawn from the canal, and completed before the opening of Navigation next spring.…
>
> In consequence of the peculiar arrangement of the outlet into the River at New Hope, by which, its connection with the canal is made at the head of a level nine miles long, the improvement to this point, will be rendered <u>unavailable</u>, unless the whole distance of nine miles is raised, or a Lock is constructed in the canal immediately below the outlet—this latter plan is proposed, in the event of the Legislature refusing the Necessary appropriation, to complete the work to Bristol—
>
> The Lock (built in a temporary manner of wood) will cost about <u>$2000</u>. and will of course be unnecessary if the improvement is Extended, but if built its cost and removal must be <u>added</u> to any future extension … if the Lock is to be constructed, it should be done before the opening of navigation in the spring.[82]

This apparently was the so-called papermill lock at New Hope.

Gay, always a strong advocate of the canal, proposed the extension of improvements to Bristol:

> two thirds of the present coal trade on this canal, passes through to Bristol, and only <u>one third</u> leaves it at New Hope. It follows therefore, that if the work is suspended at the latter place, the smallest amount of trade, paying toll on 35 miles only, will enjoy all the advantages of the improvement, while the larger amount paying toll on 60 miles, will receive none whatever.[83]

Gay's report concluded with a long explanation of why the railroads would be unsuccessful in competing with the canals for heavy freight, in which he pointed out the especial problems faced by railroads in overcoming grades compared to the level of the canal.

The sale of the canal in the spring of 1858 terminated any further state endeavors to improve it.

Sale of the Canal

During the fall election campaign of 1842, with the state facing financial disaster, the movement to sell the public works had gained wide support. The Whigs accused the Democrats of raising the state "debt to $40,000,000, raising taxes, abusing the veto power, and of bribery and corruption on the public works." The minutes of the State Senate of January 4, 1843, contain a communication from Governor David

Rittenhouse Porter (1839–1845) generated in response to a July 1842 "Act to provide for the ordinary expenses of Government, payment of the interest upon State debt, receiving of proposals for the sale of the Public Works, and for other purposes."

Under the seventeenth section of the act, the Governor was "authorized and required to receive proposals for the sale of the Delaware Division of the Pennsylvania canal." In the eighteenth section, he was to receive similar proposals for the sale of

> the North Branch, from Northumberland to Lackawanna creek, and Erie Extension of the Pennsylvania canal; also the Columbia and Portage railroads, and the main line of the Pennsylvania canal, and all other branches of railroads and canals belonging to the Commonwealth, and lay before the next Legislature at as early a day as possible, such proposals, if any, for their concurrence or rejection.[84]

Advertisements in six of the state's more important newspapers in August stimulated only two responses, one of $3,000,000 for the Columbia and Philadelphia Railroad, to be amortized with payments of $100,000 per year plus interest at 5 percent, and the other, an outright offer of $10,000 for the outlet lock at Portsmouth on the Eastern Division of the main line canal.[85]

William Bigler (a future governor) presented the senate with "An Act to authorize the Governor to incorporate the Delaware Canal company" on February 10, 1843. Over the next months, the bill went through the various necessary readings plus a conference with the house, and received an important amendment that gave the new company the right to "construct one or more out-let locks at suitable points, to form a connection with the feeder of the Delaware and Raritan canal," and set tolls for their use. Finally, on April 13, 1843, Governor Porter signed the amended bill.[86]

Similar bills had been proposed to dispose of other of the lateral canals across the state. An Erie Extension Canal Company was authorized, and with strong regional support its stock was subscribed. Property on which the state had expended some $4,650,678.87 was turned over to the new company, with the proviso that it complete the canal. This was done with the modest expenditure of approximately $782,123.72 and the canal system, which extended from Beaver Falls on the Ohio River to the city of Erie on the lake of the same name, continued in operation until 1871 when the collapse of an aqueduct ended theline's active existence.[87]

The North Branch and the North Branch Extension were combined as the North Branch Canal Company. The new company was called upon to assume 114 miles of partially finished canals. The state had already spent $1,222,011.19 on these works; it was expected that at least another million would be required to complete the effort. Sufficient stock for the new company was never subscribed, even though the time deadline was extended several times. In 1849 the works passed back to the state, which completed the navigation system to the New York State border where it would meet New York's canals, in 1855, just three years before the North Branch was in turn sold to the Sunbury and Erie Railroad.[88]

Two other lesser portions of the state system were dealt with: the Wicanisco Canal, a short canal in the Susquehanna Valley that tapped a coalfield, was sold to a private company, and the Thaddeus Stevens-inspired Gettysburg Railroad (popularly referred to by the Democrats as the "Tapeworm Railroad" because of its winding path) was simply scrapped.[89]

On April 18, 1843, a new law was passed that took the appointment of canal commissioners away from the governor and provided for their direct popular election for staggered three-year terms. In January of 1844, the newly elected board met and proceeded to organize.[90] Subsequent elections became bitter factional struggles that in many cases further undermined the efficiency of the board, which now controlled a massive patronage across the state.

In Governor Porter's 1845 annual message, the transfer of the Erie works to the Erie Canal Company was acknowledged. Appended to his message was the report of the commissioners appointed under the "act of the 13th April, 1844 … 'to authorize the Governor to incorporate the Delaware Canal Company'" —a report of the inability of the commissioners to sell the stock.[91] On December 18, 1844, Joseph R. Evans, treasurer for the board of commissioners, submitted a report of expenses for $767.31 expended promoting the sale of the stock, and amount that exceeded the $500 originally appropriated. The sale had been advertised in newspapers in Pittsburgh, Lancaster, New York, Boston, and Philadelphia. All the monies received from the sale of stock had been returned to the purchasers.[92]

The March 1845 report of the house's Committee of Ways and Means "relative to the sale of the Main Line" of the Pennsylvania Canal summarized the problems. The state was in a financial bind, unable to meet many of its obligations, including the interest on its debts, and there was a shortage of currency in parts of the state. This situation produced "irritation and discontent" among the populace:

> During this state of things, the people asked for the sale of the public works in order to relieve themselves from taxation. The time however selected for the consideration of the bill was unfortunate—the public works were unpopular—the embarrassment of the state was attributed to the bad management of the improvements. An opinion prevailed that if they were sold the Treasury would be relieved from an annual draft to support and maintain a large number of unnecessary officers … [93]

The sale had been authorized by the legislature without having been submitted to popular vote, an extraordinary assumption of power.

> The expediency of a sale might well be questioned, as well as doubts raised whether incalculable evils would not follow, both humiliating to our pride as a state, and disgraceful to us as a people, had the Legislature assumed the prerogative of transferring a work of such vast importance without a full expression of the sovereign will. If a sale is made, the improvements must pass into the hands of a company, the stockholders of which to a great extent, must be foreigners, not only to our soil, but in feeling and in interest.[94]

In 1845, the people in a popular referendum endorsed a proposal to sell the works. As the proposal—one that had demanded a full return on the original expenditures on the state works—was still active, the Committee on Ways and Means still questioned the expediency of the sale, and was particularly concerned about the capital investment that had been expended on the main line. There were still hopes that the improvements would be seen as valuable possessions in the future. The members revealed their Jacksonian orientation in their committee report:

> Corporations have generally been considered obnoxious to the public weal; their history is one of entire selfishness, monopolizing in their design and results; they always interfere with the action of individual enterprize, concentrating large amounts of capital, which necessarily operates injuriously to the interest of men with small means.[95]

The situation varied according to the eye of which beholder it was seen through. An 1845 article in *Hunt's Merchants Magazine* pointed up the "obvious" benefits from the state system:

> Notwithstanding this, attempts were made during the late financial embarrassments, consequent upon the derangement of business and the universal prostration of public and private credit, to heap odium upon the whole system of state works. At one time, popular clamer [sic] almost prevailed. But that time has passed away. The credit of the public works has revived with the credit of the state, and the voice of opposition has been drowned by the music of the boatman's horn on the canals, … Let the main line of state works, be hereafter intrusted only to honest and competent men; let the political knavery be hereafter banished from its control; let experience, economy, and wisdom, direct, regulate, and manage all its affairs, and this important work will, henceforth, be no expense to this commonwealth.[96]

The proposals to sell the public works would not die. In the January 13, 1847, session of the State Assembly, a motion was offered that the Committee on Ways and Means "be instructed to report a bill to this House, providing for offering at sale the canals and railroads owned by this Commonwealth." The resolution passed a second reading but apparently did not at this time become law.[97]

Governor Francis R. Shunk included a very specific declaration referring to the Columbia and Philadelphia Railroad in his annual message of January 1848:

Governor William F. Johnston
1848–1852

Under no circumstances should any plan or arrangement be entertained, by which the State would, for a single moment, be deprived of the ownership, and entire control of the road.[98]

In Governor William F. Johnston's annual message of January 1851, attention was called to the transportation needs of the citizens of the northwestern portions of the state. In the face of other railroads being constructed,

the people of the Commonwealth ought never to lose sight of that other great enterprise which, known as the Sunbury and Erie Railroad, was meant to connect the Susquehanna, the Delaware, and the Lakes. Besides the command of the trade of the Northern seas secured by its construction, it would bring into market for sale and settlement vast bodies of untenanted and unimproved lands, and develop treasures of inexhaustable mineral wealth now wholly inaccessible.[99]

The state, however, was unable to embark "in these various improvements."

Governor William Bigler devoted a large portion of his annual message of January 1855 to the problem of the state and its canals:

> [The Delaware Division] makes a most gratifying exhibit. The gross receipts counted $365,327.07, and the expenditures $59,738.67, showing a net profit of $305,588.40; a sum equal to the interest on six millions of the public debt, and to 20 per cent. on the original cost of the work, including the expenditures for new locks.[100]

Remembering that the canal commissioners were now elected and not appointed, Bigler suggested that the law that bound the canal commissioners to a fixed rate of tolls for the whole season should be repealed. These elected officers with the related responsibilities should "be left free to meet the exigencies in trade and commerce, as they may arise." The Governor reaffirmed his commitment to support the completion of the state works, specifically the North Branch, but expressed doubts as to the wisdom of the sale of the state works. He

Governor William Bigler
1852–1855

had, as directed in the Act of April 27, 1854, solicited sealed bids, actually proposals for purchase of the main line of public works. There had been no offers at the set prices and "public notice was again given, on the 14th of November last [1854], in accordance with the 29th section of the act, for proposals, to be submitted to the General Assembly; but none have been received."[101]

Governor James Pollock
1855–1858

Bigler affirmed that many citizens, "perhaps a majority," desired the public works to be sold, but this desire was based on the assumption that the measure would be one of real economy—that it would lessen, without the hazard of increasing, their annual taxes. Such a sale might be made at a price far too low to effect this purpose; and if so, to give away the public works would be still less likely to produce the desired result. Bigler offered a passing recognition of the benefits "resulting to the people from these improvements."[102] Proposals endorsing the sale of the state works would not go away. A scattering of petitions, resolutions, and bills surfaced in both the assembly and the senate during their 1855 sessions.[103]

In January of 1856, Governor James Pollock devoted much of his annual message to the problems of the state works. Only the Delaware Division offered a favorable picture. There, revenues less expenditures showed a net revenue of $332,575.56, more than three times the excess of aggregate revenues less ordinary and extraordinary expenditures state-wide, which totaled only $103,585.53. It should be noted that this did not include interest on the funded debt. "If all our lines of improvement exhibited a similar balance sheet," commented the Governor, "the people would have less cause of complaint and more confidence in the general operation of the system." Pollock, however, unlike his predecessor, stated his opinion forthrightly. It was:

> That the State should, long since, have been separated from the management and control of these works,... Public policy and public sentiment demand this separation; and every consideration of present and future interest requires their sale.[104]

An examination of the 1856 minutes of the State Assembly reveals some of the undercurrents present in the state. There was a good deal of resentment across the state against the Pennsylvania Railroad, chartered in 1846, which by 1852 had been built from Harrisburg west across the state to Pittsburgh. The early fifties saw the railroad institute a series of legal attacks on the state through the canal commission, whereby the railroad attempted to be relieved from paying tonnage taxes. These had been assessed as part of its charter to compensate the state for possible losses to the state system as a result of competition from the new railroad. The Pennsylvania Railroad attempted to force the state to furnish motive power and permit it to pass cars over the Columbia and Philadelphia Railroad as a matter of right.

While the state was sustained in the courts, the Pennsylvania Railroad continued its attacks, mostly in the media and in the legislature. The railroad was considered to be the principal prospective purchaser of the main line of the state works from Philadelphia to Pittsburgh. It is impossible to determine whether its legislative initiatives had any real support, but on April 3, interspersed with many considerations concerning the sale of the public works, was a memorial from the president and managers of the Sunbury and Erie Railroad Company, asking that they be considered in a bill for the sale of the main line of the public works.[105] Later the same day, the State House of Representatives received a communication from the Canal Commissioners, in answer to a resolution adopted that morning relative to the proposed lease of the main line of the canal to the Union Canal Company.[106]

On April 8, 1856, petitions were presented from citizens of Philadelphia "praying" for the passage of a law authorizing the sale of the main line of the public works to the Sunbury and Erie Railroad Company.[107] The State House's minutes of March 3, 1857, contain remarks furnished by its Ways and Means Committee supplementing the "Act for the sale of the State canals" with some specific remarks about the Delaware Division:[108]

> For several years past the receipts from the Delaware division have been steadily and rapidly diminishing, owing to the completion of railroads; ... Your committee cannot overlook the fact, that there is no instance in Pennsylvania of a canal in successful competition with a railroad in the transportation of passengers and freight ... the Lehigh Valley road is reducing the business on the Lehigh canal...

The committee felt that the idea of a sale for cash was a "sheer absurdity," and outlined the promising fiscal future of the Sunbury and Erie Railroad, which would pay for the lateral canals with $3,500,000 in bonds, secured by a mortgage for $7,000,000. The report noted that a railroad was less perishable property than a canal that could be destroyed at any time by a freshet, and had words for those who opposed the sale of the works:

> They may allege that the price is inadequate, or the security insufficient, or the time unpropitious. Such objections have been urged heretofore to the injury of the State. In 1844 it was believed that the main line could have been sold for $12,000,000, but when the bill was introduced into the Legislature it fixed the price at $20,000,000, and no purchaser could be found. In 1854 it was understood that $9,000,000 would have been given, but again it was objected that the price was too low; it was limited to $10,000,000, and no sale was effected. In 1856 it would have been sold for $7,500,000, on a reasonable credit, but the bill provided that it should be paid in yearly instalments of $1,000,000, and

no party would purchase. In the year following it was sold to the Pennsylvania railroad company for $7,500,000, on long credit, that being the highest price that could be obtained therefor.[109]

The date of the sale was June 25, 1857, and on Thursday, July 23, *The New York Times* reported that the stockholders of the Pennsylvania Railroad had approved the purchase. The Board of Canal Commissioners was virtually unanimous in its opposition to the sale. Already, on Wednesday June 10, Henry S. Mott, president of the Board of Canal Commissioners, had reported to his board that, in line with a resolution they had adopted, he had "Commenced proceedings in the Supreme Court of Pennsylvania against all proper parties to prevent the Sale and Transfer of the Main line of the Public works." [110]

By June the Supreme Court had ruled that, except for one provision, the law providing for the sale was constitutional and the legislature had acted properly.[111] In his annual message of January 1858, Governor Pollock noted that the disposal of the main line had

> directed public attention to the importance and necessity of disposing of the remaining divisions of the public improvements. The reasons and policy that required and justified the sale of the one, apply with equal force to the sale of the other.
>
> [It is] not only evident to all who have given a the subject a candid and impartial consideration, but the necessity is clearly established, by the history of their construc6tion and management.[112]

He commented that there appeared no prospect that the revenue would ever exceed the costs of repair and management. Considering the present state of taxation and the state debt, he proposed that

> A sale, at the earliest practicable period, of the whole of our public works, for a fair consideration, upon terms just and liberal to the purchasers, and at the same time amply protective of the rights and interests of the people, should be authorized by the Legislature.[113]

He added that the receipts should be applied to the state debt.

On Thursday April 23, 1858, the Board of Canal Commissioners received from the legislature a resolution to stop any expenditure of funds for repairs, deepening, or widening after "the passage of the laws authorizing the sale of the Public Works to the Sunbury & Erie Rail Road Company," or to any other party.[114]

On Thursday August 19, 1858, the board received the decision of the courts rendering the acts of the legislature providing for the sale of the state works constitutional.

About one year after the sale of the main line, following the Governor's approval of an enabling act on April 21, 1858, the lateral works were sold to the Sunbury and Erie Railroad for $3,500,000, largely in long-term bonds that the state took. The railroad company then disposed of the canals for $3,875,000, again receiving bonds that could be pledged to the indebtedness to the state.[115]

The Delaware Division was disposed of on July 10, 1858, for $1,775,000 to a newly formed Delaware Division Canal Company. This company operated the canal for a few years and then in 1866 leased it long-term to the Lehigh Coal and Navigation Company, which operated the canal to 1931. One million dollars in Delaware Division Canal Company bonds that the Sunbury and Erie had taken in payment for the canal were immediately deposited with the treasurer of the Commonwealth as a performance bond, returnable to the railroad after a certain construction level had been achieved.[116]

On Thursday October 21, 1858, the board accepted the resignation of State Engineer Edward F. Gay and acknowledged "the great ability, integrity and economy which he invariably exhibited in the discharge of his official duties." [117]

The Board of Canal Commissioners was abolished on January 15, 1859, and transferred all its books, records and property to the state auditor general. On February 26, 1885, by an act of the State Assembly, all of the records of the canal commissioners were transferred to the custody of the Secretary of Internal Affairs.[118]

So ended Pennsylvania's venture into the political morass of internal improvements.

∽ CHAPTER VI ∽

The Delaware Division Canal Company: 1858-1940

Background and Sale

By mid-century the Delaware Division of the Pennsylvania Canal, state-owned and state-operated, had been in operation continuously since opening in the 1830s. The largest portion of the traffic that passed over it was coal fed into it from the Lehigh Canal, constructed, owned, and operated by the Lehigh Coal and Navigation Company. Even after the state built an outlet lock at New Hope in 1848, providing the Lehigh Coal and Navigation Company with a long-sought route to the profitable New York market via New Jersey's Delaware and Raritan Canal, the efficiency of the canal remained a problem.

During the 1850s, at least partly in response to this concern, the state continued its efforts to expand the capacity of the Delaware Division. As the LC&N noted in its 1853 annual report, the state canal had "been much improved by the recent construction, at Uhler's and New Hope, of locks of dimensions enlarged to correspond with those of the locks on the Lehigh...." However, it was "indispensable" that the depth of water on the Delaware Division be increased to six feet. During 1853, as a result of new construction and breaches in the canal banks, LC&N had lost some seventy days' use of the state canal.[1]

In 1855, 734,729 tons of coal entered the Delaware Canal, substantially more than the previous year. Nonetheless, the company lamented that improved conditions on the Lehigh were

> in a measure neutralized by the very inferior character of the accommodations and facilities offered on the Delaware Division of the Pennsylvania canal; forming as it does practically, a prolongation of the Lehigh Canal, and constituting the connecting link between it and the magnificent navigation of the Delaware and Raritan Canal Company. In regard to this portion of the State improvements, we are obliged to reiterate the oft repeated statement of insufficient depth of water—of contracted and oneself constructed aqueducts and locks—of banks and towing paths inadequately supplied with overfalls, imperfectly and partially protected by slope walls and by paving and so little raised above the surface of the water in the levels, as to be liable to be overflowed and breached by every passing summer shower; and of a supply of water, at some seasons, dependent upon a ricketty [sic] and rotten water-wheel.[2]

In 1856, the LC&N noted favorably that the state legislature had appropriated additional funds for the much-needed improvement of the Delaware Canal.[3] This money enabled contracts to be let for sixteen miles of improvements from Easton to the Frenchtown (Uhlertown) Lock. Another appropriation of $50,000 in 1857 enabled the state to continue deepening the canal to the outlet lock at Wells' Falls. Boats carrying coal destined for the New York market crossed the Delaware River at that point and passed into the navigable feeder of the Delaware and Raritan Canal. The remaining portion of the improvements, extending from the outlet to Bristol, was left to be finished in 1858.[4]

Neither the state nor the Lehigh Coal and Navigation Company could know it, but 1855 was the peak year for carrying anthracite on the Delaware Canal. Competition from railroads had already begun, almost imperceptibly at first, to erode the amount carried on the waterway. Plans continued for making improvements to the canal.

The Democrats controlled the board of canal commissioners; according to their opponents, they ran the canals with nepotism, graft, and corruption. Doylestown's *Intelligencer* implied that the $100,000 appropriated for deepening of the canal was just squandered on

> a succession of patch-work, a quantity of riversand and gravel, scattered on the tow-path and berm-bank, in greater or less quantities, from Easton to somewhere in the vicinity of Lumberville, where the money will probably again run out, and the next Legislature will be called upon for another appropriation of $50,000. The Work is poorly done, and the materials are of the most unsuitable character.... Many men, residing along the canal in this county and Northampton, understanding the nature of the work to be done, bid for contracts, in good faith and as honest men. Great was their surprise when they found that the proposals were a mere sham and that the contracts had been awarded to personal pets, and to parties where the Canal Commissioners themselves have a large pecuniary interest.... [5]

The persons responsible for the graft and corruption were named in another article in the newspaper:

> Henry S. Mott is the senior member and chairman of the Canal Board, under whose supervision the public works are placed. Thomas L. Wilson is Secretary of the Board. William Overfield, Superintendent of the Delaware Canal, is a nephew of Henry S. Mott. John Mott, the principal contractor to execute the sham repairs now going forward is a son of Henry S. Mott. Mr. Wilson, one of the engineers in charge is son of Thomas L. Wilson, mentioned above; and Mr. Gay, another engineer, is a son of Edward F. Gay, State Engineer.... Until the sale of the Main Line, it was one great hot-bed of favoritism and venality; that outlet being removed, the operations of the contract jobbers will be concentrated upon the remaining property of the state. [6]

Following the sale of the Main Line of the Pennsylvania Canal by the State of Pennsylvania to the Pennsylvania Railroad on June 25, 1857, it would appear inevitable that the balance of the state works, the so-called lateral canals up the Susquehanna and up the Delaware, would also be disposed of by the state. In March, the *Intelligencer* reported that petitions were circulating along the line of the Delaware Division calling for the sale of all the public works belonging to the state, and the abolition of the canal board. "These petitions are readily signed by persons of all political grades, except those who are office holders along the Canal or are in expectancy of fat jobs." [7] The same paper, unfriendly to the Democrats, noted in April the passage of the bill for the sale of the state canals which

> has made a great flutter among the 'bosses' and South Carolina 'mud-sills' on the Delaware Division, who received their appointments more from their blind subserviency in 'sticking to the ticket,' than for any particular fitness for the responsible duties to be performed. [8]

Immediately upon the sale, all expenditure of state funds for improvements on the canals ended. [9]

The state, as will be recalled from the previous chapter, sold the so-called lateral canals to the Sunbury and Erie Railroad for $3,500,000 and accepted payment in the form of bonds, which would be part of the

Governor William F. Packer
1858–1861

$7,000,000 in bonds the railroad was permitted to issue and sell under terms of the deed. Among the specific mortgage bonds executed and delivered to the state to guarantee the sale was to be one for $1,500,000 on the Delaware Division Canal. Governor William F. Packer signed the agreement on May 19, 1858. [10] Among the Lehigh Coal and Navigation Company papers in the Pennsylvania State Archives is a typescript copy of the May 7, 1858, articles of agreement whereby the original incorporators subscribed the stock of the newly formed Delaware Division Canal Company. On July 10, 1858, the deed of sale of the Delaware Canal was executed between the Sunbury and Erie Railroad and the new Delaware Division Canal Company. On July 14, under the Governor's name but over the signature of the deputy secretary of the Commonwealth, the articles of incorporation, along with the deed, were apparently properly recorded with the state. On September 13, 1858, H.S.

McGraw, the state treasurer, acknowledged receipt of $1,000,000 in bonds of the Delaware Division Canal Company from the Sunbury and Erie Railroad, the canal to be collateral, and the railroad was released from that portion of its mortgage obligation. This, it would appear, formally legalized the transaction.[11]

In the issue of March 18 the *Intelligencer* had repeated rumors published in the Easton Argus to the effect that

> the Delaware Division will be purchased by the Lehigh Navigation Company. We do not know how true this may be, but hope the statement will prove correct. In the hands of this company it will be made a very profitable improvement.[12]

Apparently the expectation of the LC&N was high, for on June 8 the Doylestown paper reported

> E.A. Douglas, Esq. the eminent engineer in the service of that company, with Mr. Cox, their active manager, passing down the canal, for the purpose of making a critical examination of the actual condition of the work.[13]

However, the July 7, 1858, issue of the Doylestown *Intelligencer* reported:

> the Delaware Canal, from Easton to Bristol, has been sold by the Sunbury and Erie Railroad Company to an association of ten or twelve leading capitalists of Philadelphia, numbering among them Messres J.V. Williamson, A.S. & G. Roberts, J.G. Fell, E.W. Clark & Co., William Longstreth, the Messres Borie, Charles Henry Fisher, Judge Hepburn, Ephraim Marsh, of New Jersey and others.[14]

The price was reported as $1,775,000, to be paid principally "in 6 per cent mortgage bonds, preferred stock, and $475,000 in cash within ten months." The first payment of $75,000 had been made the previous Saturday and the company was organized as The Delaware Division of the Pennsylvania Canal Company; Jay Cook was elected its first president. The financiers who had arranged the sale were reported to have received $25,000 for their services and the stockholders to have received two shares for each one purchased. By paying a generous eight percent dividend on the stock they created a market demand which enabled them to sell their shares and clear good profits.[15]

Everyone had expected that the purchaser would be the Lehigh Coal and Navigation Company, for their canal from Mauch Chunk in the heart of the anthracite coal regions to Easton was the primary feeder of the Delaware Division. But it was reported in the Philadelphia press that the only terms ever mentioned to the Lehigh Coal and Navigation Company were "two millions of dollars, all cash within thirty months, with an assurance that no other terms would be entertained." [16]

At least part of the explanation of what was, for all practical purposes, the rejection of the LC&N as a purchaser can be found in the long-running verbal campaign waged against the state by the LC&N as it attempted to obtain an outlet lock from the Delaware Division Canal to enter the Delaware and Raritan Canal of New Jersey in order to reach the profitable New York market. This had been bitterly opposed by the capitalists of Philadelphia, who had used every political stratagem to keep Pennsylvania coal from being diverted to New York. Even after 1848, when the outlet lock was constructed at New Hope, there were still many impediments placed on this trade. In fact, New Hope had been a poor second choice, for the LC&N had hoped the state would construct the outlet lock further upriver, at Black's Eddy.[17]

The makeup of the body of the principal incorporators is interesting. Ephraim Marsh was president of the Morris Canal Company and there were innuendoes that his interest was to guarantee that some LC&N coal being shipped to the New York area would still cross the Delaware at Easton to the Morris Canal. Also among the incorporators of the new company were the presidents of the Lehigh Valley Railroad, the Sunbury and Erie Railroad, and the Bank of Commerce, along with Philadelphia financiers who had extensive interests in the coal regions, particularly in the Hazleton Company coal mines. They were judged to be "unquestionably a strong team," and it was observed that

> the purchase has been shrewdly and quietly put through. They pay $75,000 in cash, $40,000 a month for ten months, $100,000 in 8 per cent stock, and $1,200,000 in mortgage bonds. One half the surplus over $1,000,000 goes to the State.[18]

E.W. Clark & Company of Jersey City had followed the sale of the Delaware Division to the S & E Railroad with great interest, so much so that Mr. Clark asked the canal company if he and his friends should

make up a party and buy the Delaware Division of the Pennsylvania canals, [and] would the Morris Canal and Banking Company lease the said canal for twenty years, and what annual rent they would give therefor.[19]

The Morris Company responded that if such a lease were legal, they would consider $200,000 per year paid in two installments.[20]

The directors of the Morris Canal Company felt it was important to "have a control of the Delaware Division" to forestall the Lehigh Coal and Navigation Company from obtaining a monopoly on the transportation of coal out of the Lehigh region. In the process, they hoped to guarantee to themselves a portion of the Pennsylvania coal trade.[21]

The Hazelton group were the owners and investors in the Beaver Meadow Railroad and mines. Over the years they had been dependent on the Lehigh Navigation to get their coal to the markets, a situation not free from controversy and disputes.[22]

Two weeks before the date when the new owners declared an eight percent dividend on their stock, they gave

orders to stop the pay of lock-tenders along their line during the period for which navigation is closed. The practice under the State management was to give them $27 per month, and a house to live in during the winter. By this change the Company will save a large sum, but we are not so sure that they ought at this inclement season to throw so many laborers out of all employment for the winter.[23]

The new owners asked the superintendent, Mr. Overfield, and "all the other persons employed on the canal by the State, to continue discharging the duties of their respective offices, for the present." [24] In 1859, Ephraim Marsh told his Morris Canal stockholders:

the effect of this arrangement has been, to secure to this company an approximation to a proper proportion of tolls upon that branch of their business, and to make the Morris Canal as favorable an avenue as any other, for the transportation of Lehigh coal to supply the New York Market, and for re-shipment upon tide water.[25]

At the beginning of 1859 the new company began to throw its weight around with a new bill, introduced in February in the Pennsylvania Senate, entitled "An Act Relative to the Delaware Division Canal Company of Pennsylvania." It brought forth numerous remonstrances and presumably was never passed. According to the *Intelligencer* it contained

outrageous provisions … giving this Company unlimited power, permitting them to disregard the claims and rights of property holders along the canal. It also gives them authority to construct a dam across the Delaware river at New Hope, which, it is well known, will drive the shad from the river entirely.[26]

The bill would also establish a tribunal "for the settlement and assessment of damages, from whose decisions there is no appeal."

The right of trial by jury should be always secured to the citizens in such cases. This Company having made purchase of the Delaware Division of the Pennsylvania Canal at a very low rate, upon the understanding as provided for in the bill passed at the last session of the Legislature for regulating the sale of the State Canals, that they would settle and pay the claims for damages or demands against the Commonwealth in relation to the location, construction, repair, management or use of the Delaware Division ought not to have special legislation to free them from these liabilities, which entered into their purchase.[27]

In financial terms the new company started off rather auspiciously. The *Intelligencer* summarized the annual report of the Delaware Division Company for the year 1859, its first full year of operation. During the twenty months since the transfer, the canal had been enlarged and improved almost its entire length, and at Easton chutes have been made for the more easy transfer of coal by rail, to that point into the Canal, thus giving it an additional source of tonnage.... The works are greatly increased capacity [*sic*] as compared with what they were when they left State control.[28]

Over the year, the company had "earned eight per cent on its capital, over and above the interest on its bonds." The details were as follows:

Total income from tolls, rents, and interest	$222,030.76
Ordinary expenses	46,680.21
Net earnings	$173,350.55
Against which has been charged	
Interest on bonds	$ 60,000.00
Dividends paid	49,334.00
Construction	11,890.72
Land damages	2,929.13
Real estate	1,290.84
Building enlarged lock	2,530 .83
	$127,975.52
Leaving a credit balance of	$ 45,375.03 [29]

The new company apparently continued to improve the canal. According to a news item dated December 17, 1861, the canal, most of whose locks still had the original dimensions of 90 feet in length, were now able to handle boats carrying from 90 to 100 tons. In fact, one boat "lately built by Samuel Soliday, at New Hope, has carried 106 tons of coal to market." [30]

Lease and Lehigh Coal and Navigation Company Operations

A canal, and particularly one that runs along a major estuary as did the Delaware Division, inevitably had problems of flood, breaks, and even simple maintenance. While there were relatively few interruptions during the latter 1850s, there were major floods in 1862 and numerous closings on the Delaware Division Canal in 1863 and 1864, while in 1865 it was necessary for coal passing south to enter the Delaware and Raritan at the New Hope outlet lock and exit into the Delaware at Bordentown, navigation on the Delaware Division below the outlet lock having been suspended for repairs from July 16 to September 9.[31]

It was particularly in light of situations such as this that the LC&N felt it was important to control the several companies along the routes whereby the company transported its coal to the Philadelphia and New York markets

> so that they might act together as a whole and not, as heretofore, often embarrass each other and the public by failing to agree about tolls, or to unite in making necessary improvements. With the view of securing these advantages and of placing our own canal above and beyond the power of any hostile interests, a lease of the Delaware Division canal, for a term of ninety-nine years has been negotiated with the Delaware Division Canal Company and a contract entered into simultaneously with the Delaware and Raritan Canal Company, by which the through tolls to New York will be at all times during the lease shared in certain equitable proportions by the two Companies, and relations established which, it is believed, will lead to such prompt and harmonious action hereafter, as will tend greatly to benefit and promote the trade.[32]

The LC&N had agreed to pay

> the interest on the bonded debt of the Delaware Division Canal Company, amounting to eight hundred thousand dollars, at six per cent. per annum, and semi-annual dividends at the rate of four per cent. each, clear of State and United States taxes, on their capital stock, amounting to one million six hundred and thirty-three thousand three hundred dollars, together with such expenses, not to exceed five thousand dollars per annum, as may be necessary to keep up the organization of the Company.[33]

Noting the rent was high, "not much less than two hundred thousand dollars per annum," the LC&N management felt that net profits would justify the expense and that controlling the routes was essential. The lease between LC&N and Delaware Div. Canal Co. was "consummated" on August 20, 1866.[34]

Among LC&N's concerns was one that was to become a long-term threat to the ultimate vitality of the canals. It called for the completion by the end of 1867 of the rail line from Mauch Chunk to Easton and of a connecting bridge across the Delaware. This would avoid the situation whereby, because of the seasonal closing of the canals, profits were much diminished by the forced inactivity of the mines during the winter season.[35]

The 1866 annual report showed that in that year, the Delaware Division Canal had had no interruptions during the whole season and had shown a profit of $80,027.63, actually the last profit that the canal would show for the next few years.[36] In 1867, twenty-two days were lost on the Delaware Division "owing to the breaking of an aqueduct." The repairs, in addition to the ordinary work, included:

> the completion of the new [double] lock at Smithtown, the re-building of the Rocky Falls and New Hope aqueducts, several bridges, and the materials a[nd] part of the labor for rebuilding Tinicum aqueduct.[37]

(Left) Double lock 15-16 at Smithtown.

(Below) The aqueduct over the Tinicum Creek.

In 1867, the Lehigh Coal and Navigation Company made an attempt,

at the suggestion of the Superintendent and Engineer, to reduce the cost of transportation by establishing a line of boats under the charge of one party. To accomplish this the Company has leased 100 boats, which were idle last year, on favorable terms to an energetic firm, and good results are expected from the arrangement. The hope is entertained that if the experiment is successful, the boatmen who own their own boats will organize in future years, and make such savings in their expenses as to be able to reduce their freight charges; whatever is saved in this way will increase the tolls.[38]

In 1868, passage through the outlet lock at New Hope was suspended for nine days because high water in the Delaware River prevented "ferriage." An additional eight days were lost as a result of a breach in the Delaware and Raritan Canal, while "in June an aqueduct at Yardleyville gave way, stopping operations below New Hope for about a week." In September "the lower gates in the outlet-lock at Easton gave way, causing a stoppage of boats passing to and from the Morris Canal, for five days." [39] In 1869, an October freshet did damage

greatly in excess of that caused by any former flood. The Tinicum and Tohickon aqueducts were entirely washed away, and those at Durham and Gallows run seriously damaged.

The loss of these aqueducts was caused not by the rise of the Delaware river, which was then only twelve feet above ordinary level, but wholly by their affording insufficient water-way to pass the flood from the mountain streams over which they formed the canal crossing.[40]

Had the Delaware been higher (it subsequently rose to thirty feet), it would have neutralized the force of the side streams that put their force against the aqueducts.[41] The repairs to the aqueduct took longer than anticipated, and the canal was not opened for the 1870 season following their completion on April 14. The reason was

[the] frequent and heavy rains during the fall and winter, which drove us away from work on the piers by raising the streams fourteen times in about as many weeks, and delayed their completion about a month. The contractors for the superstructure did not press their portion of the work with proper vigor.[42]

Only a day after the first full day of operation on April 16, 1870, there was a severe freshet on the Lehigh on April 18 that carried away "a portion of the guard-wall at Easton.... until the river can be turned to its usual course, we have no means of transfer from the Lehigh Canal to either the Delaware Division or the Morris Canal." [43]

A detailed listing of annual problems would be endless.

The Delaware Canal remained the bottleneck in the system. In 1868 the Lehigh Canal could carry boats of 175 to 200 tons capacity and the Delaware and Raritan could accommodate boats of even greater capacities, whereas boats on the Delaware Canal were limited to a maximum of 100 tons. If thirty-four miles of that canal, the section from Easton to the outlet lock at New Hope, could be enlarged with an expenditure of $500,000, LC&N believed the expenditure would pay for itself in two or three years.[44]

In 1870, John Brown, the "Canal Manager" of the Delaware Division Canal, proposed implementing the long-held dream of the Lehigh Coal and Navigation Company to build an outlet lock at Lower Black Eddy. In his correspondence with E.W. Clark, president of LC&N, he revealed some of the residual problems of that company's canal route to the New York market. Contingent to the proposed outlet would be an agreement to be reached with the Delaware and Raritan Canal to deepen their feeder by three feet, something that he indicated engineer Ashbel Welch of the D & R was already disposed to and was ready to commence at once, not only to satisfy the Pennsylvania interest but also to guarantee "to their Canal in a dry time an adequate supply of water." [45]

During the past 1870 season, for forty-three days the water in the Delaware at the New Hope crossing had been "at the lowest stage of the river ever known," too shallow to permit passage across the river by fully loaded boats, which necessitated either lightening up at New Hope, or loading at Mauch Chunk "from six to ten tons less than we should have done." The other option was to send the loaded boats to

Bristol and into the D & R at Bordentown but there, because of limited towing capacity, the maximum that could be handled was about twenty-five loaded boats per day, plus there would be "a loss to the Boatmen of about three days to each trip." The crossing at "Lower Blacks Eddy" would guarantee adequate river depth for the crossing even at the lowest river levels, and would be completely feasible if the feeder were deepened in order to handle the loaded boats. In addition, the new outlet lock, nearly opposite the feeder of the D & R, would save passage through five additional locks, one at Lumberville and four at New Hope. The river would now be reached by three locks at Lower Blacks Eddy, two if locks 13 and 14 (Point Pleasant) were combined. Brown came up with an estimate of $24,339.92 for

> the proposed Out Let Lock at Lower Blacks Eddy, with a view of locking down into the river Delaware at that point, Lock 17 feet lift, together with the necessary work connected therewith.[46]

Probably one reason the various programs for improvement of the Delaware Division were never implemented was the extensive damage sustained by the canal as a result of flooding in the fall of 1869 and again in the spring of 1870. The net loss reported for 1869 was $143,692; this was followed by a loss of $127,020 for 1870. These losses, plus the new arrangements that were being negotiated with various railroads—notably the Central Railroad of New Jersey and the Morris and Essex—all contributed to the movement of coal traffic away from the canals.[47]

Financial Crisis and Lease Renegotiation

Over the long run, the greatest threat to the canals and to their particular function, that of carrying coal, was the development of railroad competition. It was this that, in some degree, put the Lehigh Coal and Navigation Company in the railroad business, constructing railroads that would sometimes compete directly with its own canals and, in other cases, combining railroad with canals in ways that were, at least for the moment, more efficient ways to get coal to the urban markets. However, by mid-century, the combination of the continuing technological efficiency of the railroad as a bulk carrier and the degree of entrepreneurial investment in new lines saw railroads multiply throughout the anthracite regions. The resultant business combinations were in competition with each other, all attempting to guarantee reasonable and accessible avenues to the markets.

In 1871, to guarantee outlets for its coal, particularly to the New York market, the Lehigh Coal and Navigation Company entered into an agreement, dated May 30, with the Central Railroad of New Jersey.[48] This agreement involved leasing all of LC&N's railroads to the Central Railroad of New Jersey in return for rent constituting one-third of the gross revenues of the roads. The Central would purchase all the equipment on the routes by assuming payment of interest, and ultimately principal, on $2,310,000 of the LC&N's "five million gold loan" and agreed to purchase all of LC&N's other materials on hand, and shop tools and machinery. In addition to guaranteeing the operation with adequate rolling stock, the LC&N gave the Central the option, for three years, of leasing the Lehigh Canal at a net annual rent of $200,000, and assuming in connection therewith the lease of the Delaware Division Canal and the annual obligations under the lease, amounting to $138,714.[49]

Additional propositions for the lease of the Lehigh coal lands and the maintenance and operation of the Lehigh and Delaware Division canals were considered by the board during December of 1873, and approved on December 30. The board tied a lease of LC&N mines to the Central Railroad of New Jersey's subsidiary Honey Brook Coal Company. This agreement was necessary in order to guarantee the viability of the canals and to insure that the new lessor of the mines would not divert all traffic away from the canals and onto the railroad. The canal lease called for the Central Railroad Company of New Jersey to pay the LC&N

> a net annual income of Two Hundred Thousand Dollars in equal quarterly sums, over and above and clear of all disbursements or liabilities for taxes and imposts of every description and of every cost charge and expense of maintaining, repairing and operation said canals Slack-water navigation, dams, locks, buildings and the appurtenances thereof, and also of all damages or liabilities incident to the

This train hauling anthracite on the Lehigh and Susquehanna Division of the Central Railroad of New Jersey could carry far more coal more economically than boats on the canal system. In the distance is outlet lock 30 of the Lehigh Navigation, near Treichler's and the Three-Mile Dam.

ownership or operation of said premises and of earning and collecting all tolls water rents and other income from the same; and also over and above and clear of all liabilities, charges costs or expenses arising under the lease of the Delaware Division Canal to the Lehigh Coal and Navigation Company bearing date the twentieth day of August 1866, a draft of which contract is annexed and made a part of this contract.[50]

Through these arrangements the Central Railroad of New Jersey acquired extensive coal lands, either directly from the LC&N or by sale or lease of LC&N properties to the Lehigh and Wilkes-Barre Coal Company, a subsidiary of the Central, while the LC&N passed the onerous obligations of the 1866 Delaware Division Canal lease over to the Central.[51]

It would appear that the Central had little interest in the canals, for the directors of the railroad in their 1873 report to the shareholders, after noting the desirability of having the canals as well as the railroads under a single corporate control, stated:

[By] this agreement all the difficulties arising from a divided ownership of the railroads and the canals are obviated. It being the interest of the Coal Company to send as much coal to market over both routes as the market will take profitably, it now becomes the interest of the Railroad Company also to fill both avenues as full as possible. No great profit is expected from the canals, but no loss is anticipated, and the incidental advantages will be very great. A large reduction has been made in the working organizationa of the canals, and while at least equal efficiency will be maintained, the reduction in expenses will be considerable. Whatever direct profit is to be derived from the canals will mainly result from the success of these economies.[52]

The next few years would be complicated by one of America's major economic depressions of the century, usually referred to as the "Panic of '73" (1873). In 1874, however, the Central Railroad reported a profit of $19,644.78 from their operation of the canals. The following year, 1875, showed a loss of $95,919, brought about partly because of a lengthy coal strike in the Wyoming, Lehigh, and Schuylkill regions. The effect of this loss on receipts was "very injurious" for the first six months of the year, and although there was an "immense business done after the strike was over, [the canals], limited by the equipment of boats," were unable to make up the losses during the second half of the year. The next year, 1876, saw a larger loss, which LC&N reported was "partly due to a diversion of canal tonnage to the railroads."[53]

Not long afterward, by March of 1877, the Central Railroad was unable to meet its obligations and was in receivership. Negotiations between the Central and the Lehigh Coal and Navigation Company ensued during the period from March to June of 1877. On June 30, a final settlement was reached. Under its terms the Lehigh and Wilkes-Barre Coal Company, receivers of the coal company, and the Central Railroad of New Jersey, receivers of the railroad company, had the option to surrender the coal lands and canal at any time up to January 1, 1878, following thirty days' notice. Until then the Lehigh and Wilkes-Barre Coal Company was to operate the mine and the Central was to operate the canal "at the risk and on account of the Lehigh Coal and Navigation Company."[54]

Some of the detail is as follows:

3d The letter of June 4th 1877 to Mr Bullitt to be modified as follows

    (a) Canal Boats to be taken at $75,835.60

    (b) The Rent Acct with Coal Company to continue to draw interest at 6% from June 1, 1877

    (c) Payment by Railroad Company to be Cash $200,000.

         ”   ”   ”   ”   Sept 1st   99,654.35

. . . . .

The Canal Rent account stands as follows,

Canal Rent Due Jany 1877		$50,000.
Bal & Del Div ” ” ”		13,510.12
Del Div^n Tax & dividends Feb 12/77		77,214.06
Rent due April 1st		50,000.
Proportion Del Div^n to April 1st		31,633.38
Less Water Rents Collected	9,405.77	
Personal Property at valuation	40,000	
		49,405.77
		$166,951.79 [55]

A final addendum was added on June 30, 1877, to the effect that when the receivers ceased to operate the canals, the Central Railroad of New Jersey would be "forever released and discharged from said last mentioned contract." [56]

The Central Railroad had operated the canals and collected the revenue in 1874, 1875, and 1876. LC&N's annual report of 1878 seemed optimistic about the future:

> The small revenue of the past two years does not afford a fair criterion by which to estimate the future value of the canals. They suffered in 1877, by the refusal of the Receiver of the Central Railroad to operate them, and when we assumed control it was too late in the season to arrange for business, and through navigation was closed on the 4th of October, by injury to the Delaware Division Canal.[57]

The LC&N managers protested in the same report that the 1866 contract under which the Delaware Division canal had been operated by the LC&N had "been found oppressive and onerous." This is illustrated by the following table of losses sustained by the business over the thirteen-year period of the agreement.

Year	Loss
1867	$ 80,777.12
1868	19,735.61
1869	143,692.81
1870	127,020.61
1871	77,968.16
1872	102,040.76
1873	90,872.01
1874	51,565.15
1875	88,578.08
1876	120,006.91
1877	179,479.78
1878	148,171.65
	$1,229,908.65
Less profit, 1866,	80,027.63
Loss in thirteen years	$1,149,881.92 [58]

The report analyzed losses:

> The loss in 1877 was largely due to the storm of October 4th, which carried away two aqueducts and closed navigation for the season. The cost of repairs was $38,263.73, of which $15,579.50 was charged in 1877 and $22,684.23 in 1878. The losses in 1874, 1875 and 1876 and part of 1877, were paid by the Central Railroad Company of New Jersey under their agreement to operate the Lehigh and Delaware Division Canal, and to pay us a fixed revenue.[59]

The situation had changed. The Pennsylvania Railroad, the new lessees of New Jersey's Delaware and Raritan Canal, now refused to carry out the agreement made with the Lehigh Coal and Navigation Company for the division of tolls. The deciding embarrassment came when the $800,000 in mortgage bonds matured:

> the demand was made upon this company either to pay them or to negotiate an extension. This demand we resisted as not justified by the terms of the lease and when a legal enforcement was threatened, your Board conceived it to be their duty to look closely into the legal aspects of the question and the respective rights of the companies.[60]

Counsel advised that there were serious doubts as to whether the lease contract could be enforced as the stockholders had never sanctioned the existing agreement, and because, in the opinion of counsel, neither the Delaware Division Company, nor LC&N had the power to enter into the agreement at the time it was made. After some months of fruitless negotiations:

> some of our stockholders determined to test the validity of the lease. Your Board withdrew its opposition to their action, and a bill in equity was filed by stockholders residing out of this State, in the U.S. Circuit Court, and this Company was served with notice to make no further payments pending the decision of the court.[61]

Before the case was taken to court, a new agreement was reached, dated February 1, 1879, subject to ratification by the stockholders.[62]

In 1878, the $800,000 in outstanding twenty-year bonds had come due. The LC&N, which had guaranteed the bonds, negotiated in June with the Delaware Division Canal Company. A joint financial committee of the two companies met seven times in the month of June 1878 and produced the agreement for extension, which was incorporated into the agreement of Feb. 1. The agreement reduced the rents guaranteed by the LC&N to a level that would produce only a four percent dividend rather than the eight percent under the 1866 lease. Shareholders were offered the opportunity to exchange, on a share-for-share basis, Delaware stock for LC&N stock. Further, "at any time after three-quarters of the shares of the capital stock of the Delaware Division Canal Company shall have been exchanged," the offer could be withdrawn. The Delaware Division Canal Company was given the right to extend the payment of principal on the bonds for another twenty years. Finally, the agreement authorized the LC&N to pay rent due the Delaware Division Canal Company in script and, beyond that, to permit the Delaware company to use the script to pay dividends to stockholders. The script was redeemable in five years with accrued interest. The agreement was ratified unanimously at the annual meeting of the stockholders of the Delaware Division Canal Company on February 4, 1879.[63]

The Lehigh Coal and Navigation Company announced on March 10, 1884, that it was terminating the right of Delaware shareholders to exchange their shares for Lehigh shares, more than three-quarters of the outstanding shares having already been so exchanged. The LC&N now held 29,642 shares out of 32,667 outstanding shares of the Delaware Division Canal Company. The remaining 3,025 shares were largely held by estates whose administrators preferred not to disturb their investments.[64]

A modification of the agreement between the two companies was reached in February of 1886 because of "its having been shown to the Delaware Division Canal Company that it is impracticable to earn enough money on the Delaware Division canal to pay the rental as at present agreed on between the parties hereto." The new arrangements would be guaranteed by the LC&N delivering additional first mortgage bonds to the Trustees of the Sinking Fund of the First Mortgage of the Delaware Division Canal

Company. Under the new arrangement, the whole net earnings accruing to the LC&N should henceforth be paid to the Delaware company and the LC&N would guarantee that if these earnings should fall below what was needed to pay interest, taxes, organizational expenses, and four per cent on capital stock held by others than the LC&N, they would make up the deficit. Otherwise, any surplus went to the LC&N.[65]

In 1898 the bonded indebtedness again came due. On June 20, the minutes of the Delaware Division Canal Company report that the LC&N proposed to purchase the balance of the $800,000 of still-outstanding Delaware Division bonds and to extend their life for fifty years at four percent, to July 1, 1948. Originally there had been $1,200,000 in bonds at six percent issued to cover the mortgage taken back by the Sunbury and Erie Railroad; $1,000,000 of this was then passed on to the state in order to satisfy the mortgage given by the state in the 1858 sale of the lateral canals, including the sale of the Delaware Division to that railroad.[66] The bondholders were notified in a printed announcement dated June 7, 1898, that "the said Bonds will be purchased at PAR … on or after that date." The only option offered was the opportunity for the bondholders to convert their bonds "into the Fifty Year Funding and Improvement Four per cent. Loan, to be issued July 1st, 1898, by THE LEHIGH COAL AND NAVIGATION COMPANY, by the payment of a premium of two and one-half per cent."[67] The LC&N 1898 Annual Report announced that "bonds to the amount of $479,000 were presented and purchased by this Company, leaving one bond of $1000 outstanding, the owner of which cannot be ascertained. This Company now owns all the extended bonds."[68]

Operation and Maintenance, 1878 to 1900

Floods and freshets were fairly common occurrences; wear and tear on a system that carried water was likewise a continuing concern. There were challenges. For example, the company had to guarantee a sufficient number of boats operating on the canals to adequately handle the available business, at least until such time as the railroads had been constructed and corporate arrangements were in place to offer satisfactory alternate routes to the major markets. In 1878 Superintendent of Canals John T. Stockett reported that 566 boats had passed the weigh lock at Mauch Chunk, while an additional 300 were engaged in "miscellaneous traffic, principally below Glendon, that did not pass the Weigh Lock at all." Of these, some 282 were owned by LC&N. Many were being used in New York Harbor and on Long Island Sound: "Of these, 117 are in the hands of the boatmen, who pay a certain percentage every trip, with the view of eventually acquiring ownership. During the past season 17 were thus paid for, and bills of sale given the boatmen." These activities were run as a subsidiary company, the Freight Line, under the auspices of the superintendent of canals.[69]

During the 1880s, numerous boats came from the Morris Canal into the Delaware Division carrying New Jersey iron ore to Pennsylvania iron works. From the less-than-complete statistical picture obtained from LC&N annual reports we can identify the following:

1883	168 boats carrying iron ore for Glendon and Durham furnaces	
1884	176 boats carrying iron ore for Durham Furnace	
1887	184 " " " " " " "	
1888	167 " " " " " " "	
1892	5,213.09 total tons of iron ore carried on two canals	
1893	no ore carried, 1 Morris Canal boat on "our canal" during season [70]	

The panic of 1893, which brought to an end the boom of the 1880s, had its impact on the canal, one being the increase in non-company boats on the two canals, many of them engaged in "miscellaneous trade." Some of the commodities transported were iron ore, stone, fruits and vegetables, manure, and cement. According to the managers: "This increase was probably due to the extremely bad business on the Delaware and Raritan Canal, forcing the boats to come to our canal in search of freights, and is not likely to prove permanent."[71]

(Right) Durham Furnace, the only furnace along the Delaware Canal, dates from 1848-49. Iron ore and anthracite for fuel were brought to the site and pig iron was shipped out by canal. A colonial-era furnace of the same name, which used charcoal for fuel, had existed nearby. Its products were shipped down the Delaware River on Durham boats.

(Below) A canal boat alongside the loading wharf of a stone quarry near Lumberville. Hard sandstone was shipped from here to Philadelphia for use in buildings and for paving streets.

As usual, maintenance was a continuing problem. In addition to numerous breaches in the canal walls, some of which were dozens, even hundreds of yards in extent, the aqueducts seemingly were particularly vulnerable to damage. For example, John Ruddle, general supervisor of canals, reported in 1893:

> On May 3d last the lower of the 3 spans at Taylorsville Aqueduct broke down, having been in use so long that the timber was rotten; it was repaired by building an entirely new span to replace the one broken down and building a truss on each of the other two spans to strengthen them ... This aqueduct is now in fairly good condition, and should last about 3 years more, when it should be replaced with an iron or steel structure. Yardley Aqueduct, which was strengthened during the winter of 1889 and 1890 should be replaced within the next 3 years by an iron structure. During the present winter we are building a new steel aqueduct to replace the wooden one at Point Pleasant and partly rebuilding the aqueduct at New Hope, putting the latter in condition so that it should last from 10 to 15 years longer.[72]

Ruddle's judgment was that the most pressing work along the Delaware Division was the locks and water wheels. Another concern and potential expense was the dredge boats, which were in bad condition generally:

These boats are very old and have never been thoroughly rebuilt, the hulls and deck-houses are badly rotted and in such condition that it will cost almost as much to repair them and put them in proper condition as it would to build new boats. I would recommend that the necessary arrangements be made, and that during the coming season we build at least one new boat, putting in new machinery to increase the efficiency, and that new boats be built to take the place of the other two within the next three years as by that time the old ones will be completely worn out.[73]

Despite heavy flooding on both the Lehigh and Delaware on May 21 and 22 of 1894, which closed the canals until June 22, the Point Pleasant or Tohickon Creek Aqueduct was able to be replaced:

> The old aqueduct was torn out and replaced with a new steel structure 208 feet long, in 3 spans, with a clear water way 22 feet wide on the bottom and 24 feet wide on top. The structure is designed to carry 6 feet 3 inches of water and to overflow over the top of the steel work at that height, giving a very ready means to take care of surplus water coming into the canal from rains. It is also supplied with 9 draw-off gates, 3 in each span which give further means to handle excess of water in the canal. The steel structure was erected by the Edge Moor Bridge Company of Wilmington, Del. All other work was done by this department.[74]

The total cost, including $7,500 for "Steel structure erected," was $10,624,79. Supervisor Ruddle also reported that the dredge boat on the Delaware Division built prior to 1866 was worn out and that a contract had been let to the Osgood Dredge Company of Albany, N.Y.,

> to furnish the machinery for a new one. The hull is to be built at our own yards, on plans furnished by them. It is calculated that this boat will dredge from the middle of the canal and deposit the material on either the towpath or the berm in one lift, doing away with the use of scows and a large part of the force of laborers heretofore employed in disposing of the material dredged.[75]

The boat would be ready at the beginning of the 1895 navigation season. Its value was testified to in the LC&N's 1896 annual report:

The rebuilt Tohickon Creek Aqueduct

> During the season the new dredge referred to in my last report was kept constantly at work deepening the canal at points where necessary, except when busy taking out bars the result of rains. The channel was deepened and widened for a distance of 29,500 feet, some of the material being deposited on the banks, which were raised from six to fourteen inches as required, for the distance of 27,700 feet, the balance of the material dredged being thrown over the bank and wasted. As a rule all this work was done by the dredge crew of 4 men only, and it was only in exceptional cases where it was necessary to use other men, except for the purpose of leveling the materials deposited on the banks by the dredge.

The next season, 1897, the dredge would work below New Hope, "in the 9 and 11 mile levels, where they are shallow and where we have much trouble with channel grass." [76]

In May of 1894, "a dredge for pumping, cleaning, and preparing for market the coal dirt that is dredged from the river" had been put into service on the Lehigh. This pump dredge was but the first of a number that would add reclaimed coal, dredged from behind dams, to the total coal tonnage shipped by the canals. The amount of reclaimed coal shipped in 1894, the first listed in the LC&N records, was 10,414 tons. The volume would grow: in 1935, for example, the volume reached more than 188,000 tons, and between 1893 and 1929 some 2,424,146 gross tons of coal were retrieved from the Lehigh River and sent over the canals to market.[77]

By 1897, a newer pump dredge was in operation along with a plant for processing reclaimed coal at Bethlehem Junction, near the present Hill-to-Hill Bridge, where the Jersey Central and the Lehigh and New England made a connection. With that plant in place, as much coal was shipped as could be prepared by the dredge. That year, 22,624.13 tons of reclaimed coal were shipped down the canal; it was predicted that the following year, 1898, some 30,000 tons would be shipped.[78]

The introduction of dredging on the Lehigh had a double purpose. While it was an economical way of obtaining coal, particularly the buckwheat and other small varieties, the Lehigh Canal with its many dams and many floods was subject to silting to a degree that had dredging not been instituted on a massive scale, the waterway would have become useless. New technologies in boiler design that made buckwheat and other small varieties of anthracite coal useful and developments in the design of hydraulic dredges found a happy marriage on the Lehigh and provided additional cargoes to send down the Delaware Division.

In early January of 1895 a temporary pump dredge was set up in Bristol Basin, which had become so shallow that loaded boats could get through only with great difficulty. Three men were set to work and the dredged material was deposited on the flats to the south of the basin. By March 25, the work was finished and a channel seventy feet wide, from seven to nine feet deep, had been dug for the entire length of the basin. The material handled was mud and refuse from the woolen mills at Bristol. Arrangements were made to eliminate the mill pollution—about which Bristol's inhabitants had complained—by building a drain under the canal that would discharge into a tidal stream rather than into the canal.[79]

A coal and lumber yard on the north side of Bristol Basin in October 1898, after dredging had cleared the channel. Bristol had the largest concentration of canal-associated businesses of any community along the Delaware Canal.

Unloading coal at Leedom's coal yard in Bristol. Carlton Leedom is on the unloader. "Section" boats such as this one were uncoupled to facilitate loading and unloading. The front section of the boat is being unloaded first, starting at the front, while the rear section waits behind. This photograph was taken by Ernest Finn of the Lehigh Navigation Coal Company.

New technologies would create additional problems for the "antiquated" canal:

Owing to the introduction of machinery for unloading coal from boats and the small capacity of our canal boats, we are laboring under great disadvantages with our canal shipments. Indications are … the trouble will be aggravated until ultimately we will be cut off almost entirely from shipping coal beyond our canals unless we can accommodate our boats to the requirements of the trade.[80]

In 1890, note had been taken of the decreasing freight rates on the competing railroads: "the canal rates must follow them, and the margin of profit on the canal business is therefore but small."[81] Therefore in 1897, in order to stay competitive, the company was doing everything to make the boats as "machine-friendly" as possible. This work involved

taking out the kelsons [keelsons], making a smooth floor that offers no obstruction to self-filling steam shovels, and widening out the coamings so as to give more room for the shovels to pass. By widening out as much as we dare without sacrificing the stiffness of our boats, we can barely get room enough to allow the entrance of a 1-ton shovel, the size most generally used, and we cannot increase the beam of our boats on account of the narrow locks and aqueducts on the Delaware Division.[82]

A New Century: Problems and Proposals

Soon after the completion of the Lehigh Canal, the Lehigh Coal and Navigation Company had seen the waterpower potential of the Lehigh Canal in the Easton area and had developed an industrial park at what is now Hugh Moore Park, selling waterpower to manufacturers of a variety of products. As the new century approached, and the new electrical technology burst on the scene, the managers of the LC&N looked optimistically at the hydro-electric prospects of their waterways. In 1899 canal supervisor Ruddle discussed the potential of Slippery Rock Dam, which was under consideration to be constructed above White Haven on the upper Lehigh. He was encouraged on account of the large demand for water powers that has developed during the last year. The Easton Power Company have just completed the installation of 1500 horse power at South Easton; the Lehigh Power Company has closed a contract with this Company for a minimum of 1350 horse power at Raubsville, six miles below Easton. Several smaller powers, amounting to probably 300 horse power, are either in negotiations or in process of installation, and recently we have been approached by one large electrical company to know if we can furnish 5000 horse power. There is no question about our being able to furnish all this power, provided we can, by impounding dams, hold back enough of the flood waters in the Spring to tide over the period of low water in the Summer and early Fall. [83]

Ruddle suggested "a Hydraulic survey of the Lehigh River and Canal between Mauch Chunk and Easton." In 1900 he reported more specific plans for the Delaware Division:

Surveys have been made to the improvement to the canal from New Hope to Morrisville, with a view to establishing a large water power at the latter point. If the plan should be carried out as now contemplated, it would be possible to develop a considerable water power near Yardley, where water would be used under a 16-foot head, and the same water would be used a second time at Morrisville from the canal to the Delaware River under a 28 foot head. This plan would mean the improvement of about 14 miles of canal, the removal of one lock, the raising of one lock to double its present height, and the changing of the location of the third lock. Two aqueducts would be abandoned and the streams running into them be turned into the canal; the canal would have to be widened the entire distance and the banks raised a very considerable part of the way. The limit to the amount of power that could be developed would be the available flow of the Delaware River, and the ability to pass the water through the canal as remodeled. [84]

In 1901 Ruddle suggested that, instead of aiming to sell additional waterpower, the company should carefully consider improvement of its waterpower resources. He believed it was feasible to establish small electrical plants of from 300 to 600 horsepower at each lock, using the locktenders as station men, and to sell the electricity generated to distributing companies through meters. [85]

At Raubsville, five miles below Easton, the plant erected by the Lehigh Power Company commenced using canal water on February 7, 1901, under an agreement dated January 2, 1900. A freshet in December of that year shut off water to the plant. While repairs were made, new freshets of 1902 and 1903 damaged the plant to such an extent as to put the power company out of business. The plant was sold to James H. Morris at a foreclosure sale on April 28, 1904. He in turn sold it to B.F. Fackenthal, Jr., and Lee S. Clymer on April 5, 1905. Fackenthal was one of Bucks County's most prominent citizens. He was president of the Thomas Iron Company, a major stockholder in the Warren Manufacturing Company (later the Riegel Paper Company), a pioneering industrial chemist, and noted Bucks County historian. He and Clymer put the plant back into workable order and reached agreement with the canal company on July 31, 1906. Following a reorganization and a new agreement in 1908, Clymer Power Company operated the plant until 1934 when it was merged into the Pennsylvania Power and Light system.[86] PP&L ran it until Hurricane Diane in 1955.

In 1903, Ruddle reported that despite the fact that the repairs on the five-mile level below Easton enabled the company

to pass with ease sufficient water through the level to develop more than 1000 hydraulic horse power; how much more could be passed before reaching the limit of capacity is unknown for the reason that the Lehigh Power Company cannot take and use any more power. It must be understood that though the above quantity of water can be supplied it will not actually develop the power given, on account of the low efficiency of turbines at part gate. Also the Power Company has no means of ascertaining the power it receives except by their electrical gauges and these vary greatly from the hydraulic results, giving plausible reasons for complaint and attempting to avoid the payment of water rent. [87]

He suggested the establishment of an electrical department to further the development of water power for the generation of electricity: "At least twenty-five such stations could be installed and the current sold for manufacturing or transportation purposes." Nothing further was done to implement these

Dipper dredge on the Delaware Canal

proposals, possibly because the next year, 1904, was visited by flood, the worst of the three major inundations that plagued the canals for three successive years. [88]

Losses during these years were sizeable. High water, floods, and extensive damage as a result of six consecutive years of high waters, 1901 to 1906, were the principal culprits. In 1901, a freshet on the Lehigh River closed operations from August 24 to September 16. [89] The Annual Report of the Supervisor for Canals for 1902 noted:

> The year 1902 was the only year in the history of the Lehigh Canal in which navigation was entirely abandoned. The flood of December 15th, 1901, was followed on February 28th, 1902, by a second and more disastrous flood, that on some portions of the river exceeded the memorable freshet of 1862. The canal was very badly damaged, but by energetic work might have been repaired so that navigation would have been possible in the latter part of the season.
>
> On May 12th, however, a general strike of the miners in the anthracite coal fields began, and it was soon demonstrated that this strike would last so long that, even if repairs to the canal were completed, there would be little coal shipped. [90]

For 1903 the supervisor reported that because of flood damage from the previous years, the boating season did not open until May 20 on the Lehigh, and May 26 on the Delaware. On the night of October 10, "the highest freshet ever known at Easton occurred in the Delaware River, the water reaching a height of 39½ feet above low water mark." The damage, particularly on the Delaware Division, was extensive. Both canals, "in view of the lateness of the season," were closed for the season. There were further problems that surfaced during that season. "Owing to the fact that they had been out of commission during the previous year, considerable time was required to collect the boats and boatmen necessary to operate them on a paying basis." The season was shortened, running from late May to October 10, impacting on the earnings of both the boatmen and the LC&N. In addition to the shortage of boatmen, some of the "free boats" (privately owned boats) had been destroyed or were in such condition that they could not be repaired. To make things even worse, "the very active demand for labor drew off many of the best men into other channels." [91]

In 1904, as a result of accumulated damage and new floods, the canals did not open until July 11 and closed early, on December 2. The tonnage carried by the two waterways was some 16,725 tons less than during the shortened 1903 season. [92]

In 1904, the managers announced that, despite the exceptionally heavy expenses the series of recent floods had created, which had "been a great anxiety to your Managers,... they have assumed the expenditure on the ground that the property at stake is of too valuable character to be neglected." [93]

In 1906, the fifth year in a row in which the two canals had shown losses, the board of managers continued to evaluate the prospects for the canal. The short-term problem was the lack of competent labor to handle the boats. This was the result of the loss of work as a result of the floods of the previous years and the high wages prevailing elsewhere that drew labor from the canal. "The trouble can only be overcome," the board pronounced, "by an increase in wages, which will have to be granted, although it will result in increased costs."

Careful study had been given the long-term place of the canal in the company's future. As of 1901, because the receipts on the company's Lehigh and Susquehanna Railroad had become sufficient, increased traffic on the canal no longer threatened that road. But should the canals remain in operation when the railroad was hauling a large volume of the company's coal? At a critical board meeting in January, 1902, the damage to the system wrought by the flood of December 14, 1901, prompted discussion of whether the company could justify rebuilding the canals. Lewis A. Riley, president of LC&N, gave four reasons for repairing the system:

1. The necessity of operating the canals in order to perserve our chartered rights;
2. The belief that the property is capable of producing considerable revenues from waterpowers now developed and to be developed;
3. The ownership and operation of the canals put this company in an independent position in regard to the transportation and marketing of its coal;
4. If at any future time it should be deemed advisable to abandon the canals, it is probable that they would be a valuable factor inh negotiating for additional facilities or compensation for the traffic we could place elsewhere.[94]

The board accepted these arguments and acted to repair and maintain the canals. Before the managers could make major moves to upgrade the canal, however, the series of disastrous floods had occurred:

> The destruction was so great and the outlook for future business so doubtful that some of your Managers favored the abandonment of the canals, as they had serious doubts as to the propriety of spending any more money on them.[95]

The fact that almost every one of the other canals of the nation had been abandoned or were close to being abandoned no doubt influenced this opinion. However, "your Managers have continued to operate your canals and have expended in the last few years over $600,000 out of the surplus earnings of the Company in rebuilding and making substantial repairs." Plans were under discussion "for enlarging this portion of the Company's business, and the sentiment is to give them favorable consideration." The next year, the managers reported that in addition to adding fifty boats to the company's fleet:

> A careful and systematic investigation of the problems of canal traction, with a view of the ultimate substitution of mechanical for animal towage was also carried on upon a practical scale, the conclusion being that an expenditure for this purpose will be abundantly justified with an annual traffic of 450,000 to 500,000 tons, to which point it is thought probable that the business of the canal can be developed during the next two years.[96]

During 1908, some 252,039 gross tons were moved over the canals, some 200,846 tons of which was anthracite coal. Prospects were better for the coming year, "about 150,000 gross tons of new coal business having been contracted for at satisfactory prices."[97] In 1909, 328,990 gross tons were carried on the canal and the total for 1910 was 364,971 tons, which translated into the first profit for years.[98]

An experiment in mechanical traction was conducted on September 27, 1906, when Philadelphia and Easton trolley car No. 6 "pulled four canal boat loads of coal—90 to 100 tons. Strain on trolley car terrific, moved at only four miles per hour." The test area was a one-mile stretch from Uniontown, a suburb of Kintnersville, to Lehensburg. A newspaper story speculated that even had the experiment been successful, there would still be questions, for "The expenditure in building a trolly road would be enormous" — would this be compensated for "in the savings occasioned by this novel method of locomotion?" The less-than-successful trial apparently ended any plans to extend the trolley lines. The lines already essentially paralleled the canal for a distance from Kintnersville north through Raubsville where they took their power from the turbine at Lock 22–23.[99] The canal would remain a mule-powered system with earthen banks until its closing in 1931–1932.

Another essentially unsuccessful attempt at mechanical traction was made in 1909 when the company put two tug boats on the canal. According to the recollections of the late Chester Lear, who had been raised in the lockhouse at Lock #6, they "busted up" the canal. They were inefficient—after the tug cleared the lock it lay, "snortin' and twistin'," waiting for the rest of the tow to be put serially through the lock. In the time taken the tug and the first of the tows could have been making their way through the next lock down the canal. The experiment was abandoned the next year.[100]

The 1918 annual report is particularly suggestive. The company lamented the loss of labor to the military and other industries and the death and incapacitation caused by the influenza epidemic. This was reflected on the canals. The canal department report noted that "The average number of crews operating boats on the canal in 1918 was 31 as compared to 39 in 1917 and 77 in 1916." The report observed that the boatmen's freight rate had been increased approximately fifteen cents a ton on April 1 with a view of increasing the number of men in the company's service. This did not prove attractive: only a small number of old men remained on the boats, and it was impossible to obtain new boatmen.[101]

In 1919, the average number of crews operating boats on the canal increased to forty-four, apparently in response to a bonus, "effective September 13th, to increase their weekly earnings fifteen dollars ($15.00), to continue until the close of navigation." [102]

Roughly between the 1890s and 1920 there was a national, in some ways international, inland waterways movement that encompassed grand canals. Some few segments such as the rebuilt Erie Canal, the rebuilt Soo Canal, the Cape Cod Canal and others were products of the movement, while the Great Lakes–Mississippi River–Gulf of Mexico proposals were among the many dreams, near-fantasies. Among those that never got beyond the proposal stage was a ship canal across New Jersey and the related pipe dreams of expanding and incorporating the existing canals into a gigantic eastern ship-canal complex. As LC&N Vice President Edwin Ludlow speculated in his 1918 Canal Department Annual Report:

> If, however, the State should take this canal [the Delaware Division] and make it part of the inland waterways now being developed by the Government, the Lehigh Canal could be increased in size at a minimum cost as far as Catasauqua, permitting the use of barges from the Lehigh and New England Railroad docks at Catasauqua and shipping over the inland waterways a large percentage of the anthracite coming from the Company's mines … The Lehigh Canal between Easton and Catasauqua can be made a waterway of great importance if a barge canal is built from Easton to tidewater on the Delaware.[103]

Losses on Operation of Lehigh and Delaware Canals					
Year			Year		
1890	$45,517	profit	1902	$77,036	loss
1891	38,161	profit	1903	69,039	loss
1892	31,343	profit	1904	159,456	loss
1893	16,986	profit	1905	49,190	loss
1894	16,927	loss	1906	37,885	loss
1895	2,975	loss	1907	33,010	loss
1896	16,060	loss	1908	38,304	loss
1897	11,433	profit	1909	18,904	loss
1898	6,089	profit	1910	22,264	profit
1899	7,402	profit	1911	32,897	profit
1900	10,733	profit	1912	22,916	loss
1901	9,076	loss	1913	57,645	loss

Table compiled from various LC&N annual reports.

The 1920s: a Canal in Decline

During the 1920s traffic on the canal continued to slip. The last measurable traffic through the outlet lock at New Hope was recorded in 1920 and the last shipment beyond Bristol, a minuscule 85 tons, was recorded in 1922. A major problem was that the 100-ton, 11-foot-wide boats coming out of the Delaware Division Canal were just too small to be viable among the monsters in the harbors of New York and Philadelphia. We find, as a result, that during the 1920s almost all of the coal traffic down the canal terminated in the various coal yards along the canals. No longer were the coal boats towed by tugs from Bristol Basin to Philadelphia or other destinations on the Delaware River. The table below, extracted from the 1927 annual report, illustrates the situation.

Comparative Statement of Anthracite Coal Shipments of 1,000 Tons and over to Towns Along the Lehigh and Delaware Division Canals During the Years 1927 and 1926 [104]

Destination	1927	1926	Increase		Decrease	
	Gross Tons	Gross Tons	Gross Tons	%	Gross Tons	%
Northampton	6,441.08	9,079.13			2,638.05	29.06
Catasauqua	8,099.17	12,077.07			3,977.10	32.93
Allentown	2,235.02	3,944.02			1,709.00	43.33
Bethlehem	36,881.11	32,130.13	4,750.18	14.79		
Freemansburg	2,690.01	3,098.06			408.05	13.18
Easton	24,810.06	26,880.16			2,070.10	7.70
Point Pleasant	1,216.01	1,130.13	85.08	7.55		
Centre Bridge	2,838.17	276.02	2,562.15	928.20		
New Hope	2,231.11	2,523.08			291.17	11.57
Yardley	2,153.12	1,987.05	166.07	8.37		
Morrisville	18,423.05	21,779.14			3,356.09	15.41
Bristol	13,045.01	13,991.03			946.02	6.76
Total	121,066.12	128,899.02			7,832.10	6.08
Ten points in 1927 and nine points in 1926, along Lehigh and Delaware Division canals, under 1,000 tons	4,065.09	3,473.16	591.13	17.03		
Total	125,132.01	132,372.18			7,240.17	5.47

The 1920s suffered from erratic weather patterns. The canals endured high waters and floods in 1924, 1926 and in 1928. Drought or low water could also create problems for a canal and the canals were drought-plagued in 1922, 1923, 1928, 1929 and 1930. Labor agitation was also a cause of concern; there were strikes at the mines in 1922, a particularly problem-filled year, and also in 1928. In 1922, water levels were so low that boats had to be light-loaded.[105]

Cargoes other than coal were spotty and diminishing. In 1920, for example, more than 17,000 tons of cement descended the canal from the lower Lehigh Canal to the Philadelphia harbor. The next year, no cement, but more than 23,625 tons of stone descended the Delaware Division from Lumberville to

Philadelphia. Small amounts of stone, often less than a thousand tons, continued to be sent down the canal for many years. In 1922, more than 10,000 tons of sand went north from Tullytown to Durham, but another year that stream diminished to little more than a trickle.

Economically, the canal was dying.[106]

One problem that became magnified during the 1920s and 1930s was the problem of bridge maintenance. When the Delaware Division Canal Company purchased the canal in 1858, they assumed liability for the maintenance of both road and farm bridges across the canal. The 1926 LC&N Annual Report observed that there were

> on the Delaware Division Canal 35 public road bridges and 33 farm or private bridges of the old wooden truss type with load limit of 3 tons but carrying traffic that follows improved highways,... They require constant attention and will be an increased expense until replaced with more substantial structures.[107]

The next year, 1928, the company noted that the erection of a new bridge between Bristol and Burlington, New Jersey, would throw onto the nine public highway bridges between Morrisville and Bristol loads "which they were never intended to carry." [108]

Following World War I, the patterns of canal traffic changed appreciably. The last boat reported to have crossed the Delaware from the New Hope outlet lock to the Delaware and Raritan Canal was the *W.E. Bernard*, William Allshouse, captain, which crossed at noon on November 12, 1923, and returned on November 14 at 9:40 A.M. The last statistical listing for this crossing reported by the LC&N was 1,209 tons for the year 1920.[109]

According to I.M. Church, canal superintendent, the waterwheels at New Hope, whose maintenance had been a constant problem for nearly a century, closed down the first week of June 1923, presumably limiting the capacity of the canal south of that point.[110]

In 1930, the managers informed their stockholders: "Your Company is now substantially a holding company." The next year, 1931, they reported to the stockholders:

> in recent years, the lease to your Company of the Delaware Division Canal, dated August 20, 1866, has been a liability rather than an asset, the annual operating loss for the past ten years averaging more than $50,000; and in addition your Company has paid under the terms of the lease an annual sum equal to a four per cent. dividend on the stock of The Delaware Division Canal Company not owned by your Company.[111]

And in 1931, the LC&N board of managers reported that with falling railroad rates and the prospects of large expenditures for maintenance and reconstruction of bridges in the near future, prospects for the canal were not good.[112]

Oscar Geddes of Lumberville was reported to have been "the last man to sign a contract to haul coal on the old Delaware Canal." He started on the canal at the age of 12 and was the third generation of his family to follow that waterway.[113]

While 1931 is the last year of official operation of the canal, portions were in limited use the following year as there were a reported sixteen boatloads of coal delivered to destinations along the canal—to Yardley and elsewhere—during 1932.[114]

Statistical Analysis of Coal carried on Canal

Delaware Division –

Coal entered Del Canal		entered D&R	to Bristol
1853	659,909		
1854	734,729	170,000	530,000
1855	755,265	156,340	545,480
1856	706,251	174,423	476,565
1857	530,911	147,545	351,233
1858	512,512	164,419	293,475
1859	606,506	301,419	263,745
1860	639,323	341,816	260,733
1861	582,102	267,347	288,584
1862	217,202	97,410	106,392
1863	376,996	196,559	156,018
1864	470,951	241,200	202,325
1865	588,736	399,066	160,738
1866	792,397	526,245	221,823
1867	767,998	472,751	251,483
1868	761,538	433,005	293,245
1869	468,037	247,345	185,011
1870	648,856	265,771	354,011
1871	614,085	312,185	269,426
1872	657,789	298,626	311,342
1873	624,182	271,750	313,008
1874	666,641	224,440	415,169
1875	549,628	190,968	319,834
1876			
1877	275,836	93,922	132,586
1878	341,054	175,184	131,591
1879			
1880			
1881	321,126	96,438	175,233
1882	297,926	116,079	133,058
1883	361,494	178,040	133,011
1884	422,841	238,756	128,267
1885	359,238	209,956	104,380
1886	351,403	139,243	104,398
1887	242,688	131,106	65,832
1888	286,791	174,639	62,352
1889	293,822	158,432	86,603
1890	298,044	162,062	83,703
1891	304,318	123,744	123,499
1892	278,163	105,977	148,225
1893	220,495	88,606	112,941
1894	216,983	86,175	110,674
1895	209,144	47,789	136,978
1896	211,115	47,955	143,531
1897	231,505	51,661	159,425

Delaware Division –

	Coal entered Del Canal	entered D&R	to Bristol
1898	198,088	48,992	130,149
1899	203,293	45,087	141,147
1900	197,039	42,734	139,605
1901	177,539	36,610	128,003
1902	Because of strikes and floods, only 469 gross tons of anthracite coal was carried on the Lehigh and Delaware Canals		
1903	46,927	7,085	32,504

Total of all goods carried on both canals

1904		111,096	(decrease of 16,725 from 1903)
1905		199,766	
1906		214,844	
1907		248,820	
1908		252,039	
1909		328,990	
1910		364,971	
1911	251,460	7,287	221,356
1912	154,337	4,252	128,337
1913	168,631	1,609	145,707
1914	175,427	946	154,150

	to Points on Delaware Canal	Entered D & R	Beyond Bristol
1915	21,343	754	113,439
1916	22,342	547	42,313
1917	25,380	322	not available
1918	26,397	not available	not available
1919	25,062	826	5,462
1920	28,245	1,209	not available
1921	25,695		22,038
1922	19,142		85
1923	37,446	not available	
1924	29,320	not available	
1925	30,344	not available	
1926	45,162	not available	
1927	43,829	not available	
1928	39,576	not available	
1929	37,624	not available	
1930	172,256 gross tons carried on two canals, 91,227 tons of LC&N coal		
1931	119,250 gross tons carried on two canals, 65,566 tons of LC&N coal		

Profit and Loss Statistics

Annual profit and loss on canal operations by Lehigh Coal and Navigation Company
(extracted where possible from annual reports)

Year		Lehigh	Delaware Division
1868		$312,493	($ 19,735)
1869		166,260	(143,692)
1870		177,637	(127,020)
1871	collective profit both canals		$169,190 less rent on Delaware
1872	revenue from both canals	293,788	less rent and taxes on Delaware $188,701
1873	revenue from both canals	326,753	less rent, etc. 188,701
1874	revenue from both canals	200,000	first year of Central RR of NJ operation
1875	revenue from both canals	200,000	second year of Central RR of NJ operation
1876	not available		
1877	not available		
1878	not available		
1879	not available		
1880	not available		
1881	not available		Delaware Division = Revenue
1882	not available		minus Rent and Taxes
1883		386,354	$57,745 – $81,438
1884		370,101	58,950 – 69,921
1885		396,107	9,880 – 61,964
1886		135,104	($4,279)
1887		10,363	16,685
1888		43,200	
1889		48,494	
1890		45,517	
1891		38,161	
1892		31,343	
1893		16,986	
1894		(16,927)	
1895		(2,975)	
1896		(16,060)	
1897		11,433	
1898		6,089	
1899		7,402	
1900		10,733	
1901		(9,076)	
1902		(77,036)	
1903		(69,039)	
1904		(159,456)	
1905		(49,190)	Delaware $22,646; Lehigh $23,585
1906		(37,885)	
1907		(33,010)	
1900		(38,304)	
1909	revenue from both canals	(18,904)	

Year	Lehigh	Delaware Division
1910	22,264	
1911	32,897	
1912	(22,916)	
1913	(57,645)	
1914	(35,160)	
1915	(29,973)	
1916	(38,990)	
1917	(63,343)	
1918	(52,196)	
1919	(130,272)	
1920	(203,408)	
1921	(111,112)	
1922	(103,607)	
1923	(54,394)	
1924	(91,041)	
1925	(76,182)	
1926	(71,356)	
1927	(122,825)	
1928	(92,639)	
1929	(96,779)	
1930	(116,649)	
1931	(100,498)	

∾ CHAPTER VII ∾

The Human Element

The canal breathed life into the communities along its path with the boatyards, the producing farms, the limekilns, the industries, and the quarries. At the same time it brought coal into the communities to provide an abundance of energy, and involved generations of people from the communities along and adjacent to the canal in tasks connected with the maintenance and operation of the canal. Among the jobs it created was that of operating the craft that plied the waters of the new "highway."

It is easy on the one hand to romanticize a past; it is also possible to fall into the trap of making judgments about the conditions of life and labor based on twentieth-century norms that make long hours and child labor seem somehow excessively cruel, exploitative, and abusive. Some such cases did occur, as did accidents and violent crimes of passion and brutal attacks on individuals, which often, at least from our perspectives, seem to exhibit a callous disregard for human value. These things still occur today, but the parameters have changed. Every effort must be made to keep this in mind as we attempt to understand the lives and values of the canal boatmen and those who interacted with them.

There was much in the life of the boatman who, by escaping from the limited confines of his immediate neighborhood and the restrictions enforced by a small, tight-knit community, found a life that at least to some degree provided the excitement that has been the eternal quest of the young. And it must be remembered that work from the early years of childhood with long hours, from dawn to dusk, was universal. The long hours on the canal were, for many, less taxing and restrictive than would be labors in the field or factory.

The canal operated for roughly a century. During its first half-century the level of operations approached the capacity of the canal, with boats waiting for passage through locks and for wharf space at Bristol or Mauch Chunk. Conditions of life then were far different from what they became during the last half-century of canal operation, particularly during the first three decades in the twentieth century—a period that was in some ways equally demanding, but in a far less pressure-filled and competitive environment.

For most, the life was one of excitement and the challenge of making one's way in this world as a man among men. It offered a fulfillment and satisfaction that gave the individual a sense of identity that is too often not available in today's structured existence. Even for girls and women, the canal could have its thrills, although the mores of the period confined their contributions to secondary roles. Among the canal people as well as in the communities along the canal, there were the successful and well-to-do alongside the unfortunates and ne'er-do-wells, the capable and able alongside the weak and those with physical and mental disabilities. There could also be found the exploiters, often using political chicanery and corruption, alongside the exploited, who were the losers and sometimes the victims of the political process.

The Economic Impact

What is to be considered here is the tempo and pace of life along the canal that resulted from the stimulation the canal brought, rather than trying to measure the major industrial and regional changes resulting from what has been called the "Transportation Revolution." The canal was responsible for the creation of

Three general stores along the canal were Singley's in Upper Black Eddy (above), Sigafoos's store below Erwinna (right), and LeRoy Haney's store in Tinicum (below).

Haney's General Store photo courtesy of Raymond E. Holland Regional and Industrial History Collection.

Sigafoos Store and Dwelling

active and vibrant communities, many of which have since either passed into virtual oblivion or have undergone major change. Examples might be Uhlerstown and Yardley, earlier called Yardleyville. If one waits today for a half-hour or more in the quiet yet picturesque hamlet of Uhlerstown a single car might pass over the still-extant covered bridge. The stone of the lock still remains, but the wooden gate has long since rotted away. The lime kilns, long inactive, are still in the hill, and Michael Uhler's house still stands as does the hotel, although it has been damaged by fire. One searches in vain for evidence of the boat yard and grist mill that once sent forth sounds that enlivened the community.

Yardley is, today, an active and vigorous commuter community, many of whose inhabitants travel daily to the centers of economic activity in New York and Philadelphia. But it has changed. Leedom's lumberyard, where coal was delivered by canal boats for many decades, stands idle, and the general stores and traditional hardware stores have been replaced by convenience stores and speciality shops. Both the borough and surrounding Lower Makefield Township struggle to preserve remnants of their historic identity.

Uhlertown and Yardleyville were products of the canal. Simpson Torbert, superintendent during the 1830s, reported to the board of canal commissioners in 1833, "The village of Yardleyville has become a place of trade, its containing two mills, three stores, two coal and two lumber yards together with two taverns and a lime kiln."[1] In the past, there were also in Yardley and its environs a basket factory, a boatyard, and a quarry; in the 1870s the not-yet-incorporated village had its own newspaper.[2]

All along the canal were found canal-related activities. According to Chester Lear, long-time lock-tender at Lock No. 6, there were barns or stables where the boats would tie up at night and where, for a small fee, the mules would be put up and fed. He mentioned Billy Kirkbride's Milkhouse just north of Bordon's Lock No. 7 as well as several others in the Yardley area. Similar facilities were available along the whole canal.[3]

Billy Kirkbride's daughter, the late Anna Shaudys, remembered the boats and the boatmen. Especially on weekends, for the canal was not operated on Sundays, the boatmen would tie up, first in front of Frank Bordon's barn and then at her father's barn or milkhouse. They quartered and fed the mules for 25 cents per night and on Sunday the boatmen would visit with the Kirkbride family or the Kirkbrides, particularly the youngsters, would visit and play upon the canal boats.[4]

Samsel's Boatyard at Uhlerstown and another boatyard at Yardley were two of several boatyards along the canal. There were also stores. One of the best known was Singley's at Upper Black Eddy, now a country store that retains its two entrances, one facing the canal and one facing the street. Numerous personages along the canal operated small businesses supplying the needs of the boatmen.

Edna May Reed, née Hillborn, first came to Yardley at the age of four. Her father worked in the electric power plant that supplied the trolley lines while her mother had a general store on Edgewater Avenue in Yardley, a street that still runs along the towpath bank of the canal. As Mrs Reed remembers it:

> [my mother] had a lot of canal trade—they would come down the canal on the boats and they would holler to her what they wanted and then she would get it ready for them and if they wanted a loaf of bread right away she would just throw it to them and they would catch it.
>
> … No meat but they sold bread, soda, ice cream, canned goods, cigarettes, penny candies—those kind of things.[5]

Both the parameters and the technology were similar on the Morris Canal. Jim Lee, the preeminent historian of the Morris Canal, asked Helena Stone to recall some detail of her father's operation of a coal yard and store. "Did your father extend credit to the boatmen?" he asked. "Oh yes," she responded, "We had what we called Store books and everything we put in that. I guess they didn't have the money till they came back. He trusted everybody."

Many of the boats, particularly in the latter years of canal operation, were emptied along the canals. Helena Stone described the operation:

Well, my father had a long tall pole; I think you'd call it a derrick. There was a rope with a pulley on it. A large bucket was attached to a rope on a horse that pulled that rope—went forward and pulled that bucket from the barge. There it was emptied on our coal piles and of course all that coal was brought during the spring and summer for the winter supply of those who bought from us.[6]

(Above) A canal boat being unloaded using a derrick and block and tackle at Kelchner's coal yard at Walnutport on the Lehigh Canal. This was the method used by small yards up and down the canal, while the large yards had mechanized equipment similar to that shown at Tattersall's in Morrisville (left) and at Leedom's (page 90).

Boatmen Jim Brown and Lewis Strohm supplement the story: The bucket, on a boom, was filled by men working with shovels and then swung out of the boat to be emptied. It took two men a day to empty a load of 90-plus tons of coal on the Pennsylvania canal. The work was not usually done by the boatmen, but sometimes this was a source of extra money. Jim Brown, the only black captain on the Delaware Canal, remembers a whole ten dollars to do the job. Clifford Best remembers being paid four dollars a day to drive the horses that pulled the full bucket from the boat and moved an empty one back into the boat. Normally, he remembers, there were two buckets used. During the latter years of the canal there were only two places on the Delaware Canal, Leedoms Lumber Yard in Yardley and Tattersall's in Morrisville, where there were continuous buckets so the boat could be emptied in about two hours.[7]

During the last years of the canal, almost all of the coal that entered the Delaware Canal was delivered to coal yards along the canal, and traffic on the canal was reduced to almost a trickle. Railroads had taken over from the boats except along the Pennsylvania side of the Delaware River. There, the coal yards still depended on the canal to deliver coal until trucks took over in the 1920s and 1930s

Life of Individuals

The ordinary people whose lives were spent on the canal have left little formal documentation. Reconstruction of their way of life is not a simple task: it relies largely on personal memories, with only a few written records.

Life could be hard on the canal, particularly when viewed in the perspectives of today. The youngster who put in a sometimes eighteen-hour day was usually working in less physically demanding conditions than were other youngsters working on farms or apprenticed in shops or, worse yet, trapped in a factory or mine. There was much about the life that was exciting and attractive.

And the canal was a way of life for families. Chester Lear, born in October of 1894, recalled that when he was at the tender age of one and one-half years his father left Riegelsville, where he had worked on the maintenance scow, to become the locktender at Lock No. 6 in Yardley. His father remained in that position until the canal formally closed in 1931. His was a canal family, most of whose members had worked on the canal for three or four generations. As Chester remembered it, his grandfather's brother, Barrett, was boss of the carpenter boat on the canal. Many of the canal families intermarried: for example, Frank Bordon, longtime locktender at Lock No. 7, was his father's brother-in-law. Chester recounted that when a male member of the family reached the age of 14, a job on the canal was found for him. As he said, they "lived like muskrats—born and raised on the canal," and his granddad said, if you took the job on the canal, you had a lifetime job.[8]

Canal life started even earlier for the boatmen. Simon Johnston, who started on the Morris Canal at age eight or ten, recalled many years later:

> I thought it was a pretty good life. It was a hard life when you stop to look at it now. When you stop to think of people living on a boat. It was just a little square place where you slept and ate and everything.... When you stop to think we slept on them boats, to think families were raised in that little cabin.... Now I was just saying this morning, we didn't have automatic washers, and didn't have bathtubs, and we didn't have no toilet in the house. Think what them poor boys had to do. When they had to go to the toilet, they had to go under a tree or in the bushes along the canal.[9]

Responding to questioner Jimmy Lee's observation that boating started early in the spring and continued late into the fall, he said, "It was very cold for us boys. We didn't have shoes to wear. We went barefooted." They had to keep on leading the mules, even though they had no raincoats and many times no shelter along the canal.

Frank and Howard Swope and Louis Strohn remember the frightening experience of thunderstorms along the canal. According to the Swopes, "Pop" told them to get away from the mules as their shoes attracted lightning.[10]

The Swope family, Frank Sr. and sons Howard, Frank and Roy, taking a load of anthracite down the canal. The small cabin in which the family lived when they were not on deck is at the rear of the boat. This is near Kintnersville.

W.H. Gausler, who started as a driver on the canal in 1840, working for bed and clothing, recalled:

I was first employed as a driver by John Backman of Freemansburg, Pennsylvania. Mr. Backman was the owner of two canal boats, or scows, built in double sections, with a capacity of about sixty tons, used to freight coal from Mauch Chunk to Bristol and Philadelphia via the Lehigh and Delaware canals. I drove the horse of the boat "Bear" that brought the first load of iron ore from South Easton to Catasauqua, Pa. for the Crane Iron Furnace Company in September, 1840.

About 1850 the Hokendauqua Iron Furnace was built at Schwartz's Dam above Catasauqua. I freighted pig iron from Catasauqua and Hokendauqua to Philadelphia for $1.46½ per ton up to December 1852.

Our expenses for one boat for one trip from Mauch Chunk to Philadelphia and return were $3.00 for provisions and horse feed. Bacon (or fletch) cost 4¢ per pound; shoulder 4¢; ham 6½¢; butter 12¢; coffee 12½¢; brown sugar 4¢; potatoes from 2 to 3 shillings per basket; oats from 2 to 3 shillings per bushel; hay and stabling over night, 1 shilling; other provisions and feed in proportion.

Up to 1843 the boats ran Sundays, the canal being the only means of bringing freight to Philadelphia … Nearly all boatmen kept going day and night, boats being so numerous that the canal seemed to be a solid mass of boats. The salary of a boat captain was from $14 to $20 per month; bowsman from $8 to $14 per month, and drivers $5 per month. The boatmen often encountered dangers from high winds at Easton dam at the weigh-lock, the Chain dam and Lehigh Gap.[11]

The bowsman was soon dispensed with and a two-man crew could manage a loaded boat.

When boats arrived at Bristol with their load of coal destined for Philadelphia or other towns along the Delaware, there had apparently been two procedures for turning around for the return journey. If the captain owned his boat, he left his mules stabled at Bristol and remained with the boat while it was towed to the yards where the coal was to be delivered. If he did not own the boat, as was most usually the case, but simply rented or leased it from the company, he surrendered the loaded boat at Bristol and received an empty boat for the trip north. There could be great differences in boats, in age, in ease of handling, and also in the level of housekeeping that it had received. Several of the boatmen have memories of boat cabins infested with bedbugs; the return trips were sometimes memorable for that reason.[12]

Canal boats in the Delaware River at Bristol. The heavy ones are lashed together waiting to be towed to Philadelphia; the light boats are being towed back after delivering their loads of coal in the city.

Madeline Free Rilleria recalls the pain and joy of leading the mules on the towpath, at the age of six, for an eighteen-hour day over the 106-mile trek along the Lehigh and Delaware canals. Her memories were bittersweet:

> I loved them animals [the mules] and they loved me and they used to cry for me and whinny every once in a while—when they knew I was getting tired and then I would crawl up on their backs and make a bed on there.[13]

Most commonly, the boat was operated by the captain, most often on the tiller, and his driver, who sometimes, as in the case of Madeline Free, might be as young as six years of age. The captain himself might be as young as fourteen or fifteen. Sometimes a whole family went along. Clifford Best remembers boating with his father, a lifetime boater, his mother, and five siblings on the boat during the summer months. How did they sleep? Well, there were two bunks in the cabin and four slept on them while the rest of the youngsters slept on a mattress on the floor of the restricted area of the cabin. Best also recalls that one sister was born on the boat. Asked if they didn't feel crowded, he responded that they were used to it. "Didn't know no better." [14]

On a typical day, the crew rose at about 20 minutes before 4 AM, and went to the barn to clean and harness the mules in order to have the boat ready for the 4 AM lock openings. Ordinarily the boys wore overalls, a shirt, and a hat. Most went barefooted, although Clifford Best reported that he always wore shoes. Madeline Free wore a kind of bloomer outfit that her mother, who had dress-making skills, made for her. As Best recalls, "I liked it, I really did." The only part he didn't really like was the fall of the year with the ice. When his hands split, he greased them with wagon grease and put them into his gloves. They had sheepskin coats, raincoats, boots, and hats to combat the weather.[15]

Laborers on the canal worked the same long hours as the boatmen. From sunup to sundown was universal for the laboring

Young Daniel McCollick of Erwinna in 1911 at Mauch Chunk, where he and his team started the 102-mile trip from the loading docks to Bristol. The trip from Mauch Chunk to Bristol and back took seven to eight days.

man of the day. The initial excavations for the canal were, to a large degree, contracted for by local farmers, who used their own equipment and teams and hired their neighbors. These men were perfectly capable of performing the backbreaking pick and shovel task of excavating the prism of the canal. Contractors with greater skills, many of whom worked on various of the state properties, contracted to do the "mechanical" work such as constructing locks, aqueducts, waste gates, etc.

After the canal opened it became necessary to hire men to perform maintenance. Irish names began to appear more and more often among the English, Scotch-Irish, and German names. There seems to have been a pendulum swing between hiring individuals to work under the supervision of the supervisors and their foremen, and the contracting out of maintenance, repair, refurbishing, and reconstruction to outside contractors who would bid on jobs. In either case, as noted elsewhere, the state was not always the most reliable paymaster; both the workers and contractors who contracted to do labor on the canal were often victimized in a manner similar to that illustrated by the pathetic letter penned by John H. Willhelm in 1843 to Mr. John R. Butler:

Sir, I inform you that I am back between two and three hundred Dollars on the Delaware Division for labour Dunn under Mr David Connor, Supervisor and I am in great neat for Money my family is suffering and I run my self in Dept in consequence to keep up the Canal my Creditors are suing me and say they will no wait no longer. I therefore pray that you will urge Mr David Connor, to pay of the old Claims Due on Checkrolls for which funds are to be provided on the first of July.

Please to in form me by a few lines wether there is Any interest to be paid on Money Due on Checkrolls of backstanding Money for 1840, forty-one and forty-two and whether there is any prospect that it will be paid now in July.[16]

Even when the state paid, the laborers could still be victimized, as happened in a case in 1856 when, on the Delaware Division of the Pennsylvania Canal, a dishonest contractor named Schenewalt "drew $1500 on Friday last to pay the hands in his employ, and on Saturday absquatelated [*sic*] with the money in his pocket." [17]

Deep-seated prejudice could further complicate matters. When the Democrats held the state house and dominated the canal commission, it would seem that the Catholic Irish, often the victims of discrimination themselves but now fast becoming stalwarts in the Democratic Party, were in a favored position for the "state" jobs on the canal. Most illustrative is a news item of June 1857 that appeared in the Doylestown *Intelligencer*, quoted here in its entirety:

Proscription on the Canal.— It seems that no laborers are allowed to work on the canal enlargement now in progress along the Delaware, except as are known as reliable Democrats. Until lately, we were not aware that the labor of one man, if faithfully performed, was not as good as that of another, but we have recently been informed of the dismissal of an Irishman from the work at Black's Eddy, by one of the Lancaster contractors, for the alleged reason that he was a Protestant, and had voted for Col. Fremont last fall. The luckless Paddy was assaulted by some of his fellow workmen, and would have suffered severely had it not been for the interference of some boatmen. In this shameful conduct they were encouraged by the contractor, who abused the heretic in no measured terms.[18]

A communication to the board penned by supervisor William K. Huffnagle are illustrative of the some of the needs and problems of the boatmen. He was writing on behalf of the Rev. John Magoffin of Bristol, "a truly pious, & highly respected gentleman, formally an extensive merchant of Philad^a having retired from business with an ample fortune, now wishes to devote his time & money to the good of his fellow men." Magoffin belonged to "no particular Sect but works upon the grand principles of the Scriptures, 'Faith, Hope, & Charity'." Huffnagle was writing in support of his request for permission from the board of canal commissioners to occupy

a small point now used for a flower garden near the Collectors Office in Bristol [where he proposed to erect a] Boatmens church at an expense of from five hundred to a thousand dollars ... & there deliver lectures or Sermons on the Sabbath.[19]

Magoffin would, Huffnagle wrote, be willing to accept a ten- or fifteen-year lease.

The need was there, according to Huffnagle, for in Bristol an ever-changing number, sometimes as many as two hundred, of boatmen and hands were idle on a Sunday. The boatmen would be ready to attend such a service, whereas

they are unwilling to go up into the town among better dressed people.... This dear old man has been preaching to them in the open & when I saw him a few days ago was quite ill from the effects.

The apparent end to the affair was summarized in the comment on a letter filed in the archives of the board noting that "the Board regrets that under existing laws they possess no Authority to grant this privilege" but, were such authority given by an act of the legislature, they would act favorably.

Lock Tenders

The working day of the locktender was long. During the busy years of the canal, the 1840s to 1860s, it would have been especially arduous and demanding as boats passed almost continuously, 24 hours a day, six days a week. Despite numerous petitions for increased compensation, the position, often a political plum, was sought-after for it included a rent-free locktender's house and a period of relative ease during the period when winter closed down the canal, from sometime in December until, in most years, about mid-March. During the 24-hour operation period, it was necessary to either hire an assistant or for members of the family to spell the locktender, the latter being the continuing practice during the whole active life of the canal. At many locks the locktender, or more often his wife, supplemented the family income by selling food or services, such as baked goods and other foodstuffs, or laundering. Bordon at Lock No. 7 supplemented his income by trapping muskrats.[20]

What would today be called gender discrimination is found in the canal communication which John Matheys, canal supervisor, dispatched to the board of canal commissioners in the spring of 1846, listing his roster of eighteen locktenders who would operate the twenty-six locks, the twenty-fifth being the outlet lock across the dam at Easton, and the twenty-sixth being the tide lock at Bristol. Five of the eighteen locktenders were replacements, for which he spelled out the reasons. Three of those replaced were women, Ann Brown, Susan Slack, and Catharine Cooper, who had "been on as Lock Tenders for a number of years." Matheys wrote:

> My reasons for removing the women before named are that I am satisfied that the business of the line was much impeded by keeping them on, as the business of the line is heavy it requires some person able to do the work and be at their post at all times.[21]

Another removal, Christopher Bloom, was "an infirm old man and entirely unfit to do the work required," and Christopher Lugar was accused of not paying "proper attention to his lock." The removal of Jacob Sedam was because

> there was charges made against him of taking several Tons of Coal from Boatmen during the past fall and having sold it to people in the place which on examination I found to be true.
>
> Matters of this kind has been subjects of great complaint on this line of men buying or taking coal of Boatmen consequently when Bts arriv'd at their place of destination they would fall short of weight making it unpleasant for the Shipper and raising as [sic] difficultys between him and the buyer. By request of many engaged in the business at the time I took charge of this line I gave notice to all under the employ of the Commonwealth that any person either taking or buying coal of Boatmen (except in cases where they were fully authorized to sell) would render themselves liable to immediate removal. As the above was the first case of the kind that had come under my notice I thought it best to meet it with removal as it would have the effect of preventing any thing further of this kind.[22]

Ann Brown for Lock No. 6, Susan Slack for Lock No. 7, and Catharine Cooper for Lock No. 17 had been on David Connor's list of appointments made in 1842.[23]

Catharine Cooper, who was removed as locktender at Lock No. 17, refused to leave the lockhouse following receipt of the notice served by Supervisor Matheys. He reported:

> Moses Ridge her Father a farmer about a half mile below the Lock has with his two sons attempted to resist any effort of mine to vacate the premises by arming themselves and apparently determined to shoot any person that attempts to remove theirs. On the 1st day of April the time Aron Emery the person I selected to take that Lock was about to take possession he found those three persons in the house armed and full of fight. They frightened him off the ground in consequence of my not having time to attend to it up to the present time she has remained in possession of the house and is still there. Last evening I went to Doylestown and took the advice of Thoˢ Ross Esq on the subject, he directed me to make oaths to the fact of their resisting to remove and of their threats to shoot any person that come near, which oath I made and had it served on the Sheriff of the County to attend at that place next Saturday at 12 o'clock to keep the peace while I vacated the premises. The Sheriff consented to attend this

I thought the best course to pursue in as much as they are a hard sett. I think likely there will be trouble when we attempt to remove them, but if there is any guns about the Sheriff it can soon be settled. This Moses Ridge resists giving possession of this house on the foolish pretext that he has not been payed for the ground on which the Lock house is erected, according to my understanding of the matter it would make no difference whether he had been paid or not not. [*sic*] But to the contrary I paid him last summer on a warrent [*sic*] drawn by your Board to sum of 224 Dols I think, and if I recollect right it covered the whole amt of Damage awarded to the Estate of Wm. Thomas, and Edward Ridge the money I paid to this Moses Ridge he being the surviving heir to the above named Estate. The Journal of the Bd of Appraisers will state whether such is the case or not … [24]

One of Matheys' reasons for such gender bias was the increased demands of the job:

I have made arrangements for passing Boats at all hours both day knight [*sic*] on our line. Last knight we passed at this place [New Hope] Eighteen Boats between 10 o'clock in the evening and 4 o'clock in the morning that being about the time that operations were suspended under our former regulations. Our Double lock tenders complain considerably thinking they ought to have had more than an advance of Ten Dollars for the knight work but I think they will stand it, if not I will advise you of same. The fact of allowing them an extra hand last fall at 87½ cts per day has spoiled them somewhat. I suppose it will be necessary to make some arrangement with the collectors for passing the Bts. all knight. But as that is a matter of their own I suppose they will make the necessary arrangements with you themselves. The increased pay to Lock Tenders will amount to Thirteen hundred and Thirty Dollars under the arrangement of running all knight, I have not a doubt but our increased trade in consequence of that same will amount to more than Five Times that amount.[25]

It was the very lifestyle of some of the employees that created some of their problems. Earlier, in 1841, Supervisor David Connor had reported:

The continuation of John Hamilton to tend the Locks Nos. 15 & 16 [Smithtown] would have been a dissatisfaction to the neighborhood and those who are interested in the public works as when he was first placed there I have been credibly informed and that too by the most respectable persons in that section that he has frequently insulted the Boatmen when passing up and down the Canal and threatening them with violence without any cause. He has also been in the habit of abusing and ill-treating his wife tearing her clothes and throwing them out of doors and tossing her out with them besides annoying the neighborhood continually.[26]

Connor had, he reported, appointed one who he hoped would be a satisfactory replacement. Another locktender, Hugh Dunn, who was also on Connor's list of appointments for 1842, was already in trouble by autumn of 1843. Connor wrote:

There was a Lock Keeper of the name of Hugh Dunn at Locks No. 10 & 11 [New Hope], who I notified duly to leave said locks on account of bad conduct some time since and appointed another in his stead, and that Mr Lewis S. Coryell has taken the key into his possession and says that the other shall not move into the house as it belongs to him and defies Mr. Joshua Slack to move in and prevents him from getting possession of it. Lewis S. Coryell says that the State never paid him for it and he is determined not to let them have the use of it any longer. The principal reasons for discharging Dunn was that he was in the habit of getting drunk so as not to be able to attend to his business others had to do it for him and he was continually abusing the Commissioners for reducing the wages of the LOCK keepers and actually refused to draw his money for the two last quarters and said he would lay it before the next legislature, etc. etc. so that it was impossible to continue him any longer.

I have understood that the Lock House was built by the Commonwealth and Coryell claims it because he says the state never paid him for the land on which the house is erected.

You will please advise me as soon as possible what is to be done in this matter as the Locks are now attended with some additional expense on account of Mr Slack's not getting into the house.[27]

It would seem that Lewis Coryell, onetime engineer on the canal, had fallen from political favor and was dissatisfied with settlements made by the state for land taken in New Hope and for water taken from the Union Mills, where Coryell was part owner. One summary of titles lists a "type B" settlement made with Coryell for approximately 3,300 feet of canal. A "type B" settlement involved releases after appraisals made by state appraisers, something that Coryell still did not accept, and debate continued over ownership. Another listing showed Coryell in 1855, and his executors in 1866, accepting deeds after an agreement had been reached and additional payments had been made by the Commonwealth.[28]

In later years, when the press of business was less, women regularly operated canal locks. For example, Flora Henry recalled that she helped her father, the locktender at Smithtown, until his death in August of 1931, after which she and her mother tended the lock until the canal closed down for good in 1932. According to Flora:

> Locktender houses were built close to the locks on small tracts of land belonging to the canal. The locktender was often assisted by his wife who was as skilled as he in handling the gates. If a man was trustworthy, then the job of locktender was his for life.[29]

This was the case at least during the last years of the canal. According to Chester Lear, the locktender was paid $25 per month, and lived in the lockhouse rent-free.[30] Many locktenders and their families supplemented their incomes by selling food or sometimes services such as laundry, and also boarded mules overnight. Flora Henry remembers that one of her tasks was to take care of the boatmen's mules. She also remembers that

> When a boat was about 500 yards away, the boatman would blow a conch horn so the tender would get his lock ready. If the tender had any trouble with the lock gates, he would blow a whistle of warning. This was a moment to dread, for the Captain was apt to be angry if he had to wait for his boat to be locked through.[31]

Flora Henry. Sketch by Robert J. McLellan.

Locktending must have been a hard job, for the lore is replete with stories of fights between aggressive boatmen who attempted to jump ahead at locks. The cure for this, reportedly, was for the locktender to throw both into the water.[32] The locktender's "housekeeping" tasks that he had to perform around his locks were not always the most pleasant. Harry Warford, who was born at Lock No. 9 in New Hope where his father was locktender, noted that the nastiest job was to take a dead skunk from in front of a fall gate.[33]

Louis Comfort Tiffany's photograph of a locktender's family tending the lock at Lock 6 in the summer of 1886. The "doghouse" that protected the gears is in the center.

Mules

A great deal of canal lore concerns the long-suffering mules who provided the motive power to pull a canal boat with 90 or 95 tons of anthracite coal. Sometimes 100 tons were loaded, but according to the old boatmen, this usually caused the boat to drag on the bottom so an 80- or 90-ton load was preferred. The first "job" of the youngster on the canal, sometimes at the tender age of six or eight, was the task of mule driver, that is, leading or riding the mules for an eighteen-hour day on the six- or seven-day, 212-mile round trip from Mauch Chunk to Bristol and back, and caring for the mules at the end of the long day. While the mule is a hard-working and essentially tractable animal, less prone to excitement and panic than the horse, the task for the often-tiny youngster was demanding and occasions could arise when it was dangerous.

Almost all of the old boatmen have stories of dangerous run-ins with mules. Lewis Strohm remembers one time when he was taking the feedbaskets from the mules and the back mule kicked the basket—"knocked me over the bank—if he'd kicked me I'd be dead." Jim Brown, who couldn't swim, remembers being kicked into the water by a mule; luckily he grabbed the tow line from the boat and reached safety. On another occasion, when young Jim Brown was the mule driver for John Free, John frightened the mules by using a "blacksnake" or whip and the mules broke free and raced down the towpath. They were recovered by the locktender.[34]

Mules could be frightened by locomotive engines. Clifford Best remembers when the mules of Horace Major, reputedly the slowest boatman on the canals, were scared by the railroad locomotive at Easton; the mules broke free and swam the Lehigh River. They started back but one drowned on the return trip. Madeline Free Rilleria also remembers the difficulty of keeping mules under control where the canal (the Lehigh) ran close to the railroad.[35]

The newspapers reported many drownings, among them several that were the result of unfortunate encounters with mules. In June of 1854 the Doylestown *Daily Intelligencer* reported that on the previous Friday evening

> a boat boy, by the name of COGAL, from Trenton, aged about 14 years, was kicked by a mule on the Towpath of the Delaware Canal, at Lumberville, which threw him into the river. He was found in about an hour afterwards, and an inquest was held by Joseph Hough, Esq. The report of the Jury was in accordance with the facts—that he came to his death either by the kick or drowning.[36]

In 1856, the same journal reported another drowning, in this case as a result of trying to deal with a crisis:

> [A boy who] was driving a mule team on the Delaware Canal, near New Hope, was accidentally drowned. The mules had fallen into the water, and in the effort to extricate them, he fell into the Canal. He was from Easton.[37]

Most boatmen took good care of their mules; it was only common sense, for their livelihood was directly tied to their animals and well-treated animals worked better. Only a few really mistreated their animals. Lewis Strohm remembers one who would walk along and kick the mules right above the hoof, a tender spot, and would thus avoid using a more obvious whip. According to Madeline Free Rilleria, some drivers beat their mules.

The driver, often aided by the captain, took the mules out of the stable in the morning and curry-combed them before harnessing them for the coming day. The mules were fed morning and evening by hanging a feedbag on them so they could eat as they pulled the boat. The feedbag would be made available additional times during the day. Feed could be purchased at a feedhouse established by the company at Laury's on the Lehigh Canal. Mule feed, according to Lewis Strohm, was corn mixed with oats, to which a little salt hay was sometimes added at night. According to the same source, "on Sundays you took off the collars and scraped them." [38]

There were skills that the drivers, even despite their often extreme youth, had to master quickly. Passing another boat was an art, particularly if you were driving the mules pulling the loaded boat. As several of the old-timers recall, you had to be there to unhook your mules and drop your line when your loaded boat passed beyond the nearer light boat, or risk having yourself and your mules pulled into the canal.[39] This must have been what happened in 1856, when it was reported that

A mule and horse were drowned in the aqueduct of the canal, at Point Pleasant, on tuesday night last. They belonged to a boat, and were drawn into the canal by another boat passing at the time.[40]

Every young boatman had to learn to snub a boat into a lock. This meant wrapping the rope around the snubbing post to slow the boat's speed and then bring it to a stop. Howard Swope recalls that "Pop" first gave him the rope and ordered him to snub the boat with all of the boatmen who were gathered at the "pay" lock at Siegfried's watching. He did so successfully. Jim Brown notes that if the boat was moving too fast, you could burn the rope through. It was not like a car, he said, you had to start to slow a boat, particularly a loaded boat, well before where you intended to stop it. You always had to remember that you were relying on a team of mules and manipulating a boat which, if loaded, weighed, boat and load, over 100 tons.[41]

A boy is leading the mules as a loaded boat is moving slowly into Lock 3 in Bristol. A snubbing post, showing grooves where it has been worn by ropes, is in the center front of the picture. After the rope was wrapped around the post the gates would be closed and the boat would be locked up or down.

Apparently operating the tiller required greater skill and greater responsibility than leading the mules. Madeline Free Rilleria still remembers being put on the tiller before she was ten. She also worried about being hit by bridges when she was getting on and off the boats at one of the many bridges.[42] Illustrative of the danger from bridges is the case of James Lair, fourteen years of age, who was reported drowned in the canal above Yardleyville on the night of September 22, 1853:

He was a hand on board a Canal Boat, and in passing up the Canal on that night, was employed in steering, while the Captain was asleep in the Cabin. The boat ran aground, and waked up the Captain, when it was found that the young man was missing. The boat was stopped for the night, and search made; and about noon next day his body was picked up from the canal just below a bridge. A scar was found on his face; from which it is supposed he fell asleep at his post, and was struck by the bridge in passing under, and knocked off the boat. A coroner's jury investigated the case and reported according to the facts. The young man's parents reside at Bethlehem, and his body was conveyed to them.[43]

Murders, Drownings and Other Tragic Events

Tragic events occur in the life of every community, and life along the Delaware Canal had at least its share. While many must have gone unrecorded, by using newspaper accounts and relying on the memories of those who worked on the canal we can get some sense of the temper of canal days.

There were undoubtedly sins of both commission and omission, but many tragedies were blundered into, as was the case in late August of 1851:

> [A] man by the name of WILDONGER, a resident of the vicinity of Point Pleasant, was committed to our county prison, on a charge of killing a man named Dougherty, at Bristol.[44]

It seems that Dougherty's boat was in such a position on the canal that Wildonger's craft was unable to pass. Dougherty was lying on the deck of his boat asleep, or pretending to be, when

> Wildonger threw watermelon rinds at Dougherty,… in order to arouse him, and have him make room for his boat to pass. Dougherty roused up, and threw stone coal at Wildonger and hit him. Wildonger requested him to stop it, but he threw again, and hit Wildonger a severe blow upon his back. Wildonger then seized a boat hook and struck Dougherty in the neck, producing a severe wound, and a profuse flow of blood. Dougherty jumped into the water and swam across the canal and back, but soon bled to death. Wildonger was arrested, committed, and brought to prison. We understand that he is severely bruised on several parts of his body, by the coal thrown by Dougherty.[45]

The disposition of the case is unknown.

One boat captain found that Philadelphia, where his boatload of coal had been towed, could be a hotbed of crime. It was in 1859 when

> one James McRae, of New Hope, captain of a canal boat running on the Delaware Division, while at one of the wharves at Richmond [near Philadelphia] with his boat one night last week was attacked by about a dozen rowdies, knocked down, and robbed of his watch, thirty dollars, a gold pen and silver case, and several papers of value to him. It was so long before he could find a police officer that the robbers made their escape.[46]

Many of the tragedies were apparently accidental. In 1855, on a Thursday night in July, "a boy employed on a canal boat on the Delaware canal, fell off the boat into the canal just above Yardleyville, and was drowned." It was the next morning before the body was recovered and an inquest was held. The *Daily Intelligencer* reporter

> [had] not heard the boy's name, but it is said that his parents live in the upper part of the county. His mother, who was on another canal boat, passed by Yardleyville directly after the recovery of the body, just in time to be present at her son's funeral.[47]

Accidents could be work-related, as was the case of John Gabert, captain of canal boat No. 402 of Mauch Chunk, who died when he "fell into the hold of his boat while it was entering the outlock [*sic*] lock at New Hope, and broke his neck."[48]

More poignant was the "Death of a Man and Boy by Suffocation from the Gas of a Coal Stove." It seems that George McDonald, captain of a canal boat, and his boy, named Edward Porter, retired for the night and placed the small potbellied stove just outside the door of the cabin. The door was left open to admit the heat to the cabin, but the hatches and doors above were so tightly secured as to exclude ventilation. When there was no stir on board in the morning an examination was made, and

> [upon] opening the hatch, the boy was found dead, and the man insensible. He was taken to the residence of Nelson Ryan, and medical aid procured, but which proved of no avail. On Sunday evening his soul passed from the clay tenement. An inquest was held on the body of Edward Porter, and a verdict was rendered in accordance with the facts— "that he came to his death by suffocation." The boy was about twelve years of age, and resided at Catasauqua, Pa. The man had no family; he was a Scotchman by birth.[49]

The identity of the victim was a mystery on occasion. On October 6, 1851, a stranger was drowned in the canal, below Yardleyville. He was seen by the locktender to enter the water, but then he sank. The body was found a day later and the inquest, held before George Yardley, Esq., determined that he was "deranged." About thirty-five years of age, about five foot eight inches in height, mustached, with an imperial and whiskers, and tattooed, he was presumed to be a foreigner. There was no clue as to who he was or whence he came. He was interred in the "stone graveyard, below Yardleyville." A boatman who heard the body described said "It must be that of old Hank Morris of Mauch Chunk." But this was conjecture.[50]

Sometimes accidental death occurred seemingly without explanation, as was the case of Felty Shellinger, who was steering a coal boat on the night of June 18, 1859, near Lock No. 13 at Black's Eddy. It was reported that he, "in the darkness of the night," accidentally fell from the stern of the boat and was drowned. They drew off the canal level in order to recover the body.[51]

Some accidents, while maybe equally memorable, were less tragic. One such happened at the old bridge over the canal in Yardleyville. As reported in the press:

> An empty boat, passing up the canal that morning, struck the girder of the bridge, and forced it loose from the iron fastenings, leaving the structure hanging by a very slight hold on the edge of a piece of iron. It remained in this condition until five o'clock in the afternoon, when Lamar Johnson, one of the Newtown volunteers, drove Blaker & Feaster's team on it, with a load of coal, and crushed it down, wagon, horses, driver and the wreck of the bridge, all falling into the canal together. It made a great splash, and much excitement until Mr. Johnson and the horses were fished out of the "raging water," and landed safely on the shore. The company have replaced the old bridge by a substantial new one.[52]

A more romantic rescue occurred on a Sunday afternoon in 1852 when Cyrus Stover was driving with his two sisters in a small carriage along the road on the canal bank a short distance above the Durham post office. Something frightened the horse and it

> backed till the vehicle overturned into the canal. Mr. S. sprang out before it went over. His sisters were precipitated into the water, but were saved through the exertion of MICHAEL FACKENTHALL, Esq. and others. One of them was rescued without much difficulty—the other floated down the canal about one hundred yards, and when taken out, life was nearly extinct. She was resuscitated by great exertions, and is now doing well. The horse was drowned.
>
> [The spot where] this casualty happened is said to be very dangerous from want of a guard or railing.[53]

In 1930, while the canal was still operating, a bizarre incident enfolded in Bristol. The headline in the Bristol newspaper read "Woman Attempts Suicide By Leaping Into Canal." It seems that Elizabeth Forlini of South Philadelphia, aged 36, left her husband and six children and went first to Trenton and then to Bristol with her sister-in-law. Her brother, Dominick Zupito, and their niece arrived in Bristol and found the two women "riding about town in an automobile bearing a New York plate in the company of two men." They escaped for the moment but about an hour later the brother and niece came upon the two women and pleaded with them to return to their homes and families.

> The conversation, apparently, was an amicable one, when suddenly as the four crossed the Mill street bridge of the canal Mrs. Forlini dashed away and ran to the canal bank and leaped in.
>
> The other two women screamed and Zupito went to the rescue of his sister. She was pulled ashore and taken to the hospital. Police were called and the entire group was placed under arrest. All but Mrs. Ferlini were later discharged.[54]

The same year, an act of heroism took place on the canal in Morrisville. One Charles Stiener, eighteen years of age, disregarding that his arm had been broken from a fall from a horse two weeks before, "leaped into the Pennsylvania Canal Monday evening and saved Clifford Weurpel," a six-year-old boy. With the assistance of 43-year-old John Beatty he hauled the youngster from the canal. Surrounded by several hysterical women he responded quickly to first aid and within a short time was able to go home.[55]

Surveillance and Security

During the life of the canal, some coal was legitimately made available to the boat captain and his crew for their use (boats had a cookstove and a heating stove, both of which burned coal), but during the busy years of operation additional amounts—sometimes several tons—were added to the load for the benefit of the operator of the boat.

The story is oft told as to how the farmers along the canal would line up bottles on their fences to encourage the boatmen to heave coal at these targets. The farmers could then collect the coal as a contribution to their winter supply.[56] A more specific case is that of impressionist artist Edward W. Redfield, who settled along the canal at Phillips Mill in 1898. Redfield sawed and painted the outline of a human figure with one arm rounded in a circle with a sign, "hit me," a device that challenged the boatmen and reportedly provided him with his winter supply of coal.[57]

This boat approaching Tullytown has traveled through many miles of agricultural land. Not only did the boatmen throw coal at bottles on farmers' fences, they helped themselves to tomatoes, apples, peaches, corn, and whatever else was conveniently close to the canal.

During the latter years of the canal, according to Clifford Best, the company gave you 200 pounds of coal for the boatman's use, something more than was used on a typical trip. The boatman stored the balance and took it home for winter use. During the last five years, the hatches were sealed after the coal was loaded, and woe be the boatman who broke that seal before the coal reached the consignee. Before this, according to Best, the locktenders would sometimes jump on the boat and take some coal.[58]

Complaints were not unheard of during the busy years of the canal, as is illustrated by the report of the complaint "lodged before WILLIAM KINNY, Esq., by Mr. PATTERSON, agent for the Coal company against a stable keeper, in Bristol, for taking coal from a canal boat." [59]

As years went by, and profits diminished, the Lehigh Coal and Navigation Company employed Pinkerton's National Detective Agency to try to terminate what had apparently been a kind of understood "privilege" of the captain. R.J. Linder, superintendent of Pinkerton's Philadelphia office, reported to E. Hill, general coal agent for the company. He paraphrased in great detail Captain Taylor of the *Morgan*, "one of the Uhler boats," who told the Pinkerton agent:

> he [Captain Taylor] had been on the canal for 20 years, man and boy; and that he used to make money ten years ago, but this cannot be done now, as 'things are played out.' He went on to say that in those days a captain had a fair chance of selling enough tons of coal to the farmers and others to pay his own board-bill; but that as things are at present, these people do not any longer care to risk buying coal from the captains of the boats, —besides which the coal is now weighed down so close that if any is taken it is

sure to be missed. He added that as it used to be, the men on the boat could always turn in after the loading hands at the Mauch Chuck [sic] chute had left, and shovel in a couple of tons themselves; whereas they will now give one only enough coal to burn out on his trip; and that the last time he loaded iron at Easton, he had to beg enough coal to last him down; and also, that if he is a day or two longer in making any trip than he expected to be, he will be out of the coal, as a general rule. He also said that none of the captains buy any coal out of the cargo for their own use; and if they cannot get any out of the cargo, they will have some left behind where they discharge, by giving the shovellers a half-dollar. He declared that he himself has had as much as two tons left in this way, when he had his own boat; but that now, while working for a salary for others, if he can get a ton or so from any of his friends, he charges it on his provisions bill and the Company has to pay it. Then he said that down at Bristol and Morrisville is where they used to get away with a good deal of coal; but the people there-abouts will not buy so much now, as the captains and the drivers used to sell enough to get drunk on the proceeds, so that they ran the thing into the ground, so to speak. He said that on the down trip most of the coal thus disposed is taken off under the cover of night; but on the up trip they are not so careful, regarding the coal, in a measure, as their own.[60]

Anna Shaudys remembers that her father, Billy Kirkbride, would never buy coal from any boatman.

Life Along the Canal

The canal went through the heart of numerous communities and many of them—Bristol, Yardley, New Hope, Point Pleasant, and Uhlerstown for example—had locks within their corporate limits. The canal, the reader will remember, operated from 4 AM to 11 PM, giving reality to the remembrance of Estella Everest of Yardley that the "boats would blow conchs and wake you up."[61]

Another of Yardley's senior citizens, Marjorie Cadwallader Dinges, remembers that the boats approaching Lock No. 5 on the canal seemed to blow their conch shells almost behind her main street house, serving as a signal for all the youngsters to run to the canal lock to watch the boat pass through.[62]

Children who lived adjacent to the canal enjoyed the activities. Anna Shaudys remembers getting rides on canal boats of friendly boatmen from her family's milkhouse a relatively short distance down to Bordon's lock and then getting rides back with other boatmen. She also recalled barge parties out of Yardley enlivened with music from a wind-up Victrola. Early in this century there were vacation communities along the canal, and Flora Henry recalls that the summer folks who came to Smithtown always arranged for an outing to New Hope and back. The cost of such a canal barge party in the early twenties was about $25.[63]

Flora Henry, daughter of the locktender at double lock 15-16 at Smithtown, noted on the original of this photograph that the Smithtown "summer folks" got together to pay for a barge trip to New Hope. They are about one-half mile south of lock 15-16 on their way back. The boat is a work scow.

In winter, children skated to school on the ice although Mrs Shaudys recalls that just about the time the ice was good, "Mr. Bordon would let the water out of the canal and spoil the ice." [64]

Clifford Best recalls that the people along the Delaware Canal were friendlier than they were along the Lehigh. He particularly remembered gifts of fruit and candy at New Hope but he didn't realize until later that the givers were the thespians who were turning the one-time country canal town into a drama center.[65]

The canal and its setting were seemingly a reason that Phillips Mill, just north of New Hope, became a center for artists and art. It all started when Dr. George Morley Marshall purchased the properties in 1894. In 1898 he lured William Langston Lathrop, an already recognized artist, to the site. Lathrop, who had been raised in Ohio along the shores of Lake Erie, was always an avid sailor and purchased a boat on the canal. According to his granddaughters the boat, a "put-put," could carry twelve and was named *Sunshine*. Lathrop started a school and would meet his students at the New Hope railroad station and bring them north to Phillips Mill on the canal. Lathrop's granddaughters remember as many as fifteen students outdoors along the canal receiving instruction.

Other artists found their way to the area. Edward Redfield in Centre Bridge and Daniel Garber in Lumberville also became leaders of what has been labeled "the Bucks County Impressionists."

In 1929 Dr. Marshall sold the mill to the Phillips Mill Community Association and it has been both an art museum and the site for numerous art shows. The Lathrop property was something of a social center, and some of the activities there were recorded on 1930s home movies, as was the launching of a 32-foot sailboat, which was towed down the canal then received its sails and keel. In 1938, at the age of 79, Lathrop died in this boat, named the *Widge*, during a storm at Montauk Point, New York.[66]

(Above) Aaron Phillips' home at Phillips Mill, later the home of artist William Lathrop.
(Right) Lathrop Studio at Phillips Mill. The original mill dates from 1756. Hal and Sara Maynard Clark Collection, Spruance Library.

Old-timers, both canalers and persons who grew up along the canal, remember the canal as a great swimming place. Madeline Free Rilleria remembered that the canal water was clear except after a heavy rain. Edna May Reed remembered swimming in the canal "all the time and the water used to be so clear. We'd hear the boats coming with the mules and we'd jump out. As soon as the boats got past, we'd jump back in and swim again." [67] Norman Bond, raised in Morrisville, remembers swimming in a pool below the borough. A favorite stunt was to dive under the empty boats going back up the canal, coming out on the other side. The empties drew only twelve to eighteen inches. He also remembers catching eels, impaling them on a stick and roasting them over a bonfire. Even after the canal closed down the canal was a great play area, particularly for growing boys. [68]

The author can remember that in the 1930s, the boy scouts from Philadelphia Boy Scout Camp Treasure Island, in the Delaware opposite Lock No. 17, took all their swimming and lifesaving tests in the canal. The more adventurous among the boys had their favorite stunts. One practice, according to Flora Henry, was "stemming ... a daring feat indulged in by the more enterprising, when allowed by a canal boat captain. The procedure was to lie on one's back with feet against the prow of a moving boat, which thus propelled the swimmer headfirst into the water in a seemingly rapid effortless glide." Swimmers also, "if permitted ... like[d] to trail through the water hanging to the blade of the rudder." [69]

Boys swimming and playing in the canal at Point Pleasant. Hal and Sara Maynard Clark Collection, Spruance Library.

An accident occurred at some time or another for everyone connected with the canal. Some of the boatmen, Jim Brown for example, could not swim. In Jim Brown's case, he was kicked into the water by a mule, but he was able to catch a drag line and climb to safety. Madeline Free Rilleria recalled that her father was a good swimmer, while Harry Warford reported that John Winter, who first operated the mule "barges" at New Hope, couldn't swim. Likewise Luther Evans, who operated the mud digger or dredge, couldn't swim. [70] Sometimes it was not the boatman who came to grief in an accident, but a draft animal. For example, in the summer of 1867 a team that had been detached from a boat ran away near Lower Black's Eddy. They ran into a horse towing a boat, throwing the horse into the canal. The animal was pulled out a short time later, but died soon after from the effects of the accident. [71]

Most old-timers remember that the towpath was always a thoroughfare for inhabitants along the canal. Schoolchildren sometimes used it to go to school, and adults often found it the shortest and most pleasant route to and from work or town. But life along the canal, as life everywhere, had its dangers, illustrated by the case of a twelve-year-old girl, the daughter of a man named Reigle, who in 1855 fell into the canal three miles above Point Pleasant and drowned. Probably there were numerous other such incidents that went unrecorded. [72]

Humor could be found along the canal in the names of the boats. While boat names were usually based on hero worship, pride in their craft, or humor, they sometimes bore such titles as *Rat*, *Flea* or *Fly*, and there were also some unusual names. These included *The Wooden Child*, *May Flour*, *Ladies Friend*, *Local Option*, *Sabath Rest*, *Here I Am*, and *Ubydam*. According to Flora Henry:

Folks tell of a man who called his boat *To and Fro*. Laughter after he resumed his trip caused him to investigate and he discovered that some jokester had changed the name of his boat to *Toads and Frogs*. [7]

Yardley resident Virgil Kauffman recalled youthful pranks along the canal. Some of the coal boats, he remembered, would return upstream heaped with watermelons. The boys could smell the melons,

[and] would stand on one of the camel-back bridges and wait until the barge approached, then dive into the water coming up at the prow of the boat. The man driving the mules would be far ahead. The man or woman holding the tiller could not see the boys until they climbed high enough to be seen

over the melons. Each boy would roll at least two melons into the water, then would dive in and come up far down stream safe from the wrath of the bargemen. Later they retrieved the bobbing melons and had a feast. [74]

It could be a hard life. As Jim Brown said, you had to be tough. While there were a few violent types, "bad actors," most of the boatmen and their families were decent and hardworking people who were basically moral and upright. Lewis Strohm remembers that fun was made of canal folk and the youngsters had to defend themselves with their fists in school, which they attended only from December through March while the canal was closed for the winter. Most reported little tension between the canalers and the occupants of the communities along the canal. Education was marginal for the young mule drivers although Madeline Free Rilleria, maybe an exception, was taught the basics by her father and then, in the days when few children anywhere went beyond Eighth Grade, finished high school. According to many testimonies, the boatmen were kind and supportive of one another even though, to use the words of Anna Shaudys, their language was "sometimes more expressive than elegant." [75]

Diet and Drink

Clifford Best's recollections are essentially those of the other boatmen. They ate well, not necessarily according to the standards of the modern nutritionist. The fry pan and the coffee pot seemed to be the major cooking utensils and ham and eggs, fried potatoes, coffee, and often beans constituted a large portion of the universal diet of the boatmen. Madeline Free Rilleria remembers her father prepared oatmeal, and sometimes they had fried cornmeal mush.[76] Mrs. Martha Best, Clifford's mother, remembered that during the afternoons she, with her seven children aboard, would "make sandwiches and roll them in paper and throw them out on the towpath for the kids. They would sit on the mules and eat them." [77]

Many of the boatmen had farms where the wife and the youngest children would stay and which would more than adequately supply the boat with every food necessity, with the exception of a few perishables and goodies such as candy.[78] Some canal boats had chickens aboard. Another food source, as Lewis Strohm recalls—almost with glee—was the farms and gardens along the canal. As he describes it, with explanatory gestures, they (the boatmen), without permission, "milked" peaches off the trees along the canal and also took apples and tomatoes off the loaded trees and vines, and seemingly there were no objections from the farmers along the canal.[79]

Frank Swope, maintenance division chief for the canal park since 1994, is the son, nephew, and grandson of canal boatmen and the recipient of many of their tales. One suggested that chickens along the canal had to beware of the canalers, "most of whom were fishermen.... They would bait their hook with a kernel of corn, so any chicken wandering off a nearby farm might become dinner for the night," —boiled, Swope was told, in a pot of canal water.[80]

The two-burner cookstove was always on the deck, usually at the hinge, and cooking was normally done there although there was a smaller second stove in the cabin that could be used in cold weather. The captain maneuvered between his tiller at the stern and the stove in the mid-section in order to supervise the cooking, then usually traded places with the driver so that the driver could eat. There are stories of letting the mules go by themselves during mealtime on quiet canal stretches while both ate.[81]

Intoxicating beverages are always a problem for some members of every community. The boatmen on the canal were no exception. Most of the old-timers interviewed admit to having known only one or two boatmen who drank heavily—but almost always added that they still did their job.[82] However, there were numerous "watering places" along the canal and the evidence is that these were visited by many boatmen. Fighting and violence often resulted.

Pinkerton investigator R.J. Linden one evening stayed in the hotel in Bristol and commented on the drinking of the boatmen:

> I took another round among the captains after supper, and as all of them had been drinking pretty hard meanwhile, there was some one knocked down every twenty minutes or so.[83]

The cast-iron coal-buring cookstove was kept chained to the boat, and was generally used on the deck during most of the year. In the cold-weather months it would be moved to the cabin at the rear of the boat, where the boatman and his family would share small living quarters. Next to the stove is its fuel supply, a box of coal, and next to that is the water barrel. The towing post is on the far right. This photograph shows the front section of a hinge or section boat. The feed box containing oats and corn for the mules, in which ham and bacon would be stored to keep them cool, was on the rear section.

Alcohol and water did not necessarily mix when it came to operating a canal boat. In 1854 this was the case with "JAMES GALLAGHER, aged about 40 years." It was supposed that he fell from his boat while intoxicated and "Drowned in the Canal a few miles above Bristol." An inquest verified this judgment.[84]

One account recalls that one Aaron LaRue, who kept a store in a canal storehouse in Yardley, was converted by one of the great anti-liquor crusades that swept the country. In response, one morning he rolled out all of his barrels of rum, broke them open, and dumped the contents into the canal. To complete his reformation, he ignited the rum. The whole canal was on fire and, according to the account, put the town in jeopardy.[85]

The canal provided a life style, now passed, for both the boatmen and those who daily watched the boats pass and often envied the boatmen. For it was easy for those who watched the boats disappear into the distance to imagine that those operating the boats were escaping the drudgery of everyday routines.

PART TWO
1931 – 2000

∽ CHAPTER VIII ∽

Transition:
The Tangled Web of Transfer to the State

During the 1920s traffic on the Delaware Canal declined with each year. The decrease in the number of boats navigating the canal can be attributed largely to the advent of heavy-duty motor trucks and the improvement of roadways. Anthracite was still the predominant fuel for homes and industry in the early part of the twentieth century and canalside coal dealers in Pennsylvania needed to be supplied with anthracite from the mines of Carbon and Schuylkill counties. Unlike the New Jersey side of the river, where the Belvidere and Delaware Railroad paralleled the river for much of its length, there was no railroad running parallel to the Delaware Canal. Commerce on the canal, already significantly less heavy than it had been toward the end of the nineteenth century, all but ended with the general economic downturn of the Great Depression. The Lehigh Coal and Navigation Company formally ended commercial navigation on the Delaware Canal during the autumn of 1931.

Strong circumstantial evidence exists that sixteen boats made deliveries of anthracite to coal yards in the Delaware Canal in 1932, after the formal closing of the canal. This is based on the recollections of the late Carleton Leedom, a member of a family that operated coal yards along the canal during this period.[1] Regardless of which year is correct, 1931 or 1932, the ending of commercial navigation on the canal marked the beginning of a period of uncertainty.

The story of the Delaware Canal since 1931 has many facets. First is the story of preservation efforts, which prevented the canal from sliding into the oblivion that was the fate of so many other towpath canals. Second is the story of the process of turning it into a useful recreational, environmental, and historical resource that would justify its existence. Third is the running narrative of the relations of the now state-owned canal with the Lehigh Coal and Navigation Company and with adjacent property owners and the communities that border it. There was also an economic dimension, for, because of its attractiveness, the canal brought tourist and recreational dollars to the area and stimulated upscale development in its environs. An unmaintained canal, on the other hand, would become a detriment to property values. And finally, it was, and still is, necessary to engage in politics to provide at least part of the funds necessary for the canal's survival and upgrading as well as for the organizational structure to implement its preservation. The canal, part of a region's and nation's heritage, could provide a basis for the kinds of pride and grassroots support that contribute to civic well-being.

Great Expectations

In 1931, with the canal long passé as a competitive transportation system, the State of Pennsylvania on June 26 approved an act that relieved the Delaware Division Canal Company from its charter obligation of maintaining a commercial navigation system. The company

> by deed dated September 30, 1931, conveyed to the Commonwealth all its right, title and interest in and to the canal bed, towing path and berm bank of the Delaware Division canal between Raubsville and Yardley, a distance of about forty miles, reserving the right to lay and maintain mains and pipes in

May	Boat.	Captain	Consignee	Destination	Lading	Tons	Cwt	Kind	Time	Remarks	
18	269	Wm. B Winters	O Donnell Bro	Bristol	Coal	92	17	Pea	3.20	P.M. 5/6	1
27	274	F. D. Swope	"	"	"	93	09	¾ Buck	12.	noon 5/7	2
29	271	Jno Minder	Luis Leedon	Yardley	"	91	09	Ches	7.	P.M. "	3
39	228	Jno Rymond	Tattersall	Morrisville	"	90	-	¾ Buck	3.	" 5/8	4
48	223	C. S. Dreher	"	"	"	92	19	Stove	5.25	a.m. 5/9	5
45	272	C.A. Cook	O Donnell Bro	Bristol	"	95	18	Ches	5.25	" "	6
51	200	Jos Reed	"	"	"	95	14	Stove	9.25	" "	7
50	227	Howard Reed	Tattersall	Morrisville	"	93	10	Ches	10.	" "	8
53	280	H. E. Andrews	Luis Leedon	Yardley	"	90	13	Pea	3.40	P.M. "	9.
55	206	Jos Gengley	O Donnell Bro	Bristol	"	92	09	Pea	5.50	a.m. 5/12	10
58	150	Thomas Nace	Tattersall Co.	Morrisville	"	93	11	"	5.50	" "	11
59	275	John Winters Jr.	S Le Leedon	Yardley	"	96	11	Stove	10.	" "	12
63	226	N. J. Belts	O Donnell Bro	Bristol	"	93	19	¾ Buck	12.30	a.m. 5/13	13
64	269	Wm. B Winters	"	"	"	94	-	Ches	3.10	P.M. "	14
65	284	Chas White	Tattersall	Morrisville	"	95	17	"	8.15	a.m. 5/14	15
69	285	Frank Kilonner	O Donnell Bro	Bristol	"	95	19	Pea	10.	" "	16
67	274	Frank Swope	Tattersall	Morrisville	"	92	04	"	10.40	" "	17
68	271	Jno Minder	O Donnell	Bristol	"	95	13	Stove	3.45	P.M. "	18
79	205	Jno Allen	"	"	"	91	15	"	12.	noon 5/15	19
	269	Wm. B. Winters		Slate Dam	Empty				7.25	P.M. 5/8	1
	271	Jno Minder		"	"				5.40	a.m. 5/9	2
	274	Frank Swope		"	"				9.30	" "	3
	228	John Rymond		"	"				3.	P.M.	4
	223	C.S. Dreher		"	"				5.	a.m. 5/12	5
	227	Howard Reed		"	"				2.45	P.M. "	6.
	280	H.E. Andrews		"	"				3.15	" "	7
	272	C.A. Cook		"	"				7.	" 5/13	8.
	200	Joseph Reed.		"	"				8.45	a.m. 5/13	9
	150	Thomas Nace		"	"				3.45	P.M. "	10
	275	Jno Winters Jr		"	"				3.45	" "	11
	206	Jos Gingley		"	"				6.30	" "	12
	226	N. J. Belts		"	"				9.30	a.m. 5/15	13
	284	Chas White		"	"				3.50	P.M. "	14
	269	Wm. W Winters		"	"				5.70	" "	15

The last coal boats to use the canal in 1931 are listed above. The name of the captain, the name and location of the coal yard receiving the cargo, the weight and type of coal, and the time the boat passed the New Hope office are listed. Remarkably few boats were using the canal by this time. All the boats were returning to Slate Dam, near Laury's Station on the Lehigh River. By the early 1920s the Lehigh Navigation had become so clogged with coal silt that no coal was shipped out of Mauch Chunk. Instead, trains would be used to carry it to a transfer station at Slate Dam, where it would be loaded into boats. The following types of coal are listed: pea, buckwheat, chestnut, and stove. The list was compiled by Harry Warford Sr., the locktender at New Hope.

the towing path for the transportation of water; and also agree to supply part of the water required for the portion of the canal conveyed, subject to the right to take water from the canal to fulfil existing and future water supply and power agreements.[2]

The LC&N retained the right "to use, sell or otherwise dispose of the remaining portions of its property as it may determine." The six miles of canal from Easton to Raubsville remained in the company's ownership because of the substantial income the company received from the sale of electricity generated by the hydroelectric generating plant at Raubsville.

On October 18, 1931, the ceremonial transfer took place at historic old Neely's Mill, today restored in the upper Thompson-Neely House segment of Washington Crossing State Park. Governor Gifford Pinchot accepted the deed from William Jay Turner, general counsel for the Lehigh Coal and Navigation Company. They were joined by a representative for New Jersey's governor, by Secretary of Highways Samuel S. Lewis, and representatives of numerous preservation, historical, nature, and artistic groups. Pinchot announced that all the old bridges across the canal in the newly named Roosevelt State Park would "be preserved just as they are so that their picturesqueness shall continue to help make the historic canal one of the beauty spots in the United States." LC&N's Turner said the company had deeded the stretch to the Commonwealth to "assure perpetuity of the beautiful landscape we have all enjoyed these many years." Secretary Lewis announced a survey to "determine the best method of preserving all of the old bridges and yet provide adequately for highway crossings by new bridges at other locations." He said the locks and towpaths ought to be kept up for a century, and suggested that "some of the old barges be restored and preserved." He endorsed the suggestion of Morris L. Cooke of Philadelphia that "the park should be kept free of filling stations and 'hot dog' stands," and rejected proposals that "its ancient bridges" be replaced by "earth 'fills' carrying pedestrian or vehicular crossings" as these would not only destroy the beauty, but do irreparable damage to the canal's value as a center of water recreation.[3]

The occasion was marked by a piece of verse penned by Catherine Curren Smith, which was printed in the *Intelligencer*:

The old canal was taken over
By the State the other day,
To perpetuate its memory
In a rustic old parkway.

Its scenes of rural splendor
Are portrayed by artists' touch;
Its winter landscapes immortalized
By the mighty Redfield's brush.

What a flow of memories it recalls
To men now aged and grey,
Who trudged along the tow path
In their happy boyhood day.

Early in March, as spring appeared,
They left their books and schools
To tramp from Bristol to Mauch Chunk
Behind a pair of stubborn, balky mules.

It served mankind a century
But now its days are spent
We must preserve its beauty
And leave nothing to repent.

Oh, old canal, flow serenely on,
And may beauty grace your way,
Throughout the coming centuries,
As she does at the present day![4]

In 1931, when the state took over, there were some grandiose plans for the new state park centered on the canal. In 1932, the state contracted with landscape architect James R. McConaghie for a plan entitled "A Report on a Proposed Recreational Development Roosevelt Park." His completed plan called for a forty-mile park between Yardley and Raubsville. It proposed three major centers, at Yardley, Erwinna and Riegelsville, plus four minor centers and five special centers, all with canoe and boat concessions. There were also plans for passenger boats including two dance barges, repair barges, small barges and cabin boats which would "make it possible for family or organization groups to spend vacations on the canal." Administration and maintenance was broken down into four sections, with one supervisor, four foremen, fifteen laborers, carpenters, and a variety of additional private concessionaires who would provide maintenance, staff facilities, and operate locks. These ambitious plans were never acted upon.[5]

The plans became superfluous when the steel-reinforced aqueduct at Point Pleasant (over Tohickon Creek) collapsed in 1934 and the wooden flume that replaced it did not survive a great storm in 1936.[6]

Company Problems and Policies

The 1931 deed to the state canceled the 1866 lease and subsequent agreements. It also removed the obligation whereby the Lehigh Coal and Navigation Company agreed to indemnify the Delaware Canal Company against losses resulting from its operations. LC&N consented to pay the canal company an annual dividend on that portion of the canal company's stock that was not owned by LC&N. The obligations of the existing $800,000 mortgage were also extinguished.[7] On October 1, 1931, The Delaware Canal Company and the Lehigh Coal and Navigation Company reached an agreement whereby the lease of 1866 and its amendments of 1879 and 1886 were canceled. The new agreement stipulated that LC&N was to assign to the Delaware Division Canal all of its waterpower leases and crossing licenses in the Delaware Canal, and that all crossing licenses should be transferred to the state.[8]

On July 21, 1931, Henry H. Pearse described the situation in response to questions posed by the trust department of Philadelphia's Real Estate-Land Title Trust Company.

For many years past the business of the canal has steadily decreased, and the losses in operation over a period of 10 years have exceeded $50,000 per year, so that it has become imperative to abandon the operation of the canal. In the accomplishment of this a portion of the canal will be transferred to the State in accordance with a Bill recently passed by the Legislature, and the lease to The Lehigh Coal and Navigation Company cancelled.

Conditions are such that at present indications upon the expiration of the lease the stock of the Delaware Division Canal Company would have no value, and the Navigation Company is, as you know, offering $45. per share for the Delaware Division Canal Company stock, or an exchange of two shares of The Lehigh Coal Navigation Company stock for each share of the Delaware Division stock, in order that the stockholders may not suffer any loss.[9]

Efforts had been made to obtain the last of the outstanding shares of Delaware Division Canal stock, that is, those that were not by now held by the LC&N. As of July 24, 1931, out of a total of 32,887 shares of stock issued, all but 899 were owned by the LC&N. The list of additional holders is interesting, for the LC&N had "assurances from outside holders of a large part of the 899 shares that they will accept our offer of either $45 per share or two shares L. C. & N. Co. stock for each share of Delaware Division [Canal Company]." They included

Henry Disston	5 shares
Estelle Pardee Erdman	20 shares
Fidelity-Philadelphia Trust Company, various trusts	44 shares
Francis E. Green (Corn Ex. Natl. Bank Tr. Co.	6 shares
Real Estate Land Title Trust Co.	21 shares
Ludie Warden McMillen	11 shares
Ario Pardee, Trustee etc.	1 share
Herbert W. Warden Jr	11 shares
The Penna. Institution for Instruction of the Blind	9 shares
Jessie Hannis Perot	2 shares
Mary W. Shoemaker	22 shares
Emma A. Stephenson	8 shares
Trustees of the Methodist Episcopal Hosp. Etc.	115 shares
Trustees of Phila. Yearly Meeting of Friends	598 shares
Charles N. Welsh	8 shares
Edward L. Welsh	12 shares
S.J. Welsh	6 shares [10]

The Lehigh Coal and Navigation Company retained control of the section of the Delaware Canal between Raubsville and Easton. Revenue was being generated in this section from the Raubsville hydroelectric plant and the company felt there was potential for additional power plants.

The LC&N continued to receive some income from the canal from sales of water and small amounts from utility licenses. The company had apparently given up any idea of maintaining the waterway for navigation, for it recorded an agreement dated September 14, 1931, which granted the engineering department of the United States Army the right to deposit material in the canal basin at Bristol in connection with its dredging of the channel of the Delaware River between Philadelphia and Trenton.[11]

The Borough of Bristol appears to have been party to the arrangements. On Tuesday, October 13, a local newspaper reported:

Burgess Clifford L. Anderson and the borough authorities have been busy negotiating for the filling in of the basin. They were anxious to eliminate this spot for a long time but the expense of filling it was always a problem to meet ... The filling of the basin will make available a large area of land directly to the south of the business section.[12]

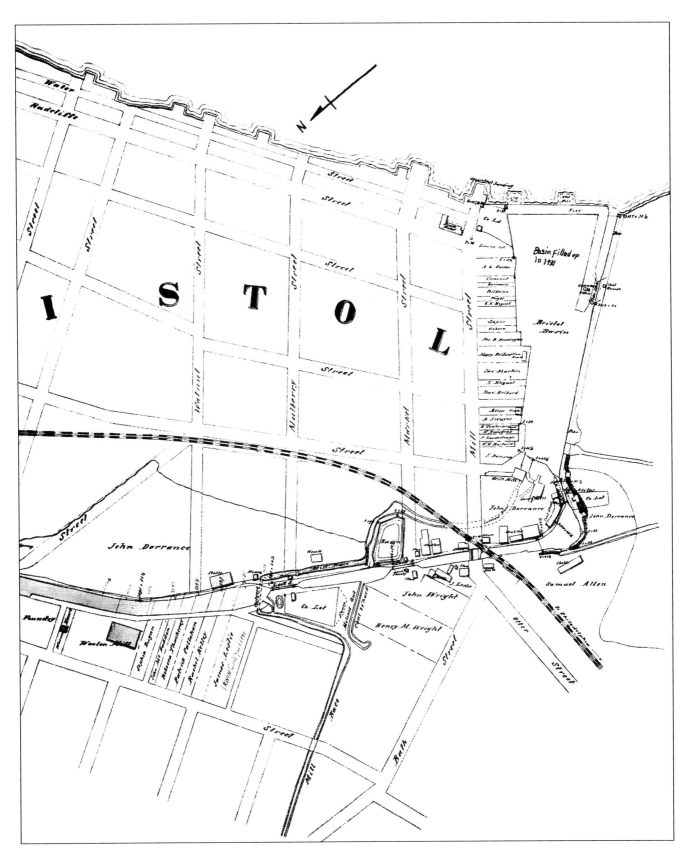

Lehigh Coal and Navigation Company of the Bristol section of the canal, showing the large basin that started to be filled in shortly after the canal was closed in 1931.

Borough officials hoped to obtain title to the property by purchase or by gift, so they might create a public park. This was to happen a half-dozen years later, when they succeeded in obtaining title to the basin and eventually filled it in and transformed it into a large parking area. At a later date the Bristol authorities filled in additional portions of the canal with waste such as coal ashes. Many years later this was perceived to have been a mistake and during the 1990s efforts were planned to remove this fill and rewater the canal.

A major encroachment was permitted on the canal right-of-way in 1932 through a lease, dated April 1, from the Delaware Division Canal Company of Pennsylvania to the Lehigh Coal and Navigation Company. It called for a "Portion of the Towing-path and Canal Bed to be used as a railroad siding and coal handling plant from the Pennsylvania Railroad Company to the Tattersall Coal Yard at Morrisville."[13] The 1932 Annual Report of the LC&N reported that

> During the year, certain bridges crossing part of the canal retained by The Delaware Division Canal Company of Pennsylvania were replaced by fills and culverts, resulting not only in reducing the danger of accidents but also in decreasing the cost of maintenance.[14]

The loss of portions of the canal continued. The event that brought the perennial problem of maintaining water in the canal to a crisis was the collapse of the Point Pleasant aqueduct at about 5 p.m. on Tuesday, September 4, 1934. This was in the state-owned portion of the canal, which was no longer operating. It was, however, still marginally maintained and was a popular swimming spot. Two boys and a man had been seen swimming in it a short time before the collapse. Two persons had been on the aqueduct when "they felt the structure sway under their feet" —they escaped by running. It was this event that focused the attention of the newly formed Delaware Valley Protective Association on the canal.[15]

Within weeks, four thousand individuals had signed petitions requesting repair or rebuilding of the aqueduct over Tohickon Creek.[16] After this agitation, largely spurred by the recently organized DVPA, "the State authorities made a temporary repair consisting of a 4' x 2' flume which carried the water across the broken aqueduct and gave us a fairly good flow during 1935," according to Sara Maynard Clark. "This furnished enough water for pleasure barges to operate as far as Cuttalossa—but the damage from the flood of 1936 put an end to these picturesque parties."[17]

The one continuing force that struggled to see that the canal continued to exist was the Delaware Valley Protective Association. It had been organized in 1933 when it appeared that the canal might be given up and paved over. The prime mover was artist-publisher William F. Taylor, who served as its first president. He filled various other offices over the years and published the periodical *Towpath* during several periods between 1940 and 1963. The DVPA mounted a grassroots movement, almost unprecedented at the time, and could claim that the subsequent 60-mile canal park and adjacent Ralph Stover Sate Park were a result of their persistent efforts. In 1957 the organization, now with some 2,000 members, elected Hal H. Clark president, an office he more than filled for the next quarter century. He was an almost irresistible force in support of the canal and of the valley.[18]

The piers for the Tohickon Creek aqueduct, which collapsed in September 1934. The temporary repair, a wooden flume, was destroyed in the flood of 1936. The aqueduct was replaced in 1948.

Who Owns the Canal?

On October 4, 1935, the *Intelligencer* reported on a meeting of the previous evening at which Dr. James F. Bogardus, Deputy Secretary of Forests and Waters, had announced that the attorney general's department had declared that a part of Act 352 of 1931, granting a portion of the canal to the Commonwealth, was unconstitutional. This was the reason the state had failed to take any measures to restore the canal or the fallen Point Pleasant aqueduct, and had failed to seek federal aid to restore the canal. The rationale behind this decision was that the original transfer of the Delaware Division Canal to corporate ownership in 1858 was predicated on the condition that the waterway would be properly maintained at all times, or it would revert to state control. However, the lower portion of the canal still depended on the Lehigh Coal and Navigation Company for water, which came from the slackwater pool on the Lehigh River at Easton. State authorities construed this dependence to mean that the canal still in fact belonged to the LC&N.

The "gift" of 1931 contained a provision that after July 1, 1936, the state would be obligated to pay the LC&N the sum of $6,000 per year for the use of water in its portion of the canal. The state Department of Forests and Waters was making a survey to determine whether it would be cheaper to purchase water from LC&N after July 1, 1936, or to install and operate a pump to lift water from the Delaware River.

According to Bogardus, the canal still belonged in its entirety to the LC&N, but if the LC&N did not immediately repair the entire aqueduct at Point Pleasant as it had been, and restore the canal in its entirety, then it would automatically revert back to the state in its entirety and would become state property.[19]

Rumors circulated during late winter and early spring of 1935. It was reported that the state's budget had been made up and that there were no funds in it for maintenance, nor for the water rent which would become necessary during the coming season, nor to replace the aqueduct. Fears were expressed that an attempt was being made by the state to have the canal abandoned.[20] A letter from Governor George H. Earle, in which he stated that he had been informed by his secretary of Forests and Waters that "a pipe or flume would be all that is necessary to repair the present break in the aqueduct and carry the water across so that the canal between Point Pleasant and Lumberville can be filled," appeared to be evidence of this intent.[21]

The state's attempt to escape the expense of repairs was expressed in a letter dated March 5, 1936, from Governor Earle, informing William F. Taylor, secretary and prime mover of the Delaware Valley Protective Association, that as of the previous October 16 the state had turned the whole canal back to the Delaware Division Canal Company, saying that the state expected the company

> to perform the terms, conditions and duties imposed upon it by the Act of April 27, 1888 [1858] including particularly those duties and conditions which require the company to maintain the canal in its entirety as a public highway or waterway and to keep same up, including the public and private bridges crossing said canal, in good repair and operating condition.[22]

This whole episode is a classic example of "buck passing." The Lehigh Coal and Navigation Company refused to assume responsibility again. By the end of May, it was rumored the LC&N had announced that it would make no repairs and that the company, faced with repairs that were estimated at $200,000 and an annual upkeep of $30,000, might once again try to surrender the whole tract to the state.[23] Actually, the LC&N rejected the state's contention and refused to make any major repairs or restorations, although the company did provide minimum maintenance, apparently to avoid creating additional legal liability.

In March of 1936 "certain taxpayers" of Bucks County initiated a suit in the Pennsylvania Supreme Court to finally determine the constitutionality of the 1931 act. On May 25, 1936, the court ruled that the act was unconstitutional and the forty miles of canal returned by the state remained in the possession of the Lehigh Coal and Navigation Company. On February 2, 1937, the attorney general of Pennsylvania instituted proceedings in equity in the Court of Common Pleas of Dauphin County seeking forfeiture of the canal under provisions of the 1858 acts that had transferred ownership of the canal from the state to private interests.[24] The floods "of unusual magnitude" in March of 1936 probably hastened the final solutions, for the damage to the canal was extensive:

[It] was estimated that the cost of restoring navigation would approximate $125,000, exclusive of the amount of $47,510.54 expended by the Canal company because of the floods, in repairs between the Easton dam and Raubsville and below that point.[25]

As a result of the floods, there was no water in the canal from Point Pleasant to New Hope during most of the balance of 1936. This brought numerous protests from property owners along that portion of canal. Among the more articulate was that of Morris L. Cooke of the Rural Electrification Administration, to the LC&N, dated June 2, 1936.[26] While he, along with the nearly two thousand members of the Delaware Valley Protective Association, was certainly concerned about the aesthetics of the valley, his particular concern was fire protection.

"The apparatus of the Stockton (N.J.) Fire Department" across the Delaware from Centre Bridge, Pennsylvania, where Mr. Cooke lived, "was capable of pumping water out of the Canal but not out of the River," Cooke wrote. The risk was of "not having any water at all in the Canal."[27] The cause was the two dams "which you have built—one at Centerbridge and one opposite the Johnson Farm." The likely reason for the construction of these dams was that "the tow path bank had been scoured by floods [and] some troublesome leaks developed which delayed the water reaching Center Bridge until August 5th. and New Hope a day or two later." The construction of coffer dams was a normal procedure when major repairs were embarked upon.[28]

Because of the floods and a damaged towpath bank at Rocky Falls and Riegelsville, the National Slag Company, located below Raubsville—which was probably already using canal water in its operations—had erected "two bulkheads" or dams across the canal to create a basin from which water could be pumped into its plant. These kept water from flowing down the canal.

> On July 20th. the Slag Company was notified to remove the obstructions within 48 hours after receipt of notice. By agreement with the Slag Company sluices were cut in the bulkheads or dams by our forces on July 25th and 26th. Water was started down the canal immediately, viz. on July 26th. and reached Point Pleasant on July 31st.[29]

This action was at least partly in response to the state's contention that the company was legally obligated to maintain a waterway. As Thomas Ross, counsel for the Delaware Valley Protective Association, wrote the deputy attorney general of the Commonwealth:

> it is now intended by the canal company to cut five foot openings through these dams and frame those openings so as to permit a three or four foot water level to flow through the dam obstructions in the canal, and to make it possible for the sand and gravel company to close those openings in the dams with planks and resume pumping water from the river, in the event that floods should again breach the canal walls or the flow of water through the canal should again be interfered with, with the result that the sand and gravel company would be deprived of the water from the canal for its purposes. This condition and the situation at Morrisville, where the canal has permitted a railroad to be laid in its bed and water is piped down the canal to Bristol to supply the mills there, very obviously put the canal in a condition where it cannot be used for water transportation for its length.[30]

The canal, particularly its upper end, with a future that was less than guaranteed, was under pressure from another source. On March 17, 1936, the engineer of the Delaware Canal Company, L.C. Conant, wrote to William Jay Turner, his company's general counsel, to say that the district engineer for the state Highway Department had contacted him concerning repairs to State Highway #611, which abutted the canal for a long distance below Raubsville. Conant informed Turner that the canal south of Raubsville had been given to the state; Turner responded that he understood that the attorney general "had rendered an opinion that the act was unconstitutional but at the present time the canal still belonged to the state." The highway engineer had proposed repairs "from Coffeytown, one mile south of Raubsville, to Riegelsville and was going to fill out into the canal in order to provide sufficient shoulders for the highway." He was informed that the canal company had no objections for it "had nothing to do with that section of the canal."[31]

A further threat to the continued existence of the Delaware Canal was the Philadelphia to Easton Highway Improvement Association. This group was lobbying the state to fill in portions of the canal in order to widen Route 611 between Easton and Kintnersville. The association's secretary, J.W. Bliss, contacted the legal counsel of the Delaware Division Canal Company in an attempt to gain the company's cooperation.[32]

In September of 1936, the Board of Directors of the Delaware Division Canal Company met

to determine definitely whether it desires to retain the canal and restore the same to navigable condition, or whether it will surrender it to the state. If it determines on the latter course it desires to be protected concerning certain existing railroad spurs in the region of Morrisville which have encroached into the bed of the canal.[33]

The following February, the *Intelligencer* reported that the LC&N, faced with the state's suit to invalidate the corporate title because of the company's failure to observe the proviso in the original agreement to maintain a navigable canal, was agreeable to surrendering the whole canal to the state, particularly as local citizenry and the state's Water and Power Resource Board judged that the Morrisville encroachment would not interfere with the future use of the canal by the Commonwealth.[34]

However, before the end of March, 1937, the LC&N, through the Delaware Division Canal Company, had reneged on a supposed agreement and was contesting the state's attempt at forfeiture. "It is alleged," the newspaper reported, "that the canal company is attempting to sell a right of way for the conveyancing of water to the City of Philadelphia and, with that in view, is holding whatever title it may possess to the canal as long as possible."[35]

Aqueducts, locks, banks and towpaths all suffered damage from the flood of 1936. The canal was not being used by the Lehigh Coal and Navigation Company to carry coal by this time, and the necessary repairs would be costly to the company. This is the lock at Lumberville following the flood.

Rumors continued to recur and circulate. In July of 1938, it was reported that the canal would be rejuvenated by a project to bring coke by tractor-drawn barges on the canal to Bristol where it would be processed into "saleable products including gas and the residue to be sold for fuel in the form of brickettes." The *Intelligencer*, which carried the story, said there was both interest and skepticism on the part of "people familiar with the valley." The column noted the great expense necessary to restore the canal. "One section in Morrisville is completely filled and used as a railway spur. The street crossings in the borough have also been lowered by filling the canal and removing the bridges." The Point Pleasant aqueduct, the deterioration of towpath walls, the need for deepening the canal, and the condition of the locks all were mentioned in the newspaper's story.[36]

When the LC&N replied negatively in 1936 to the state's inquiry as to whether they intended to restore the canal as a public waterway, the Commonwealth instituted a suit on February 2, 1937, in the Dauphin County Court of Common Pleas seeking forfeiture under the provisions of the 1858 act.[37] The "bill in equity" was dismissed on March 21, 1938. The Commonwealth appealed to the state Supreme Court which on October 3, 1938, affirmed the decision of the lower court and on November 23 denied the Commonwealth's petition for re-argument.[38]

The Delaware Division Canal was still a losing proposition for the LC&N, with little prospect for any future reversal. In September of 1940, the LC&N's comptroller compiled figures for the period from January 1, 1930, to December 31, 1939.

		REVENUE	EXPENSES	NET INCOME
Year	1930	40,830.89	96,207.17	(55,376.28)
	1931	34,801.34	61,741.17	(26,939.83)
	1932	22,239.20	11,080.84	11,158.36
	1933	20,437.33	13,630.66	6,806.67
	1934	17,262.74	33,264.53	(16,001.79)
	1935	17,663.46	16,615.26	1,048.20
	1936	13,085.94	81,203.10	(68,117.16)
	1937	13,772.52	23,738.35	(9,965.83)
	1938	14,874.29	24,025.21	(9,150.92)
	1939	15,128.68	21,370.95	(6,242.27)

The canal had been fully operational during the years 1930 and 1931 and for a brief period during 1932. From October 1, 1931, to October 16, 1935, forty miles of the canal were maintained by the state, a situation that somewhat skewed the figures. "Since October 16, 1936, expenditures for maintenance have been kept to a minimum," the comptroller reported. The floods "of unusual magnitude" during March of 1936 required extraordinary maintenance costs. There had been heavy floods in the spring of 1940; repairs amounted to $16,987.49— "paid from advances made by the Pennsylvania Power and Light Company," the water-power customer of the canal at Raubsville. These advances were to be applied against subsequent water-power rents payable by PP&L.[39]

New solutions were necessary. On June 21, 1939, the state assembly passed a bill authorizing the secretary of Forests and Waters:

> (1) With the approval of the Governor, to acquire by donation any part of the property formerly constituting a system of canals, the use of which for transportation has been abandoned; and (2) To utilize such properties for park purposes, to sell for industrial or domestic purposes the waters of the canal, as heretofore, and to transfer to the Department of Highways such part of the property as he may deem undesirable to retain.[40]

According to the board of managers of the LC&N, negotiations were under way.

On April 22, 1940, the representative of the *Intelligencer* was informed by Secretary G. Albert Stewart of the Department of Forests and Waters that the Commonwealth had notified the Lehigh Coal and Navigation Company that it had decided to accept the gift of the canal: all that was awaited was a final decision of the corporation. It would be a complete transfer "including all income from the sale of water for power and other uses with the gift of the property." While this income would not fund restoration of the Point Pleasant Aqueduct, it would "take care of maintenance and minor repair." There were expectations "that barge parties, hiking, boating and fishing will be enjoyed by the public this summer."[41]

Many details had to be taken care of before the deal could be finalized. Internally, both the Lehigh Coal and Navigation Company and its subsidiary, the Delaware Division Canal Company, had to perform a number of actions before the transfer could legally take place. Among the suggested methods for transferring the canal to the state was by sale for a nominal sum or by preparing the proper proxies; finally it was resolved that the title to twelve small tracts of land acquired apart from the original deed from the Sunbury and Erie Railroad should also be conveyed to the Delaware Division Canal Company for ultimate transfer to the state.[42]

On October 28, the president of the Lehigh Coal and Navigation Company wrote to "The Pennsylvania Company for Insurance on Lives and Granting Annuities, Trustee under Consolidated Sinking Fund Mortgage of the Lehigh Coal and Navigation Company dated July 1, 1914" requesting authorization to validate the donation. Both their legal counsels and accountants were consulted. Ultimately it was decided that a donation was the proper procedure for a stock transfer; apparently a sale for even a trifling consideration would entail a Stock Transfer Tax. The potential liability was summarized in a LC&N internal document.

Stock Transfer Tax: 5 cents per $100 par value, if selling price

is under $ 20. per share $801.75

Penna. Tax   2 cents per $100 par value   320.70

$1,122.45 [43]

On October 18, 1940, Luther C. Conant, corporate engineer and real estate agent of the Lehigh Coal and Navigation Company and the Delaware Division Canal Company of Pennsylvania, furnished the Provident Trust Company, holder of 30,000 shares of the Delaware Canal Company under a mortgage bond, a summary of the negative aspects of continuing to hold the Delaware Canal, citing both operating losses and continuing liability. He recommended transferring ownership of the property to the state without compensation, noting his opinion was "fortified by the fact that the Morris Canal, and the Delaware and Raritan Canal, similar properties situate in the State of New Jersey, were acquired by the State of New Jersey from the owners, without compensation."[44]

The Board of Managers of the Lehigh Coal and Navigation Company passed a series of resolutions at a meeting on October 24, 1940. First, it was resolved that all the shares of the Delaware Division Company held by the LC&N would be voted at the Special Meeting of Stockholders of the Delaware Division Canal Company scheduled for October 31, 1940, in favor of conveyance to the state. Procedures were approved for voting all the shares of the Delaware Division Canal Company at a special meeting as a donation "without consideration" to the Commonwealth of Pennsylvania. Proxies were prepared appointing Robert V. White, president, or Henry H. Pease, secretary, respectively, of the two companies' proxies to vote the stock.[45]

Exit the Company

There had been talk about a celebration of acceptance by the state back in May, but it would be months before all of the corporate problems could be ironed out. The deed was subjected to long study, and title searches were necessary before the attorneys on each side would approve consummation of the deal. Thomas Ross, attorney for the Delaware Valley Protective Association, spelled out some of the complications in a letter of November 27, 1940. His investigation revealed that two deeds were needed. The first, whereby the LC&N conveyed all pertinent property to the Delaware Division, had been prepared and was ready for execution. The other deed, about forty-two pages long, included all the property to be conveyed, including that received from the LC&N. It was time-consuming, as certain liens were disclosed from the searches of title and Mr. Adams [Deputy Attorney General] says these have all now been cleared including some judgements and an order of the Public Service Commission, so that the liens are out of the way. The Attorney General's department has been carefully checking all the provisions of the deed and all lengthy descriptions of real estate property. Some errors and defects, largely of a typographical character, have been shown, and these have to be corrected by the Canal Company in the deed.[46]

Ross reported that final approvals could be completed within ten days.

It would be December 19 before the *Intelligencer* could proudly announce, that the "Delaware Valley Parkway Is Now Property of the State."[47] The 1940 Annual Report of the Lehigh Coal and Navigation Company noted that "during the past ten years [the Delaware Division Canal Company] has been endeavoring to dispose of its canal property because transportation by canal had become obsolete." The conclusion was the donation of the entire canal property to the Commonwealth of Pennsylvania by deed "duly executed by the Canal Company [and] signed by the Secretary of Forests and Waters on December 18, 1940,… and on the same day the Governor noted his approval thereon."[48]

In 1940, still a few months before the state would resume title to the canal, there was apparently a good deal of confusion as to what the future held for the canal. This is vividly revealed in a letter penned by Ida G. Leavitt of Morrisville, Pennsylvania, to the Delaware Valley Protective Association. From her letter, it would appear that there was a possibility that the canal might be "drained off or filled in." She complained for herself and her neighbors living north of Morrisville's Calhoun Street Bridge that the flow of water had diminished:

> the two or three bridges between the Calhoun Street Bridge and Yardley were taken down and roads made, so that the flow of water in the canal was reduced almost to a standstill and it can no longer be used for canoeing as formerly, when we could paddle up to Easton.[49]

The *Towpath*, the publication of the Delaware Valley Protective Association, during the summer of 1940 contained letters protesting the stagnant canal and asking when? WHEN? would the state take over. Among the laments was this very illustrative verse:

MOSQUITOS ALONG THE TOWPATH

They pester me from morn till night
They never do give up the fight.
And when you hear their motors hum
There is no use to dodge or run
For all too soon you're sure to feel
The gentle touch of their bills of steel.
And yet we mortals would like to live
Amid the pleasures the canal did give.
Who is it holds the waters back
And makes the canal a stagnant sewer?
How we'd like to have them feel the gentle touch
Of the little birds they love so much.

Frank White

to which editor William F. Taylor added

> Good "Blankety-blank" verse, Frank
> With sympathy—Bill [50]

L.S. Conant was primarily responsible for the final transfer of the canal property to the state. In his January 1941 memorandum of a conference with Albert Stewart, Pennsylvania's Secretary of Forests and Waters, he noted that as of the previous December 18, the state had assumed the salaries of all the employees on the canal except for two foremen:

Foremen Harry Wismer and Harry Warford will continue as employees of The Lehigh Coal and Navigation Company as the Commonwealth has a man they wish to put on as Foreman and also will probably use George Wismer as Foreman on the upper end.[51]

The Commonwealth's Water and Power Resources Board issued a report in 1942 of its attempts to measure the damage to the canal resulting from the floods of 1936 and 1940, published under the somewhat cumbersome title "The Delaware Division Canal, Report Upon Its Present Condition and Its Relation to the Control of Floods in the Delaware River." In it, the board made a detailed suggestion as to restoration, further use, and development of the canal.[52]

In the 1945 to 1947 period, the canal was under the supervision of the District Forester, whose office was in Norristown, Pennsylvania. In 1945, this was E.F. Brouse; in 1947 it was W.P. Moll. In 1945, Mrs. Robert A. Hogue, secretary of The New Hope Public Health Nursing Association, penned a letter to Pennsylvania's Department of Forests and Waters expressing concern about "the present state of the barge canal." She wrote that there was no water in the canal "in some places and in others the water is stagnant and filthy, a breeding ground for mosquitos and a possible source of disease." What, she asked, were their plans for the canal?[53] Brouse, who was directed to respond, apologized that the canal in New Hope and above was not all that it should be, but he insisted that the conditions were not totally the result of state action or inaction:

> In spite of protests, dozens of those living along the canal drain their sinks and lavatories into the canal and not only that, it is a depository for refuse of all kinds including leaves, brush, dead animals and whatnot.
> … Many of the residents of New Hope Borough are not without fault and if we were to name names I believe that a good many otherwise reputable citizens would be very much embarrassed.[54]

Those who lived along the canal would also have to cooperate.

In a follow-up letter written to Mrs. Hogue several weeks later, he noted that although some progress was being made toward getting water through the canal, there was still "a very bad break to fix in the vicinity of Uhlerstown before there is a chance of maintaining a normal flow at New Hope." He estimated that the canal could not be completely watered before the following spring, heavy rains during the previous July having caused "terrific damage." That many of the residents along the canal were less than enamored of the canal park was validated by the district forester:

> I want to tell you that during the past five years we have had quite a good deal of trouble with residents along the canal below the aqueduct in New Hope and that is the principle reason until last July why there has been no water in the lower sections of the canal. We are bedevilled one way or the other it seems. The residents along there claim that the canal through leakage was driving them out of their homes which of course was an unhealthy and unsatisfactory condition. One or two of them got lawyers on us in spite of the fact that I disclaim leaks after having spent a good many hundreds of dollars on repairs immediately above Templetin's lock in the Fall of 1943. I think the cellar water they are getting is hillside drainage but no one will agree to this in spite of the fact that there is water in their cellars when there is none in the canal. It seems like an impossible situation all the way around.
> I presume the only way of arriving at a solution is to turn the water through the town and then let the matter be worked out with the proper legal authority. This we propose to do in the Spring.[55]

Rebuilding and Restoring — Saving the Canal

In the fall of 1947, Bill No. 33 was pushed through the Pennsylvania legislature. As finally passed, it appropriated $200,000 for work on the canal and the Department of Forests and Waters initiated the engineering studies preparatory to the final construction.[56] The Doylestown *Intelligencer* reported on June 3, 1948, that State Senator Edward B. Watson had notified them that his bill had been passed and money was available and could be expended. With the approval of the Department of Forests and Waters, the Department of Property and Supplies was ready to advertise for bids. Within the next few days it would award the contract for the construction of a new aqueduct at Point Pleasant, and every expectation was that there would be water in the canal by the end of the season. Within the article was this statement:

> Due to the increased prices of labor and materials, the complete restoration of the canal cannot be accomplished during this biennium, but the building of the Point Pleasant aqueduct will at least put water into the canal which will wash away the mud and refuse and make the area more attractive.[57]

Hope was expressed that the "barge" parties, swimming, fishing, and boating that had ended in 1935 following the collapse of the aqueduct could be resumed.

With completion of this work, the canal appeared to be in good shape, at least from Point Pleasant to New Hope. Among the many spots that were restored and repaired under the 1948 appropriation of $200,000 were the Tohickon Creek (Point Pleasant) Aqueduct, the Paunaucussing or Milton Creek (Lumberville) Aqueduct, Locks No. 12 (Lumberville), 13 and 14 (lower and upper Point Pleasant) as well as several wall areas, waste gates and stop gates. Unfortunately, the three locks were restored with canal gates and hardware that did not conform to Delaware patterns, gates and hardware that the state salvaged from the Schuylkill Canal.[58]

In 1949, just when it seemed that all the most pressing problems had been met, the Durham Aqueduct collapsed, again depriving the canal of water from Durham to New Hope.[59]

In 1950 the state contracted with consulting engineers Damon and Foster for another study of the canal, this time from mile 24 (New Hope) north to Easton. The loss of the Commonwealth's interest in the

Lock 13 near Point Pleasant. Locks 13 and 14 at Point Pleasant and lock 12 at Lumberville were restored with hardware salvaged from the Schuylkill Canal. Courtesy of The Intelligencer/Gian Luiso.

"lower end" of the canal—Bristol, Levittown and even Morrisville—could already be seen at this date. Damon and Foster's detailed study was complete with engineering drawings and cost estimates for restoration, north of Morrisville, of locks, aqueducts, waste gates, stop gates, overflows, canal walls, coping to top canal walls, canal bridges, the dam at Easton, and dredging. There were two levels of estimates, one that would put the canal back into working order, while the other would attempt only a stabilization of the canal for water control and flood protection but would not restore it to navigational condition. Some of the locks were still operational at this time. Complete restoration was estimated to cost $3,000,000, not taking into consideration any replacement pilings that might be needed.[60]

In the July 1951 issue of the DVPA's *Towpath*, president Dr. W. Wilson McNeary reported that "the Durham Aqueduct, so long under reconstruction, is now completed. The Gallows Run Aqueduct is also completed and water is now flowing as far as Tinicum."[61] In 1952, McNeary, now secretary of the DVPA, noted "Our chief objective at the present time is to see that the old canal so long an eyesore may soon be filled with water." [62]

In the meantime, the aqueduct over Tinicum Creek had collapsed and reconstruction was underway. As at Durham, the reconstruction would be by massive steel I-beams. At Tinicum they would be 8'6" apart and connected with steel flooring.[63] In January of 1952, the *Towpath* noted a delay in obtaining steel plates for the decking "because of the exorbitant price charged by the sellers of the material." Secretary of Forests and Waters Milo F. Draemel noted that less-permanent wood construction might be substituted, an/d it was hoped that water might be flowing by February. The steel did become available.[64] The 1952 May-June issue of the *Towpath* carried the legend "Tinicum Aqueduct Complete" under an illustration showing the removal of the temporary dam at that site.[65] Work was also started on the aqueduct at New Hope and on a retaining wall below Lumberville where the towpath had been completely washed away.[66]

The valley was devastated by one of the worst floods in its history in 1955, triggered by hurricane Diane. Repairs would be extensive, more than $315,000 according to the estimates of DFW Secretary Goddard.[67]

In 1955, Maurice Goddard was appointed Secretary of Forests and Waters. He would become one of the Delaware Canal's best friends for the next several decades. By training a professional forester, Goddard had registered "no party" for 20 years and was a non-political appointment made by Governor George M. Leader. He had been head of the School of Forestry at The Pennsylvania State University. He would serve under two Democratic and two Republican governors before being named by Governor Milton Shapp to be secretary of the new Department of Environmental Resources (DER), which was created in 1970 to replace and enlarge the functions of the Department of Forests and Waters.[68]

The 1955 flood provided another opportunity for the enemies of the canal to rise to the attack. In June, Senator Joseph J. Yosko, Democrat from Northampton County, introduced a bill calling for the transfer of the canal to adjoining property owners. The bill had been introduced at the urging of Jacob A. Raub, former Northampton County district attorney, who contended that the canal was being maintained for the benefit of a few people at the extreme end of the canal, particularly the artist colony at New Hope. State Senator Edward B. Watson, who had led the fight for funds for the canal since 1936, promised that the bill had no chance in the Senate and offered an expert engineering opinion that filling the canal would only increase flood danger as the river bank would be pushed back to fill the canal, an operation that would cost more than would repairs.[69]

Even with all of the monies expended on the canal following the 1955 flood, the canal was still not put back to its previous condition. Six of the eleven bridges swept away by floodwaters were "promptly replaced 'with concrete pipes and fill' in order to quickly restore normal transportation." This statement, offered in 1976 by C.P. "Bill" Yoder, curator for the Pennsylvania Canal Society, continued: "It is understood that as State money becomes available these culverts will be replaced by camel back bridges." For, he noted, "each reduction to the cross sectional area of a stream introduces resistance to the normal flow of water" and a culvert with one-tenth the flow of the original body of water not only restricts the normal flow but also "acts as a trash barrier and collector to further restrict normal flow of the stream." Since that time the pledge to replace, has been largely ignored by the state bureaucracy.[70]

In 1957, the state announced a policy for the state park. As a goal, the policy stated:

The Delaware Canal shall be developed to its maximum use as a recreational area for the general public and as a conveyor of water to various consumers at a minimum cost to the Commonwealth of Pennsylvania.

In the short term, the policy for the lower 10 miles of the canal from Bristol to Morrisville was for it to be used solely for the purposes of conveying water with a minimum of maintenance, with an emphasis on recreational development and improvement of water quality.

Long Range Policy Number 4 was, over the years, to be often ignored and violated, and yet at the same time often quoted to the state authorities in face of threats to the canal. It read:

All requests for encroachments on the waterway area of the canal shall be considered in terms of the reduction in recreational use and water conveyance ability. In no case shall the top width of the canal water be less than 25 feet, except at aqueduct crossings or cross drainage features. The clear height of structures shall be determined by the towpath requirements. If no towpath exists, a minimum of 8 feet above normal high water shall be required.[71]

There was a good deal of interest in some kind of zoning along the canal. As "The Gossiper," a weekly columnist in the *Intelligencer*, noted, with water back in the canal, and

> the increasing number of visitors it is not unlikely that mercenary persons, who are less interested in preserving the undiluted beauty of the valley, will seek locations of State owned land for certain types of commercial projects which will detract seriously from the lure of a protected area of that sort.[72]

Unfortunately, the DVPA failed to act because of disagreement as to how zoning was to be accomplished.

Depending upon whom you believe, the canal may have come closest to extinction during 1957 as a result of both legislative action and inaction. In the spring of that year, the appropriations committee of the Pennsylvania House of Representatives excised from the budget a request from Governor Leader for $229,000 to maintain the Delaware Canal; in fact, the committee even removed the minimal operating funds from the budget. Most members of the legislature were unaware of the action until May 27, when the Department of Forests and Waters, which had run out of funds, ordered that the canal be drained on June 1. At six o'clock on the evening of the twenty-seventh, after an official from that department phoned the DVPA, president Hal H. Clark moved into action.[73] Pat Greene, in the August edition of the *Bucks County Traveler*, quoted Bucks County representative Marvin V. Keller's assessment of Clark's persistence:

> On the afternoon of May 27th, not fifteen legislators were aware of the Delaware Canal; by the following morning all of them were—and some even wondered if uranium had cropped up in its channel.

As it was reported, "For ten days—backed by the press, TV and radio—the lovers of the canal never let up until they'd won their point." Two days before the legislature adjourned for two years until its next biennial session, it approved a maintenance appropriation of $78,000, $14,000 less than the amount used during the preceding two years.

That evening, Clark, an ex-newspaperman, had made phone calls to state legislative and administrative leaders. He released the story to the morning press across the Delaware Valley, and by the following morning had sent press releases to twenty-six influential dailies and weeklies all over the state. The story was picked up by the wire services, putting it on radio and TV, and individuals and groups were almost immediately registering their protests.

In a follow-up story, the *Bucks County Traveler* reported that when James Camp of Centre Bridge had gone to the local telegraph station to send his protest he had found eight hundred similar telegrams piled up on the agent's desk awaiting their turn.[74]

Senate leaders arranged a hasty conference with Dr. Goddard. It was agreed that the order to drain the canal would be rescinded. State and county leaders were heard from, even the County Labor Council. The State Fish Commission announced it could not salvage the 10,000 fish it had stocked in the canal, which brought pressure from sportsmen's groups and the 400,000-member-strong Pennsylvania Federation of Garden Clubs joined the fray. Certainly an example of the effectiveness of grass-roots action!

State Assemblywoman Margarette Kooker gave a slightly different account, in which the situation was the result of scare tactics by Governor Leader, who was unhappy with the Republican budget recommendations. She listed current DFW appropriations and unexpended funds totaling $15,000,000, an existing oil and gas lease fund of millions set aside for flood control, recreation, and conservation—which would be supplemented by additional millions in royalties—along with nearly $10,000,000 still unexpended, left in an emergency flood fund established following the 1955 flood. She promised to "see that the canal is properly taken care of so that the citizens will continue to enjoy its advantages."[75]

Maintenance

When one goes through the collections of newspaper clippings, really the only extant history of the post-1940 canal, one can only be struck by the vulnerability of a structure carrying water. The canal's history is the story of a series of breaches in the walls and other structural collapses and of the efforts to perform the repairs necessary to get the water flowing again. The sequential nature of that flow depended on only two real sources of water: the pool at Easton that provided the flow—if there were no interruptions—from there to New Hope and, for the lower end of the canal, the outlet lock at New Hope, which accepted water from the pool created by the wing dam, thus guaranteeing the flow from that point to Bristol—again, provided that there were no breaks or other interruptions in the waterway.

In 1966, Dr. Goddard spelled out some of the problems in a letter which praised the DVPA for its efforts, including those connected with the rebuilding of the wing dam at New Hope during the 1960s, which should keep the lower end of the canal filled even during a season of low water in the Delaware River. He noted: "Major projects cannot be constructed in a short period of time and hence, the only alternatives are to either spend money to bypass the water or leave the Canal dry for an extended period … Because of the excessively high cost involved in diverting water or bulkheading numerous small sites," the water in the canal would be drawn down in mid-November to permit completion of a number of small projects along the canal. Both water users and the Fish Commission would be notified.[76]

Maurice Goddard, known throughout Pennsylvania as Doc Goddard. Courtesy of Pennsylvania Historical and Museum Commission.

It is impossible to list and document all the problems, floods, breaks, droughts, etc. that have occurred and to list in detail all of the results, fish kills, citizen anger, etc., so let the following plus those that are referred to incidentally elsewhere in this volume, suffice as examples.

Both the newspapers and the DVPA have had their moments of concern over the lower end of the canal. Theodore Elonis' letter to the editor of July 2, 1965, described the canal in Morrisville as

A long hole or channel about three feet deep and 12 feet wide and even less in places. Fish, where are they? Clean water? Well, no, it isn't there long enough to get clean. In the past three years I have seen the Canal go from its fullest to bone dry. This is one reason for no fish, less muskrat and frogs. Also, no more people hiking or having fun on its banks.[77]

The water was so low because of the deteriorating wing dam at New Hope, according to Superintendent Bailey. Water could not enter the canal, and several big leaks had developed in it between Washington Crossing and Yardley. Bailey warned that many fish might die unless removed. "There are not many game fish there, but they're the kind that children could have a lot of fun fishing for." The ability to fight fires in the Yardley-Morrisville area was also reduced, while the welfare of several small industries and farms that used canal water were threatened.[78]

In 1968, the Bucks County Department of Health pronounced that it had, along with the Department of Forests and Waters,

expressed concern over the number of persons, primarily children, bathing in the Delaware Canal. These agencies have stated that the water in the canal is unsuitable for bathing and that bathing in the vicinity of the lock and water control structures presents a grave safety hazard to the bathers.[79]

There was danger from both disease and underwater hazards.

Following heavy rains in late June of 1973, the canal suffered its fourth major break since 1936, when a 200-foot-long section of canal wall collapsed between Riegelsville and Raubsville, 3.5 miles below the Easton lock. There was great additional damage, silting, fallen trees and other litter, undermined concrete structures along the canal, and "Extensive damages to canal banks, caves-ins, etc. caused by river breaking into canal and eroding banks." The state brought in much regional equipment and manpower, but funds were still short and estimates were that water would not be restored at best before late autumn. Superintendent Holland asked for help in trapping fish in the drained canal in order to transfer them to the river. Canal employees and Point Pleasant residents were already so engaged.[80]

The continuing series of breaks—two in 1936 following storms, and breaches due to Hurricane Diane in 1955, Hurricane Agnes in 1972, and the big rain of June 1973—caused Hal Clark to reevaluate his previous opposition to the proposed Tocks Island Dam on the Upper Delaware and become a strong supporter of a solution that today seems like an anachronism. "I am not for damming up our rivers," Clark emphasized, "The DVPA was one of the first to come out for the Delaware as a wild river above Tocks, but the Delaware Basin is a small river basin with limited water resources. None of the critics of the dam tell us where the water is coming from for the needs we can see coming."[81]

River Road and New Hope

Tied to the canal were the problems of River Road, Pennsylvania routes 32 and 611. Paralleling the canal, River Road and its ambience were closely tied to the aesthetics of the canal on the one hand and to its basic physical integrity on the other. Ever since the canal had been abandoned as a navigational waterway, continuous efforts had been made to fill the canal or at least to make major encroachments upon it to improve and upgrade River Road. The number one watchdog protecting the canal from these threats was the Delaware Valley Protective Association.

The state engineer's survey of 1950 noted that for some eleven miles, the canal wall served as a retaining wall for the highway. It was made up of dry walls, of which many sections had collapsed. The collapse of the stonework had undermined the highway, creating dangerous conditions since the highways were used by increasing numbers of trucks and a large number of motorists.[82]

One spot on the canal begging for improvement was the south entrance into New Hope. Sometimes called "Death Corner," it was where Windybush Road entered River Road from a sharp grade just a few yards south of where River Road made a 90° right turn onto a camelback bridge over the miter gate at the lower end of Lock No. 10, and then a sharp left turn onto Main Street. In 1952, the DVPA protested that a plan as extensive and expensive as that proposed by the state, for which there was no funding, was unrealistic and suggested a simple angle bridge across the lock and some widening of the angles at the curves.[83]

It was not until near the end of the decade that plans were formalized and work was anticipated. The division still continued between the highway department, which would fill in the canal and pipe the water through a 300-foot pipe, and the DVPA and presumably most of the citizenry of New Hope and its leadership. The Department of Forests and Waters had a definite policy that the canal was recreational and a park facility, and must not be used for other purposes.

The DVPA still was lobbying for a much cheaper and environment-saving angled bridge. It protested the hearings scheduled by the state Department of Highways for 1:00 p.m. in New Hope Borough Hall, which would hold a maximum of twenty-five persons, rather than a meeting at night in the high school gymnasium. Members of New Hope Borough Council were reported to have been threatened with loss of federal funds for the project unless they gave their support to an elaborate plan for modernizing River Road, a plan that included the destruction of Lock No. 10 in New Hope.[84] Apparently the highway department won, at least in New Hope: in about 1960, the lower half of Lock No. 10 was filled in so that the road could angle across the pipes carrying the canal.

As early as 1958, the DVPA was intervening and persuading the state Department of Highways to abandon plans to cut the sharp corner at Phillips Mill. The plan would have damaged the Bucks County art colony and invaded the canal up to 14 feet in order to widen River Road. This intervention also forestalled the highway department's effort to build a truck road for heavy-duty sand, gravel and cement transportation. Hal Clark, now president of the DVPA, protested that there had been no consultation on the part of the highway department with the Solebury Township supervisors or any other group. Even the Department of Forests and Waters' district engineer had not received any plans. Finally, he protested the "high-handed and indefensible procedure" of holding a formal hearing, then being told it had only been held because a hearing was required by federal law but that it was unnecessary, for "under the particular federal grant upon which the project was based, the Highway Department could take state land and even federal land."[85]

In 1967, serious efforts were made to attack another major problem along River Road. The highway department would, as part of an experimental program, construct a mile of retaining walls along the highway between Centre Bridge and Lumberville in order to hold up the road, which was gradually slipping into the Delaware Canal. The solution designed by state highway engineers was to plant I-beams along the bank at eight-foot intervals. Six-inch reinforced-concrete slabs would be slid into the beam channels and toed to pilings into the road center. They would not excavate into the cliff wall but would increase the shoulder on the canal side. The initial bid was $298,698 by Roland G. Tiracorda of Madera, Pennsylvania, and the state was reviewing the bid. In 1977 the construction was implemented by the Miller and Brown Construction Company.[86]

In May of 1961, the DVPA successfully mobilized sufficient opposition to forestall a proposed 28-acre shopping center along the canal in Lower Makefield Township.[82] In another issue they were less successful, for DVPA and local Morrisville officials lost their fight to prevent the highway department from filling a 100-foot stretch of the canal "to provide a roadway beneath the proposed Route 1 Super highway." Today the canal is piped under the highway, with one of the piers encroaching upon the canal right-of-way.[87]

Under the leadership of Hal Clark the DVPA was credited with successfully coordinating the efforts of the Bucks County Park Board, the Bucks County Planning Commission, the Pennsylvania Department of Highways and the DVPA to find an alternative to widening River Road and the destruction of the Palisades in Bridgton, Tinicum, Solebury and Plumstead townships.[88]

Clark, writing about the long-term struggle, noted that Governor Pinchot had addressed a group of citizens in 1931 and urged them to organize and fight to protect and develop the canal and scenic River Road because it would become one of the finest treasures of the Commonwealth. The DVPA, according to Clark, had organized and kept the faith. In the 1950s, he recounted, Governor Leader and the LC&N had abandoned the project but

> In the Martin, Duff and Fine administrations cooperation resumed with the exception of the highway engineers who have steadily sought to destroy the canal and the scenic River Road. Their ally was the late Senator Joseph Yosko who always carried a bill in his pocket to fill in the canal. Each time he introduced it, the late Senator Edward Watson put it on ice.[89]

Clark and supporters achieved some success at Phillips Mill about 1960, during the Lawrence administration. Secretary of Highways Park H. Martin, with staff and parks engineers, visited the area and announced their conclusions. "No major reconstruction can be done on this road without destroying vegetation and endangering the old canal." The highway department committed itself to "resurfacing and limited pavement widening starting in 1961."[90]

The high cliffs of the Palisades drop almost into the canal. A narrow road runs along this area of exceptional natural beauty, made more beautiful by the proximity of the canal.

However, in 1962 Clark learned from a New Hope-Solebury school administrator that the highway department had withdrawn the $770,000 appropriation for these limited improvements

> because the Delaware Valley Protective Association would not allow them to build the kind of road they wanted to build. Our understanding of the road they desired to build is a 20 ft. road with 8' or 10' berms. Such a development, as Mr. Martin himself stated, would destroy the scenic values of River Road and very likely would destroy the Canal as well.[91]

Part of the problem was that federal funding would be available only if the road were rebuilt to the more generous dimensions. Clark, however, pointed out there were other state road projects, Old York Road for example, that were being constructed with state funds that met the federal guidelines for subsidies.[92]

By 1967, Clark had recruited Pennsylvania's two United States senators and Bucks County's congressman and state senator along with three members of the state assembly to contest another proposed widening of River Road. Broad-based local citizen and community backing supported this coalition. According to then-United States Senator Joseph Sill Clark, he had been advised

> by State Highway officials that we should make every effort to get the United States Bureau of Public Roads to reduce its standards in order to save as much of the scenic River Road's natural attractions and beauties as possible.
>
> The River Road at first was to be built with 50 per cent Federal Aid requiring secondary major highway right-of-way standards of 42 to 44 feet and up to 26 feet width for cartway.[93]

The department's original plan would have eliminated 40 business places and residences between Yardley and Kintnersville and would have "denuded stretches of the Palisades to a height of 60 feet." In Point Pleasant the existing bridge would have been replaced, the road would have been straightened, and many houses and businesses "including Kolbe's brick apartment house" would have been eliminated. According to Clark, to rebuild River Road was "like trying to put a trunk through a transom."[94]

Another problem had to do with the construction of a new Route 202 bridge. Originally 202 had been routed through the main streets of New Hope and Lambertville, New Jersey—overtaxing busy streets and an antiquated bridge. The plan called for a new multi-lane toll bridge well north of the borough. Almost from the beginning, the DVPA went on record against the highway department's plans. It did not join the few locals who protested that the bridge was unnecessary, but protested the toll aspect (it wanted a free bridge) and opposed any exit from the toll plaza onto River Road. DVPA claimed it had an agreement with Dr. Goddard that the toll booth would be a distance beyond River Road, where the road joined the original Route 202. If the toll bridge were built, Clark warned his membership,

> it will damage one of the finest scenic areas of the Commonwealth, destroy valuable property and endanger the development of the internationally famous and historic Delaware Canal in Theodore Roosevelt State Park and its scenic River Road. It will attract truck traffic on River Road and it will not solve the traffic problems in New Hope.[95]

The highway department denied knowledge of any such agreement and the toll booth and entry onto River Road were supported by the officials of the Delaware River Joint Toll Bridge Commission. Clark and the DVPA lost on this one, but the interchange apparently has not done permanent and irreparable damage to River Road.[96]

Mule "Barges"

A *New York Times* article of May 31, 1942, reported that "Permission has been granted for the revival of barge parties ... and one John Winter and his mule are looking forward to a busy season." The reconditioned boat would run from Centre Bridge to Washington Crossing Park, presumably passing through locks 8 through 11 at New Hope. The writer, Ethel Davenport, noted that when she had lived along the canal some thirty-five years earlier, approximately 1907, sometimes a week would pass on the dying canal between boats.[97]

An item in the March 1954 edition of *Towpath* entitled "Scow Party" noted that the appellation "Barge Parties" was a misnomer, for, according to an old canal boatman, the boats that had been used were not barges. The boats on the canal had been steered and their motive power, the mules, were under the control of the boat "captain." The so-called barges at New Hope were actually former LC&N maintenance scows. However the writer noted that "Scow Party" would never suit the publicity, so that as the boat rides now resumed they should still be called "Barge Parties." The use of the word "barge" for the low-hulled vessels that carried passengers on the Delaware Canal has long been a source of annoyance to knowledgeable individuals.

In 1954, with the aqueducts restored and the canal re-watered, the mule-drawn canal "barge" rides were resumed. The operator was Peter Pascuzzo and the boats were

> piloted by John Winters and his brother Floyd, two New Hope residents who are third generation bargemen. They are well versed in the lore of the canal, John having begun working around 1917 as an apprentice mule skinner. He earned 25 cents a week helping to guide barges loaded with coal. The barge captain was paid $1 a day plus his meals.[98]

On March 4, 1962, John F. Winters, who was listed in his obituary as the "well-known ... foreman of the excursion barge crews here," died at the age of 52 years.[99]

Pete Pascuzzo built his first 50-foot steel boat in 1953, after years of persuasion by the leaders of the DVPA. He had a first-year total of only about 400 passengers. In 1961, he built two additional boats, making a fleet of three. In 1964, he recounted some of his problems for a *Philadelphia Sunday Bulletin* reporter. He learned early, on the five and one-half mile run north to the picnic area, that a 63-inch-tall mule would get wedged under one of the footbridges across the canal. Another frightening recollection was an incident that occurred when he was leading two mules across the canal on a plank walk in New Hope. One mule fell in, pulling Pascuzzo after him. The second mule fell in on top of Pascuzzo. "I could've got killed right there," he recalled.

He had problem years. In 1954, pipeline construction emptied the canal for much of the year. The following year, 1955, was the disastrous flood year. "And in 1956, it was so cold that on the Fourth of July you needed an overcoat." By 1964, however, he had four barges and eight mules, employed six boys to lead the mules, and for that year expected nearly 12,000 to ride his barges.[100]

Pete had more than his share of problems. Sometime in the spring of 1969, a newsman's camera recorded one of his mules that had fallen into the canal between the Canal House and the Towpath House in New Hope. Between one of the handlers, tourist volunteers, and the rescue squad, the mule was righted and half-swam, half-walked to a spot from which he could get out of the canal. According to the legend, "Pascuzzo, barge owner, says he's sending Jack back to where ever he came from, his country manners leave something to be desired, swimming in the canal, indeed!"[101]

In 1973, a 200-foot-long break occurred in the canal between Riegelsville and Raubsville, keeping the canal largely in an un-watered state for most of the season. According to Pascuzzo it was "the eighth year in a row I've been out of business because of breaks in the canal. How much more can a guy take? I've cancelled out so many private parties that I'm in a hole already." Were it not for his trucking business, Pascuzzo said, he would not be making a living.[102]

The mules that pulled the "barges" at New Hope, to quote an old boatman, "had a personality" —and that could be mean. Peter Pascuzzo certainly had occasional mule problems, some that were sufficiently newsworthy to be recorded, as for example in *The Philadelphia Inquirer*. The paper reported it was "a mule named Maud that's giving 67-year-old Pascuzzo ulcers." Unlike his other nine mules, Maud refused to cross a small bridge at Lock No. 9 to get across to the towpath. Neither a tug-of-war nor shocking her with a cattle prod worked. Pascuzzo offered a former partner $25 if he could get her across the bridge. His solution: a blindfold. Halfway across, Maud stopped, and the former partner's situation "brought Pascuzzo his only smile over the incident."

" 'But that damn one,' Pascuzzo snarled, glaring at Maud, 'She's got to go. You know anybody who wants to buy a mule cheap?' "[103]

Pascuzzo was followed by subsequent concessionaires. He sold out to Jim Newman who ran the operation for several years, then in 1977 George Schweickhardt and Leo Ramirez became the concessionaires.[104] Leo died on September 21, 1994, presumably leaving George in total charge. They had elaborated

Barges at New Hope, a popular tourist attraction for many years.

their offerings to include catering and musical entertainment, although not historical interpretation. Whether or not the canal is watered remains a constant threat along with their more routine concerns about vulnerability to the vagaries of weather, etc. Faced with the uncertainties of water in the canal during the last several years, the concessionaires have expended $10,000 a year to pump water into a canal that was lacking its normal and adequate flow.[105]

The partners had a sense of humor. In 1988 they held a small ceremony where they named two of their mules, one Peter and one Jim. Their famous namesakes, then-Congressman Peter H. Kostmayer and State Senator James "Jim" C. Greenwood were in attendance. In 1992, Peter successfully challenged Jim for his congressional seat.[106]

The Lower End

The abortive 1931 park grant to the state had extended south only to Morrisville; in 1940, the last year the canal was under the control of the Lehigh Coal and Navigation Company, serious consideration had been given to a plan to terminate the canal into the Delaware River at Morrisville. The tidal basin at Bristol had been filled in the early 1930s and a section in Morrisville was filled for a railroad siding.

In 1988, the detailed legal analysis of the status of the ownership of the Delaware Canal in the Bristol section of the Roosevelt State Park, requested by Superintendent Douglas Hoehn, was prepared by William W. Shakely, director of the Bureau of Legal Services of the Pennsylvania Department of Environmental Resources, for William C. Forrey, director of the Bureau of State Parks. It recounted how the old canal basin, already filled in by the LC&N, had been transferred by an act of the legislature and a subsequent deed in 1947 to the Borough of Bristol to be used "only for a park and for parking facilities." The deed was amended under a subsequent act of the legislature to "include public purposes, including a sewage pumping station and a marina." It was in 1954, while the canal was under state control, that the state leased for $1 a year a portion of the canal from Lock No. 1 to Beaver Dam Road, including locks 2 and 3, to Bristol to facilitate construction of the Warren Snyder School.[107]

By an act of 1961 the Pennsylvania Department of Property and Supplies, with the approval of the governor, was authorized to convey to Bristol the entire length of the canal in the borough. "As conditions of this conveyance, the Borough was to build and maintain suitable structures for diverting water from the canal into Adams Hollow Creek and to provide for adequate channel capacity in the Creek." As these conditions have never been fulfilled, a deed was apparently never executed. The property ownership from

Aerial view of Bristol, 1941. Locks 2 and 3 can be seen. Lock 2 and the section of wide water as far as Lock 3 were filled in for Warren Snyder Elementary School. Compare this with the company map of Bristol on page 129.

Lock No. 1 to Adams Hollow, which flows through Bristol from the borough's northern fringe eastward to the Delaware River, is retained by the state; but under the lease, the borough is still responsible for the maintenance of the Adams Hollow Waste Gate.[108]

The Borough of Bristol, in addition to allowing a school to be constructed on the canal right-of-way, extended the life of the borough dump by trucking excavated material out of the dump and depositing it in the old canal bed between the school and the basin, now filled with dredged materials by the U.S. Corps of Engineers. Carl Nelson, a retired Bristol contractor, remembers that in the 1950s he and his brother-in-law, Hubert Nelson, were approached by the borough. to excavate material from the dump, to fill and level the trash, and add trainloads of cinders shipped by the railroads.[109]

In 1953, five-eighths of a mile of canal was leased for the proposed Levittown Shopping Center. Water would be piped under the parking lot through an inverted siphon.[110] The Morrisville railroad siding for Tattersall's Coal Yard was removed by the state in 1961; the contractor was Eugene E. Edwards of Langhorne.[111]

Maurice Goddard, secretary of the Department of Forests and Waters, visited Bucks County in the spring of 1962 to discuss the lower end of the canal. Goddard was, according to the *Towpath*, "ready to amputate it." The secretary met with various county and local officials, most of whom expressed support for the canal. Goddard, on the other hand, complained "we have tried to get cooperation from the people who live near the canal. But we haven't seen much enthusiasm in Falls Township and below." The Delaware Valley Protective Association was less than enthusiastic; its president, Hal H. Clark, noted it had received little cooperation from groups in the lower end and opined, "if we can't get enthusiasm, you might as well take the water out of the lower end."[112]

Clifford McConnell, an engineer for the Department of Forests and Waters, spoke to a DVPA meeting in Morrisville in 1964. He lamented the condition of the so-called "lower end," noting that it had cost the department "$325 a mile last year to clear the canal of dead animals, discarded cans and cartons, shopping carts, old mattresses and other debris." Also, "vandals have damaged waste gates, locks and other devices on the lower reaches of the canal,… [and] 'unauthorized persons' had tampered with release gates, reducing the water supply to nearby industries." He threatened that the whole lower end might, as was already the case in a few short sections, be covered and run through culverts. McConnell categorically stated: "The future of the canal in this section is in jeopardy because of this misuse. I can make that a very plain statement."[113]

The fate of the lower end continued to concern many. In December of 1965, Secretary Goddard penned a letter to John Rogers, president of the Bristol Borough Council. The department had studied the problems and determined that it was "not feasible to reopen the Canal through the Borough for park and historic purposes." The estimated $200,000 cost, twice what was annually spent on the whole canal, was excessive. Goddard summarized:

> Rehabilitation of the existing structures in the Borough would still not restore this Canal historically correct. The section of Canal which was filled for construction of the school would have to be enclosed in a pipe. The Tide Lock, Lock No. 1, Lock No 2 and the Tidal Basin have also been altered or destroyed beyond recovery for historical purposes.[114]

Trash, likewise, despite the borough's efforts, was still a major problem; and there were those in the borough who "have requested approval for filling additional sections of the Canal because of the trash and sanitation problems." Because of this, the department would approve of filling from Grundy's Lake to the spot already filled, although, Goddard noted "consideration must be given to providing an overflow from Grundy Lake to the adjacent Adams Hollow Creek." For this, he promised state cooperation.

Hal Clark, in 1967, noted that one of the state's recent clean-ups of the canal had netted four hundred truckloads of junk, including seventy grocery carts.[115]

In 1969, state engineer McConnell, in response to renewed agitation, listed the money spent on the canal, noting that only its upper portions had been kept clean by the localities. According to Thomas May, another state engineer, it was necessary for the lower end to show "that they would do proper maintenance of the canal, while we would take on any capital improvements." The state would then make costly improvements to insure the continued flow of the canal. May cited as an instance the lock near Edgely, which needed improvement.[116]

A new group, the Lower Bucks County Conservation Committee, was formed in Bristol Borough in the late 1960s. It was spearheaded by Ralph Ratcliffe and Naomi Tomlinson and supported by a committee of twenty-five who stimulated a great deal of activity in a very short period of time starting in 1969, despite the opposition of many local officials. First they persuaded the Grundy Foundation to encroach on only about one-third of the Grundy Lagoon for the construction of the Grundy ice rink. They persuaded the Pennsylvania Department of Highways to decide "that the spur road to Interstate 95 would not require that the canal be piped or filled in at that

An abandoned section of the canal near the Grundy Mills in Bristol.

highway's intersection with the Pennsylvania Turnpike and Route 13." The I-95 connection that concerned the Bristol group and Dr. Goddard in 1969 is only today, in 2001, being realized, but at the turnpike interchange the flow of the canal has been severely constricted by passing it through culverts under the four-lane Route 13, under the four-lane Levittown Parkway, and again under Route 13 north of the Parkway. A similar restricting passage is found further north under the massive embankment on which is constructed the four-lane Tyburn Road.

Ralph Ratcliffe coordinated his efforts with those of Boy Scout leader Bud Stahl, who promoted a major clean-up day. Clean-Up Day, Sunday June 29, 1969, embraced much of the canal, with scouts, Jaycees, Red Cross, rescue squads and others involved in what was eventually to become an annual event along the whole canal, from Easton to Bristol.[117] Subsequently, during the following January, a Conservation Patch was created for those Boy Scouts who had participated in three canal clean-ups.[113]

Ratcliffe, a most vehement spokesman for the canal in Bristol, was described in the *Courier Times* as an avid fisherman and, in 1974, as "a middle aged postman with thinning black hair." That year he was quoted in the *Courier Times*:

Volunteers from the Falls Township Fire Company assisting with a cleanup in April, 1999. Courtesy of Friends of the Delaware Canal.

> I've lived in Bristol all my life. I grew up along the canal—that's where I used to go swimming in crystal clear water without any clothes on. I just got tired of seeing the canal go.[119]

His two main projects were "an old fashioned lock restoration on the canal near Edgely Ave. [Lock No. 4] and construction of a 'waste-water gate' in Bristol to rejuvenate the Adams Hollow Creek and control the waterflow on the canal's lower level. Ratcliffe was bitter about the desecrations to "his" canal: "That school was built illegally, on land belonging to Roosevelt State Park. It wasn't until four years later the state legislature passed a bill deeding the land to the school district." What he saw as the particular tragedy was that an alternative site would have served equally as well for the school. "There was a big field down there, but the planners didn't want to use it because of the adjoining freight yard. This is where Grundy Tower is now."[120]

It was Ratcliffe and his group who obtained Goddard's pledge in 1969 not to close down the canal. And it was Ratcliffe and Naomi Tomlinson who approached politicians at every level.[121] According to a *Philadelphia Inquirer* article,

> [When] U.S. Supreme Court Associate Justice William O. Douglas, an avid conservationist, was told of the group's efforts, [he] pledged to support [them] and walked the canal to promote its restoration.
>
> Douglas and his wife Cathy hiked the six miles of canal in the Bristol-Morrisville area two days before he went into the hospital to get a pacemaker put in his heart.
>
> 'It was a worthwhile cause,' Douglas said after the walk and most people were shocked to hear of his being hospitalized a day after the hike, in which he had set a hard pace.[122]

These activities brought about the support of the DVPA for preservation of the lower end. Goddard announced in 1971 that plans for a $350,000 improvement for Adams Hollow Creek were underway.[123]

Ratcliffe has remained vocal and active and has been joined on occasions by other equally demanding and uncompromising spokesmen for Bristol and the lower end of the canal.

Wing Dam

A wing dam across the Delaware had been erected at Wells Falls (New Hope) in the 1830s to guarantee a flow of water into the Delaware Canal south from that point. (See map on page 33) Waterwheels had been used to lift water into the canal when it was busy and boats were constantly going through locks. But after the termination of navigation, when activity on the canal slowed to a halt, the dam itself was sufficient to provide a flow of water for the use of New Hope's Union Mills and into the lower sections of the canal. Until the 1960s, Union Mills maintained the dam; by then they no longer utilized the water and therefore stopped maintenance. In 1964, Mrs. Harold F. Lodge of Washington Crossing wrote to Dr. Goddard complaining about the condition of the canal, particularly the three miles between Taylorsville and Woodside Road, between Washington Crossing and Yardley. She had been told by the superintendent that "the causes are the deterioration of the Wing Dam at New Hope," along with lack of rain and vandalism at Borden's Lock (Lock No. 7) where the overflow was left open, often for days.[124]

Efforts to resolve these problems were already underway and on Wednesday, February 24, 1965, a Delaware River Basin Commission news release announced that Governor Richard Hughes of New Jersey and Governor William Scranton of Pennsylvania had agreed to a bi-state plan for the restoration of the Lambertville-New Hope wing dam, under the supervision of the Delaware River Basin Commission. Under the agreement, the two states would share the $280,000 estimated construction cost. Design and engineering fees would raise the total to $320,000.[125]

On April 19, 1967, Herbert A. Howlett, chief engineer for the Delaware River Basin Commission, wrote Hal Clark expressing satisfaction with the Ganscer Construction Company, contractors for the work of rehabilitation of the Lambertville-New Hope wing dam, which was to be completed within 365 days. He commended Clark, noting that it was "the combined efforts of your organization [DVPA], the States of Pennsylvania and New Jersey and this office" that had finally gotten the work underway.[126] Clark was made a life member of the Delaware Valley Power Boat Association, a group that had worked with him seeking the rebuilding of the wing dam.[127]

The wing dam cost $50,574 less than had been appropriated, so the balance was returned to the coffers of the two states, an almost unheard-of phenomenon in public finance.[128]

Since the 1960s the restored wing dam, apparently left without any maintenance or even any periodic examination, has again deteriorated. In the 1990s it is even less functional than it was before it was restored in 1967, and getting water into the canal below New Hope during periods of low water in the river is problematical at best.

Superintendents

In 1963 Russell Paetzell of Upper Black Eddy retired as superintendent of Theodore Roosevelt State Park after having held that position since 1941. Paetzell had guided the state park during its difficult early years, but in the process he had alienated many former boatmen and maintenance workers. He was replaced by James W. Bailey.[129]

Bailey, by trade a construction engineer, had been employed by the state for nine years and had, as district engineer for the Department of Forests and Waters, been called in to direct the clean-up following hurricane Diane. With his wife and two children he lived in a trailer behind his "official" residence, the old Lodi Lock House, which the state was restoring. The lock house subsequently became the canal headquarters.[130]

By 1973, Richard L. Holland was superintendent.[131] Eugene Giza became superintendent in 1975. It seemed to take a special kind of person to survive as canal superintendent. Each in his way had a kind of love affair with the canal. Eugene Giza expressed it well: "I like to think of the canal as the biggest and best aspirin in Bucks County.... An hour's walk along it will take care of a lot of problems." Giza came to the job from the director's role at Delaware's Seashore State Park. A native of Clearfield County in central Pennsylvania, he desired to return to his home state.[132] He had been on the job only eight months when he confided to an interviewer: "One thing which has really impressed me so far is the way local people feel about the canal. Our crew [then numbering 16] is very dedicated. They see it as their canal. Their grandfathers built it and they work hard to keep it up. I've never seen anything like it." When he left in 1979, at the age of only 36, it was to become superintendent of Presque Isle State Park in Erie.[133]

He was succeeded by John Nuss, already regional park engineer. For the next few months he would continue as engineer along with his new role as superintendent of Stover and Roosevelt state parks. The park superintendent position paid a thousand dollars more in salary than his regional engineer's salary, which was at the maximum. This may have influenced him to take the park position with its combined staffs of seventeen in winter and nineteen in summer. Among his goals: "I plan to have a lock operating in each of the reaches of the canal—north, south and central. The planned first operational lock is Ground Hog Lock at Raubsville."[134]

Speaking to the Canal Property Owners, a group that had fought with his predecessor, Nuss, perhaps a bit more realistic, announced after less than two months in office: "A lot of the repair work which this canal desperately needs must be done when the canal is dry—bone dry" to allow heavy equipment to drive in the canal bed without sinking in the The repair work if done properly would take at least two years and up to $60 million.

Nuss would move up the next year to chief of maintenance and environmental management for the Bureau of State Parks. where he would pursue many of his concerns for the canal.

His replacement was Douglas Hoehn, then aged 35, who had been superintendent of Crooked Creek State Park for the previous six years. He stayed for nine and a half years before moving on to Ohiopyle State Park in Fayette County in 1989.[136]

Activities

The canal has been a favorite destination for visitors and tourists for many years. Not the least-interesting attraction was Pete Pascuzzo's mule-drawn "barges" in New Hope.

The canal ride has become a popular setting for special events. For example, in 1961 Governor Robert B. Meyner of New Jersey celebrated his fiftieth birthday with a party on the canal.[137] The canal barge is an attractive and unique place to celebrate weddings and to hold engagement or anniversary parties. This author has been privileged to be in attendance at one each of the latter.

Among the more noteworthy groups to party on the canal were the forty members of the teaching profession from Ireland who visited Bucks County on August 9, 1964. Shepherded by the vice president of America's Friendly Sons of St. Patrick, John Thornton of Blue Bell, Montgomery County, and Bucks County Commissioner Walter Farley, they boarded the barges had a clam-bake at the picnic grounds along the towpath and exchanged citations and commendations.[138]

Hal Clark commented on the visit:

A large group of Irish educators, upon returning home from an extended tour of America, wrote to Governor Scranton that their finest day in this country was spent along the River Road on a mule drawn canal boat ride on the Delaware Canal. They said, "never let this treasure be destroyed." Dr. Goddard warned us never to excite any more Irish since he had to answer all of the letters.[139]

Hal Clark subsequently received a letter from Dr. Stephen Daly of Dublin, Ireland, one of the educators, in which Daly noted: "There is a movement on foot in this country to close down some of the canals. Already there is an Association formed to fight the Government." Daly was furnishing them with material on the history of the DVPA and its struggle for preservation of the canal.[140]

Ownership

The problems of maintaining and policing a sixty-mile canal park are continual. Residents along the canal, were ever-ready to protest when the state, regardless of cause, failed to maintain water in the canal, or when the property owners along the canal felt that they were being imposed upon, or their privacy invaded, by "outsiders" using the canal and the towpath. A number of property owners along the canal had deeds dating from the mid-nineteenth century specifying that their property extended to the center of the canal, even though the issuers had never had the legal right to execute such deeds.

Periodically the owners organized and attempted to exercise what they conceived as their legal property rights as leverage in an attempt to get the state to improve maintenance on the canal. In September of 1968 an *ad hoc* group calling itself the Delaware Canal Property Owners Association threatened to start a court suit to determine whether the state even owned all the canal. Two of the leaders, Emery Nemethy and Joseph Butera of Point Pleasant, appeared at the regular meeting of the Bucks County Commissioners to protest. According to the two, the state had destroyed plantings and in one case had ripped down a $600 post-and-rail fence.

The dispute dragged on. According to Carl R. Mapel, Jr., an assistant state attorney general, the property owners were not really ready to question the state's title; rather, "they just want to put as much pressure as they can on the state to spend as much money on the canal as it can." He expressed the state's willingness to try to increase the inadequate number of men assigned to police the canal, and to enforce the ban on motorcycles on the towpath. He also said that he would talk to the barge concessionaires and tell them, "Listen Charlie: Stop letting those people throw beer cans from the barges."[141]

Secretary Goddard, apparently exasperated by the claims of the "harassed" residents and the sympathetic hearing given them by the Board of County Commissioners, fired off a "hard-biting" letter telling the commissioners that "reports of harassment by maintenance workers on the canal were 'biased, distorted and rarely are objective.'" He noted that if Bucks County was dissatisfied with the state's efforts, he "would be glad to transfer its [the canal's] ownership to the county." The state had, he reiterated, spent more than $1.7 million since 1955 on the canal. Goddard's message was supplemented by a telegram from Assistant Attorney General Mapel, more succinctly laying down the same challenge. The Bucks County commissioners, in response to Goddard's letter, replied, "we no longer support what we now believe is an unwarranted and continuous attack upon your department." The gauntlet had been thrown: if a suit were entered, all maintenance on the canal would end.[142]

The several newspapers published by the Delaware Valley Publishing Co. in New Hope and Lambertville editorialized on March 20 noting that, happily, the Canal Property Owners Association had become silent. The editorial noted this was positive, for

> they were haggling with the head of a department who has a record of doing his best to maintain the canal in excellent condition despite efforts in Harrisburg to cut costs. If Goddard ever loses interest in the Delaware Canal, you can rest assured the Canal Property Owners will beg him to come back, imperfections, if he has any, and all.[143]

In May of 1969, the Canal Property Owners Association prepared a position paper that outlined its concerns. Couched in less-abrasive language, they set forth their concerns, many of which were real and not particularly extreme. Without giving up their contention of ownership, they requested boundary markers and special exceptions for those who needed to use the towpath with motor vehicles to reach their homes or properties. Under "maintenance," they hoped efforts would be made to stop erosion along the canal, to maintain the water level at all times, and to restore the locks. Under "housekeeping," they requested regular mowing, clean-up of "trash, beer cans, etc." and the "strategic placement of 'litter' baskets," and called for rest rooms, because "present practice is to use the bushes, often on private property in a rather indiscriminate manner." Finally, under public relations, they listed their grievances:

– curt and often sarcastic remarks in answers to questions
– attempts to license or remove private docks
– refusal to allow property owners access to their land by vehicle
– indiscriminate raising lowering of water levels
– threatened and actual removal of trees and shrubbery on private property.[144]

Many of these concerns, real or imagined, continue, even down to the present day.

Vandalism, Accidents and Surveillance

It is impossible to calendar all the numerous acts of vandalism and misuse of property that have been committed and continued to be committed along the canal, but let a few examples suffice.

On the night of February 7, 1961, the 205-year-old Centre Bridge Inn was destroyed by fire. The temperature was +2° Fahrenheit and the canal was almost completely frozen, which deprived the firefighters of the ability to use the canal as a water source. They used a chain saw to cut through two feet of ice to get a little water, too little to save the historic building. An important reason for keeping water in the canal had always been for the potential to fight fires but freezing was a further problem. In 1977, during a deep freeze, the New Hope Eagle Fire Company cut holes in the 18" ice on the canal, holes which they covered with plastic and kept open for firefighting purposes. The park superintendent expressed concern over the 2' x 3' holes and asked that the holes be covered and clearly marked. Most years such extreme measures were unnecessary.[145]

On Sunday, June 16, 1963, vandals dynamited a tree into the canal in Solebury Township north of New Hope. Township Police Chief John Wagner said Primacord, a rope-like explosive, had been wrapped around the tree, dropping it in such a way as to block the canal. Pete Pascuzzo charged that the dynamiting was deliberately aimed at interfering with his canal barge operations.[146] Following this and other incidents a $25 reward fund was set up independently by members of the DVPA in an effort to offset the activities of vandals. As Hal Clark noted, "vandals no longer confine themselves to such acts as throwing picnic tables and park benches into the canal." Some three weeks after the tree was dynamited the canvas top and some of the chairs of one of the barges was destroyed by fire.[147]

A DVPA news release of March 29, 1966, reported racing cars and motorcycles on the towpath, which was becoming a nuisance to people living in the area and a danger to pedestrians on the towpath, as well as damaging the towpath. Some were reported as actually racing while others were using it as an auxiliary highway. The canal superintendent reported that gates and warning signs erected to prevent these practices had been sabotaged. The DVPA asked citizens to report license numbers of both cars and motorcycles.[148]

Trashing and dumping remain eternal problems. The debris could take many forms—shopping carts were legend. During 1966, the clean-up crew took from the canal .0north of Upper Black Eddy parts of Corvettes, some old and some new, which they turned over to the police.[149]

Residents along the canal certainly had reasons for concern. The canal had become to Emery Nemethy and many of his neighbors, "a royal pain in the anatomy. The motorbikes (at least in the past), the Great Unwashed with their beer cans, soda bottles, candy wrappers, and other trash—the screamers, the nitwits with their air rifles shooting at snakes—I'd cheerfully see them all (and this goes for Maurice Goddard, too) dead at my feet."[150]

Trash dumped into the poorly watered canal was a constant source of irritation for those living alongside the canal.

Gravel Pits and Quarries

During 1966 and 1967 the subject of quarries along the canal became a matter of concern. Leading the fight, as usual, was Hal Clark and the DVPA. His letter to Governor Raymond P. Shafer succinctly summarized his concerns:

> Gravel pits are dispoiling *[sic]* the scenic River Road and Theodore Roosevelt State Park causing gradual deterioration of one of Eastern Pennsylvania's most scenic tourist attractions. This will eventually lead to loss of revenue to the area and to the state by loss of the tourist dollar—one of our largest sources of income in the state.[151]

There were still numerous spots along the canal that were either possible park sites or sites for "uncontrolled gravel pits," Clark told the governor.

Secretary Goddard responded that the situation was being considered, but as the major concern was aesthetic, the DVPA and local governments would be most effective through passing suitable zoning ordinances.[152] Goddard also called for support of State Senate Bill No. 492, a measure that would subject gravel pit and quarry owners to the same obligations as the coal strip miners, with requirements for backfill and reclamation.[153]

Chief engineer McConnell's response to a note from Edmund A. Scotch of Rocklidge illustrates the problems and the frustrations. Yes, trees had been cut near the Lumberville lock and bulldozers were removing gravel from the edge of the canal. The trees were on private property but "Despite this, we had tried for several years to dissuade the owner from taking this action and digging the gravel on the property." The canal property was only about 70 feet wide and the returns for exploiting the sand and gravel deposits were attractive. It was also happening in Uhlerstown, Upper Black Eddy, Kintnersville and other places. The Commonwealth did not have the power to stop these activities, McConnell pointed out; local ordinances were the most effective weapons.[154]

Tragedies

A detailed history of the canal could be a litany of drownings, ever since the original construction of the canal. Most were, at best, small news items if they were reported at all, especially those that involved young victims, or were work-related tragedies. However, in the second half of the twentieth century, when a drowning occurred in a state park it was news. It was also maw for hungry lawyers.

In 1967, two-year-old Jacqueline Clardy of Yardley, Pennsylvania, wandered away from her mother and drowned in the canal. Reacting to the tragic event, William Detraz, also of Yardley, collected over 100 signatures on a petition asking Yardley to "get rid of the canal or at least have it fenced off." He dispatched his petition along with a registered letter to Governor Shafer. The canal's long-time defender, Hal H. Clark, president of the DVPA and member of the Bucks County Park Board, argued in defense of the canal. He lamented the loss of a child's life, but

> … destroying historical beautiful landmarks is not the answer. If the canal was converted into a road, for instance, many more children would die, with the speeding trucks, which come roaring through Yardley.[155]

The cost of draining and filling the canal would be tremendous, he said, and commented on the utility of the canal: had there been no canal half the town would have been burned to the ground in the late 1950s.[156]

By the 1970s, new forces, both intangible and tangible, would impact the complex questions of the canal and its survival. The nation was being swayed by forces, often of gloom, calling for the necessities of preservation and of ecological awareness. Professional park, wilderness, and environmental managers were appearing on the scene and seemingly there would be at least some greater degree of public awareness of the canal and the state park as players in the new game plan.

~ CHAPTER IX ~

From Theodore Roosevelt to
Delaware Canal State Park

Passing the Torch

In 1974, Hal Clark expressed opposition to a proposal to discharge effluent or other waste material into the canal. His comments succinctly summarized the accomplishments of the Delaware Valley Protective Association, which had been strongly supported by a partnership with Dr. Goddard of the Pennsylvania Department of Environmental Resources. The canal provided fire protection and irrigation water, it supported recreation, nature and tourism, and on four occasions it had been refurbished by the Bureau of State Parks after having been broken and filled with debris. Additionally, the DVPA itself

> [had] reduced pollution in the upper region of the Canal by 65% in one month. The Boy Scouts helped us. We have faced dumping from State Highway trucks, also crank case oil, garbage, etc., etc., Systematically we have contained it by vigilance.
>
> The dumping from the Levittown Shopping Center was stopped only when refinancing required Dr. Goddard's okay. To open a Canal blockade at Morrisville several years ago, Dr. Goddard removed thousands of yards of dumpage, etc. Shortly afterward the Highway Dept. planned to fill it in with dirt, run a small pipe through and build an unnecessary access road over the Canal for Rt. #1. We are the only group that fought it and stopped it. Otherwise the lower end of the Canal would have been in immediate jeopardy. Many other major pollution emergencies occurred including when flue dust tanks at Bethlehem Steel Corp. poured heavy cyanide pollution into the Lehigh River. It then polluted the Delaware Canal and the Delaware River at Easton. DVPA checked this out to a successful conclusion in cooperation with the industry and the states involved. There was a great loss of fish life.[1]

During the next few years, Clark, who reached the ripe old age of 90 in 1980, saw leadership of the movement pass to other organizations.[2] Virginia Forrest, still active in the DVPA and increasingly the canal historian and a spokesman for the Bucks County Conservation Alliance and C.P. "Bill" Yoder, curator of the collections of the Pennsylvania Canal Society and Easton's Hugh Moore Park, were becoming more visible advocates for the canal.

In 1979, Superintendent Giza wrote Hal Clark, asking him to meet with Mrs. Betty Orlemann, who had lived along the canal for two years. Mrs. Orlemann, at the time a newspaper reporter, was doing research on the canal for future publications. In 1982, "Betty of Smithtown," who would become the major force in founding a new group, the Friends of the Delaware Canal, was reported in the *Intelligencer* as challenging the state Department of Environmental Resources to provide adequate funding for the canal. Reporter Florence Schaffhausen quoted Betty in an article:

> [It is] costing DER hundreds of thousands of dollars because work cannot be done when trouble is first spotted. Take the cave-in at Durham Lock. This situation was spotted five years ago, when a minor repair would have prevented expensive damage. By the time bids are advertised, the cost goes sky-high.[3]

There was a maintenance crew of only 16 and too little money, according to Mrs. Orlemann. Further, when the Delaware River was low, as it had been a few days earlier in September of 1982, water was observed in the outlet lock running from the canal into the river instead of from the river into the canal: "A few-inch drop in the Delaware River level means no water in the southern end of the canal."

Weary of watching the deterioration that was occasioned by there never being enough state money to deal with pressing needs along the canal, Mrs. Orlemann announced a meeting on Wednesday evening, October 13, 1982, at the Towpath House in New Hope "and was astounded when 30 people showed up." She had scheduled a barge ride and her slide presentation, along with conch shells blown by former boatmen Frank and Howard Swope. Lance Metz of the Canal Museum in Easton showed the 1952 Roy Creveling film, "Paradise Ditch," and Doug Hoehn, superintendent of the Roosevelt State Park, gave an address. Out of this meeting came the Friends of the Delaware Canal.[4]

Mrs. Orlemann said the purpose of the group was "to bug Harrisburg and try to get money for a project. We got tired of seeing an empty canal." Some of the plans may have been a little too exalted: according to an *Intelligencer* article, when "warmer weather returns, Mrs. Orlemann and her group will dig out shallow parts of the canal and try to strengthen its borders."[5]

Maintenance

The valley again was pelted by heavy rainstorms over the second weekend in July of 1975. The more than two-and-a-quarter inches of rain caused heavy flooding in Upper Black Eddy and Erwinna, where flood waters entered a number of buildings and devastated the planted fields of farmers in the area. At Upper Black Eddy it caused a heavy flow of water from Lodi Creek "over the canal lock and debris then blocked the lock-raising mechanism … the lock could not be raised until four men could join in the effort. A large log was reported in the lock early today." According to Superintendent Eugene Giza, stones, gravel and mud in the canal north of Menders Creek formed a dam, and culverts were stopped up south of Tinicum Park. More than 4,500 fish were reported rescued from the drained canal during the following week.[6]

In 1978, Giza spelled out part of the problem:

Because of some 300 road drainage pipes from Routes 32 and 611 and some 175 tributaries emptying into the canal, large debris bars have been deposited. To provide adequate flow of water in the canal, it is necessary to overflow these debris bars with a full head of water. A makeshift aqueduct cannot supply the necessary amount of water to accomplish this, nor can pumps maintain an adequate flow.[7]

The amount of hydraulic engineering required to sustain the canal was sizeable. In 1978, after Erwinna Creek broke through the canal walls, not only were the walls repaired and the gravel and other debris in the canal dredged, but the creek was permanently rerouted.[8]

It was in 1978 that the state brought in a pump in response to the pleas of New Hope borough officials who worried about fire threats, and also to provide water for the mule barge concession, a major tourist attraction. Superintendent Giza noted that the pump would "provide about three feet of water, compared with the normal level of 4½ feet. The six-inch pump will have to operate 24 hours a day…and George Schwieckhardt who owned the barge ride concession, would be responsible for security and maintenance of the equipment."[9] Unfortunately, however, the pump was not operated on a constant basis.

Portions of the Kenwood section of Levittown were flooded by a break in the canal on Sunday, July 27, 1980. A hole about the size of a basketball was discovered about 9:00 AM and by 1:00 PM it had grown to "a gaping eight by four-foot gusher that would have drained all of the 60-mile canal into Levittown had not locks been closed at Edgely and Mill Creek by the fire company." The park ranger suggested that a muskrat might be the culprit. Streets were flooded to several feet but damage was limited to several lawns. A fishy smell pervaded the neighborhood for a short time.[10]

The canal was again empty during the fall and winter of 1981 and into the following spring. A leak and a dangerous weakness in the canal wall was discovered by a jogger who fell into a three-foot-deep hole in the towpath on the weekend of October 25. Luckily, he was not injured.

Betty Orlemann's account in the *Delaware Valley News* provided the detail:

> ... the park employees ... lowered the water level from Easton to Lumberville ... by shutting the guard lock at Easton.... Dye tests ... proved that canal water is leaking into the Delaware River from the base of the canal slope ... "I want to keep at least a low flow of water in the canal for the fish," says Hoehn, "but it is essential to have a very low flow at the site of the collapse to keep the water from breaking through the towpath and blowing out the entire section of canal and towpath." [11]

Some of the lining was missing and 50 yards or more of towpath were threatened in the same spot as the 1973 collapse. At that time, the holes had been filled with dirt, the hole in the canal plugged, and a lining put in. The proposed solution this time was to fill the holes with concrete, pumped across the canal from Route 611. When a seal was formed the channels were to be pressure-grouted. The canal had be dry for the entire reach, a process that takes about a week. Then the six-inch clay liner had to be replaced. Regional Superintendent of State Parks Robinson estimated it would take a day or two to replace the liner using a crane. If it was found necessary to use heavy equipment on the towpath side of the canal, earthen coffer dams were to be built to road level as transportation routes for the trucks. This would take several weeks. The work was estimated to take at least two months and possibly much longer.

By April the job was completed. Then a rainstorm caused a washout of a waste gate in the work area, delaying the refilling of the 60-mile-long waterway until June. On July 18, a wall collapsed at the Durham aqueduct and Roosevelt State Park authorities said it would be autumn before the wall would be repaired. There was no chance that the canal would be carrying water in time for fall foliage and its accompanying tourists.[12]

In 1984, six months after a sensational drowning, Bruce Dallas, public information officer for the DER, described the state's plans for upgrading the canal. These plans were placed on a speeded-up schedule because of the drowning six months earlier of Jessica Savitch, a young NBC anchor, and her companion in the canal at New Hope. The state had decided to build three bridges at a cost of $60,000 each to replace culverts across the canal. These were among the 45 culverts across the canal that had been installed after the hurricane floods of 1955 wiped out bridges along the canal. The culverts impeded the flow of water, and, according to Superintendent Hoehn, during the previous four months the result had been three floods and $250,000 damage to canal property, mostly canal walls.[13]

In 1985, the state purchased two larger pumps to replace a smaller, inadequate one to maintain the water level at New Hope. The Friends, the barge operators, and many of the residents along the canal challenged William C. Forrey, director of the Bureau of State Parks, to put the pumps into operation, particularly as after heavy March rains repairs of the resulting flood damage were lagging.[14]

During the commercial years of the canal, the state or the company had paid a bounty for the muskrats and water snakes that would burrow into the canal banks and create leakage. They still plagued the canal in 1979. According to then-canal foreman Sandy Miller, when muskrat damage was reported a workman was dispatched to the spot. There, "the workman places broken glass in the hole to discourage the return of the muskrat. He then mends the hole with mud and clay to prevent further leakage." If the muskrat burrowed too close to the surface, the towpath might collapse into the burrow; it would then be necessary to use a backhoe, to dig out the hole, fill it, and pack it securely. Miller estimated that in the previous year, 1978-1979, about 1,500 to 2,000 traps had been set along the 60-mile canal, yielding close to 14,000 muskrats. Pelts at that time brought $5.00 to $5.30 and sometimes even $6.00. For gourmets and gourmands, Miller noted that muskrats were "sometimes called 'Marsh rabbits', and are considered by many to be a delicacy ... that is because they eat only the finest vegetation."[15]

Plant growth in the canal had become a major problem because of the fluctuation of the water level. *The News* of Frenchtown, New Jersey, published a photograph on September 2, 1976, showing park employees spreading weed killer on the canal.[16] Plant growth has since become an even greater problem, and by mid-summer, water primrose and duckweed have in many places almost completely choked the canal and new environmental regulations have severely narrowed the options for plant control that were

Members of the Pennsylvania Canal Society examining the guard lock, feeder channel and weigh lock at Easton during a field trip in May of 1968. The guard lock is the entrance to the Delaware Canal. The overhead structures are bridges of the Lehigh Valley Railroad and the Central Railroad of New Jersey, which crossed from Pennsylvania into New Jersey at this point. These were major coal railroads that would have put the canals out of business had it not been for coal dealers along the canal who had no other means of getting their supplies until roads were improved and trucks were used for delivery.

Below is the feeder dam at the mouth of the Lehigh River, which raised the water level so the Delaware Canal could be watered. This photo was also taken during the PCS field trip in 1968.

available in 1976. This became a particular concern for Ralph Ratcliffe, a Bristol-based spokesman for the "lower end."[17]

Alternating floodings and droughts have continued, and waterless and low-water periods along the canal have encouraged sometimes rank plant growth along its 60-mile length. Together, they have reduced the actual water depth to a now-usual two or three feet and sometimes only a few inches.

Superintendents

This was one hell of a year; labor scarce, high water, no boatmen, food high, cost sheet going wrong way and everybody with chips on their shoulders. Nothing but fight, fight! Hell has no terror; can't be anything worse than trying to run a damn old ditch like this.

1917 Canal Superintendent

This has been one hell of a year; labor scarce, water high, union troubles, high prices, budget book going wrong way and everybody with chips on their shoulders. Nothing but fight, fight! Hell has no terror; can't be anything worse than trying to run a damn old ditch like this.

1984 Canal Superintendent

These quotes were appended to the agenda of a state meeting held in January of 1984.[18] Being a superintendent was not an easy job.

Douglas Hoehn, who served from 1980 to 1989, expressed the hope that during his tenure progress had "been made between neighbors and the park.... I think we're getting away from the syndrome of fix it in my back yard and that's all that matters."[19] It was during his tenure that, despite a diminishing staff and budgetary reductions, a new optimism surfaced for the canal's future with the creation of a Friends of the Delaware Canal organization, the development of the Master Plan, and the creation of the Delaware and Lehigh Canal National Heritage Corridor, discussed in the next chapter.

Design and Restoration

In January of 1968, Clayton P. "Bill" Yoder, curator and spokesman for the two-year-old Pennsylvania Canal Society, sought the support of the well-established DVPA. He wrote Bruce Singer, vice president of the DVPA, to oppose what appeared to be prospective alterations by the state park to Lock Number 24, the guard lock at Easton. The original configuration included the guard lock, which was 22 feet wide by 100 feet long; a weigh lock, the only one on the line of the canal; and a feeder channel for supplying water to the canal. The feeder control gates at the upper end had a massive and very interesting operating mechanism for the gates. Yoder believed these facilities were the most massive and well-preserved examples of fine masonry to be found on the canal.

Yoder opposed the proposed maintenance program, in which the state planned to remove all these facilities and replace them with a single lock 11 feet in width and enclose the feeder in a tube, thus entirely eliminating its visual presence and historical integrity. He documented the history of the structure and shared with Hal Clark his judgments on the plans of the parks department:

It would be a veritable crime to destroy at this late date those examples of fine engineering and stone masonry that have existed since the beginning of the canal. It is unfortunate, but true, that through the commendable process of maintenance, the old canal is gradually losing its identity. It is evidently the policy of the Department to replace the open feeders that exist at most locks for supplying down stream water with underground tubes.... In addition to introducing added restrictions to the flow of water, the sight and sound of the water flowing through these open streams has been eliminated. I am aware that a limited budget is available for canal maintenance; why squander a portion of it in eliminating these open feeders that have been adequate for one hundred and forty years and which add so much to the beauty of the lock areas.[21]

Chief Engineer McConnell informed Hal Clark in March of 1968 that there was but $125,000 planned for the Easton lock project, which limited the options. To restore the lock authentically would take $400,000, "yet we must repair the lock immediately to prevent deterioration of the structure with subsequent detrimental effects on the entire canal."[22] Yoder's letter had its effect. When restored, the central lock received "new stone-faced walls over the present walls, reducing the width from 22 to 17½ feet."[23] Reconstruction of the guard lock was completed in 1971 by the Belmont Contracting Co. of Pottstown for a final cost of $174,141.[24]

At least until about 1980, canal superintendents planned to restore the canal eventually to working condition. Certainly as early as 1974, the dream was being actively pursued. In December of that year, DER employees Eugene Mulitsch and Louis Agosta were at work at Groundhog (Raubsville) Lock constructing replicas of canal gates. Without blueprints, they pulled old gates out of water and mud and made exact replicas using long-leaf yellow pine and wooden dowels.[25] The *Easton Express* ran a photograph of the gates lying on the ground in December, and another one in January showing the gates being installed, apparently unsuccessfully. In the spring of 1979 another set of gates was being constructed.[26]

A story in the April 29, 1979 *New York Times* promised that

Five miles from the northern end of the canal, at the Ground Hog lock in Raubsville, the springtime work holds potentially the biggest summer treat of all. A working lock, which will be the only one on the canal will be installed there.[27]

This time the construction material was pressure-treated hemlock, put together with handmade dowels and mortises plus iron bands from hardware original to the canal. Superintendent Giza said that with the specially treated lumber that was used, the gates would last 100 years. Every attempt was made to duplicate the original hardware, drop gate, wickets, etc.[28] The gates were installed and water was let in. Unfortunately, they failed to hold. George F. "Sparky" Cochran, retired from maintenance in the State Park, did not see the mishap, but remembers the disappointment registered on his fellow workers' faces as they reported that the gates had "washed out."[29]

In 1981, the state committed much of its park budget to adapting park facilities for use by the handicapped. Roosevelt Park received some $30,000 which went for an "easy-access latrine" at Centre Bridge, low charcoal grills at spots along the canal, and special picnic tables with handrails and one clear side for wheelchairs, plus fishing ramps for handicapped anglers. This postponed the construction of a new park headquarters until the next year, when $150,000 was budgeted for a new structure at Lodi. The plans were made public in February. The 150-plus-year-old locktender's house would be refurbished with the hope that at some future date it would be made into an interpretative center. The new building, replacing the existing shed, would resemble an L-shaped ranch house with the short side facing Lodi Hill Road. This portion would contain offices and a visitors center while the long side, hidden from the road, would house workshops and garage bays. The narrow, .9-acre lot along the canal had been donated by former Tinicum Township supervisor Bill Darrow. Because of the dimensions of the property, the structure would not conform to the township zoning codes and a variance was necessary.

In August the state modified the plans, possibly influenced by the petition signed by 45 neighbors opposing the structure, claiming "it would change the character of the neighborhood," but even more because the bureau discovered their $150,000 was insufficient to implement the plans. The restrained plan would replace the existing long shed with a single cinderblock building containing shops, an employees' lunchroom and lavatories.[30]

Not everyone was enamored with this concern for 2the staff and the commitment of resources for the new headquarters. The structure was never built. Virginia Forrest, activist environmentalist and defender of the canal, wrote Wilson Oberdorfer, legal counsel for the DER:

One other thing I can't understand is, we have 14 or 16 working men trying to keep the canal and locks in as good condition as possible. Meanwhile, I've been told, a whole new building is being put up for the staff along with a place for them to eat. If we have waited this long without spending so much money, wouldn't it be better to put extra men on the job?[31]

Registry and Landmark Designations

In 1974, the canal was placed on the National Register of Historic Places, culminating the work of many. Working under the chairmanship of Virginia Forrest of the Bucks County Conservation Alliance, the application was prepared by C.P. Yoder, curator of the Canal Museum at Easton since its creation in 1970 and curator of the collections of the Pennsylvania Canal Society. The materials came from the files under Yoder's supervision and from the accumulations of the DVPA, which had been working to preserve the canal for thirty years. The application was then dispatched to the Director of Historic Preservation of the Pennsylvania Historic and Museum Commission, where a map was prepared, the application completed, and forwarded to Washington. When acceptance finally resulted, all of those involved felt an important step had been taken in their long fight to preserve the canal.[32]

In 1975, the Boy Scouts of America (Minsi Trails Council), taking advantage of the historical designation, brought out a 45-page guide book for the 60-mile trail following the canal. They tied this trail into a network of historic trails across the United States. Artist William Tompkins of Solebury Township designed a shoulder patch to represent the Scouts' achievements. [33]

Preservationist and advocate for the Delaware Canal, Virginia Forrest. Courtesy of the Friends of the Delaware Canal.

The proponents of canal preservation were not satisfied. By 1975, they were pushing for "National Landmark" status, which "would protect [the canal] from federal encroachment in the name of progress." [34] Virginia Forrest announced on December 20, 1976, that the formal papers had been signed by the interior secretary in Washington on December 8 and that the official announcement would soon be forthcoming.[35]

On June 21, 1978, a ceremony was held at New Hope dedicating the canal as a National Historic Landmark. The dignitaries present used the occasion to pay tribute to the volunteers who over the years had worked to preserve the canal. The designation should, according to New Hope's mayor, "write an end [to any attempt] to fill the canal in order to widen River Road (Route 32)." Dr. Maurice K. Goddard, secretary of the Pennsylvania Department of Environmental Resources, praised the work of those who had labored so long and hard to preserve the canal and noted that the state had, since 1955, spent $3,838,329 on maintenance, repair, and restoration of the canal.

The venerable Virginia Forrest, chairman of the historical committee of the Bucks County Conservation Alliance, urged letter-writing to the legislature that was cutting state-park funds. "The people who use it [the canal] should take care of it," protested one New Hope resident who finger-pointed at the mule-drawn barge concession at New Hope and the canoe concession at Point Pleasant. "Most of the junk and stuff in the canal comes from people on the barges or in those canoes. They should be made to clean up," said another New Hope resident.

Three bronze plaques were distributed. One was to be mounted at New Hope. A second was presented to Bill Yoder, curator of the Canal Museum at Easton, for mounting at the upper end of the canal. The third, for Bristol, was accepted by Naomi Tomlinson of the Lower Bucks Canal Conservation Committee.[36] These markers soon had to be replaced, since the Heritage Conservation and Recreation Service, which administered the National Register and Landmark programs, was reabsorbed by the National Park Service.

Above left is one of the plaques that mark the designation of the Delaware Canal as a National Historic Landmark. Above right is one of several state historic markers that are found along the canal.

The Persisting Question of Ownership

In 1977, the question of ownership of the Delaware Canal resurfaced. Wilson Oberdorfer, director of legal services for the state Department of Environmental Resources, announced that as a result of lengthy research through canal commissioners' records from the early nineteenth century, the state's title to the Delaware Canal was confirmed. He suggested a campaign of education to try to offset the long-held contentions of property owners along the canal to the contrary. While there had been deeds issued during the nineteenth century granting property rights to the center of the canal, these had been issued without any authority.[37]

In September of 1978, Edward J. Encelowski, who designated himself as corresponding secretary for the Canal Property Owners (CPO) wrote Governor Shapp complaining that Wilson Oberdorfer had made

> extensive use of people and time in research of deeds, etc. and therefore has undoubtedly caused great expenditures of tax payers monies. We question the propriety of this and therefore ask you to determine who among the officials, whether elected, appointed or hired, authorized such expenditures. There is a mockery here inasmuch as some of the monies expended were provided by us to be used against our interests.[38]

On behalf of the organization, its president George English, and the writer, the letter claimed harassment and challenged the legality of the expenditure of public funds.

The agitation continued and in March of the next year, 1979, residents of Tinicum and Plumstead township who owned property bordering the canal finally formally organized the Canal Property Owners. George English of Smithtown was elected president; Elinor Robbins who lived next to the canal in Uhlerstown despite a Frenchtown, N.J., post office address, became one of the officers. One of her children had drowned in the canal and she and her husband had shored up the berm bank next to their house with old tires. "Until the state can prove that it owns the land, we own it," said English, who claimed support of the majority of the property owners along the thirteen miles of canal in the two townships. Residents along the canal were concerned not only because of the state's claim to ownership of both the towpath and the berm bank, but also because

> [they] have been asked to remove so-called encroachments on the land bordering the canal, including structures, patios and walls. They also have been told they must have docks on the canal licensed and must remove or renovate docks which are in poor repair.[39]

A break in the canal wall in Upper Black Eddy in mid-August of 1978 drained the canal for an 18-mile stretch from that point to New Hope, including Plumstead and Tinicum townships. This gave George English, CPO president, an opportunity to talk of a "war" and to accuse the state of land theft and harassment.[40]

On August 15 of 1979, park superintendent Eugene V. Giza, exasperated at what he apparently conceived as continuing harassment, released a letter to the *Delaware Valley News* of Frenchtown, New Jersey. He accused English of baiting the state over the previous four years but now, as the final straw, "he has gone one step too far in threatening to 'blow a hole' in a State park employee."

Giza listed a bill of particulars. The English property had been purchased in 1973, in the name of his wife, Betty, and the deed did not read to the center of the canal. In 1974, when he was questioned about driving on the towpath, English claimed to have an agreement permitting him the right—which he could never present, always claiming it was "somewhere inside the house." According to Giza, this triggered the organization of the Canal Property Owners and the appeal to the press. This effort had been abortive: both attorneys and a cooperative title insurance company had recommended against further pursuit of any idea of suing the state. Then, in July of 1979, a citation was finally issued to Mrs. English because her car "was frequently parked on the towpath in front of her house." This had been preceded by complaints of area residents who had been forced to leave the towpath in order to pass the obstructing vehicle to continue their walk, and the complaint of a neighbor who was concerned that the vehicle blocked any emergency use of the towpath. Mrs. English had been issued many courtesy notices, and Giza noted that as citations were also issued to others for such violations, these could not be ignored. Since that time, English had planted hemlock seedlings on the towpath in an area normally mowed and had twice prevented the mowing of the area with intimidating threats to the canal worker. After being subjected to profane language and threats, Giza returned with a trooper who ordered the plants removed, at which point English proclaimed harassment in the press. Giza said, "Enough," but added that he could now work with the newly elected officers of the Canal Property Owners.[41]

Some of the virulence seemed to die after a meeting held at Conti's Restaurant in Doylestown on October 4, 1979, apparently called by Virginia Forrest. From the meeting's minutes, a mix of detail and careless editing, it would appear that those present were Virginia Forrest, her daughter Virginia Hutton, William C. Forrey, director of State Parks, Wilson Oberdorfer, legal counsel for DER, and members of the Canal Property Owners. Except for a "Linda," the members of the CPO are not identified in the minutes.[42]

There was a great deal of give-and-take. Oberdorfer presented a most detailed history of canal ownership and offered to document, if requested, any particular piece of property. He also explained how, in condemnation procedures, title could pass with no specific deeds being executed. One question he fielded concerned home ownership:

— I think we are concerned about the people whose houses are there. Do they own their houses?

Oberdorfer: Of course!

— They do, even if it is on the bank?

Mr. Oberdorfer: Now wait a minute. There may be a couple of encroachments but we have never told anybody to remove anything. The question is what are we going to do now about the encroachments that were made years ago. The policy that has been announced and that has been told to all the township commissioners is that we are going to try to prevent new encroachments and deal with old encroachments as time and resources permit.[43]

The meeting appears to have ended in agreement on one thing, that there was need for cooperation and collective action on behalf of the canal, but no one really seemed anxious to step forward and provide leadership for the organization.

The issues have not died, for there are still some property owners who are convinced that their deeds give them ownership to the center of the canal. There are hundreds of minor encroachments on canal property, and a number of major ones, where construction has impinged on state property or which have created obstructions that limit passage over the full extent of the state property. Most are in abeyance, awaiting eventual state legal action.[44]

River Heights Towpath Towers

Rumblings of what was to occur surfaced in January of 1973 when M.H. Apartments, Inc., sought permission to build a bridge across the canal. The DER held a public hearing in Morrisville and denied permission. The issue reappeared in May. Now the developer, Edward B. Boyer, was seeking various exceptions from the Morrisville ordinances for a proposed fourteen-story apartment house along the canal at the northern boundary of the borough. The exceptions sought dealt with on-site sewage disposal, entry grades, and density. The area totaled about nine and one-half acres, six and one-half west of the canal on which the high-rise would be constructed and approximately two and one-half on the east (River Road) side of the canal. Most of the six and one-half acres had 15° to 25° grades and were covered with old trees, some 150 years old.

Morrisville Councilman John Hofmann said the plan, particularly the provisions for parking, bothered him, and that "completion-wise, it's going to be nothing but a lot of asphalt with a big building in it." The Lower Makefield Township supervisors were already on record opposing the plan, thus denying the developers any outlet other than across the canal and depriving them of adjoining acreage in Lower Makefield for supplemental parking. Morrisville had already denied an entry from Crown Street to the property.[45]

Even so, in July, Morrisville borough council approved the plan by a 5-1 vote. The carrot on the stick held out to the council was the lure of additional tax receipts, estimated to be about $114,000 in borough taxes and over $300,000 in school taxes. In September of 1973, M.H. Apartments, listing former Bucks County Commissioner Edward Boyer, Morrisville CPA Arthur M. Nicholson, and Philadelphia attorney Melvin Bank as principals, entered an appeal to encroach on the canal for the building of a bridge to the Pennsylvania Environmental Hearing Board, the review body for the DER. Oral arguments were held in February and in September. According to the DER lawyer, Timothy Weston, a "gentleman's agreement" was reached whereby the Morrisville parties would withdraw their appeal and the DER agreed not to oppose any special legislation granting "a license" to M.H. Apartments.[46]

It had now become a political matter. In December of 1974 Representative Marvin Weidner from Upper Bucks County and three other Bucks County representatives, Republicans Edward F. Burns, Jr., John S. Renninger, and Benjamin Wilson and one Democrat, James A.J. Gallagher, introduced House Bill 3724 to support the developers. It died in committee. Republican State Representative James Wright, Jr., who represented Morrisville, did not support it. Assemblyman Weidner, when questioned, said that when he was approached by Bucks GOP Chairman Harry Fawkes to help out the partners in M.H. Apartments by introducing the bill he agreed, but "I'm not pushing it. I did what was required of me, and that's it." He did, however, say that part of his reason for seeking the special license to cross the canal was retaliation for what he considered an unattractive bridge built about four years before across the canal in Tinicum Township in his district.

Weidner reintroduced his bill in May of 1975, now labeled House Bill 1231 and written in identical language, into the lower house of the Pennsylvania legislature. The bill authorized the DER "with the approval of the governor to grant a license across the Delaware Canal and through the Theodore Roosevelt State Park in the Borough of Morrisville, Bucks County for bridge purposes."[47] This time he had five different co-sponsors, all Democrats, four of whom were from outside Bucks County. During the next few months, more newsprint was expended on this bill than on anything else that had happened to the canal during the last five decades.

By this time the opposition was mobilized. The DVPA, the Bucks County Conservation Alliance, and the Lower Bucks Canal Conservation Committee formed a coalition to oppose the plans for the bridge and as these organizations pressed, most of the local political leaders joined their ranks.[48] Hal Clark pointed out in a news release that despite an attempt to make the bridge appear as temporary, the fact was "It is a flat, not a standard canal type."

> [In addition to the] traffic of nearly 1,000 people, their friends and services come down to a proposed 24 foot bridge over the Canal, [it was] the only entrance and exit in case of a fire or other emergency.[49]

The bridge would also carry sewer lines and storm drains across the canal. Clark noted: "Sewer lines over the bridge make it permanent. Would they close out the toilets while they build a new bridge?" By the time the bill came up for a vote three of its sponsors, from Altoona, Summit Hill and Mahanoy City, withdrew their sponsorship, leaving only Theodore Berlin, a Bucks County Democrat, and Jack A. Arthurs, a Democrat from Butler, as co-sponsors.[50]

However, the bill did pass the house on June 1, 1976. Bucks County Representative Jack Renninger reported how the bill was "railroaded" through the house. He recalled:

> Mr Fineman opened the House of Representatives at 1:00 P.M. sharp and by 1:35 when I got to the floor this bill and several others had been voted upon. The Speaker was about to adjourn the House … I asked to be recorded on the Master Roll call…. Needless to say, I was surprised that the whole Session was over that promptly…
>
> Mr. Wright, (as the property is located in his District), spoke against the bill. The majority vote of 102-72 reflects the effectiveness of Mr. Wright's appeal.[51]

Marvin Weidner, the bill's originator, was absent and did not vote. Two of the original sponsors voted against the bill. The margin of victory was one vote, 102 votes being needed for passage.[52]

In the senate the bill was sent to the transportation committee, chaired by Frank J. Lynch of Philadelphia, who quickly got the bill reported to the senate floor.

> Senate sources said that lobbying by the Philadelphia Construction Trades Council (which is reported to have spent $20,050 in the effort) and support from the Philadelphia Democratic City Committee influenced the quick action.[53]

Bucks County State Senator H. Craig Lewis said he had been approached on the floor by Philadelphia's Senator Henry J. "Buddy" Cianfrani, who told him the Philadelphia Building Trades Unions were for the bill.[54]

Bucks County state senators Lewis and Edward Howard were able to get the bill recommitted to the environmental committee and then referred to a sub-committee chaired by Howard. He called for hearings. In the meantime, Howard was seeking more information in preparation for the senate fight—he had received some 400 calls and telegrams from residents opposing the project. Residents in Lower Makefield Township had started a letter-writing campaign and the township supervisors had written Governor Milton Shapp asking him to veto the special legislation if it should pass the senate.[55]

Howard noted that based on the figures given, each resident of the new River Heights Apartments would be paying $1,000 annually in taxes. Never had he "seen a bill move with the speed this one has. It's a marvel." On August 11, the sub-committee held hearings in Morrisville. The opposition was mobilized. Trenton's *Evening Times* headlined its story, "Canal bridge hearing draws quite a throng."[56]

Representatives of the DVPA, the Bucks County Conservation Alliance, the Pennsylvania Canal Society, the Society to Preserve River Road, and the Lower Bucks County Canal Conservation Committee spoke, along with numerous elected officials, almost all, except for those from Morrisville, in opposition.[57]

Following the hearings, Morrisville leaders complained that they should be able to control their own affairs. One council member expressed the support of the whole council for the bill "from a purely economic viewpoint." He noted that

> 20 per cent of the town's 11,309 residents are above the age of 65 and cannot endure rising property taxes. If the building is constructed at the cost of $15 million, the borough would gain $114,400 a year and the school would pick up $427,500 in new taxes.[58]

On September 20, 1976, *The Daily Intelligencer* editorialized: "Our Opinion, Senate Resources Committee must uphold canal bridge ban.... The bridge would be a case of letting private interests benefit by permitting a violation of the historical integrity of the canal." This newspaper clipping, in the files at the Delaware Canal State Park Office, has a handwritten marginal note, "They [the committee] did! 12 to 1 [to uphold the ban] about 9/22/76.[59]

In January of 1978, Morrisville Borough gave a "tentative OK to build Ferry Arms complex." Boyer and Nicholson were at it again, this time with plans to construct a seven-story, 57-unit building complete with penthouses overlooking the Delaware River. This time the structure and the parking would be on the two and one-half acres between the canal and River Road. In October, Congressman Peter H. Kostmayer told the *Trenton Times* that "it would be a 'mistake' to permit construction of high rise apartments in Morrisville." Despite claims by the borough council that the legislator's remarks did not influence their decision, they tabled approval at their council meeting the next day. In November, however, they did approve by a vote of five to three. The plans called for 120 parking places and dedicated two acres, located in neighboring Lower Makefield Township, to open space. According to Morrisville's zoning officer, the project could be built with only the one access to River Road. Ferry Arms was never constructed.[60]

Arthur Nicholson, attempting the role of the silent partner, was back in 1987 with new plans, this time for a fourteen-story structure, the first five floors of which were to be parking levels, on the same two and one-half acres. After a series of highly publicized actions involving clearing trees without permission on state property, starting without obtaining necessary permits, and then rumors of bankruptcy, the project mercifully died.[61]

The Pump

A long-time goal of those who sought to protect the canal and the valley was flood control. To achieve this, the Delaware estuary would have to be brought under control. For many years the anticipated high dam planned at Tock's Island near the Delaware Water Gap was assumed by many to be a cure-all for the river and the canal's problems. Hal Clark, the driving force in the DVPA, was sure this should be the solution. Dr. Goddard was likewise a supporter, something that caused environmental groups to oppose his appointment as head of a Department of Environmental Resources, which replaced the Department of Forest and Waters. Ultimately, the Tock's Island project, scheduled for groundbreaking in 1971, was defeated—possibly wisely, for a number of reasons—but the action left the valley and the canal still vulnerable to floods.[62]

Another project, also developed by the Delaware River Basin Commission, called for the diversion of Delaware River water at Point Pleasant and the construction of a pumping station to provide water for areas in Bucks and Montgomery counties and—in order to obtain future revenue and provide a broader funding base—to provide water for the cooling towers at Philadelphia Electric Company's nuclear reactor power plant at Limerick on the Schuylkill River. This project, the result of years of study and hearings, now became a *cause célèbre* for environmental activists. Because the pumping station would be constructed adjacent to the canal and because pipes would be necessary to carry the pumped water under the canal, the canal supporters' community became involved.

In 1974, the engineering firm, E.H. Bourquard Associates, Inc., and DER regional engineer John H. Nuss discussed the agreement for passing water under the canal. The engineering firm indicated agreement in August on everything except watering the canal. They were proposing to eliminate the pumping of canal water around the work area. Nuss, in a letter several weeks later, agreed that sufficient water could be pumped from the river, but "we originally suggested piping rather than pumping since a gravity system is certainly more reliable than pumps. What type of pump do you propose? Will you have a stand-by pump?"[63]

The engineer's proposal was accepted and the final agreement contained a detailed description of the project. Crossing the 60-mile canal "would certainly not be unique or unusual.... [There were] at least 127 water, sewer and other utility crossings, along with 135 public and private bridges and culverts providing access and transport." In order to work under "dry" conditions, Lock No. 14 (Upper Point Pleasant lock) and the canal water would be diverted by a weir into the Delaware River while still maintaining normal water depth in the canal. A small cofferdam, eight feet high, would be erected just below Lock No. 13 (Lower Point Pleasant lock) and temporary pumping facilities having a capacity of 25 cubic feet per second would be installed to deliver river water to the canal just downstream of the cofferdam. Detailed specifications, apparently provided by the DER, were given for canal restoration:

> ... segregated impervious soils will be used, if deemed suitable by the Department, for replacement of the canal lining. This backfill shall be placed in 8-inch layers and compacted to a density of 95% per modified Proctor tests. Rock in backfill shall not exceed 12 inches and will be placed in 18-inch layers separated by 12-inch thick layers of overburden material.[64]

The pump became a bitter, divisive issue. In 1976, Joseph Catania, Democratic member of the Bucks County Board of County Commissioners, protested the board's endorsement of landmark status for the canal, not because of any roadblock it might put in the path of constructing the high-rise apartment in Morrisville; rather, he accused the Republican majority of using landmark status "as a 'back door' way of blocking construction of the Point Pleasant pumping station."[65]

Opponents attempted to use the canal to halt the pump project, apparently unsuccessfully. In September of 1981, Wilson Oberdorfer responded to questions from Virginia Forrest, a bitter pump foe, saying that he had inquired about blasting and had been advised that similar rocks were routinely removed by blasting at greater depths in cities, without damaging structures. "The experts are confident that the state of the art of blasting is such that it can be done successfully under the Canal without causing damage to the Canal." Furthermore, he pointed out, the agreements guaranteed that the Neshaminy Water Resources Authority (NWRA) or their contractors would ensure any necessary repairs.[66]

In the statement of the NWRA, which would consume much of the water from the pump and pipeline, supplementing their applications to the Corps of Engineers was this disclaimer: "It has been claimed that emptying the Pennsylvania Canal during construction would create hydrostatic pressure which will damage this historic landmark," actually, the canal had been "emptied at least once each year over the last 2 years for maintenance without damage."[67]

In 1982, construction bids were sought and the accepted bid was that of the Mergentime Corporation of Raritan Township, New Jersey. Construction was underway in 1983. The next few years were ones of turmoil. Demonstrations, a referendum on the pump where a "yes" vote was recorded as a negative and vice versa, and the election of a Democratic-dominated Board of County Commissioners occurred in the meantime. The NWRA members were replaced and work was stopped on the pump amid lawsuits and questionable expenditures of public monies for public lobbying against the pump. The canal, which had suffered minor damages at the hands of the demonstrators, was sloppily reconstructed by the contractors under orders of the anti-pump NWRA board, something that brought charges, lawsuits, and a second reconstruction of the canal to the specifications in the agreement.[68]

Ultimately, the political pendulum swung again and the pump was built. The canal today flows, apparently unscathed, past the structure that houses the pump. However, politics and the specter of the debts incurred during the years of controversy remained. Political issues and the pump issue resurfaced in 1994 when the government of Bucks County agreed to sell the pumping station, the transmission main, and the water rights to the North Penn and North Wales water authorities in Montgomery County for $55.2 million. The receipts relieved the taxpayers of extensive legal and punitive damage obligations remaining from the pump episode but the county surrendered control over the water, something that put the former opponents of the pump in opposition to the sale.[69]

Vandalism and Mischief

In October of 1979, a fire of "suspicious origin" consumed a 12' x 16' locktender's shed at the Easton end of the canal. The structure, built in 1920, had neither heat nor electricity and caught fire on a rainy day. It was, according to canal superintendent Nuss, of no historical significance.[70]

In June of 1980, Olive Pellegrini, whose property on Mill Creek Road in Falls Township bordered the canal, was standing in her front yard when she was nearly run over by a car. When teenagers driving illegally on the towpath, sometimes drag-racing, reached Mill Creek Road only to discover the exit onto that road blocked by an iron gate, "the trapped drivers ride down the embankment into the Pellegrinis' yard." Putting up a fence was permissible, according to canal superintendent Nuss, but it could not be put on the embankment on canal property, where, according to the Pellegrinis, it would be effective. Teens had "been using [the canal] for beer parties, a drag strip and 'general horsing around'." An iron gate that would have protected the Pellegrini property had been taken down by vandals the previous year. " 'They pulled it right out of the concrete,' an exasperated Randy Pellegrini [the son] said."[71]

What was a convenience to one individual could be an offence to another. In 1982, Virginia Forrest wrote William Forrey, Director of State Parks, protesting "A most shocking thing ... two portable toilets on the towpath between Centre Bridge and Phillips Mill." These, along with two picnic tables and eight benches, "have attracted motorcyclists and other passers-by, off the River Road.... I cannot believe that anyone from your organization would approve the placement of such a monstrosity along the canal. How can we deny permits to home owners to expand and/or repair their property when this type of action is allowed?" It was a "blight to the esthetics of the area."[72]

In July of 1982, a headline reported "Canoeists Steal $50,000 In Jewelry Beside Canal." The theft took place in the home of George English. The thieves "apparently used a canoe to gain access to the house and to make their escape along the canal."[73]

Policing the canal has been a continuing problem. Questions kept arising as to jurisdiction between local law officials and state park authorities. In 1977, DER legal advisor Wilson Oberdorfer essentially spelled out the situation for the New Hope authorities: park police have primary jurisdiction on state property, and state police have power to enforce "the general criminal laws of the state" but not municipal ordinances.

Finally, the pronouncement was made: The canal was unlike other state parks but was a water-use area and therefore remained open twenty-four hours a day. Oberdorfer said that the state had no liability for damage to private property, the state's "sovereign immunity" was a complete bar against any claims. The latter question had arisen because of flooding and property damage to business places on Mechanic Street in New Hope.[74]

Threats

In 1978, a not completely unfounded rumor was abroad, suggesting, in the words of Virginia Hutton, that "Harrisburg tired of problems with the Canal ... suggests National takeover."[75] The *Delaware Valley News* of Frenchtown, New Jersey, headlined the rumors in October of 1979 but in its account noted that while the DER had dispatched a letter with such a suggestion the previous May, neither William Forrey, parks director, nor John Nuss, park superintendent, saw any interest on the part of the federal government. Congressman Peter Kostmayer opposed federal ownership.[76]

In the 1970s and 1980s, real-estate developments in the central portions of the canal became major concerns for some of the canal's defenders. Bucks County during the post-World War II decades, in addition to being the locale for basic steel manufacturing, was also becoming a prime bedroom community for commuters to Philadelphia and New York. Some of the new developments were in Upper Makefield Township, adjacent to Washington Crossing State Park and the Delaware Canal. In 1973, developer Chris Gigliotti, Jr., was seeking approval for his "Shires of Buckstone" proposals. Of particular concern were the plans for sewerage and groundwater runoff. In June of 1973, the Upper Makefield supervisors approved plans that included a name change to "Shires Crossing," a reduction in the number of houses, and the creation of a "restrictive preservation" area along the adjacent Delaware Canal.[77]

In 1975, the DVPA and the Bucks County Conservation Alliance entered the fray to oppose planned drainage from detention ponds directly into the canal. The permit had been granted by C.T. Beechwood of the Regional Water Quality Manager's office upon the advice of a state engineer, Steve Finkel. Apparently Superintendent Giza and State Engineer Nuss as well as local residents were concerned about the permit, which would permit an overflow across the canal bank, threatening the canal. A final decision was made by William C. Forrey, who laid down stricter regulations for stormwater management, including a proviso that the emergency overflow conduit from the detention ponds should be directed away from the canal.[78]

In the early 1980s a nearby development was opposed by the DVPA and the Conservation Alliance as a matter of principle. A 245-unit project was proposed to be constructed by Michael Lamelza, who would also operate the existing sewage plant in Washington Crossing State Park and pipe the treated water under the canal for emptying into the Delaware River. These questions were raised: Should a private developer have the right to cross public park land, and should the Washington Crossing Park sewage plant, built with tax payers' monies, be 'leased' to a private party to share capacity?[79] At the February 1982 meeting of the Washington Crossing Park Commission, area resident Nate Golub, a retired National Park Service administrator, expressed "utter disbelief" that the proposal would be even considered by Pennsylvania's Historical and Museums Commission (PHMC). He called it a serious precedent and concluded by saying "It would be an unconscionable betrayal of trust if your commission 'sold out' our heritage for a few pieces of silver."[80]

Ultimately the developer gave up his plans and sought permits to pass an eight-inch sewer line along State Route 532 through the village of Washington Crossing to the river. Protests and questions raised and addressed to the DER and the PHMC were politely rebuffed: precedent did not rule out crossing the canal, in this case on the Route 532 bridge, provided the proper permits were obtained.[81]

Tragedies

On the foggy night of May 18th, 1977, Caron Ehehalt, a businessman from York, Pennsylvania, left Chez Odette, a New Hope restaurant and watering place, and exited the parking lot past warning signs and onto the towpath and into the canal. In March of 1982, an eight-member Bucks County jury, in a civil suit filed on behalf of Ehehalt and his five children, awarded the survivors $1.05 million in damages, mostly against the Commonwealth. The state appealed. According to Superintendent Hoehn, he was, in view of the appeal, ordered not to alter the parking lot exits.[82]

Before the appeal reached the courtroom, another tragic drowning occurred that put the canal into national headlines when, on a rainy evening on October 23, 1983, a 35-year-old rising NBC news anchor, Jessica Savitch, died as a car driven by *New York Post* vice president Martin Fischbein exited the Chez Odette parking lot past two warning "no exit" signs and onto the towpath. The car slid into the canal lock and flipped over. Fischbein, Savitch, and a dog in the car drowned. In a settlement reached in 1988, the estate of Jessica Savitch received a cash settlement of $8.15 million from the *New York Post*, the Chez Odette, Pennsylvania's Department of Environmental Resources, and Fischbein's estate. The *Post's* liability was established by business papers in the car proving that the trip was being deducted by the newspaper as a business expense. The greater portion of the settlement, the *Post's* and Fischbein's portions, was covered not by the state of Pennsylvania, but by a $100 million insurance policy on Fischbein that covered his personal driving and his business driving for the *Post*.[83]

It was not until September of 1984 that an announcement was made that Commonwealth Court had heard an appeal on the Ehehalt case. The court upheld the decision that the state was primarily to blame.[84]

One month later, in October of 1984, a new barrier was erected to protect others from taking the wrong turn at the end of the Chez Odette lot. According to Superintendent Hoehn, the towpath beyond the parking lot was also the entry drive for several persons living along the towpath and they protested at having their entrance impeded. Finally a barrier, opened with a padlock, was installed.[85]

There is not the space to record every tragic occurrence along the canal. Motor vehicles, or at least their operators, were responsible for many problems. A few examples must suffice. On February 16, 1976, the *Easton Express* ran a picture of a heavy truck from Ottsville with its rear wheels hanging off the crumpled metal retaining barrier while its front bumper extended just above the water of the canal. The damage to the empty truck was estimated at $150. No estimate was made as to the damage to state property.[86] Also in 1975, a huge dump truck backing along the canal to reach the Upper Black Eddy repair site nearly ended up at the bottom of the canal when a wheel went over the edge. "We had to dump the load from the truck to keep it from going into the canal," according to canal foreman Sanford Miller.[87]

In May of 1977, another *Express* photograph shows a car in the canal, still upright, but with water up to the level of its windows. The car was being driven south on Route 32 by 82-year-old Robert Martz when he lost control and the car slid into the canal under the Route 32 bridge in Bridgeton Township. He was rescued by the Milford, New Jersey, Fire Department and Rescue Squad, who found Martz sitting on the hood of his car, shaken but unhurt.[88]

In August of 1978, a horse named Aragon slipped into the canal one Sunday morning in New Hope, just south of Odette's. Thanks to the efforts of the Heavy Rescue Unit of the Lambertville Rescue Squad and New Hope's Eagle Fire Company, rigging was erected in place and the poor animal was extracted from the mud of the canal to a joyous welcome from all the participants in the rescue.[89]

In August of 1979, one Karel Mikolas, 40, of Slatington, Pennsylvania, was traveling north on River Road in Plumstead Township when his car went out of control. It struck a concrete bridge, veered and went over an embankment, then hit two trees before coming to rest in the canal, which was dry at the time. He was treated for minor bruises at the Doylestown Hospital.[90]

In October of the same year, a murder victim's body was recovered from the Delaware Canal near Easton. Charles H. McKean, a Lockheed employee assigned to the Naval Air Development Center in Warminster, Bucks County, had been beaten and robbed, then carried to Easton where his body was disposed of in the canal. The attackers were apprehended, charged with the murder, and subsequently pleaded guilty.[91]

Let the newspaper record of the demise of 23-year-old Mark Carey of Erwinna serve as a further example. The accident occurred between home and work sometime after 7:45 AM on Wednesday, January 31, 1990. Traveling south on River Road north of Treasure Island Boy Scout Camp, he lost control, possibly after striking a large pothole in the road, and "then skidded on the guardrail 35 feet before flipping over into the embankment—collapsing the roof of the car—and rolled into the bottom of the canal, coming to rest upside down in about a foot of water." The car in the canal, hidden from River Road, was not discovered until after noon the next day.[92]

On Saturday, February 27, 1993, what appeared to be a tragedy in the making brought fire, police, and ambulance crews racing to the canal in the lower end between Route 13 and the Levittown Parkway following a report that a child had fallen through the ice and was floundering in the frigid water. Upon arrival, they discovered bystanders and police trying to shepherd a paddling dog through broken ice to the shore. After much effort and concern, the dog—a mutt described as a German shepherd mix—was guided to shore and then he was carried by ambulance to an animal shelter where he was dried with a hair drier and pronounced in good condition. Divers subsequently confirmed that the dog had been alone in the water.[93]

On Monday, June 12, 1995, Joseph McGurrin, aged 69, hit a pole on Wheatsheaf Lane off Old Route 13, and flipped his silver Chevrolet S-10 pickup into the canal. He was trapped in his cab and the efforts of two 13-year-olds to release him were unsuccessful. Fire fighters responding to a 911 call got the door open and the victim was carried to St. Mary Medical Center in Newtown.[91]

∾ CHAPTER X ∾

The Delaware Canal State Park:
Its Present and Future

By the time that Superintendent Doug Hoehn left for a new post in 1990, a renewed optimism had surfaced for the canal's future with the creation of a Friends of the Delaware Canal organization in 1982, the development of a Master Plan in 1987, the appointment of an Advisory Committee in 1988, and the implementation of the Delaware and Lehigh Canals National Heritage Corridor the same year.

A New Superintendent

Douglas Hoehn was succeeded in March of 1990 by Ken Lewis, 40 years of age, a veteran of 14 years in the state park service. His immediate past assignment as superintendent of Sizerville State Park in Potter County had been preceded by years as chief of park rangers for Ridley Creek in Delaware County, where drug and alcohol control were crucial, and he had also served as training and safety coordinator in Harrisburg where he developed a water rescue program. "Lewis describes himself as a flood manager in charge of public relations," according to one newspaper reporter, and certainly he took to the job with its many public relations problems ably and without hesitation.[1] In 1992, under a departmental reorganization plan, Superintendent Lewis's title was changed to Park Manager.[2]

Lewis took charge immediately, pushing existing initiatives to restore the canal and expanding on them. At the end of his first summer, the *New Hope Gazette* could editorialize: "luckily for the canal, it has a keeper in the person of Ken Lewis." The virtually universal judgment has been that he continued to be both hard working and a diplomat who, despite relatively few real permanent successes and numerous frustrations, has dealt in a most even-handed manner with the often outspoken vocal critics who only too often proclaimed themselves to be friends of the canal.[3]

Lewis has been a major instigator of new initiatives and has given the park a new, broader philosophy. He viewed his role and that of the park as being more than the preservation of an historical site but rather he saw the dynamics of tourism and also the preservation and expansion of the natural areas of the sixty-mile park. He said, "There is a bigger picture here … The picnic areas and ramps can be a link between the canal and the river and its islands." He certainly helped push the state in its acquisition of islands in the river off Bucks County as well as pushing for tourist and convenience facilities at convenient spots along the canal park. He was aware that the state park had, in 1995, the sixth-highest attendance of the 110 state parks, an estimated 1.25 million visitors.[4]

Ralph and the Lower End

Activities had finally begun to refurbish the lower end of the canal by early 1982. In the late 1950s the canal had been covered by the parking lot of the then-new Levittown Shopping Center and since that time, canal water has been piped under the shopping center through an inverted siphon. The office of State Senator H. Craig Lewis noted in a conversation with this author that the state's lease with the shopping center would terminate on July 31, 1988, and that reopening the canal was under consideration. Maintenance of

The towpath can be seen on the right of the canal, which enters a culvert where the two people are standing.

the siphon (culvert), was the responsibility of the Bramlee Corporation, then the owners of the shopping center, but according to the superintendent of the state park, maintenance had been less than adequate, if not nonexistent. When Superintendent Hoehn ran a dye test in late 1988 to determine the length of time it took canal water to flow through the pipe, he discovered that it took an unacceptable two-and-a-half hours.

Senator Lewis's office supported the agitation of a group of Bristol residents who wanted the last southerly portion of the canal, which had been leased to the Borough of Bristol by an agreement dated December 7, 1954, returned to the state.[5] In 1994 the lease of canal right-of-way on which was constructed the Warren Snyder Elementary School was at a cycle where either party could end it. Prior to that date, a Bristol Borough group briefly pushed for termination of the lease, but the date passed and now the programs seem to be to develop and interpret the canal around the school rather than pursuing the more extreme call for the school's removal from the old right of way of the canal.[6]

Bristol native Ralph Ratcliffe, active and vocal, was joined by other equally demanding and uncompromising spokesmen for Bristol and the lower end of the canal. Hard working Elaine Beck, head of a more recently formed Association for the Restoration and Preservation of the Delaware Canal, in late spring of 1989, when speaking in opposition to half-way measures to open the canal through the Levittown Shopping Center parking lot, offered the somewhat visionary goal "that the entire 60-mile length of the waterway be opened someday for navigation."[7] Another particularly strident voice was that of William Pezza of Bristol Borough, who styled himself as the only Lower Bucks member appointed to the 21-member Delaware and Lehigh Canal National Heritage Corridor Commission. A legislative aide to Democratic Assemblyman Thomas Corrigan and a Bristol School Board member, he protested loudly that he would not "sit back quietly and allow Lower Bucks to be ignored." Ignoring the fact that a large percentage of the proposals in the Friends of the Delaware Canal master plan were committed to projects that would stabilize the canal and keep it watered rather than ones that would enhance any particular locale, Pezza and his fellow spokesmen protested that not enough money was designated for the lower end because, as Ratcliffe proclaimed, "the lower canal will remain neglected as long as populous Lower Bucks is under represented."

In the summer of 1990, Ratcliffe and a group of fellow protesters picketed one of Congressman Peter Kostmayer's constituent meetings carrying signs reading "The Canal starts in Bristol, not New Hope" and "The Lower end wants a voice in Canal decisions." They protested the expenditure of $325,000 by the state for the purchase of the lockhouse in New Hope, which the Friends of the Delaware Canal, largely through their own efforts and financing, would turn into an office and interpretive center. Lower-end spokesman Pezza expressed a concern that fairness should give Bristol a museum, such as that of the Hugh Moore Historic Park and Museums, Inc. (now the National Canal Museum) at Easton. This demand ignored the fact that the canal museum came into existence as a result of the efforts of enthusiastic unpaid volunteers of the Pennsylvania Canal Society and the generous donations of Hugh Moore, the Easton industrialist whose legacies created what is now Hugh Moore Historical Park and Museums, Inc.

As a result of massive volunteer efforts, it is now known as the National Canal Museum and is in a new setting married to the Crayola Factory in the heart of Easton. It has continued to be sustained by the hard work, efforts, and generosity of many plus the herculean efforts of volunteers and a small paid staff.[8]

Among the more positive programs of the Bristol Canal Conservation Committee and their allies was the 1989 restoration of the gazebo on its original spot, complete with Mercer tiles. Along with the clock on the Grundy textile mill, this had been a landmark for canal boats entering Bristol. The replica of the original 1915 structure, a $20,000 project sponsored by the Bristol Parks and Recreational Authority, was primarily the result of the leadership of Joseph Sagolla. The Bristol preservationists had fished battered stone steps out of the canal, columns of concrete were poured into molds constructed to match recovered shreds of the originals, and Mercer tiles were copied from "crinkled turn-of-the-century plans." There were also elaborate plans at the time, never fulfilled, for land acquisition and the development of the filled-in area of canal in Bristol Borough. Bike and hiking trails and landscaping along with visitors' centers with interpretation were part of these plans. Initial funding was solicited through a RIRA (Recreation Improvement and Rehabilitation Act) Grant, from the Grundy Foundation, and through a Local History Projects Proposal.[9]

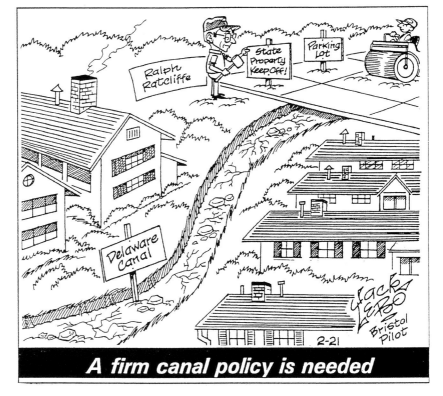

As development encroaches on the dry canal, Ralph Ratcliffe, the enduring protector of the lower end of the canal, is portrayed sympathetically in an editorial cartoon from the Bristol Pilot, dated February 21, 1991.
Author's clipping collection.

In August of 1991, unfounded charges were made by Ralph Ratcliffe that water from the reportedly well-watered upper end of the canal was being cycled back into the river at New Hope and denied the lower end. Gene Comoss, then chief engineer for the Bureau of State Parks, rebutted, spelling out the water situation for the sixty miles of canal. Nine miles below Easton, water was being diverted into the river because of the reconstruction of the Durham Aqueduct. Below the construction, the contractor was pumping river water back into the canal. At Lumberville, water was again being diverted into the river as a result of a court order obtained by the Black Bass Inn, which claimed that their structure had been damaged by the canal. The Black Bass dispute was finally settled out of court with a payment of $495,000 by the state to the inn owner, a virtual lawyer-arranged surrender on the part of the state.[10] The canal was dry to Centre Bridge, where water was again pumped into the canal by the owner of the canal barge concession at New Hope. Below that point, water was sent down the canal, and Comoss could not explain what happened to it. He suggested there may have been leaks, and said an investigation was underway.[11]

In 1992, Ratcliffe achieved a coup when he persuaded Waste Management, Inc., to pipe treated water into the canal above Wheatsheaf Road. Waste Management was the successor to the Warner Company, which had created extensive lakes in the Tullytown area by dredging for gravel and sand. This example of a public-private partnership provided a more-or-less adequate water level in the last several miles of existing canal.[12] However, Waste Management changed their activities within two years and the flow stopped. The company suggested that the state find funds to purchase the pumps in order to maintain the water supply for the lower section.[13]

In October of 1992, it was announced that the National Heritage Corridor Commission had granted Bristol Borough a matching grant of $24,000 with which to develop a walking path from Mill Street to Green Lane along the canal. With a matching donation from the Grundy Foundation, there was $48,000 available for the project. The January 24, 1993, edition of the *Bucks County Courier Times* announced that a grant totaling $304,000 had been awarded for a pedestrian towpath project in Bristol. It was made under the Intermodal Surface Transportation Efficiency Act (ISTEA) and would be supplemented by $67,000 from the Grundy Foundation and $9,000 from Bristol Borough. According to the borough's planning consultant, the intention was to create an interpretive path. No decision had yet been made on whether it would be a defined pathway or not, but there would be continuing activity at the lower end of the canal, according to the consultant.[14] The canal from Morrisville to Bristol is now part of the East Coast Greenway, a Maine-to-Florida hiking trail.

River Road and the Valley

In 1988, after more than a decade of scenic road discussion and proposals, Pennsylvania House Bill No. 1982 designated those portions of routes 32 and 611 that constitute River Road as the Delaware River Scenic Drive. In 1992, the state finally placed signs along that road recognizing the designation, but at their June 1992 meeting the Delaware Canal State Park Advisory Committee, speaking both for themselves and for the residents and the communities they represented, still expressed concern about trucks on a road that was definitely not constructed for heavy modern truck traffic. Concern was also expressed that in planning to replace bridges, which was probably needed, the Pennsylvania Department of Transportation would be straightening out the road and thereby encouraging both the already excessive speeds and even greater truck traffic.[15]

The *Philadelphia Inquirer* of September 24, 1992, carried a story on River Road and its problems. Phillips Mill in Solebury Township, with a hairpin "S" curve, was possibly the worst of many trouble spots. The article described how, three years before, Nora Grimisom was awakened in the middle of the night:

Another truck had hit the historic Phillips Mill ...

"A driver from Montana had taken half the corner of the building down," she recalled... "He said that where he came from they didn't have corners like that."

According to James R. Grosholz, vice president of the Phillips Mill Community Association, "It cost us $5,000 to repair the corner when that truck from Montana hit it. Our insurance used to cover it. Now there's a $1,000 deductible."

There were other spots along River Road—canal bridges, one-lane bridges, sharp curves, and other projecting buildings—and the concerns were not just long-distance tractor-trailers but also the local gravel and quarry trucks. The state did agree to designate River Road as a scenic highway on its 1993 maps but PennDOT said additional restrictions could only be justified where the traffic threatened the existing road structure.[16]

While the problem of heavy trucks on a scenic two-lane road continues, there has been some improvement in the relations of the canal and PennDOT. The threat to pave over the canal no longer exists and PennDOT has agreed to use their resources to help remove underbrush that has sprouted between the River Road and the canal and is consulting regularly with the State Parks people about how they can cooperate to maintain the integrity of the canal wall where the canal has been encroached upon by the roadway. However, there are long stretches of road bordering the canal in the narrow constricted spaces between the cliffs at Palisades and the river with no alternate routing where the often heavy and continually increasing traffic will remain a problem.

In 1995, "Scenic America," a conservation organization based in Washington DC, named the Delaware River Scenic Drive (River Road) as one of America's "10 Most Scenic Byways." They also described the roadway as being "endangered":

> … the road is in grave danger. The stone canal walls, which support the road, were not built to withstand modern vehicular traffic and are falling into the canal. The crumbling walls endanger the road's stability and prevent the canal from being watered … But without strong and effective action by responsible agencies, in time it may be neither scenic nor a drive. [17]

It is impossible to catalogue all that took place along the canal so let a sampling suffice. On October 12, 1988, a 17½-ton oil truck driven by one Jonathan Wilder, 39, destroyed the Tebola-Beans camelback bridge south of Washington Crossing. The bridge, clearly marked "Two Tons," collapsed and the truck and driver plunged into the canal. The unfortunate driver claimed to have received debilitating back injuries and sued the state Department of Environmental Resources along with the owners of the property beyond the bridge and the renters on that property who had ordered the oil. The judge dismissed the charges against the owners and the renters during the same year; when it came to trial, it took a jury only ten minutes to decide the DER was not liable.[18]

A leak in the canal developed at Indian Rocks and when the contractor started repair work on Monday December 18, 1989, a major piece of his equipment got bogged down in the bottom of the canal. Its removal posed a major problem. There have been trucks and cars that have lost control and have ended up in various precarious positions impaled on railings overlooking the canal and sometimes in the canal itself— on several occasions with fatal results. Trucks have lost their loads—on at least one occasion garbage was dumped into the canal—and there has been more than one episode when materials, sometimes toxic, have been deposited into the canal.[19] Along the lower end, according to one media article, there are "Rats—lots of rats" residing along the Delaware canal who come forth in packs, particularly as darkness descends, to forage about the fast-food eateries and the teeming dumpsters where litter is unconsciously and sometimes consciously scattered. Their numbers have become sufficient to be a concern to the local health authorities.[20]

Many utilities cross the canal and innumerable agreements are in place to govern these. In some cases they too could create problems, although on the whole they have successfully come to terms with the Bureau of State Parks. In 1989, the Columbia Gas Company bored beneath the canal for a pipeline and caused a collapse of the canal bottom. Then their boring head got stuck in the towpath, which necessitated excavation of the bottom of the canal in order to remove it. Sub-freezing weather in the winter of 1989–1990 held up their activities. The advisory committee minutes of March 13, 1990, reported that all repairs had finally been completed, "inspected and approved by Bureau engineers … at no cost to the Bureau."[21]

A downpour in September of 1989 dumped from four to six inches of rain on central Bucks County. A section of canal wall collapsed at Smithtown and it was reported that possibly a total of two million dollars in damages were suffered by roads maintained by PennDOT in the area. The new canal supervisor had not yet been appointed, leaving something of a vacuum at the top and, while this may have not been the cause, only one of two appropriate waste gates had been opened. According to park maintenance manager Sanford Miller, "sometime during the night the gate had come closed." Repairs were started almost immediately, possibly because of the intervention of then-State Senator James Greenwood, an area resident.[22] Similar accounts—maybe only just a little less disastrous—could be produced for almost any year in the canal's recent history.

By the fall of 1991 the river was low. This, along with breaks, had left the canal empty over most of its length for several months. Sustained periods without water can over time be as disastrous as flood waters. Floods are at their most dangerous when combined with ice, which the maintenance crew considers responsible for the greatest havoc of all.

Superintendent Lewis could proclaim early in 1992 that almost the whole canal, with the exception of the one portion drained as a result of a lawsuit and the related court order, was watered, but his optimism was short-lived.[23] New problems soon appeared and emergency maintenance and repairs were required.[24] Then, in the late spring of 1993, came the bombshells: restraining orders from the U.S. Fish and Wildlife Service and the U.S. Army Corps of Engineers, seemingly to protect the environment, stopped all work. The Corps's edict was completely unexpected.

The state of Pennsylvania had received a notice from the Fish and Wildlife Service stating its position that "the canal is U.S. water and the dredging, which had been under way since the previous January, required a permit from the Army Corps of Engineers to deposit the dredged materials."[25] The Bureau of State Parks and its engineering staff was particularly hit by the demand of the Corps of Engineers for a permit for maintenance of the Delaware Canal. Park Manager Ken Lewis in his report to the Friends of the Delaware Canal can be quoted:

> On January 11, 1994, at the Friends' general meeting, the dredging permit application was presented to the Army Corps of Engineers.... The fact that DER's engineers were able to compile the massive amount of information required in only five months is noteworthy...[26]

It seemed obvious to many that a waterway, and particularly a man-made waterway with an artificially raised towpath on the river side, is always vulnerable to washouts and other damage. Equally obvious to those concerned about the canal was that continuous emergency maintenance was essential and that, even after coal boat traffic ended and locks fell into disuse and were replaced with concrete dams and spillgates, the vulnerability remained. And for each period of time that maintenance was postponed, the problems were aggregated, often to a disastrous degree.

When the Corps of Engineers was approached by Senator Specter's and Senator Heinz's offices to see if they could do something to help with maintenance, according to the legislative offices, the Corps repulsed the solicitations, saying this was not under their jurisdiction. Then-Congressman Kostmayer and personnel for the Corps did look at the canal and there was some discussion that the Corps might improve the flow of the canal around the Route 1 bridge abutment in Morrisville that had encroached on the line of the canal. Nothing came from this, only the assumption of authority to award permits without assuming any responsibility for maintaining the canal and, incidentally, the wetlands created by the canal. What resulted from the moratorium on any work on the canal that was most damaging to the canal was the loss of watered areas and the resultant deterioration, particularly to woodwork that had been kept moist—sometimes for more than a century—and was now threatened with destruction by dry rot.

The damage resulting from the moratorium could be added to the existing problems such as the multiple places where bridges over the canal have been replaced by culverts, the area where the canal is under the parking lot of the Levittown Shopping Center, and the condition of the wing dam at New Hope. New Jersey, which is taking more water from the river at Bull's Island (Lumberville) and which is receiving more income selling water from their Delaware and Raritan Canal than they did from tolls when America's busiest canal was at the height of its operation, has constructed a new, higher wing dam to provide a more reliable flow into the D&R feeder and in the process undercut the towpath wall of the Pennsylvania Canal. The wall has been repaired and the D&R feeder has been guaranteed its flow, something that cannot be said for the deteriorating wing dam downstream at New Hope which should guarantee an adequate flow of water into the Delaware Canal. The New Hope dam originally directed water to a set of water wheels that lifted water to supply the lower portion of the Delaware Canal but they had deteriorated to such a degree that the wheels were abandoned in 1925. After the Union Mills at New Hope stopped using the water about 1960, it became necessary for the states of Pennsylvania and New Jersey to cooperate to rebuild the dam in 1967 in order to provide a flow into the canal and raise the water for recreational activities in the river. At that time, both the Delaware Valley Protective Association and the Delaware River Power Boat Association lobbied for the restoration.[27]

Congressman James Greenwood, Park Manager Ken Lewis, preservation advocate Betty Orlemann, and Susan Taylor, executive director of the Friends of the Delware Canal, by the canal in New Hope. Courtesy of Friends of the Delaware Canal.

The dredging was essential to stabilize the canal and maintain a flow of water from Easton to Bristol, a drop of only 164 feet in 60 miles. However, there were many other threats: walls that needed attention before they collapsed; tree roots and other plant materials destroying the walls; streams debouching into the canal and creating buildups of sand and other debris.

A *Courier Times* article dated June 13, 1994, labeled "The deteriorating Delaware Canal" as a "testament to red tape." Its opening lines came directly to the point,

> Bureaucracy sits as a dam, literally holding up water from flowing down the Delaware Canal.
> And each day it sits dry, its condition worsens and the cost to repair it skyrockets.

The article noted, correctly, that the clay bed, puddled into the canal as lining to make the canal watertight, was cracking and that wood deteriorates quickly when exposed to air. Some had been preserved for one hundred and fifty years in a moist state. Waste gates, cribbing around locks and other woodwork, some dating back to 1832, were threatened because the canal was drying up as a result of the Corps order. Park Manager Ken Lewis noted that there were already six waste gates that needed replacement. The roots of plants and trees were penetrating the clay lining. He further noted that some of the berm banks were structured to be supported by the pressure of water running in the canal. George Schweichardt, operator of the New Hope barge concession, observed of the canal, "It's a very old structure that's falling apart. A lot of walls are caving in, nature is starting to reclaim it." Lewis summed it up: "Meanwhile, the canal is falling apart,... And the price tag to fix it is getting bigger and bigger."[28]

The frustrations from oh so many quarters was captured in the fall, 1993, newsletter of the Friends of the Delaware Canal, which reprinted a July editorial from the *Bucks County Courier Times*. Under the cryptic legend "Clean Out the Process, Canal isn't the only thing that needs dredging," they wrote, and we quote:

> and a wet, green smell rises from the waterway, nearly stagnant. The odor is a hint of what one will see at 10 a.m.
> But canal lovers in the center of Yardley, where a stream feeds the nearly nonexistent flow, are lucky. Just north of the borough and south of Washington Crossing State Park, there's barely been a

canal for at least the last four years. "It's as blocked in Washington Crossing," according to Ken Lewis, Park Manager, "[that the water is] about 24 inches wide and about 4 inches deep." And if his estimates are correct, those residents probably won't be floating on the canal until at least next summer.

That's because of a version of spy vs. spy—more precisely, bureaucrat vs. bureaucrat, state vs. feds, environmentalists vs. environmentalists.

The state and the Friends of the Delaware Canal bought a dredge … But someone called the federal government to complain when the first dredging segment near Bowman's Tower piled silt in what turned out to be a wetland. Lewis said the state simply was storing the silt for later use in repairing the canal.

But the well-meaning citizen's report to the U.S. Army Corps of Engineers may add at least a year to the final part of the restoration project, intended to get 'hot spots' flowing, Lewis said.[29]

Possibly the most bizarre example of bureaucratic bungling occurred in Bristol borough on August 15, 1993, where a break occurred that according to Susan Taylor, executive director of the Friends of the Delaware Canal, "looks like a cave—a real enticing opening that could potentially eat up a child who crawls in and gets stuck." Because of the need for a repair permit, nothing could be done—a request for specific permission to make repairs was initially rejected; finally the red tape was bypassed and a permit was forthcoming on the following March 7, 1994, although repairs were held up due to weather and the condition of the towpath.[30]

Illustrative of the degree of bureaucratic complexities that complicated the process of getting a permit (or permits) to continue what had been pro forma for a century and a half was the list of agencies (fourteen in number) involved. They were:

FEDERAL | STATE
(DER= Department of Environmental Resources)

Corps of Engineers   DER   Dams & Waterways
U.S. Fish & Wildlife Service   DER   Waste Management
Environmental Protection Agency   DER   Facility Design & Construction
National Advisory Council for   DER   Wetlands
     Historic Preservation   DER   Forestry
National Park Service   Pennsylvania Historical & Museum Commission
Soil Conservation District   Pennsylvania Fish Commission
     Pennsylvania Dept. of Transportation

COUNTY
County Conservation District

The following permits, plans and understandings were generated as a result of the 18-month "hassle."

FEDERAL | STATE

COE (Corps of Engineers) — Joint Permit   DER   Waterways permit
EPA — NPDES Permit*   Dept. of Transportation Categorical
     Exceptions Memorandum of
     Understanding

FEDERAL/STATE
Historical Memorandum of Understanding

COUNTY
Erosion and Sedimentation Plan

The permits were designed to allow at least normal maintenance for the following several years.[31]

---

* National Pollutant Discharge Elimination System Permit, required for discharging runoff or other effluent from a pipe or swale into a body of water.

With the arrival of the permits, dredging resumed on October 18, 1994, in the Washington Crossing area where the worse silting had taken place, with work to continue southward into the Yardley area during the first year. Part of the irony was that state funds for moving the dredged material had run out in late 1994 and, on top of that, G.R.O.W.S., Inc., the landfill of Waste Management, was designated as the only acceptable designation for dredged material in the permit, despite the fact that there were locals who said they would be happy to take it at no cost or possibly even pay for it. At the landfill there would be an acceptance fee of $3 to $5 per ton. Things change almost hourly and within hours after the foregoing sentence was originally written, additional state funds were found to resume dredging when the weather cleared and the permit had been amended to permit soil to go to Evansburg State Park in Pennsylvania's Montgomery County to help build up their golf course.

About the same time that the permit came, so did the "convenient" discovery in the lower section of the canal of endangered species. The red-bellied turtle plus two forms of endangered plants were responsible for further restrictions on dredging, at least in certain portions of the canal, and also kept the same areas from being stocked with trout. The turtles can reach a length of more than twelve inches and, according to a newspaper article, they spend much time in the water but often emerge to sun themselves on logs. It was considered necessary for the canal to be drained in the fall, prior to the turtle's winter hibernation period, which would cause the red-belly to hibernate elsewhere. After a proper period of time dredging and other maintenance was resumed.[32]

Everyone has not been convinced of the significance of the turtle, as was the case in the spring of 1998 when canal dredging in the Yardley area was held up by what an engineer from the new Department of Conservation and Natural Resources (the successor to the Department of Environmental Resources, which was divided into two agencies, DCNR and the Department of Environmental Protection, by Governor Tom Ridge), referred to as "legalese." What had occurred was a disagreement between the lawyers representing the Pennsylvania Department of Transportation and the Pennsylvania Department of Public Services, which would hold up the start of the dredging. Matt Sinberg, a Yardley dentist, had already nicknamed the canal in Yardley the "muddy hole." When informed by park officials that the canal had been drained to meet the requirements necessary to avoid the hibernation period of the endangered red-bellied turtle he responded, "I even question that story about the red-bellied turtle … I've lived here 19 years and I've never seen a red-bellied turtle." He also noted that borough residents had spent a day the previous fall trying to rescue wildlife, mostly giant carp, when the canal was drained.[33]

It would appear that the permit did not wholly solved the problems but maybe just initiated a new set. Further, dredging requires draining portions of the canal and negotiations became necessary with the state Fish and Game people, which forestalled the stocking of the canal with trout, something that caused at least some resentment among the fishermen types.[34]

Friends of the Delaware Canal

As has already been noted, the prime mover in the Friends of The Delaware Canal was Betty Orlemann of Smithtown, who settled in upper Bucks County in 1977. Over the years she and the Friends have remained a force working for the canal and its preservation. After a brief involvement in the anti-pump movement at Point Pleasant,[35] the activities of the Friends have been canal improvement projects, fund raisers, canal tours by bus and by barge, annual canal walks, lectures, and regular meetings. They have been the major participant in the annual canal clean-up. By the mid-1980s, they published a newsletter and produced a calendar and a cookbook. In April of 1991, a part-time executive director, Susan Taylor, was hired.[36] In 1983, teams of volunteers from the Friends repainted and landscaped three canal bridges in Tinicum Township, a prototype effort for future projects.[37] Also a team, usually composed of Betty Orlemann, the late Howard Swope, a former boatman, canal superintendent Hoehn, and sometimes Lance Metz, historian from the National Canal Museum, carried their message about the canal to service clubs, schools, and other organizations in the region.[38]

A group of volunteers, members of *Friends of the Delaware Canal*, preparing a camelback bridge at Smithtown for repainting. *Courtesy of Friends of the Delaware Canal*

In 1983, the Friends became, more or less officially, the inheritors of the mantle of the Delaware Valley Protective Association as well as the recipients of the approximately $3,000 DVPA treasury.[39]

Thanks to the efforts of the Friends, in March of 1986 the Pennsylvania Department of Commerce awarded the organization $50,000 to support the preparation of a master plan for the Delaware Canal. Following some twelve months of research and hearings, conducted under contract with Urban Research Development Corporation of Bethlehem, Pennsylvania, and Hugh Moore Historical Park & Museums, Inc., of Easton, Pennsylvania, the final Delaware Canal Master Plan was published in July of 1987. Essentially the plan provided a blueprint for action, both public and private, to preserve, stabilize and, possibly, ultimately to restore the canal; additionally it provided guidelines and direction for the development of the areas through which the canal runs. Most importantly among the specifics was the call for the state of Pennsylvania to form an advisory committee for the canal. It presented what would basically be a bare stabilization budget that required an expenditure of some $32,000,000 over the next ten years.[40]

In 1989, the Friends were recognized with the first of their four "Take Pride in Pennsylvania" awards, while the following year they were invited to the White House for the first of three consecutive "Take Pride in America" awards.[41]

Among the other accomplishments of the Friends was the obtaining of a grant and the preparation by Urban Research and Development, a Bethlehem engineering and land-planning consulting company, of a model ordinance for canal enhancement that would enable communities along the canal to cooperate with the understaffed state park personnel. It considered zoning, property setbacks and stormwater management. Several communities endorsed the plan very soon, while others placed it under study.[42]

Another grant the Friends received would permit signage along the canal.[43] In his November 10, 1992, report to the Friends, Park Manager Ken Lewis announced that during the coming summer, interpretive signs would appear at significant spots along the canal.[44] To be created by the design firm of Chermayoff and Geismar under contract with the National Heritage Corridor, their content would be the product of State Parks. The primary funding came about as a result of the efforts of the Friends of the Delaware Canal and a grant they had received from the McLean Contributionship. In July 1996, the first of the often-postponed wayside signs and the three-sided kiosks were placed along the 60-mile Delaware Canal portion of the corridor. They described "Life along the Canal," "Men and Mules," and "Canal Boats."[45]

Possibly the Friends' most outstanding accomplishment was the successful completion, to a large degree as a result of the efforts of Zabel Davis of Yardley, of their "Pledge for the Dredge" project, through which they raised $100,000. They presented their check to the state in November of 1991 and the state furnished the necessary additional funds and contracted for a John Deere track excavator with a long arm attachment. It was scheduled for delivery in October 1992, at which time the long-overdue dredging of the canal was expected to commence.[46]

In December of 1992, following a brief ceremony at the Bowman's Hill Nature Center in Washington Crossing State Park, the dredge was dedicated. It was given the name The Zabel Belle and was immediately put into operation in the Bowman's Hill area of the canal.[47] The much-needed dredging was brought to a halt on March 31, 1993, initially because of fishing season regulations. In June, the U.S. Fish and Wildlife Service issued a violation notice citing several federal Clean Water and dredging of navigable waters acts and the U.S. Army Corps of Engineers entered the picture, for it would be necessary to gain a permit from them to clear the violations. The Friends were most active along with congressmen, state legislators, the staff of the Department of Environmental Resources, and the Bucks County Conservation District, among others, in overcoming the bureaucratic hurdles.[48]

Above, a group of canal walkers are standing in front of the Zabel Belle.

Right, Zabel Davis and Randy Apgar at the Yardley Canal Festival in 2000.

Courtesy of Friends of the Delaware Canal.

In June of 1990, the Commonwealth announced the purchase for $325,000 of the locktender's house alongside Lock #11 in New Hope. The Friends agreed to raise the funds to do the major restoration necessary that would turn the house into an interpretation center as well as serving as a headquarters for the Friends. Some $36,400 of these funds came from the Historic House Museum Challenge Grant Program and the Friends were required to raise at least $7,225 to qualify for this source, but their goal was the $74,000 total necessary to complete the restoration.[49]

Part of the locktender's house complex had included a store, the Basket Company, on Main Street adjacent to the house proper but this was gutted by fire on February 24th, 1992. The surviving portions of the structure were razed. The back walls, still standing, were cleaned and the Friends contracted with artist William Selesnick to paint murals, actually five separate scenes along the canal, with total dimensions of eight feet high and sixty-four feet long. One of the five illustrations of the historic canal and its activities focuses on a team of mules pulling an LC&N canal boat; this has become a favorite spot for camera-carrying tourists, who use the working mules as a backdrop. The artist's work was executed on sign painters' board so that, if the area in the future is designated for alternative uses, the murals can be moved.[50]

In January of 1994, thanks to grant monies and donations, particularly from the National Heritage Corridor and the Pew Charitable Trusts and implemented by two groups of young workers from the Pennsylvania Conservation Corps, a state-funded "serve, earn, learn" program, major restoration started on the lockhouse. On January 11th by 3 PM "the 1960's vintage wood paneling, two layers of linoleum flooring, and a maroon toilet and sink" were on a refuse pile. Then "removing wallpaper, installing temporary lighting, and cleaning-up the debris" lay ahead as the next steps in the long process of refurbishing and restoration. After bids, overbids and rebids, contracts were finally in place and by December of 1994 the carpenters and plasterers were at work. The Friends were still seeking funds to replace a porch and to install a security system. These funds were found and on September of 1995 the dedication of the renovated lockhouse as a visitors' center for the canal took place.[51]

In May of 1996, the Friends' restoration of the Locktender's House was one of twelve projects in the five-county Philadelphia area to receive an achievement award from the Preservation Alliance of Greater Philadelphia for its restoration. The same year, the Locktender's House and its project architect, Richard E. Brown Associates, received two awards for Excellence in Design in the competition sponsored by the Bucks County Chapter of the American Institute of Architecture and by the Central Bucks Chamber of Commerce. In 1999 the Friends received the first Franklin Wood Award, "created to recognize a Bucks County public entity that exemplifies innovative partnership in or sponsorship of a community project."[52]

In 1993, the Friends initiated a "Canal Tenders" program. An imitation of the widespread "adopt a highway" program, the canal tenders would adopt a section of canal and commit themselves to "watching for and reporting on significant changes or unusual conditions, picking up trash, and removing any obstructions from the towpath." They would also be required to complete a short questionnaire about their activities and the canal twice a year. It would provide a useful form of volunteerism and a supplement to the incredibly understaffed park employees.[53]

In 1995, the Friends were recipients of a Local History Project Support Grant from the Pennsylvania Historical and Museum Commission to support an Oral History Project. Names were sought of old-timers who remembered the canal in operation or who had included the canal and the subsequent state park in their lives and memories. Lance Metz, historian at the National Canal Museum and your author conducted interviews and audio- and videotaped the interviewees over the next several years, collecting much lore that enriches our knowledge of the canal and its people.[54]

The Point Pleasant Community Association obtained three Timber Bridge Initiative grants from the U.S. Forest Service, in 1995, again in 1998, and the third one in 2000 to develop engineering and general drawings and specifications for three prototypical timber camelback bridges with three different carrying capacities. The Bureau of State Parks, as a match, committed itself to the construction of one replacement bridge over the canal using one of the three designs.[55]

The fully restored lockhouse at Lock 11, New Hope, headquarters of the Friends of the Delaware Canal. On the left are interpretive signs. Courtesy of Friends of the Delaware Canal.

In 1997, the 10th annual five-segmented walk of the canal occurred and Willis Rivinus, who had inaugurated them, gave up his role as leader. He was replaced by Susan Taylor, executive director of the Friends.[56]

During the summer of 1996, the Friends of the Delaware Canal, aided by a grant from then-State Representative Joseph Conti and the Pennsylvania Department of Conservation and Natural Resources, instituted what would become an annual summer day camp for students entering fifth and sixth grades. The instructors were teachers Dr. Vince Profy and Mrs. Patricia Reines and, starting the second year, Bonnie Tobin, educational specialist for the Canal State Park. Meeting in the Old Library (headquarters of the Yardley Historical Association) on Lake Afton in Yardley, they explored the canal and its history using photographs, maps, and artifacts, supplemented by daily field experiences and walks along the canal.[57]

The Friends have continually projected themselves into the role of implementing canal improvement. On September 15, 1994, they hosted a "Meeting with Legislators and Bureau Director" designed for the purpose of educating the elected representatives as to the problems created by the dredging hassles, the future needs of the canal, and to create a "legislative caucus" to provide continuing support for the goals of the master plan and of State Parks 2000. The caucus as constituted at its first meeting on January 31, 1995, in Harrisburg, elected State Senator Dave Heckler as chair. The initial membership included, in addition to six assemblymen and three state senators, congressmen Jim Greenwood of Bucks County and Paul McHale of the Lehigh Valley, Lieutenant Governor Mark Schweiker, and, from the friends, Allen Black, Esq., Executive Director Susan Taylor, and Betty Orlemann, president. It was soon limited to the legislators only. When Heckler was elevated to a judgeship, assemblyman Joseph Conti (who became a state senator in 1997), took over the leadership.[58] The Friends, although no longer members of the caucus, remained committed and active.

Released in 1995

DELAWARE CANAL STATE PARK CAUCUS

PREAMBLE

The Delaware Canal State Park is the only remaining towpath canal in the United States capable of being fully watered. It lies within a designated National Heritage Corridor which was created largely because of the canal's continued existence. The canal and its towpath serve the Commonwealth as an invaluable environmental, economic, educational and recreational resource. The canal and adjacent historic, natural, and cultural sites constitute a tourist destination of international significance. The canal is a fragile structure requiring constant maintenance, much of which has been long delayed. This delay has led to deterioration which can only be reversed by expensive reconstruction.

MISSION STATEMENT

The mission of the members of the Pennsylvania General Assembly who have joined together to form the Delaware Canal State Park Caucus will be:

- To identify those federal, state, and local governments and agencies whose work impacts upon the canal or whose resources may be harnessed to benefit the canal;
- To provide organized advocacy for the needs of the canal;
- To assist in planning and coordinating the actions of the many government and private entities which impact the canal.

OBJECTIVE

Our objective will be restoration of the canal to a structurally sound and fully watered state with historically correct structures in place, preservation of the canal in that condition permanently and creation of the ancillary facilities and programs required to realize the canal's recreational, educational, economic, and environmental potential.

Cleanups

The initial credit for the annual spring clean-up along the canal goes to Ralph Ratcliffe and his Bristol compatriots, who recruited 200 Boy Scouts in November of 1969 to pull fifty truckloads of trash and junk from some ten miles of the canal. The Boy Scouts were recognized with shoulder patches. The following year they recruited more than one thousand participants to work on the canal from Bristol to Morrisville. However it was basically the Friends who would turn the efforts from a somewhat localized commitment at the lower end into a canal-long effort that was coordinated with the annual Earth Day. The involvement over the years by many groups is mute testimony to the extent of support—often silent—for the canal in the communities along its extent.[59] The Friends have assumed the leadership for coordinating the cleanup over the whole sixty miles of canal. An excerpt from the announcement in the Friends' newsletter about an upcoming clean-up is descriptive of the extent of the project:

> All Clean-Up Day workers should bring along their equipment of choice. Trash bags will be provided at the sites. It is anticipated that since there may not be much water in the Canal, this Clean-Up Day might be a good opportunity to clear out trash and debris that is usually submerged in the bottom of the waterway. Mud gear will be in order.

An article in the *Yardley News* elaborated:

> Experience has shown that high boots, gloves, rakes, saws, shovels, and branch snippers are useful tools to bring along to Canal Clean-Up Day.[60]

Betty Orlemann, founder of the Friends of the Delaware Canal, has participated in every clean-up. She reported in the *Delaware Valley News* following the 1992 effort:

What a mess! The area next to and just south of the bridge looked like a mini-dump.

Besides the inevitable beer cans, I picked up beer bottles, some broken, many other pieces of glass of various colors, and pieces of broken headlights …

I also bagged rotting trash bags, building materials (including a huge nut and bolt), a plant hanger, a six pack carrier, liquor bottles, a champagne cork and a filthy old empty pocketbook.[61]

Presumably her experience was not atypical.

That not all the efforts were necessarily on the scheduled clean-up day is illustrated by the following example. On Saturday June 1, 1991, about 100 members of a motorcycle club called ABATE, an acronym for Alliance of Bikers Aimed Towards Education, arrived in Bristol, armed with chain saws, axes, rakes and shovels, to help local volunteers clean-up the towpath side of the Bristol portion of the canal. Despite 90° temperatures, backbreaking labor and poison ivy, they were responsible for removing thirty dump-truck loads of branches and several more truckloads of trash.

According to the newspaper report, the leader of the volunteer cyclists pledged "if they need us we'll be back," despite, according to the press report, the fact that "most of the workers came away with poison ivy." They did come back: on Saturday November 2, some thirty returned, this time to do the berm. This time they filled sixteen dumptrucks with loads of trees and roots to be sent to the chipper, along with another five truckloads of trash and debris.[62]

The annual clean-ups continue.

Advisory Committee

The Friends' Master Plan of 1987 did bring some results. The state seemingly took note of the recommendations and, while the authorities were somewhat less than optimistic as to where the proposed millions would come from, they did create the advisory committee recommended in the Master Plan. In late autumn of 1987, Secretary Arthur Davis of the Department of Environmental Resources solicited names for committee membership "in order to schedule the first meeting in January, 1988."[63] Nine "public sector" members were nominated by the state legislators in the area; they were joined on the committee by eighteen elected officials representing the eighteen political entities adjacent to the canal. At an organizational meeting, held in Washington Crossing State Park on May 29, 1988, Steven Humphrey, executive director of Easton's Hugh Moore Park, was elected first chairperson of the committee. Over the subsequent years his successors, Betty Barr of the Friends of the Delaware Canal, Frank Boas, supervisor from Solebury Township, Bill Mullen, longtime canal activist in Morrisville, and William Mitchell, director of Bucks County parks, continued to provide leadership.[64]

The quarterly meetings were attended by William "Bill" C. Forrey, longtime director of state parks who, at the end of 1991, took advantage of the state's very attractive early retirement act. He was accompanied to meetings with Eugene "Gene" J. Comoss, engineer for state parks and Rayford E. Williams, legal counsel for state parks. They, on occasions, called on the advisory committee for advice and suggestions and have listened and attempted to act upon the desires and concerns of the members and of the communities insofar as they were able.[65] On June 2, 1992, Roger Fickes was appointed director of the Bureau of State Parks and he continued in the pattern of his predecessor, attending the advisory committee meetings and calling on the committee for their support and advice.[66]

It was upon the recommendation of the advisory committee in 1989 that the name of the park was changed from Theodore Roosevelt State Park to Delaware Canal State Park and the name "Theodore Roosevelt Conservation and Recreation Area" was assigned to a picnic and recreational area at Raubsville along the canal.[67]

In November of 1993, some 550 neighbors of the Delaware Canal State Park received letters from the Bureau of State Parks that, according to Susan Taylor, executive director of the Friends of the Delaware Canal, should have been labeled, "Caution—Bureaucracy at Work." The letters were notifications of encroachments, most, but by no means all, of a minor nature. The notifications were something that members of the Advisory Committee had been suggesting for a long time but even they were taken somewhat

"Encroachment" or privacy screen? Some homes that were close to the towpath had plantings to provide a modest amount of protection from the public who walked the canal.

aback by the almost implied punitive threats, for the letters unfortunately contained the rather bluntly stated warning: "Failure to remove the encroachment could result in further action by the Bureau." It was signed by Gary K. Smith, Chief, Park Operations and Maintenance Division. For many, it again raised the question of ownership and questions about deeds that placed property lines to the center of the canal.[68] Phones rang off the hook as the recipients of the letters, whose emotions ranged from anxiety to anger, called anyone they conceived as having any connection with the canal or state government. A number of property owners organized the Association of Delaware Canalside Property Owners. Since that time there have been a series of meetings held at spots along the canal.

The association presented a series of demands and statements of their rights, to which the state responded. The meetings ended without complete agreement and with further meetings in prospect but one thing that was agreed upon was that all parties felt they were working for the betterment of the canal, and at least minor and sometimes simply technical encroachments were discussed in more conciliatory terms, particularly as the state made clear its need to be able to use the banks of the canal in the prospective program of dredging. There has been no widespread implementation of the implied threats by the state.[69]

In August of 1996 the Advisory Committee was reorganized, at least partially because of the difficulty of getting a quorum at many of its earlier meetings. The number of public interest members was reduced, and the balance were representatives of larger political areas and of agencies, chambers of commerce, preservation groups, parks and state offices. At its first meeting, Jerry Bastoni, executive director of the National Heritage Corridor, was elected chairperson and Susan Taylor, executive director of the Friends, was chosen to be vice chair. During the fall of 1996, Park Manager Ken Lewis conducted a three-part tour of the sixty miles of the canal and the revised committee was challenged to examine the future of the waterway.[70] Following the demise of Bastoni in 1998, Tim Brought, a township supervisor from Solebury Township, served until his removal to Florida opened the position and Susan Taylor of the Friends was elected during the September 1999 meeting of the Advisory Committee. In the spring of 2001, William Mitchell resumed the chair for a second time and Susan Taylor accepted the position of vice chair.[71]

The Delaware and Lehigh Canal National Heritage Corridor

On February 17, 1988, Congressman Peter Kostmayer of Bucks County and Congressman Donald Ritter of Northampton and Lehigh Counties introduced a bill, HR 3957, calling for the creation of the Delaware and Lehigh Navigation Canal National Heritage Corridor.[72]

An act of Congress signed by President Reagan on November 18, 1988, created the corridor and called for the creation of a Corridor Commission. This would be the third such heritage corridor to be brought into existence by the National Park Service.[73]

In June of 1990, at a Saturday ceremony held near Bowman's Tower in Washington Crossing State Park, National Parks Service official Carl Jester "bestowed the designation of 'Delaware Canal Heritage Trail' on the 60 mile canal towpath." Thus it became part of the National Trails System, originally created under an Act of Congress of 1968.[74]

In March of 1990 the Pennsylvania legislature passed an act designating the corridor as a Pennsylvania Heritage Park Planning Area and followed this by recommending the personnel for the Heritage Corridor Commission to the Secretary of the Interior for appointment. Central to the charge given to the corridor commission was to develop over the next two years a "Cultural Heritage and Corridor Management Plan."[75]

According to the corridor's own literature, "A national heritage corridor is an alternative to a conventional national park, which normally requires the federal acquisition and management of large amounts of land." While in the park system, it was unlike other "parks": the land was not federally owned, and "the land and resources within the corridor are managed cooperatively with state and local governments and through voluntary agreements rather than exclusively by the National Park Service."[76] Reflective of this, the 1992 Draft Management Action Plan of the National Heritage Corridor Commission included a major plank, the development of a Delaware & Lehigh Trail for hiking and a Delaware & Lehigh Drive, a program to develop patterns for visitors to partake of the canal's environment and its ambience.[77]

After a certain amount of political infighting, the commission members were finally nominated by Pennsylvania's Democratic governor and then appointed by the federal Republican Secretary of the Interior. Prior to the first organizational meeting of the commission on April 19, 1990, much groundwork had been laid by the personnel of the National Park Service, particularly Deirdre Gibson. At that organizational meeting, Willis Rivinus of Solebury, already the author of a walking guide to the Delaware Canal that had gone through several editions and the leader of the well-publicized annual canal walks sponsored by the Friends of the Delaware Canal, was elected chairman. At the next meeting, Allen Sachse of Pennsylvania's Department of Community Affairs was named interim executive director and it was determined that office space should be obtained in Bethlehem.[78] By 1992, Will Rivinus had been succeeded by Donald Bernhard of as commission chairman. David A. Witwer was on board as permanent executive director and had been joined by Sue Pridemore as interpretive specialist and Millie Alvarez as administrative secretary.[79]

The first and primary charge to the new commission was to produce over the first two years a Corridor Management Action Plan. After several drafts and public meetings to discuss this, the final edition appeared, dated January 1993, titled "Delaware and Lehigh Canal National Heritage Corridor and State Heritage Park Management Action Plan." As the commission itself put it in its own newsletter, it describes four basic purposes:

- Providing Physical Linkages
- Creating an Interpretive System
- Protecting Key Resources
- Capitalizing on Heritage Development Opportunities

The Corridor Commission has attempted to work with and stimulate local governments and groups such as conservationists, preservationists, and developers to identify with the corridor, both its present and future. To do so, they have produced a newsletter, an Historic Resources Study, awarded their own grants, and supported other grant applications. Their summer internships have helped to develop and aid in the interpretation, although more has been achieved in the Lehigh areas than along the Delaware Canal. Along with the Friends, they have been a major player in the effort to obtain signage and interpretation along the Delaware Canal.[80]

It is probable that many readers stopped to examine the headline in the Sunday issue of the *Bucks County Courier Times* on April 18, 1993, which read: "Canal to get $157.6 million to lure tourists." Upon probing the article, the reader discovered that the newspaper was referring to the newly released "management action plan" that called for this amount to be spent over the next ten years. It projected that there would be $37,000,000 in federal monies expended while $120,000,000 would be state, county, local, and private money that would restore deteriorated sections of the canals, build a canal visitor center in Bucks, establish scenic drive and loop tours, restore historic structures, and promote tourism.[81]

Also in April of 1993, Governor Robert P. Casey of Pennsylvania finally gave the federal corridor designation as the Keystone State's third State Heritage Park. The State Heritage Park Program, administered in cooperation with a number of other state agencies, gave the federal corridor, local governments, and other participating partners access to planning and developmental grants from previously unavailable state and outside agencies.[82]

In 1994, a portion of the $2,800,000 released by the state to fund the National Canal Museum and the State Theater in Easton was made available to the corridor to establish an interpretive center. The Two Rivers Landing program in Easton included, in addition to the canal museum and the Two Rivers Landing Interpretive Center, the Crayola Factory™, a visitors center for Binney and Smith, makers of Crayola-brand crayons.[83]

On Friday July 6, 1994, the Pennsylvania Historical and Museum Commission announced that the National Trust for Historic Preservation had agreed to begin a study of the potential for tourism on the southern reaches, that is the Bristol–Morrisville area, of the Delaware and Lehigh National Heritage Corridor. Entitled the "Canal's End Reach," this was one of four such studies in Pennsylvania and Pennsylvania, according to the newspaper report, would be the fifth state in which the National Trust was making such studies. The Heritage Corridor contributed $30,000 to the cost of the three-year study, the total cost of which was not announced. Also involved were the Pennsylvania Department of Commerce's Office of Travel Marketing, the Center for Rural Pennsylvania, and the Pennsylvania Heritage Parks Program of the Department of Community Affairs.[84]

In the spring of 1996, Gerald Bastoni was selected by the twenty-one-member Corridor Commission as the new executive director. The 45-year-old resident of Bethlehem expressed his optimism following the appointment:

> It's a tremendous opportunity, because this project is going to leave a big footprint on all of eastern Pennsylvania for years to come.

The goals that Bastoni called to be implemented included the establishment of ten landings— "places where visitors would get area information and directions to attractions" —the upgrading of hiking and biking trails, plus the placing of interpretive signage.[85]

The goal to establish trails received attention when in February of 1996 the Heritage Corridor Commission produced The D & L Trail Workbook with the assistance of the Rivers, Trails and Conservation Assistance Program of the Chesapeake System Support Office of the National Park Service. It was subtitled An Inventory and Assessment of the Delaware & Lehigh National and State Heritage Corridor Trail System. The workbook title was accurate, for it was an outline or possibly a proposal for implementing a system of trails from Bristol at the southern end, through Easton, and on to Wilkes-Barre at the northern end of the corridor, extending the entire length of the route by which

Jerry Bastoni, executive director of the National Heritage Corridor Commission from 1996 to 1998. Courtesy of the National Heritage Corridor Commission.

the Lehigh Coal and Navigation Company carried coal from the Wyoming coalfields to the Delaware River at Bristol.[86]

In the summer of 1997, Helen Mahan-Forester, a planner with the National Park Service, was in the area, paying particular attention to the portion of the proposed trail between Philadelphia and Morrisville in Pennsylvania and a route between Palmyra and Trenton in New Jersey that had been proposed as an adjunct to the Corridor trail.[87]

Grants from the Corridor Commission to provide seed money for local initiatives have been numerous. They have included a grant in 1991 of $40,000 for the preservation of the Bristol Marsh to be managed by a partnership of the Silver Lake Nature Center and the Nature Conservancy. $100,000 went to the Bristol Lagoon in 1995 and 1996. In 1990 $21,000 was granted the Bristol Spurline Park and in 1992, the Heritage Conservancy, based in Doylestown, received $20,000 for a Historic District Study. In 1992 there was a $22,500 grant for Canal's End Reach Tourism and Preservation. In 1995 Morrisville received

$30,000 for a Water Works Restoration and the next year another $30,000. In 1997, $50,000 was provided towards the purchase of Graystones in Morrisville and $27,000 for the study of a heritage visitor's center in Bristol.[88]

In August of 1997, the Bristol lagoon was visited by Senator Arlen Specter. Up for re-election in 1998, Specter praised the volunteer efforts that were then going on and promised to use his influence to seek $20 million in federal funding for the development of a 150-mile recreational trail from Wilkes-Barre to Bristol.[89]

The Morrisville grant has borne fruit: by 1997, under the leadership of the Morrisville Heritage Development Association, an observation platform was constructed enabling visitors to see the river and the skyline of Trenton, New Jersey. The platform is level with the levee constructed after the 1955 floods. Work is underway to restore the 100-year-old pump house at the waterworks along the canal and it will be converted into a community/tourist center while an adjacent borough garage is planned to be a canoe/bike rental shop. A home for a performing theater group has also been established.[90]

In 1998, the original ten-year term for the Heritage Corridor Commission expired. Jerry Bastoni and many others successfully issued the call for support of a renewal of the Corridor Commission.[91]

In December 1998, Bastoni died suddenly, a shock to all who knew him. A momentary void in leadership resulted. However the commission and its staff moved forward actively and Allen Sachse was named as his replacement.[92]

Bureau of State Parks

The Bureau of State Parks, while less than successful in maintaining budget levels sufficient to adequately maintain and police the park, has been relatively successful in obtaining capital funds for major restorations on the canal. Whereas personnel, which numbered twenty-one (permanent and seasonal) during the 1980s, had shrunk by 1990 to seven full-time, supplemented by several seasonal employees, the result of shrinking operating budgets, the picture for capital and major maintenance appropriations was far less grim. Illustrative were the figures placed before the Advisory Committee which revealed that between the years 1981 and 1988, out of a total of nearly $22 million the BSP had in construction monies for the whole state, $1.8 million was expended on the canal. Judged on any basis other than the canal's need, this was most generous. Among the projects addressed were wall repairs at New Hope, the Lumberville wall, the Woodside Bridge, and the Stoney Run Aqueduct. Since 1988, more than two million dollars was expended on the Durham Aqueduct and the Overpeck Bridge near Lodi. Work started in 1991 and was completed in 1993, the contractor being Allan M. Meyers, Inc., of Worcester, PA.[93] The Lodi lock and bridge have been completed, although unfortunately scaled down, while a $2 million replacement Tohickon Aqueduct and the Riegelsville waste gate were in the planning and design stages. After several overbids and some redesigning, the contract was let for the aqueduct. The dedication of the completed work took place on September 15, 2001.[94]

Prior to the season of 1989, Pennsylvania's Bureau of State Parks conducted an extensive survey to provide a basis for an "initiative" to be prepared as the State Parks entered their second century in 1992. The planning document was called "Pennsylvania State Parks 2000: Directions for the Next Century." The publication, produced in 1992, was an enlightened summary of goals and aspirations. One page, entitled "Investing in the Future," featured a pie graph showing "State Parks Capital Funding Needs" at $125 million, which contained a very generous slice entitled "Delaware Canal Restoration $30 million." This was essentially the figure in the master plan for the canal. On the next page was the note: "An additional $30 million is needed to repair and stabilize one special historic resource park—the Delaware Canal." The Delaware Canal State Park was the only one out of 114 state parks to be named in the document. The recommendation was added for the whole State Parks 2000 program, that "the Commonwealth should undertake a major capital improvement program financed by a bond issue or other long-term funding mechanisms."[95]

Department of Conservation and Natural Resources

In 1995, under the new Thomas Ridge administration, there was a reorganization of the cabinet departments and the state Department of Environmental Resources was replaced by two successors, a new Department of Environmental Protection and a Department of Conservation and Natural Resources. State parks, state forests, and related agencies came under the jurisdiction of the latter. It was hoped that the concerns of the canal would be even more central to the purposes of the administrators of the new bureau. On November 22, 1995, John C. Oliver, formerly of the Western Pennsylvania Conservancy, was appointed the first secretary of the new department.[96]

The creation of the new department, presumably able to give much more attention to the state parks, can be credited, at least partially, to the efforts of the previously noted legislative caucus. And, as hoped, things started to happen. Park Manager Ken Lewis led a group of interested persons on a canal-long tour, which inspired the formation of a revised advisory committee. A plan entitled "Delaware Canal State Park: Opportunities for the Future" resulted. The plan was introduced at a meeting of the Legislative Caucus, the Advisory Committee and the director and representatives of the DCNR held July 31, 1997, at the Bucks County Conservancy in Doylestown. Then State Senator (now Judge) David Heckler, chair of the caucus, presided at the meeting and at the press conferences that followed. As reported by the media, "The Delaware Canal State Park will undergo a $7.65 million face lift with trails, water fountains and even canoe launches." Ken Lewis was reported as saying that "Studies done by park officials in recent years show that refilling the canal, a plan considered by the Delaware Canal Advisory Board, would cost $100 million, without additional costs of maintenance and other projects." He said that the "longest dry section of the canal—a 12-mile stretch though Lumberville—would remain empty for now under the project."[97]

The plan incorporated three options. Option one, or "plan one" as it was called by Ken Lewis, was, also in the words of the park manager, "pie in the sky," as it would call for the expenditure of $100,000,000 for major improvements to the canal plus new bathrooms, drinking fountains, and improvement of the towpath for hikers and joggers. The whole canal would be watered and traversable by canoe. "That's a dream," according to Lewis.

Plan two, described by the park manager as "Plan one on the installment plan," would upgrade the recreational facilities as in plan one, adding toilets, drinking fountains and a tow path hikers/bikers trail. Lewis noted, "There are sections of this canal that historically carry water all the time. Why don't we focus on the sections that hold water and make them the best they can be." The rest of the watered canal would receive only temporary repairs to stabilize it and these areas would be restored only as funds became available.[98]

Plan three called for permanently stabilizing "some sections of the canal by filling in where the prism needs support." According to the plan, "All three options focus priority on development of recreational facilities," something that according to many longtime supporters of the canal was in error. They thought and still think that the number-one priority should be historical preservation of the watered canal, although maintaining a watered prism can be achieved for much less than the projected $100 million with some compromises but without ignoring the recreational dimension.[99]

The choice of the options created controversy but, according to the DCNR, "Both the Delaware Canal State Park Caucus and the Advisory Committee adopted Option 2 of the plan."[100] The concerns of many longtime canal supporters were reflected in the plan's objectives listed as number two and four, which read as follows:

2. To develop those sections of the Canal that historically demonstrated a reasonable degree of water carrying sustainability into optimum examples of a historic watered canal environment.

4. To control vegetation in the canal prism in areas unable to sustain water.

Objective number six was somewhat ambiguous:

6. To initiate projects designed specifically to increase the total length of "Optimum Historic Watered Canal Environments," thereby increasing the possibility of realizing a fully watered, historically appropriate canal for the entire 60 miles.[101]

Among the plan's critics was Will Rivinus, instigator of the annual canal walks and the first chair of the Delaware and Lehigh Navigation Canal National Heritage Corridor Commission, who, the Allentown *Morning Call* reported, said, "the plan sounds like the state [is] favoring parts of the canal while letting the remainder return to nature." He was further quoted as asking, "Are we giving up watering for a flush toilet? Some of us feel water in the canal is paramount."[102]

The plan spelled out a five-year "plan of action," with specifics for the first four years. It is worthwhile to present the stated goals for the first year.

> In this exciting voyage into the future, the park's mission as a regional tourism destination will unfold.
>
> A significantly more user friendly bicycle and pedestrian trail in Pennsylvania will parallel what already exists across the river in New Jersey. A 60-mile bi-state regional trail system, connected by six river bridges will be a reality. Recreational and visitor comfort facilities at two of the park's largest recreational areas will be upgraded to modern, first class status. Several easy and safe canoe access points along the river will provide the linkage to a river "water trail" and the park's islands. Visitors' first impressions of the park at the popular Mule Boat Concession in New Hope, will be improved immensely through modernization of this area's comfort facilities. Enhanced historical interpretation will be offered. In Bristol Borough, a dynamic community park will be opened as a result of lagoon restoration and rehabilitation of the canal.
>
> In the canal, water will flow south from Easton. The all-wooden aqueduct will majestically tower over the waters of Tohickon Creek in Point Pleasant. The forest that has taken over the canal in historic Lumberville will be removed and the canal restored. In Yardley, the towpath trail will be widened. Dredging will reduce the risk of flooding and increase the flow of water through lower Bucks County.
>
> Most importantly, a new water intake system will be installed that will provide adequate water flow year round from New Hope to Bristol.

The estimated cost for year one was set at $2,650,000.

Dredging, bikepath-surfacing, vegetation-clearing, upgrading and establishing recreational and comfort facilities, signage and canal rehabilitation were scheduled during years one through four. The estimated further costs were: for year two, $2,130,000; for year three, $1,036,000; for year four $871,000; and for year five, $946,000.[103]

On November 26, 1997, the Bureau of State Parks announced that a new company had been formed that would take over the canal boat concession in New Hope from 20-year operator George Schweickhardt. The principals in the new venture are Paul F. Raywood, a New Hope businessman who specializes in historic restorations, and Alexander M. Urbani, president of the Urbani Family Enterprises of North Wales, Pennsylvania. They have engaged managers and have named Susan Taylor, presently executive director of the Friends of the Delaware Canal, as consultant, particularly for the historical interpretation. Two new boats were ordered from a Chesapeake Bay boatbuilder. The proposed new boats are modeled in aluminum after the *Molly-Polly-Chunker*, a vessel that a party of aristocrats, including amateur photographer Louis Comfort Tiffany, equipped for an 1886 outing on the canal from Bristol to Mauch Chunk (Jim Thorpe) on the Lehigh Navigation. The boats were delivered in time for a start in May of 1998. There has been some opposition to the change, particularly from a group of New Hope residents who have designated themselves as "Friends of George"—the former concessionaire. The state parks bureau indicated that they desired a greater historical/educational component, in the hopes of attracting more tourists.[104]

In 1996, the canal museum in Easton, renamed the National Canal Museum, was moved from its location at Lock 24, the northern terminus of the Delaware Canal, to the new Two Rivers Landing complex on Centre Square in the heart of the City of Easton. There it shared space with the Crayola Factory and the Delaware and Lehigh Canal Corridor. It opened on June 14, 1996. Subsequently, after much negotiation, preliminary arrangements were for the City of Easton to lease the old museum to the state for $1.00 a year for a minimum of twenty years. Barbara Kowitz, administrative assistant for the city, and Ken Lewis, park manager for the Delaware Canal State Park, discussed the possible agreement which would commit some $600,000 in state money for building renovation, modernizing the restrooms, connecting to city water, and an upgrade of parking and landscaping. Other possible partners were suggested: the state Fish and Wildlife Service, the Delaware River Greenway, the Corridor Commission, and also local groups.[105] The preliminary transfer took place during 1999 and it was to be finalized in June of 2001. Construction of the "River Center," as it will be designated, was to have begun in October of 2001, but has been delayed indefinitely.[106]

Dredging was underway in 1998, contracted out to James T. O'Hara, Inc. For the first year, projections were for work to be done from New Hope north to Lumberville, on a five-mile stretch in Yardley, and also on sections in Bristol and in Falls Township. The dredged areas were to be lined with clay. Once the work was underway, in the Yardley section alone about one hundred truckloads of dredged materials were removed.[107] The dredging in Yardley was completed by September 9, 1999, while the Lumberville area was completed by the spring of 2000.[108]

In September of 1998, Park Manager Ken Lewis announced that an electric pump would be installed at New Hope. According to Lewis, "when the river is low, the pump will send water across a flume under the Waterworks into the canal." This was the spot where a pair of wooden waterwheels had operated during the active years of the canal. Following further surveys it was determined that the bed of the river, even at low water, was two feet higher than the canal so a gravity system was instituted, whereby gravity-fed river water reached the canal through two pipes. This system was in place by the fall of 1999.[109]

In the meantime, the state acquired seven islands with an area of 102 acres in the Delaware River. They are designated as part of the state's natural areas program— "areas that protect unique scenic, geologic or ecological resources within the state park system.[110]

In 1998 the DCNR produced a document entitled "Delaware Canal State Park Private Investment Plan," designed to supplement the five-year plan. Whereas the state's plan called for the expenditure of $7.6 million along with the approximately $5 million currently underway for a total of $12.6, the new plan called for a broader vision and the ultimate expenditure of more than $64 million. It noted that to fully realize the broader vision, monies beyond the public tax dollars were essential and, therefore, private partnerships. The canal was broken into three sections. Projects such as an Easton visitors/environmental center, lock repairs, land acquisition, wall repairs, aqueduct replacement, construction of canal and trail crossing, restoration and interpretation in the Raubsville power plant, and enhanced staff and equipment are but a few of the items proposed. At the March 26, 1998, meeting of the Advisory Committee it was reported that CEO of Air Products & Chemicals, Inc., agreed to furnish the corporate leadership, while the committee unanimously endorsed the goals of the plan.[111]

The partnership has begun work. The minutes of the Advisory Committee for March 2001 noted that the Historic Delaware Canal Improvement Corporation had raised $100,000 to match U.S. Army Corps of Engineers funds for the replacement of the Yardley Aqueduct.[112]

Continuing Problems

It was during the second week of January, 1996, that a flood hit the Delaware Valley, the result of the melting of heavy snows. Despite the fact that the staff of the canal park had anticipated possible trouble and had drained the canal, still the rising river and the ice that it carried overflowed the banks and created flooding. In several places the water and the debris it had picked up as it surged downstream spilled into the canal, damaging banks, stone walls, and waste gates. The efforts of the park staff were heroic as they freed waste gates that were frozen, sometimes locked into two feet of ice. Had they failed in their efforts the flooding, which was disastrous in Yardley borough and elsewhere, would have been much worse. In Yardley and Morrisville, emergency crews and volunteers had opened the gates. As it was, major flooding took place and numerous residents along the canal and river, at least 1,200 in Yardley alone, had to be evacuated. The initial estimate of damages was set at $1.7 million. Later estimates of damage to the canal park were $10 million in the Northampton County section and $4 million in the Bucks County portion. The canal in Northampton County, just south of Easton, suffered the loss of portions of an 8,800-foot-long stretch of towpath that was washed away. Nearby, an aqueduct was lifted off its abutments by ice and the fish ladder at Easton, also a concern of the park and its employees, was filled with some 500 to 600 tons of silt and 450 tires. The watering of the whole canal, which had been so optimistically predicted in the autumn of 1995, would now have to be postponed for at least a year for the necessary repairs.[113]

Then on June 12, an unprecedented 11-inch downpour at Yardley created a flash flood that, according to the park manager, "caused a massive towpath blowout at the Afton Avenue aqueduct and deposited a huge siltbar where Silver Creek flows directly into the canal." The rain continued off and on for a week and spread havoc and flooding throughout lower Bucks County. Yardley was probably the hardest hit spot in the valley. At the Yardley Aqueduct over Brock Creek, according to the *Courier Times* reporter, "Tons of earth were washed away on both sides of the canal aqueduct ... severely damaging the towpath that borders the waterway." According to park manager Ken Lewis, the fast-rising waters of Brock Creek overwhelmed the waterway. "The waters rose above the aqueduct's waste gate (which was open), so there was no place to dump the water." [114]

The summer of 1996 was plagued by heavy rains that prevented the watering of the upper reaches of the canal, causing a dirty canal bed containing litter and a heavy stand of weeds. The efforts of the park staff were interrupted by the rains and were much behind schedule. They also had the task of clearing the fish ladder at Easton, a victim of the January flooding. Roger McChesney, assistant park manager, told a reporter, "Last year, we were all set [to reopen the canal], we thought. Then, January came." With the ice, snow and floods, much of the work of the previous year was washed away and had to be repeated.

It was expected that the Federal Emergency Management Agency, which inspected the area following the floods, would cover 75 percent of the estimated more than $1.5 million that it would take to repair the canal.[115]

Concerns did not disappear and the role of the canal in the floods remained a concern. Repairs to overcome flood damage had depleted the annual appropriation. Manpower required for dredging and silt build-ups and the continuing deterioration could create new financial problems.[116]

Another result of the floods was the need for emergency road repairs, particularly between Centre Bridge and Kintnersville. The Pennsylvania Department of Transportation apologized that, because of the emergency nature of the repairs, they had been unable to hold hearings and notify everyone who might be affected. The innkeepers, who operated numerous popular eateries and watering places, protested the closing of the road and pleaded that at least one lane might be open on weekends, their most profitable period. But George Koch, PennDOT's assistant construction engineer, responded:

> It would be too dangerous. ... We're going to be doing some excavation [of the road] ... The west side of the canal supports the roadway. When that failed as a result of the storm, it undermined the roadway.... [At most sites] we're going to come at least to the middle of the road,

tearing out the road to rebuild the canal. He did promise that the work would be done in small stages, closing only part of the road at a time but, as this author can attest, for all practical purposes, as long as the work continued, the detour encompassed the whole section.[117]

In August of 1997, residents complained about "Green Slime" on the canal. According to Arthur Frey of Riegelsville, "You can't see the water; it's all green." Roger McChesney reported that this was just one of numerous similar complaints about the water and also about overgrown vegetation. The "green slime" was caused, he noted, by duckweed, a free-floating plant that forms a green blanket on the surface of the water. Instead of leaves it has one or two green, leaflike fronds and a one-inch white root, and can grow as thick as one or two inches on the top of the water. According to McChesney, it is not hazardous and does not clog the waterways since it is carried by the currents. It is food for ducks and other waterbirds. It appears in the summer and will die with the arrival of frost.[118]

About the same time, seniors in Morrisville complained. Elsie Winder, a resident in the Presbyterian Towers apartments along the canal, opined, "Someone should come out and look at this stagnant water before we all get sick.... I'd rather see trees growing in it." She was seconded by Charles Gallagher, an environmental landscaper and founder of Morrisville-based Canal Kids Klub, which was devoted to beautification of the canal. He noted the need for flowing water and said "Without it, alien invasive plants like the purple loose strife, are taking over." Park Manager Ken Lewis agreed and explained that the lower end of the canal was supplied with water from the Delaware River from the pool of water at New Hope created by the wing dam, which had fallen into a state of disrepair. Earlier, water had been lifted at that spot into the canal by a pair of waterwheels, gone since the 1920s, but state park engineers were, according to Ken Lewis, designing a new intake system. As to the trash that the seniors referred to, Lewis noted that he had only three employees to remove trash from the whole canal and that volunteers and communities must be cooperative.

Another problem that summer was an oil spill on the Lehigh River that forced the closing of the stop gate at Easton. However, state employees accidentally broke the gate, forcing the temporary use of stop blocks, and subsequently had to repair the gate.

On January 13, 1998, in Falls Township, a 26,000-gallon tank of the Wonder Chemical Company sprang a leak and released some 8,000 gallons of a chlorine bleach solution into the canal. The Falls Fire Marshall described the result as "the worst fish kill I've ever seen." There was another spill from the same source on February 9. An estimated nearly 5,000 fish were killed, mostly in the first release, for, as one of the contract cleanup workers, Debra Poppel, observed, "We didn't find too many dead fish this time. They're all dead from the last spill." The kill of fish and frogs continued until a heavy rain could dilute the toxin.[119]

As sections of the canal were dry or nearly dry with no flow of water, the many pools that remained became breeding ground for mosquitoes, something that would be eliminated when water again flowed to the canal. This brought a further concern, and park personnel began testing chickens for the new "epidemic," the West Nile Virus.[120]

Sections of the canal that were heavily silted and dry or poorly watered attracted four-wheelers and other vehicles not only on the towpath but in the former bed of the canal.

Fish kills and, more often, the fish loss that resulted from the necessary periodic draining of the canal frequently resulted in a newspaper headline such as the one that graced the *Courier Times* issue of Wednesday September 26, 1990. It read "Residents say canal draining left fish high and dry," and the story told how 16-year-old Matthew Green of Edgewater Avenue in Yardley with "at least a dozen young men and children worked for at least six hours Monday netting perch, trout, bass, carp and other fish and carrying them to nearby Buck Creek." In 1993, when the canal was drained because of dredging, the headline read "Dead fish stinking up Delaware Canal," and the accompanying story again described how youngsters worked against odds to save a few fish. Presumably it made for good news, as did another account the next year of three youngsters aged 14, 9, and 6 who, according to the account, "decided to take the fish out of the canal by hand, but didn't know what to do next." After taking them home, they then followed a mother's advice and released them to a lake behind a housing development. Park Manager Ken Lewis, according to the article, admitted responsibility for saving the fish, but noted, "It's up to us to get them out, or volunteers. But it's tough on us because we only have two rangers and eight maintenance men." Appended to the newspaper article was a notice that "Those interested in volunteering their time" could contact the canal office.[121]

In May of 1996, another situation that threatened the dredging and other maintenance of the canal developed. The new concern was a canalboat graveyard located in the canal near Tullytown. As a *Courier Times* article reported, "Over a span of more than 60 years, the decks and their accessories either deteriorated or were scrapped, while the bottoms of the barges sunk deeper into the silt." Attention to the hulks was called by Mark Smith, who remembered as a teenager in the 1960s that "You could walk out on the deck, lift the hatch, and see a mud-filled cabin." Curious as to what had become of them, he found evidence of their existence and told an aunt, who then informed the Friends of the Delaware Canal. The Friends sought funds, some $2,500, to sustain the preservation and interpretation of the remains of the canal boat. The Tullytown Council voted to pay a share of the cost of an archaeological survey, some $1,300, and Waste Management, Inc., with property adjacent to the site, promised also to contribute $1,200. The hulls of the boats had become visible when the canal was drained to permit work on the Bristol lagoon. There were four boats, according to the archaeological firm's operator, Lee Cox, and the remains consisted primarily of 40-foot-long planks that had constituted the hull of the boats.

The find caused some interest, and Susan Taylor, executive director of the Friends of the Delaware Canal, was reported as saying that, because there were no surviving boats, "This is why we want these barges recorded for history." Cox, in a preliminary summary of his report, wrote that the hulks "possess sufficient significance [*sic*] criteria to be eligible of nomination in the National Register of Historic Places."

All this furor was particularly troublesome as the Tullytown stretch, which was leaking like a sieve according to park manager Ken Lewis, was scheduled for dredging and relining. Will Rivinus expressed wonder at the fuss, observing that "In theory it would be great to preserve everything taken from the canal, but there are more important issues, like making it water-tight." He continued stating that today's visitors could learn more from photographs and drawings made of the wrecks than by "looking at timbers which were left there to rot." On Wednesday, January 29, Ken Lewis reported that "We can work around them." The dredging could be continued and the hulks embedded on the west bank could and would be bypassed and it was not necessary to consult with the Pennsylvania Historical and Museum Commission. Bristol's Ralph Ratcliffe noted that "When we were kids. we called that section of the canal 'the widdies' meaning it widened at that point" and that was the reason they abandoned the boats there: "They were never in the canal." Susan Taylor promised that the Friends would place a marker at the spot.[122]

A letter from Parthenia M. Carabelli to the editor of the *Yardley News* raised an additional problem. She questioned the maintenance of the proposed public toilets along the canal, particularly the one at Black Rock Road in Lower Makefield Township, saying that without 24-hour attendant service they could be "an invitation to loitering, drug drops and vandalism." Even gas stations, she noted, lock their toilets, so if the state wants facilities for hikers it should move them to locations away from convenience and ease of access by road. Eventually, the decision was made to locate the facilities at the renovations in Morrisville rather than at Black Rock Road.[123]

In the summer of 1999, hurricane Floyd did extensive damage to the canal and communities along the towpath.

As the master plan was being implemented and a three-foot-wide path of crushed stones was inserted into the towpath, criticism surfaced. Despite the fact that this kind of surface was widely and successfully used on national, state and local trail areas, Linda Lori and Valli Rothaus appeared and protested at a meeting of the Delaware Canal State Park Advisory Committee meeting. According to Rothaus, "The historical beauty and integrity is being raped. … It is no longer scenic. … It's a 21st century material, we're a 19th century park." Their protest to the park staff, the advisory committee, and state legislators was unsuccessful. At each level the paths were supported—as they were by this author, who prefers crushed stone with drainage to muddy earthen ruts.[124]

The rewatering of sections after dredging created new problems. In the Tullytown area, water was let into the canal in late April of the year 2000. Several businesses were flooded as a result of seepage from the canal. After protests to State Senator Tommy Tomlinson, DCNR chief engineer Gene Comoss arrived from Harrisburg. The solution would be to "dry out" the canal, and while it was dry a contractor would be hired to repair the leaks. Comoss estimated the costs to be between $50,000 and $100,000.[125]

Positive attempts to improve the canal did not always meet with positive reactions. Congressman Jim Greenwood took the initiative and, duplicating former Congressman Peter Kostmayer's action, brought the Corps of Engineers to examine the spot where the canal is piped under U.S. Route #1. This time he suggested that he could find some $275,000 in federal funds to reopen the canal and bypass the pillars supporting overpass over the roadway.[126]

This resulted in a letter exhibiting the negative attitude shared by some members of the community along the canal. One Norman Enslie, in the *Yardley News*, expressed surprise that $275,000 would be used for such a purpose:

> The canal, as I remember it, is a ditch, large, long, surrounded by scenery, equipped with a footpath of sorts, and always littered with debris—pop bottles, soda cans, paper, cigarette packs, plastic trays, metal, an occasional tire and more. Green scum clings to objects thrown or blown into the water. Still the canal is history, and as such, it should be maintained, but only at a reasonable and justifiable cost. In my opinion, $275,000 is not either justifiable or reasonable. So the highway supports stand in the canal! Who would notice, and if they did, so what?[127]

The *Bucks Courier Times* of May 8, 2001, carried the headline "1,400 obstructions along canal's path." It noted that several were black-topped driveways and parking spots. Many more were like benches obstructing the towpath, or sheds or dog houses anchored "within the canal's right of way." According to Ken Lewis, any obstruction that inhibited the movement of people or maintenance equipment would have to removed, while other infractions would be dealt with on a case-by-case basis.[128]

Personalities

While note has been made of the superintendents and people like Ralph Ratcliffe and Naomi Tomlinson, saviors of the lower end of the canal, and of C.P. "Bill" Yoder, historian and defender of the canal, there are others of whom some note should be taken. There are the members of the Swope family, the late brothers Howard and Frank, who learned canalling under their father, a canal-boat captain, and who as teenagers captained their own boats. Howard started on his father's boat at the age of ten as a mule driver, and then captained a boat until the canal closed down in 1931. In more recent years, retired, he found a new life advising the Canal Museum in Easton in its interpretation of the Delaware Canal. And for about thirteen years he was a member of the team from the Friends who presented programs throughout the area until his death in 1995 at the age of 80. His nephew Frank, son of Howard's older brother, also Frank, has, in a very real sense, continued the family tradition of working on the canal. He became a member of the park staff in 1963 and thirty-one years later, in 1994, was appointed to be a "supervisor" in charge of a portion of the Delaware Canal State Park. The younger Frank Swope retired in 2001.[129]

On May 19, 1991, a grand old lady, Virginia Forrest, passed away. She had been a lifelong conservationist and during her later years had made the Delaware Canal one of her major concerns. Moving from the Delaware Valley Protective Association, she founded the Bucks County Conservation Alliance and was the recipient of the first membership certificate of the Friends of the Delaware Canal. She received numerous recognitions for her work and was honored posthumously when the "Barge Stop" picnic area (Route 32 and Paxon Road) was renamed the Virginia Forrest Recreation Area.[130]

In a volume by Kate Mulligan entitled *Canal Parks, Museums and Characters of the Mid-Atlantic*, the author pays tribute to "Three Stubborn Women." They were Betty Orlemann, Zabel Davis, and Susan Taylor, all of whom have been noted by this author. Correctly, she gave them credit for much that has occurred on the Delaware Canal and in the state park.[131]

Local Initiatives

Since its inception, the National Heritage Corridor, following the line of the National Park Service (NPS) has been emphasizing partnerships and local initiatives. While certainly the thrust has a long way to go, there has been some response. Of course the efforts of the Friends of the Delaware Canal and the Lower Bucks Conservation Committee long preceded the arrival of the NPS but since the creation of the corridor, activities have increased. Especially worthy of note were the volunteer efforts at the Bristol Lagoon. The lagoon, at the terminus of the now-filled canal, was graced by a gazebo, already restored, and was the setting for the Grundy skating rink which was burned in 1995. As it was rebuilt at another site, the whole basin area was available for restoration and what has occurred is an example of local initiative. More than 275 volunteers, many from Local 542 of the Operating Engineers along with representatives from other locals, have worked at the site. Supported by some $200,000 in state funding, half from the Heritage Commission, they have removed some 125,000 cubic yards of muck, mostly from the canal, recreating the lagoon and an adjacent island. A concrete wall more than 960 feet long has been constructed to protect the banks. Concrete, other materials, and the cost of running donated equipment consumed most of the state funds. During the spring of 1997 there were more than thirteen pieces of equipment in use at one time. According to State Representative Thomas Corrigan, "There isn't one group or company which was approached that refused to help," and the volunteers included the young who among other things painted over graffiti on the walls of the railroad that spanned the canal.

On Saturday, November 1, 1997, the restored and watered lagoon was dedicated with a coterie of state and local officials plus union representatives present, cutting a ribbon to the restored footbridge.[132] The euphoria was short-lived, as leaks developed four miles upstream that virtually drained the lagoon. Representative Corrigan became the spokesman, reporting that the state was going to plug the leak with clay. Park Manager Lewis said there were really three problems: first, the state must guarantee that the nesting places of the endangered red bellied turtles would not be disturbed; second, they must bring in another state agency that would guarantee the remnants of a buried canal boat would not be disturbed; and, third, it wasn't just one leak but there were a number of leaks along a stretch of the canal.[133]

Unfortunately there has been some controversy about what should have been a happy commitment. It was Edna Roth, a former executive/mayor of Bristol Township, who penned a guest editorial in the *Bucks County Courier Times*, "Give credit—and respect—where due for canal project." She opened by recalling

> Thirty years ago, the Delaware Canal was almost destroyed by short-sighted politicians. A group of people led by Ralph Ratcliffe and Naomi Tomlinson formed the Lower Bucks County Canal Conservation Committee. This group saved the canal and has been responsible for keeping it from being raped by other short-sighted politicians.[134]

She then went on to attack State Assemblyman Thomas Corrigan, accusing him of opposing the opening of the canal at the Levittown Shopping Center. "In 11 years as state representative, not one positive thing was done by him for the canal," she charged. She credited State Senator "Tommy" Tomlinson with seeing the potential of the lagoon and the canal, and then Corrigan hopped aboard and with his ally, Bristol Borough Council President Joe Coffman, assumed authority and prevented the Lower Bucks County Conservation Committee from participating in the dedication of the lagoon, despite earlier promises. She presented a list of the many she credited of having worked to save the canal. It follows:

> … Sen. Grundy, U.S. Supreme Court Justice William O. Douglas, Virginia Forrest (who had the canal declared an historic landmark), Milton Berkes, Judge (then congressman) Pete Beister, Boy Scouts and students from Girotti-Snyder, F.D.R. and Pen Ryn and the other volunteers for yearly cleanups of the canal, Joe Smith, former Borough Councilman, James Amon, director Raritan Canal, Walter Farley, Charles Meredith, Matt and Jim Wright, Lt. Gov. Mark Schweiker, Fidel Esposito, Bruce Singer, the many members and friends, living and deceased, who did so much for years, and Sen. Tomlinson and his staff.[135]

Controversy continued as the borough council ruled that the watered lagoon, now stocked—thanks to borough money and a $250 contribution from the Knights of Columbus—with bass, catfish and perch, was off-limits for fishing and swimming. According to the *Bucks County Courier Times*, council President Joe Coffman said that the bans were "designed to keep the area clean and protect it environmentally." Borough manager Fidel Esposito was reported to have said that signs might be posted banning bicycles and dogs. The police had already evicted, in addition to fishermen, two sun-bathers who, Coffman reported "had their blanket all spread out and were blasting their music. They were out there swimming." This raised the hackles of Ralph Ratcliffe, who proclaimed that the park was for the benefit of the people. On Wednesday, June 3, 1998, the *Courier Times* carried a photograph of Ralph fishing in the lagoon backed by Edna Roth and Billy Bartle. However, the borough officials apparently were winning as they were preparing a sign that would read, "No fishing, swimming, alcohol or bicycles."[136]

Thanks to the efforts of the Friends, partnership efforts were crowned by progress achieved by the spring of 1998. One was the stabilizing of the walls of lock #18 at Uhlerstown. The $13,000 needed was raised through a $10,000 legislative initiative grant from State Senator Joe Conti, supplemented by contributions made by Uhlertown residents, the Pennsylvania Canal Society, and the Canal Society of New Jersey. The second was the Smithtown Repair Partnership, which saw more than $10,000 raised by local residents and businesses and a legislative initiative grant of $25,000 secured by Senator Conti. Thanks to these efforts, permanent repairs were made at double lock 15 and 16, which will enable it to withstand the full head of water that will flow now that the Tohickon Aqueduct has been replaced. The Friends are looking for other areas where their efforts can contribute to the well-being of the canal.[137]

Canal Kids

During the spring of 1996, 7th and 8th grade students at the Franklin D. Roosevelt Middle School in Bristol Township started working on a research project about the canal as they prepared for an environmental sciences competition. Guided by faculty members and encouraged by Ralph Ratcliffe and Naomi Tomlinson of the Lower Bucks Canal Conservation Committee, they interviewed local businessmen seeking to learn how the canal has affected business. Among their plans were for 150 students to work cleaning litter and debris from the canal on April 9 of that year.

Local businesses pledged support by donating hot dogs, candy, drinks, supplies and restroom access. On Tuesday, April 23 they presented their project to an audience of parents, and state and local dignitaries. The 20-minute program included hand-outs, videos and slides demonstrating the historical and environmental significance of the canal. They proposed dredging, bridging the canal at significant road crossings and summarized their interviews, with homeowners, politicians and business people. It was their dress rehearsal for the competition against sixteen other schools in the Symposium for Environment and Education, a national science competition to be held in Concord, New Hampshire. To their surprise and that of their teachers, they discovered that, because of their efforts, they and the participating students of the seventeen competing schools, some 400 in all, were being awarded future full scholarships for environmental studies at Fisk University in Nashville, Tennessee. All that was necessary was that the participants maintain a B average throughout high school, get satisfactory SAT scores and have no criminal record. It is still to be seen how many of the forty Bristol Township students will ever attend.[138]

In 1997, these same "canal kids" were joined by their contemporaries of the "Kids Conservation Klub" of Morrisville. Their coordinator, Charles Gallagher, a landscape designer, led the two groups in planting canal-friendly plants along the canal, something the Morrisville group had been doing for several years.[139]

Cartoon from the Bristol Pilot, April 1999, praising students from two local high schools for caring about their community enough to organize and conduct cleanups along the canal. Author's clipping collection.

In May of 1998, the "FDR Middle School, Bristol Township Symposium Kids" were awarded a $2,850 grant by the Bucks County–based Heritage Conservancy "for the Environment and Education Sharing Knowledge to Save Our Wetlands." Kathleen Horwatt, the FDR Middle School counselor, was reported as saying, "This will help pay for the transportation to take their message on the road, including Harrisburg."[140]

In June of 1998, the same "Canal Kids" again hit the news when they wrote letters protesting engineering plans designed in such a way that they would cause a new I-85 interchange to destroy a part of the canal. They wrote letters to KCI Technologies, the engineering firm, and one of their letters was published in the *Courier Times*. They apparently disturbed the firm for the teacher, Lynn S. Roccograndi of FDR Middle School, a week later wrote a letter of apology to the engineering firm.[141]

In April of 1999, the clean-up activity of the Kids was supplemented by members of the Army Reserve 465 Transportation Company, who parked a Humvee at a nearby gas station and joined in the Kids.[142]

By the year 2000, the "Canal Kids" had added other environmental projects to their activities and renamed themselves "The Flood Kids," but they still did their turn at cleaning the canal. On April 25, 2000 Ralph Ratcliffe and the Canal (Flood?) Kids were hard at work cleaning the canal in Bristol Township. At lunchtime they were called and assembled by Gary Smith of the DCNR staff for a presentation. Noting his over 2,500 hours of volunteer time in the previous fifteen years as well as his activities with community and schools, Smith, accompanied by the cheers of the Kids, presented Ralph with a plaque recognizing him as one of three Pennsylvania "Conservation Volunteers of the Year."[143]

In May of 2001, Steven Cousin, a now a senior at Bristol township's Truman High School, received a four year, full-tuition scholarship to Fisk University. He is the first of the fifteen Canal Kids to qualify.[144]

Prospects

At the November 1994 meeting of the Advisory Committee, Park Manager Ken Lewis revealed his ambivalent feelings, that on the one hand the condition of the canal had never been worse, and that on the other, the prospects had never been better. To illustrate, he listed the numerous breaks in the unwatered canal and the plant growth in and along the canal that had established itself in the sixteen month period of confusion and debate between the various bureaucracies. He and Eugene Comoss, the state engineer for the Bureau of State Parks, collaborated to describe the inanities of the permit finally granted by the Corps of Engineers that prevented anyone taking (or purchasing) the rich dredge material taken from the canal before it had been deposited on the G.R.O.W.s landfill, an expensive operation for which the state funding was virtually exhausted. The questions of the potential for interference on the part of state and federal historical overseers was discussed by the committee and there was at least some foreboding of potential future problems. However, Lewis expressed his optimism for the future, for the permit was in place, state capital funds seemed to be in place for several major projects on the canal, there was some $3,000,000 in prospective ISTEA money and much greater input from the Corridor Commission seemed to be in the offing.[145]

Progress has been continuous since the installation of the master plan. With $3,000,000 in ISTEA monies and a $7,200,000 appropriation from the state, a $3,000,000 dredging project was initiated and as part of the first stage of the plan, a start had been made in installing a four-foot-wide path of crushed stone for hikers and bikers, down the middle of the towpath. Additionally, the contract was drawn up for the construction of the replacement aqueduct over the Tohickon, "of wood," and the design reflects the historic character of earlier aqueducts. This was finally achieved, after overbids and redesign delayed the project for at least a year. The contract was finally awarded to J.D. Eckman of Atglen, Pennsylvania. By summer of 2000, the old aqueduct had been demolished and work was underway on the replacement.[146] The completed aqueduct was dedicated on September 15, 2001.

The Friends have restored the Locktender's House at New Hope and turned it into an interpretive center. Monies seemed to be available for more major restoration and interpretation at both Bristol and at Easton. While Lewis didn't mention it, the incorporation of the Canal Museum (renamed The National Canal Museum) at Easton into the multi-million-dollar Two Rivers Landing project, where it was combined with a Crayola visitors center and a National Heritage Corridor interpretive center in downtown Easton, a complex that draws several hundred thousand visitors a year, was something that would also contribute to the enhancement of interest in the Delaware Canal, its history and its lore.[147]

The realignment of political power structures as a result of the 1994 elections, both in Harrisburg and Washington, contributed to an enhancement of efforts for the future prospects of the canal and, thanks to the efforts of the Friends, there is in place a "Delaware Canal Legislative Caucus" that has already created a Mission Statement and has been able collectively to carry sufficient weight to enhance protection and support the canal, the state park and their various related interests.[148]

Thanks to public officials, private citizens, and innumerable volunteers the future of the state park as a watered greenway seems secure and one can hope that the active, watered canal may be somewhere in the future.

APPENDIX I

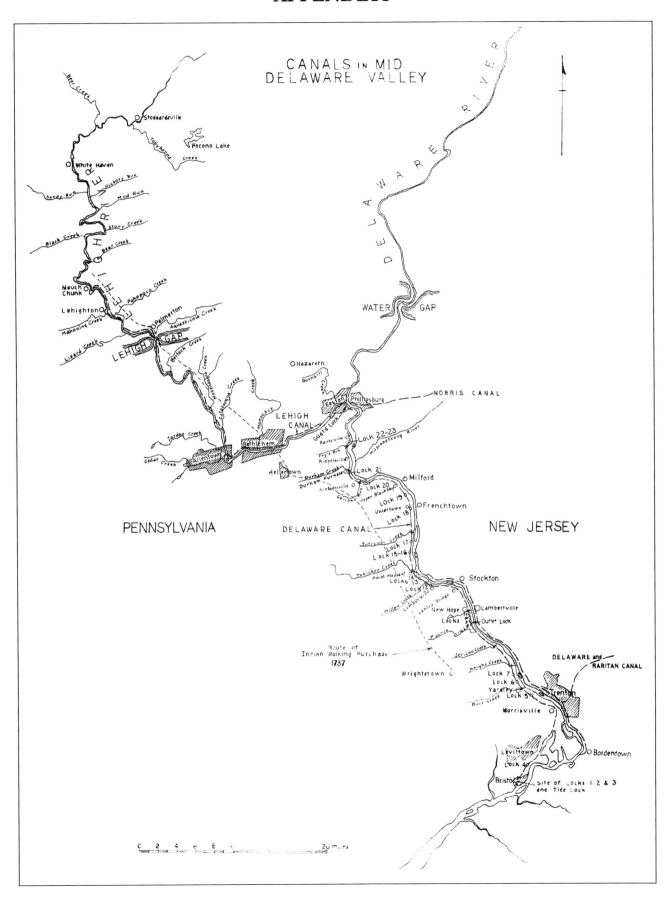

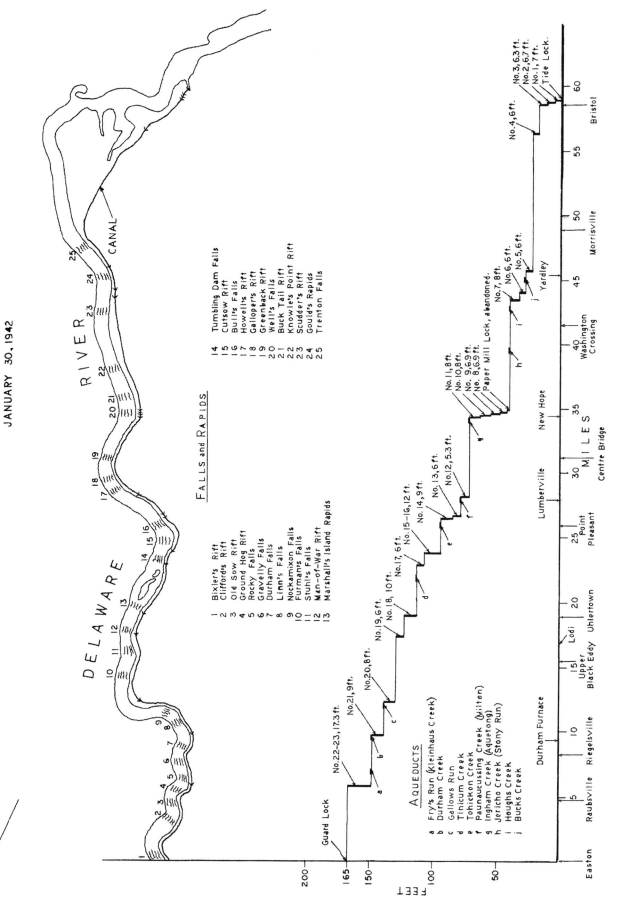

DELAWARE DIVISION CANAL — PLAN AND PROFILE

FROM

WATER AND POWER RESOURCES BOARD — PLATE I.

JANUARY 30, 1942

FALLS and RAPIDS

1   Bixler's Rift
2   Clifford's Rift
3   Old Sow Rift
4   Ground Hog Rift
5   Rocky Falls
6   Gravelly Falls
7   Durham Falls
8   Linn's Falls
9   Nockamixon Falls
10 Furmans Falls
11 Stuhl's Falls
12 Man-of-War Rift
13 Marshall's Island Rapids

14 Tumbling Dam Falls
15 Cutsow Rift
16 Bull's Falls
17 Howell's Rift
18 Galloper's Rift
19 Greenback Rift
20 Well's Falls
21 Buck Tail Rift
22 Knowle's Point Rift
23 Scudder's Rift
24 Gould's Rapids
25 Trenton Falls

AQUEDUCTS

a   Fry's Run (Kleinhaus Creek)
b   Durham Creek
c   Gallows Run
d   Tinicum Creek
e   Tohickon Creek
f   Paunaucussing Creek (Milton)
g   Ingham Creek (Aquetong)
h   Jericho Creek (Stony Run)
i   Houghs Creek
j   Bucks Creek

C. P. Yoder 1972

202 ∽ Delaware Canal

APPENDIX II

ARTICLE OF AGREEMENT, entered into this   day of   one thousand eight hundred and   by and between the COMMONWEALTH OF PENNSYLVANIA, by   Superintendent on the

Division of the Pennsylvania canal, of the one part, and   of the other part,

Witnesseth, That the said   do   promise and agree to dig, embank, puddle and construct, in a substantial and workmanlike manner, all that part of the   Division of the Pennsylvania Canal, known and designated as the   section, upon the plan of the   line of said Division, in the following manner, to wit:

The canal banks to be so constructed, that the water may at all places be at least forty feet wide at the top water line, twenty-eight feet wide at bottom, and four feet deep. Each of the Banks shall be at least two feet above the top water line, and such a slope shall be preserved on the inner side of the banks, both above and below the top water line, as that every foot perpendicular rise shall give an horizontal base of eighteen inches, the towing path shall be on the river side of the canal, its surface shall be at least ten feet wide, and the bank opposite the towing path shall be at least seven feet wide, and both banks shall have a declination from the inner to the outer edge thereof, equal to half an inch for every foot of surface; the banks shall be constructed of pure, solid and compact water proof earth, and they shall be made smooth and even, with a slope on the outermost side, not less than is above mentioned. And it is further agreed, for the purpose of giving to the banks the necessary connexion with the earth upon which they are to be erected, that all the grass, trees, bushes and stumps, on the space to be occupied by the canal banks, together with all logs, brush, roots and vegetable matter of all descriptions, shall be wholly removed at least fifty feet from the centre of the canal; and it is further agreed that al necessary grubbing shall be executed according to the directions of the engineer appointed by the canal commissioners of Pennsylvania, and when required that a puddle ditch shall be excavated under the seat of each bank, of such breadth and depth, and shall be carried up to such a height within the embankment, as may be designated by the engineers.

And the said   to be paid for completing this contract as follows:

For grubbing and clearing, the sum of

For all necessary excavation within the banks of the canal, puddle ditch and towing path of the same of earth, gravel, loose stones, clay, loam or sand   per cubic yard.

For embankment, when removed over one hundred feet, and to be measured in the banks,   per cubic yard.

For cemented gravel or hard pan, strictly such,   per cubic yard.

For solid or blast rock,   per cubic yard.

For detached rock measuring more than one cubic foot, and for slate rock,   per cubic yard.

For puddling,   per cubic yard.

For vertical wall,   per perch of 25 cubic feet.

For outside slope wall,   per perch of 25 cubic feet.

It is understood by the parties, that under the term excavation, are included all drains that may occur on the section; and under the term embankment is included the filling in of bridges, and that in all cases the earth for embankment shall be taken from such places as may be directed by the superintendent or engineer on the line. It is also understood that no allowance shall be made for the bailing of water.

It is further agreed, that any items of work, that may necessarily occur on this section, not already specified in this contract, shall be estimated by the engineer, and paid for accordingly. And it is further understood by the parties that all stone quarried from the bed of the canal is the property of the commonwealth of Pennsylvania, and not of the contractor, and may be disposed of by the superintendent as he thinks proper; and that all timber, buildings or fences on the track of the canal, are the property of the landholder, and the said contractor to be responsible for the safe keeping of the same from the depradations of   hands and laborers.

The payments to be made in the following manner: On or about the   day of   next ensuing the date of this contract, the said engineer shall estimate the quantity of work done, and upon his certificate being presented to the superintendent, the amount thereof shall be paid, deducting therefrom fifteen per cent.; and on or about the   day of each succeeding month, within the limits of this contract, the like estimate shall be made, certificate granted, and payment in like proportion made thereon. The fifteen per cent directed to be retained to be withheld until the contract is completed, unless the board of canal commissioners shall direct the same or any part thereof to be sooner paid: And further, at the expiration of the stipulated period for the completion of this contract, if the whole work shall be finished to the satisfaction of the said superintendent, the said engineer shall estimate it, and within twenty days after the presentation of his certificate to the superintendent the balance which may remain due shall be paid.

It is further agreed between the parties, that when the superintendent on this division shall give notice in writing, or by public advertisement, that the sum of money appropriated towards the expenses of this division, for the present year shall have been expended, that any subsequent labor performed under this contract, shall not be considered as incurring a debt against the state, contrary to the true intent and meaning of the 7th section of the act of the 21st of March last.

And the said   do   further promise and agree, that   will from time to time during the progress of the work conform to such deviations from the present line of the canal, and to such alterations in the form, slope, and dimensions of the banks, towing paths or any other part of the works, as the said engineer may direct. And it is mutually agreed that the decision of the said engineer shall be final and conclusive, in any dispute which may arise between the said parties.

And the said   do   further agree, that   will not re-let or transfer said con-tract, or any part thereof, to any other person or persons whatever. And that   will personally superin-tend the work during its progress.

It is further agreed between the parties, that in case the work upon this section shall not be commenced within   days from this date; or if at any subsequent period the said   should, in the opinion of the superintendent or engineer, refuse or neglect to prosecute this contract with a force proportional to the quantity of work to be done, and the period within which it is to be completed; or shall sub-contract or re-let said section or any part thereof; or shall not give personal superintendence to the work, the said engineer shall have power with the consent of one of the canal commissioners to determine that this contract has been abandoned, and such determination shall put an end to this contract, and exonerate the commonwealth from every obligation thence arising; and the superintendent may immediately proceed to dispose thereof in the same manner as if it had never existed. And to avoid disputes, as well as interruption and hindrance to the regular and peaceable progress of the different parts of the work, and to prevent unnecessary injury to the rights and property of the neighbours in the vicinity of the canal, the superintendent, engineer, or assistant engineer will dismiss from the service, every quarrelsome disorderly person, and such as shall be addicted to habits of intemperance, or who shall wantonly commit any unnecessary trespass, either upon the person, land, or property of citizens living, travelling, or working upon or near the works of the said canal, or be guilty of other offensive misconduct; and every contractor shall dismiss all similar persons employed under him, whenever thereto directed by the superintendent, engineer, or assistant engineer.

And the said   do   promise and agree to finish and deliver up this contract on or before the   day of   in the year 183

This contract not to be binding on the commonwealth, until approved by the board of canal commissioners.

In witness whereof, the said parties have hereunto set their hands and seals the day and year first above mentioned.

    W ITNESS   [L. S.] Superintendent.

                                        [L. S.]

                                        [L. S.]

                                        [L. S.]

———

Extract from the 6th Section of the act of the 25th February, 1826.

"No extra allowance shall in any case be made for the performance of any such contract beyond the sum stipulated therein."

NOTES

PART ONE

Many citations refer to the microfilm rolls available from the Pennsylvania Archives, RG-17, Records of the Land Office, Records of the Board of Canal Commissioners. The Minutes of the Canal Commissioners are found in the General Records, reels #1–5, numbers 3608 to 3612. The minutes are also found in print in the separate Annual Reports of the Board of Canal Commissioners and in the respective volumes of the state House of Representatives and Senate, and after 1845 in the Reports of the Heads of Departments. Because they are available from so many sources, they are cited only by date. The same is true for the citations from the minutes of the state House and the state Senate, which are available in their annual reports.

The following rolls of microfilm are classified as Divisional Records, Delaware:

Reel #7 [#3438]	7(1), Reports & Misc. Documents, vol 2, 1827–1835	
	7(2), Reports & Misc. Documents, vol 1, 1836–1844	
	7(3), Reports & Misc. Documents, vol 2, 1836–1844	
Reel #8 [#3439]	8(1), Reports & Misc. Documents, vol 2, 1836–1844	
	8(2), Reports & Misc. Documents, vol 1, 1845–1858	
Reel #9 [#3440]	9(1), Reports & Misc. Documents, vol 2, 1845–1858	

The following rolls of microfilm are classified as General Records:

Reel #26 [#3633]	Collectors' and Supervisors' Reports
Reel #27 [#3634]	Collectors' and Supervisors' Reports
Reel #28 [#3635]	Collectors' and Supervisors' Reports
Reel #29 [#3636]	Collectors' and Supervisors' Reports

Notes to Chapter One

1. *Niles Weekly Register* XXXII, 17 March 1827, 37.
2. Peter Wallner, "Politics and Public Works: A Study of the Pennsylvania Canal System, 1825–1857," unpublished Ph.D. Thesis, Pennsylvania State University, 1973.
3. *Compilation of the Laws of Pennsylvania Relative to the Canal and Railroad Regulations as Established by the Board of Canal Commissioners* (Harrisburg: Barrett and Parke, 1840), 27.
4. Originally, Simon Guilford was employed as engineer on the Delaware Division, but apparantly rejections of employment by other engineers caused the commissioners to reassign him to the Juniata Division. See "Report of the Canal Commissioners," 28 Dec 1827, House Journal II, No. 49, 98, also in *Hazard's Register* I (1828), 21; Minutes of Canal Commissioners, Harrisburg, 2 May 1827; "Copy of answer from S. Guilford, Lebanon, May 2d, 1827," House Journal, 1827, II, 120. A critical observer characterized Henry Sargent as "a gentleman of respectable talents and character, who has seen some service as a sub-engineer on the New York canals. He has never, we believe, been employed in a superior capacity, and has no direct experience in making estimates for a canal on the margin of a large river. That gentleman is a stranger to Pennsylvania: he brought with him a preconceived idea of the value of materials and labour, founded on New York estimates, and totally irrelevant to our country," "Delaware Trade and Canal," *Hazard's Register* I, 184. An 1836 item in the *American Railroad Journal* cites H.G. Sargeant [*sic*] as publishing "The Report of 1831" for the Hudson and Delaware Railroad, "Newburgh, or Hudson and Delaware Railroad," *Amercan Railroad Journal* V (1836), 561.
5. "Canal Documents," in *Hazard's Register* I (1828), 118–122, from Canal Commissioner's Reports including Thomas G. Kennedy's report of 5 Nov 1827 and Henry G. Sargent's several reports; reprinted from House Journal, 1827, II, 239–248.
6. "Report and estimate on the Survey of a canal line, from Easton to Carpenter's Point by D.B. Douglass, Engineer," *Hazard's Register* III, 101–108; House Journal, 1828–29, II, 241; "Thomas F. Leaming, One of the Representatives of Philad. To the Board of Canal Commissioners," Harrisburg, 14 Dec 1829, *Hazard's Register* V (1830), 12–14.
7. John Johnson deposition, 1 Sep 1827, reel #6, item #28; Bristol Committee petition, 11 Sep 1827, reel #6, item #18.
8. "An Incorporation of a Company for opening a Lock Navigation on Neshaminy Creek, in Bucks County, from Tideway to Bridgetown on the said Creek," passed 11 Jan 1832. Thomas G. Kennedy Papers, Spruance Library, Bucks County Historical Society.
9. J.N. Simpson to Jonathan Roberts, member of the Board of Internal Improvements of Pennsylvania, New Brunswick, 28 July 1827, item #97; minutes of the Senate of Pennsylvania, 24 Jan 1831.
10. Sargent to Canal Commissioners, 20 Aug 1827, House Journal, 1827, II, 244–245; also *Hazard's Register* I, 120.
11. Journal of the Canal Commissioners of Pennsylvania, Philadelphia, 10 Sep 1827, 214, RG-17; Records of the Land Office, Divisional Record, Delaware Division, 1826–1858, reel #1, Minute Book (copy).
12. Thomas G. Kennedy had served Bucks County as sheriff, prothonatory, and member of the state assembly and had been an unsuccessful candidate for Congress. He had been one of the incorporators of the Neshaminy Lock Navigation and owned property in Bucks including a farm at Erwinna and at one time a tavern in Bristol. When he left the canal he became a major

figure in the construction of the Philadelphia and Trenton Railroad. Warren S. Ely, "The Samuel Hart Collection of Manuscripts 1777–1877," *Papers Read before the Bucks County Historical Society*, V (1926), 717–731, Kennedy, 719–721; J.H. Battle, *History of Bucks County Pennsylvania*, reprint edition (Spartanburg, South Carolina: The Reprint Co., Pub., 1985); George MacReynolds, *Place Names in Bucks County Pennsylvania* (Doylestown, Pennsylvania: The Bucks County Historical Society, 1942, 1945), 88–89, 100–104.

13. Minutes of Canal Commissioners, Philadelphia, 11 Sep 1827; Ely, 719.

14. Thomas G. Kennedy to Canal Commissioners, Bristol, 5 Nov 1827, *Hazard's Register* I, 118.

15. H.G. Sargent to Canal Commissioners, Philadelphia, 10 Sep 1827, *Hazard's Register* I, 121.

16. Map, J. Edgar Thompson: Proposed extension of Delaware Division Canal from Bristol to Philadelphia—1832, Map Book #7, "Communication from the Board of Canal Commissioners, accompanied with a Report of J. Edgar Thompson, Civil Engineer, Relative to the extension of the Pennsylvania Canal from Bristol to Philadelphia," 6 Feb 1833, House Journal, 1832–1833, II, 474–486.

17. William Strickland, "Reports on Canals, Railways, Roads, and Other Subjects made to The Pennsylvania Society for the Promotion of Internal Improvement" (Philadelphia: H.C. Carey & I. Lea, 1826), 10, plus related drawings.

18. Jon Fell to Joseph McIlvaine, Philada, 5 mo. 30th 1827, reel #6, #44.

19. James Clarke to Joseph McIlvaine, Canal Office Millerstown, January 4, [1828].

20. "Memorial of members of the Legislature recommending stone locks on the Delaware," n.d., reel #6, item #34; Sargent to Pres. of Board of Canal Commissioners, New Hope, 25 May 1828, reel #6, item #36; minutes, Board of Canal Commissioners, 28 March 1828.

21. Sargent to Board of Canal Commissioners, 31 July 1828, reel #6, item #42.

22. Sargent to Board of Canal Commissioners, 17 March 1829, reel #6, item #47.

23. Minutes of Canal Commissioners, 5 June 1829; "Proceedings [Relative to the connection of the Delaware Div. with Lehigh Canal]," 5 June 1829, reel #2, 1–4.

24. "Proceedings [Relative]," 8 June 1829, 7–10, 13–15.

25. "Contract for Dam and Lock at Easton," "Proceedings [Relative]," reel #2, 24–27.

26. Receipt, "Proceedings [Relative]," reel #2, 28; contracts, 28–31.

27. Minutes of Canal Commissioners, Harrisburg, 29 Nov 1830.

28. "Petition of the Owners of Mills propelled by water power in the Borough of South Easton," 22 Oct 1856; Report of the State Engineer, Edward F. Gay, Philadelphia 20 Sept 1856, reel #2: Kennedy to Canal Commissioners, Bristol, 5 Nov 1827, House Journal II, 239–240.

29. Battle (ed.), *History of Bucks County*, 399–400; MacReynolds, *Place Names*, 101.

30. Canal Commissioners Report, 28 Dec 1827, 127, 136.

31. Senate Journal, 1828–1829, II, 5; "Report of Thomas Kennedy," 1 Nov 1830, House Journal, 1830–1831, II, 228.

32. Pennsylvania Canal Papers, Land Office, Harrisburg, Surveys and Correspondence, 1824–1829, I, item 124, specific item is missing from microfilm reel #6, Delaware Division and also in the Archives at Harrisburg, so the author is forced to rely on the quotation from same in Hubertis M. Cummings' typescript "State-Owned Canals of Pennsylvania."

33. "Progress of Internal Improvements," Doylestown, 29 Sept, *Hazard's Register* II (1828), 207; Sargent to Canal Commissioners, 31 July 1828, 17 March 1829, reel #6, items 41 and 47.

34. Kennedy's Report, 20 Nov 1828, House Journal, 1828–1829, II, 145–146; "Pennsylvania Canal," Doylestown, Sept 9, *Hazard's Register* II (1828), 207.

35. Kennedy's Report, 20 Nov 1829; Sargent's Report, 20 Nov 1829, House Journal, 1829–1830, II, 287–288, 294–295.

36. Advertisement of King and Livingston with printed endorsement and handwritten correspondence, dated variously March, July, August and October 1829, reel #12, Misc. Papers, II, 106.

37. Memorandum signed by Orvill B. Dibble, General Agent, dated 27 Jan 1835, reel #12, Misc. Papers, II, 83; Report of Simpson Torbert, 1 Nov 1835, Appendix to Vol. II, House Journal, 1835, No. 25, 106.

38. Kennedy's report, 20 Nov 1829; Sargent's report, 20 Nov 1829, House Journal, 1829–1830, II, 287–288, 294–295.

39. "Copy of an agreement between the states of Pennsylvania and New Jersey, for the mutual use of the waters of the River Delaware, for canal purposes," Senate Journal, 1829–1830, II, 198–204.

40. "Pennsylvania Loan," *Niles Register* XXXVI (1829), 297; "Temporary Loan," *Niles*, XXXVI, 317; "Pennsylvania," *Niles*, XXXVII (1829–1830), 399.

41. Lewis S. Coryell to Canal Commissioners, New Hope, 2 June 1829, reel #6, item #77.

42. Canvass Wnite to Kennedy, Philadelphia, 31 Dec 1829, reel #6, item #66.

43. Kennedy to David Scott, Pres. Board of Canal Commissioners, Erwinna, 15 March 1830, reel #6, item #67.

44. Report of the Board of Managers of the Lehigh Coal and Navigation Company presented to the Stockholders, 11 Jan 1830, hereafter cited as LC&N Annual Report, with appropriate date.

45. Kennedy to David Scott, Pres. of Board of Canal Commissioners, Erwinna, 3 March 1830, reel #6, item #70.

46. House Journal, 1830–1831, II, 227–245.

47. LC&N Annual Report, 1831, 11.

48. George MacReynolds, *Place Names*, 109–110.

49. Report of John Barber, 28 Nov 1831, Senate Journal, II, 202–204.

50. Minutes of the Board of Canal Commissioners, Harrisburg, 9 April 1831.

51. Ibid.

52. Quoted in *Early History of New Hope, 1922* (The Free Library of New Hope and Solebury, 1982), 19.

53. Canal Commissioners Report, 15 Dec 1831, 15–16; "Cost, Revenue and Expenditure of the Public Works of Pennsylvania," 30 Nov 1852.

54. Sarah A. Gallagher, *Early History of Lambertville, N.J., 1703–1903* (Trenton, N.J.: MacCrellish Quigley, Printers, 1903, reprinted by Lambertville Historical Society, n.d.), passim; see also biographical notes of Hubertis M. Cummings, reel #6, index.

55. Kennedy to Board of Canal Commissioners, Erwinna, 25 March 1829, reel #6, item #43; Minutes of Canal Commissioners, 27 Dec 1830.

56. Minutes of Canal Commissioners, Harrisburg, 31 Dec 1830; Kennedy's report, 1 Nov 1830, House Journal, 1830–1831, II, 229.

57. "River Delaware," *Hazard's Register* XVI (1835–1836), 94.

58. Minutes of Canal Commissioners, 15 Dec 1831; Coryell to Clark, reel #6, item #121; for more detail on some aspects of the interstate problems see "Damming the Delaware, Speech of Mr. W.B. Reed," *Hazard's Register* XVI, 169–174, particularly 170–171.

59. Lewis S. Coryell to James Clarke, 13 July 1831, reel #6, item #119; Coryell to Canal Commissioners, 6 July 1831, item #130; to J. Clarke, 25 Nov 1831, item #121.

60. Josiah White to James Clark, Pres., Board of Canal Commissioners, Phila., 16 April 1832, reel #6, item #II, 14.

61. "A Trip on the Pennsylvania Canal," from American Daily Advertiser, *Hazard's Register* X (1832–1833), 342–343.

62. "Delaware River. Report of [New Jersey] Commissioners, … February 7, 1835," *Hazard's Register* XVI (1835–1836), 113–115.

63. *Ibid.*

64. "Report of the Commissioners, accompanied with documents, relative to the use of the waters of the Delaware River, READ IN SENATE, December 13, 1834, [etc.]," Senate Journal, 1834–1835, II, 50–75, 644–668. See also "River Delaware," *Hazard's Register* XVI (1835–1836), 93–95, 102–105, 113–116, 152; "Damming the Delaware," 26 Feb 1835, *Hazard's Register* XVI, 169–174; "Report upon the Feeder, att or near Black's eddy, upon the Delaware division of the Pennsylvania Canal," House Journal, 1833–1834, II, 554–555.

65. C.P. "Bill" Yoder, *Delaware Canal Journal* (Bethlehem, Pa: Canal Press, Inc., 1972), 216–217, 264.

66. See printed contract for contractors, Appendix II.

67. White, quoted in Wallner, "Politics and Public Works," 113.

68. Kennedy to McIlvaine, Bristol, 4 Feb 1828, reel #11, item #89.

69. "J.M. Downing of Barker Downing, contractors for building a section of the Del Div Canal, Bond of indemnity to protect Dr. John Philips [*sic*]," signed, J.M. Downing, Bristol, Oct 20 [1830], The Thomas G. Kennedy Papers, Spruance Library, Bucks County Historical Society, item #40.

70. "J.M. Porter, Atty for Barker to Thomas G. Kennedy," Kennedy Papers, item #42; "J.M. Downing—Receipt for $1,000 from Thomas G. Kennedy, Supt. Del Division Canal and Bond of indemnity from Downing & Wood," Kennedy Papers, item #41.

71. Report of Canal Commissioners, 15 Dec 1831, Senate Journal, 1831–1832, II, 44; Albright G. Zimmerman, "The Columbia and Philadelphia Railroad: A Railroad with an Identity Crisis," *Proceedings of the Canal History and Technology Symposium* III (1984), 77–78; Act of April, 1830, Compilation of Laws, 65–67. J.M. Porter of Easton became secretary of the Board of Appraisers, see "Extract from Journal of Board of Appraisers," "A Correct Extract," certified 18 Oct 1831, signed J.M. Porter, acting secretary, reel #6, item #113; J.M. Porter to F.R. Shunk, 21 Oct 1821, reel #6, item #114.

72. "Petition to Board of Canal Commissioners," n.d., reel #6, item #72; Jacob Stover, Jr., to David Scott, Pres. of Board, Nockamixon, 22 June 1829, item #75; Minutes of Canal Commissioners, June 3, June 13, 1829, see additional items 70, 74, 79, 80, 81, 91.

73. See the runs of minutes of the canal commissioners.

74. *Josiah White's History.*

75. *Josiah White's History* 1–14.

76. *Ibid.*, 21–23

77. *Ibid.*, 37–45, 70.

78. *Ibid.*, 55–58.

79. Josiah White to James S. Stevenson, Pres. of Canal Board, Mauch Chunk, 3 mo 12 1831, reel #6, item #121.

80. *Ibid.*

81. Canal Commissioners Journal, 1 Aug 1831.

82. Coryell to Clarke, Pres. of Canal Commissioners, 25 Nov 1831, reel #2, item #121.

83. Canal Commissioners Report, 15 Dec 1831, 15; Coryell to Canal Commissioners, 13 July 1831, reel #6, item #119; Coryell to Sec'y Fr. R. Shunk, New Hope, 26 Sep 1831, reel #6, item #148.

84. Josiah White to James Clarke, Easton, 4th mo 4 1832, reel #6, item #148.

85. White to Stevenson, item #121; White to James Clarke, New Hope, 11th mo. 25 1831 reel #2, item #139.

86. Canal Commissioners Report, 29 Nov 1832; "Cost, Revenue and Expenditure" (1859), 8.

87. White to Canal Commissioners, 9 mo 3 1832.

88. Josiah White to J. Clark & Mitchell, Philad, 9 mo 3rd 1832, reel #2, item #128. The gravity railroad became known as the Switchback in later years.

89. Minutes of Canal Commissioners, 25 Oct 1832

90. White to Clark & Mitchell, 9 mo 21 1832, reel #2, item #129.

91. Canal Commissioners Report, 2 Dec 1833, House Journal 1833–1834, Appendix to Vol. II, 12.

92. Canal Commissioners Report, 2 Dec 1833, 12.

93. Report of Simpson Torbert, 1 Nov 1833, Senate Journal, 1833–1834, Appendix to Vol. II, 209.

94. Canal Commissioners Report, 12.

95. "Report of the State Treasurer on the Finances of the Commonwealth," 7 Dec 1832, House Journal, 1832–1833, II, 58.

96. *Niles Register* XLV (1833–1834), 181.

Notes to Chapter Two

1. In actuality, even though the canal was declared to have been completed in 1832, full operation of the whole line was not achieved until 1834.

2. Bristol Committee petition, 11 Sept 1827, Reel #6, item #18; Petition from Citizens of Easton, 2 Sept 1827, Reel #6, item #26.

3. J.N. Simpson to Jonathan Roberts, Member of the Board of Internal Improvement of Pennsylvania, New Brunswick, 28 July 1827, item #97; Minutes of the Senate of Pennsylvania, 24 Jan 1831.

4. Thomas F Kennedy (1783-1836) was "the leading spirit in the building of the Philadelphia Trenton Railroad from Kensington to Trenton, … He, with Richard Morris (the contract standing in name of Morris, but a supplementary agreement between Morris and Kennedy shows that they were equal partners) entered into a contract on January 1, 1833, to grade a double track road bed and construct all bridges for the Sum of $1,561,047. They agreed to take in part pay any or all stock that the directors had subscribed for which they themselves did not want to retain and pay for. Later Mr. Kennedy was secretary and treasurer of the road." B.F. Fackenthal, "Col. Arthur Erwin and James Fenimore Cooper's Novel 'Wyandotte or the Hutted Knoll'," *Papers Read before The Bucks County Historical Society* V (1926), 433–445, quote from 436n; see also Warren S. Ely, "The Samuel Hart Collection of Manuscripts, 1777-1877," *Papers Read before The Bucks County Historical Society*, V, 717–731, particularly 719–720.

5. James A. Ward, *J. Edgar Thomson: Master of the Pennsylvania* (Westport, CT and London: Greenwood Press, 1980), 10–11; "Thomson, J.Edgar," *The Biographical Encyclopedia of Pennsylvania of The Nineteenth Century* (Philadelphia: Galaxy Publishing Company, 1874), 300–302.

6. Ward, *J. Edgar Thomson,* 13–14.

7. *Ibid.*, 17–21.

8. *Ibid.*, 22-23; *Biographical Encyclopedia*, 301; for American engineers in Europe, see Darwin H. Stapleton, "The Origin of American Railroad Technology, 1825-1840," *Railroad History* CXXXIX (Autumn 1978), 65-77; Darwin H. Stapleton, *The Transfer of Early Industrial Technologies to America* (Philadelphia: American Philosophical Society, 1987); Barbara Benson (ed.), *Benjamin Henry Latrobe, Moncure Robinson: The Engineer as Agent of Technological Transfer* (Greenville, DE: Eleutherian Mills Historical Library, 1975).

9. Ward, *J. Edgar Thomson*, 17-23, quote on p. 22.

10. *Ibid.*, 22; "Communication from the Board of Canal Commissioners, accompanied with a Report of J. Edgar Thompson [*sic*], Civil Engineer, relative to the extension of the Delaware division of the Pennsylvania Canal from Bristol to Philadelphia," James Clarke's letter of Transmittal dated 6 Feb 1833, No. 135, House Journal, 1832-1833, II, 474–487, Clarke's letter, 474–475.

11. Report of William B. Mitchell, Superintendent, November 26, 1832, House Journal, 1832–1833, Appendix to Vol II, 185.

12. Lock #4 today lies just north of the Borough of Bristol and above Airport Road (former Beaver Dam Road) just west of present Pennsylvania Route #13.

13. Thomson's Report.

14. John Harrison was established as early as 1806 as a manufacturer of oil of vitriol (sulfuric acid) and was one of the founders of Harrison and Company. Presumably this was the laboratories located in Kensington in 1832.

15. Edgar F. Smith, *Chemistry in Old Philadelphia* (Philadelphia: Lippincott, 1919), 101–102.

16. Thomson's Report, 134–135.

17. Report of Wm. B. Mitchell dated 26 Nov 1832, appended to "Report of the Committee of the Senate Appointed to View the Contemplated Line of Canal from Bristol to Philadelphia," Mr. (Mich.) Snyder, Chairman, read in Senate, 26 Feb 1838 (Harrisburg: Thomson Clark, Printers, 1838), 9–10.

18. Thomson's Report, 484–485.

19. Thomson's Report, 185.

20. Thomas F. Kennedy to Canal Commissioners, Bristol, 7 Feb 1833, Reel #12 Miscellaneous Reports, II, 89.

21. "Report upon a Steam Towing boat, on the Delaware division of the Pennsylvania Canal" No. 131, read 28 Jan 1834, House Journal, 1833–1834, II, 553–554.

22. *Ibid.*

23. House Journal 1837–1838, Minutes, Tuesday, 22 March 1838, I, 852.

24. Sullivan to Dewart, 28 March 1838, No 165, House Journal, 1837–1838, II, 786.

25. "Report of the Committee on Inland Navigation relative to the extension of the Delaware Division of the Pennsylvania Canal, from Bristol to Philadelphia," read 14 January 1836, I, 248–249, House Journal, 1835–1836; House Minutes, 24 Jan 1838, I, 277, House Journal, 1837–1838.

26. Lehigh Coal and Navigation Company Annual Report, 1838, 20.

27. House Minutes, 13 Feb 1838, I, 478, "Index" I, 11, House Journal 1837–1838.

28. Snyder Committee Report, 1838, 4–5.

29. Citizens committee report, 7.

30. Snyder Committee Report, 7; Citizens committee report, 8–9.

31. Isaac Van Horn, Collector at Bristol, to Mr. Hartshorne, 15 April 1846, Reel #8(3), item #193.

Notes to Chapter Three

1. "Report of Edward Gay, Engineer," Nov 1834, in Canal Commissioners Report, *Journal of the Senate, 1834–35*, Appendix to Vol II, 74–75.

2. Martin Coryell, New Hope, 25 May 1839, Reel 7(1), item #70.

3. Minutes, Board of Canal Commissioners, 12 March 1834.

4. [Annual "Report of the Canal Commissioners, Dec 8, 1836, *House Journal*, 1836, Appendix to vol II, No. 13, 16.]; Report of John P. Bailey, relative to Enlarging Delaware Division," 18 Nov 1837, *House Journal*, 1837, Appendix to Vol II, No. 2, H.R. 11, 50–52.

5. Report of the Canal Commissioners, 6 Dec 1837, *House Journal*, 1837 Appendix to Vol. II, No. 9, 8.

6. Miscellaneous Local Events in 1836, New Series, No, 8, 102, in Spruance Library's collections.

7. "Annual Report of the Canal Commissioners," *Reports of the Heads of Departments*, 1846, 85–87.

8. See C.P Yoder, *Delaware Canal Journal* (Bethlehem: Canal Press Inc., 1972), 138–140 and Chap. 7 and note 32.

9. Deposition of John Kain, 13 Jan 1834; of William Fritz, n.d.; of Reuben Simson, n.d.; of John Wood, 8 March 1834, DD Reel #7, Reports and Miscellaneous Papers, II, 155.

10. Isaac Van Horn to Simpson Torbert, 10 March 1834, DD #7, Reports and Miscellaneous Papers, II, 158.

11. Robert P. Lovett to E.J. Pennypacker, 29 April 1836, DD #7, Reports and Miscellaneous Papers, Vol 1837–41, 5; Lovett to Moses Sullivan, President, Board of Canal Commissioners, Vol 1837–41, 8.

12. Lovett to Sullivan, 3 Jan 1838, DD #7, Reports and Miscellaneous Papers, Vol 1837–41, 15.

13. William Rogers to Canal Commissioners, 24 July 1835, DD #7, Reports and Miscellaneous Papers, II, 185.

14. William Muirhead to Clarke, 11 Sept 1835, Clarke to Muirhead, 20 Sept 1835, DD #7, Reports and Miscellaneous Papers, II, 172.

15. Coryell to Canal Commissioners, 13 July 1831, Reel #6, item #119; Coryell to Sec'y Fr. R. Shunk, New Hope, 26 Sept 1831, Reel #6, item #148.

16. Joseph Hough to Canal Commissioners, 26 March 1836, DD #7, RM, 1837–41, 4.

17. Petition dated 28 June 1837, DD #7, RM, 1837–41, 7.

18. Robert P. Lovett to Moses Sullivan, Mar 12, 1838, DD #7, RM, 1837–41, 18, Isaac B. Williams to Sullivan, Mar 12, 1838, 17.

19. For accounts of Pennsylvania's political situation, see Charles McCool Snyder, *The Jacksonian Heritage: Pennsylvania Politics, 1833–1848* (Harrisburg: Pennsylvania Historical and Museum Commission, 1958); Peter A. Wallner, "Politics and Public Works: Study of the Pennsylvania Canal System, 1825–1857"(Ph.D. diss. Pennsylvania State University, 1973), and Louis Hartz, *Economic Policy and Democratic Thought: Pennsylvania 1776–1860* (Cambridge: Harvard Univ. Press, 1948).

20. Minutes, 20 Feb 1836.

21. Minutes, 25, 26 Feb 1836; in 1844, Hough, who was in the process of being appointed as a foreman on a 12-mile segment of the canal, was described as one of "a certain set of men that are opposed to Democracy," and the Democratic-controlled board should avoid such, particularly Joseph Hough. He was further described as "the very worst man that ever was on the canal… He could be found almost at any time in some public bar very drunk instead of attending to his duties he placed another man on the spot where he ought to be and attends all places where he thinks he can get drink." The Democratic critic added, "I have nothing personley [*sic*] against the man but I think that we should have sober and industrious men to manage our public affairs." John Spear to Canal Commissioners, 3 March 1844, Reel #8(2), Doc #114.

22. Minutes, 14 March 1836.

23. Snyder, *Jacksonian Heritage*, 124; Minutes, 16 May 1838.

24. Quotes in Snyder, *Jacksonian Heritage*, 125; "Report of the committee appointed to investigate the conduct of the late board of canal commissioners," *House Journal*, 1838, No. 220, 1–296, particularly p 10.

25. William C. McPherson to John B. McPherson, 30 May 1838, quoted in Snyder, *Jacksonian Heritage*, 125.

26. Snyder, *Jacksonian Heritage*, 131–135.

27. Minutes, 1 Feb 1839.

28. Minutes, 13 Feb 1840.

29. For examples see Doc. No. 133, "Report of the Investigating Committee on the Columbia and Philadelphia Railroad.—Accompanied with Testimony," *House Journal*, 1840, II, 285–419 and Doc. No 168, "Report of the Select Committee, appointed to Investigate the Expenditures upon the Canals and Railroads of this State, accompanied with the Minority Report and Testimony upon the subject," *House Journal*, 1841, II, 547–744. These investigations were not without precedent, for example see the report of the Whig legislature, Doc. No. 242, "Report of the select committee relative to the management of the Canals and Railways of the commonwealth, together with the testimony taken in relation thereto," Doc. No. 243, "Report of the minority of the committee," Doc. No. 244, "Testimony," *House Journal*, 1836–1837, II, 801–814, 814–829, 830–965.

30. Minutes, 21 May 1839. For examples see Doc. No. 133 (note 29).

31. David Connor to Messrs Clarke, Hubley and Packer, Canal Commissioners of Pennsylvania, Easton, 4 March 1839, [Del Div] Reel #7(1), Doc No. 67.

32. Josiah Calvin to G. Espy, 20 April 1840, Reel #12(1), Doc No. 45.

33. Report of the Committee on Roads, Bridges and Inland Navigation Relative to the Canals and Railroads of the Common-wealth, Mr. Strohm, Chairman, read in the senate, May 24, 1839 (Harrisburg: printed by E. Guyer, 1839), 21; hereafter cited as Senate Committee, 1839.

34. Senate Committee, 1839, 19, 20ff.

35. Philadelphia *Public Ledger*, 28 Jan 1839.

36. *Public Ledger*, 28, 29, 30 Jan 1839.

37. *Public Ledger*, 29, 30 Jan, 4 Feb 1839.

38. Canal Commissioners Report, 31 Oct 1839, 172–173; Report of the Commissioners," H.R. No. 32, 21 Jan 1840, *House Journal* 1840, Appendix to Vol. II, 8–11.

39. Canal Commissioners Report, 31 Oct 1839, 172–173; "Report of the Canal Commissioners," H.R. No. 32, 21 Jan 1840, *House Journal*, 1840, Appendix to Vol. II, 8–11.

40. Huffnagle's Report, 1839.

41. In 1860 Solon Chapin was listed as a bridgebuilder residing at 63 N. 2nd Street, Easton, in *Boyd's Directory of Reading, Easton, Pottsville, Allentown & Lebanon together with a Business Directory* (compiled and published by William H. Boyd, Directory Publisher, Phila and New York, 1860); Solon Chapin was awarded bids over the next several years for work on the Easton Dam and elsewhere, see Huffnagle to Board of Canal Commissioners, 11 Aug 1839, [Del Div] Reel #7, Doc No. 37; Huffnagle's Report 1839; Huffnagle to E.B. Hubley, Eng. Off., Lancaster, 21 Jan 1840, [Del Div] Reel #7, Doc. No. 123.

42. For a biographical sketch of Porter, see M.S. Henry, *History of the Lehigh Valley* (Easton: Bixler and Corwin, 1860), 417–423.

43. Porter to James Clarke, 16 Feb 1839, [DelDiv] Reel #7, Doc. No. 86.

44. *Easton Democrat and Argus*, 28 Feb 1839.

45. Huffnagle Report, 1 Nov 1839, 173.

46. Robert P. Lovett, Supt., to Hon. John Dickey, Pres. of Board of Canal Commissioners, Sup. Office Del. Div. of Canal, 28 Jan 1839, [Del Div] Reel #1, Doc. No. 73.

47. *Mauch Chunk Courier*, Thursday, 18 April 1839, quoted in *Public Ledger*, 20 April 1839.

48. Martin Coryell to James Clarke, Pres. of Board of Canal Commissioners, 5 July 1839, [Del Div] Reel #7, Doc. No. 47.

49. *Public Ledger*, 6 Sept 1839; Huffnagle's Report, 1 Nov 1839; Report of Canal Commissioners, *House Journal*, Appendix to Vol. II, 176.

50. Huffnagle Report, 1839, 174–175.

51. William Innis to Board of Canal Commissioners, Easton, 10 July 1839, [Del Div] Reel #7, Doc. No. 51.

52. *Easton Democrat & Argus* 25 April 1839; Huffnagle Report, 1 Nov 1839, Report of Board of Canal Commissioners, Jan 1840, *House Journal*, Appendix to Vol. II, 175.

53. Huffnagle Report, 1839, *House Journal* 1839, Appendix to Vol II, 174–177.

54. Ibid., 178–179.

55. Senate Committee, 1839, 19–21.

56. Minutes, 7 May 1839.

57. "Trade in a New Channel; Millers, Distillers & Others Using Spring Freshet River," *Easton Democrat and Argus*, 4 April 1839.

58. "Extract from the Minutes, Feb 20, 1839, Pennsylvania Archives, RG17, Delaware Division," Check Rolls & Repair Receipts, Box No. 14; Minutes, 20 Feb 1839.

59. See "Check Rolls & Repair Receipts," Box No. 14.

60. Most of the check rolls and the individual receipts along with vouchers, etc., are in the archives at Harrisburg, see RG 17, Mss "Check Rolls & Repair Receipts," Box No. 14.

61. Pennsylvania Archives, RG 17, Del Div, "Check Rolls & Repair Receipts," Box 14.

62. Solon Chapin to Mr. Hobart, Esq., Auditor General, Easton, 22 April 1839, RG 17, [Del Div] Mss "Check Rolls & Repair Receipts," Box No. 7.

63. Connor to Auditor General, Easton, 12 April 1839, RG 17 [Del Div] Mss "Check Rolls & Repair Receipts," Box No. 7.

64. Connor to Auditor General, Easton, 12 April 1839, RG 17, [Del Div] Mss "Check Rolls & Repair Receipts," Box No. 7.

65. Connor to Commissioners, 22 May 1839, [Del Div] Reel #7, Doc. No. 71.

66. Ibid.

67. Ibid.; *Democrat and Argus*, 25 April 1839.

68. J.M. Porter to Col. Henry Reeder, Easton, 15 July 1840, Reel #12, "Miscellaneous Papers," Vol I, Doc. No. 67.

69. Harmon to____, 9 July 1840, Reel #12, Doc. No. 145.

70. Connor to Commissioners, Easton, 19 July 1839, [Del Div] Reel #7, Doc. No. 42.

71. Daniel Y. Harmon to____, 25 July 1840, Reel #12, Doc. No. 133.

72. See Chapter IV for detail.

73. *American Railroad Journal and Mechanics' Magazine*, XII (Feb 1841), 65.

74. J.M. Porter to E.B. Stuckey, Esq., Easton, 8 Jan 1841, [Del Div] Reel #1(2), Doc. No. 28.

75. "Annual Report of W.K. Huffnagle, Engineer," n.d. [ca Dec. 1841], in Annual Report of the Canal Commissioners, 15 Jan 1842, *Senate Journal*, III, 49.

76. Newspaper account quoted in I. Daniel Rupp, *History of Northampton, Lehigh, Monroe, Carbon, and Schuylkill Counties* (Harrisburg: Hickok and Cantine, 1845), 55.

77. J.M. Porter to Canal Commissioners, Easton, 11 Jan 1841, [Del Div] Reel #1(2), Doc. No. 27.

78. Huffmagle's Report, 1839, "Report of the Canal Commissioners," H.R. No. 25, 1 Jan 1841, *House Journal*, 1841, Appendix to Vol II, 12–13; Philadelphia *Public Ledger*, Monday, 11 Jan 1841.

79. Henry, *History of the Lehigh Valley*, 415.

80. LC&N Minutes, 12 Jan 1841; Report of the Canal Commissioners, 15 Jan 1842; Huffnagle's Report 1841; *Senate Journal*, 1842, III, 6–7, 49–53.

81. LC&N Minutes, 19 Jan 1841, 2 Feb 1841.

82. LC&N Minutes, 16 Feb 1841; Memorial reprinted in *Public Ledger*, 27 Feb 1841.

83. For a particularly detailed statement from among many, see Josiah White to James Clarke, Philadelphia, 6 mo 3d 1839, DD #7, Doc. No. 77b.

84. *Public Ledger*, 27 Feb 1841.

85. Reel #25, Doc. #7.

86. Connor's report, 1 Dec 1841, Reel #25, Doc. #7.

87. Reel #25, Doc. No. 30.

88. Rogers' report of 1 Dec 1841, Reel #25, Doc. No. 30.

89. Neeley's Creek enters the canal in today's Bowman's Tower segment of Washington's Crossing State Park.

90. Huffnagle's Report, 1841, Canal Commissioners Report, 15 Jan 1842, Senate Journal, III, 51; undated diagram, RG 17, Map Book #43, map No. 24; Neely's Creek is today known as Pidcock's Creek.

91. Rogers' Report, 1841, reel #25, Doc. No. 30, 3.

Notes to Chapter Four

1. Stuart J. Reid, *A Sketch of the Life and Times of The Rev. Sydney Smith* (New York: Harper Brothers, 1885), 378–381; *A Memoir of the Reverend Sydney Smith by his Daughter, Lady Holland, with A Selection from his Letters*, ed. Mrs. (Sara) Austin (New York: Harper Brothers, 1855), 2 vols., II, 458; Sheldon Halpern, *Sydney Smith* (New York: Twayne Publishers, 1968), 125; also quoted in Leland H. Jenks, *The Migration of British Capital to 1875* (New York: Alfred A. Knopf, 1927), 104–105 and in Reginald C. McGrane, *Foreign Bondholders and American State Debts* (New York: The Macmillan Company, 1935), 58–60.

2. Smith to Countess Grey, 19 Sept 1842, Austin, ed., *Smith*, 446.

3. Smith to Countess Grey, 10 Dec 1843; Austin, ed., *Smith*, 474.

4. Charles Lyell, *Travels in North America in the Years 1841–2: with Geological Observations on the United States, Canada, and Nova Scotia* (New York: Wiley and Putnam, 1845), 2 vols., I, 172–174; Governor David R. Porter, "To the Assembly Concerning Certain Financial Interests of the Commonwealth," 4 April 1842, Pennsylvania Archives, Papers of the Governors, 4th series (hereafter cited as P.A.) VI, 898–899; Governor Francis R. Shunk, "Annual Message," 20 Jan 1846, P.A. VII, 63.

5. Lyell, *Travels*, I, 173.

6. *Punch*, VII (1844), 247.

7. William Wordsworth, "To the Pennsylvanian," in *The Complete Poetical Works of Wordsworth*, ed. A.J. George (Boston: Houghton Mifflin, 1932), 784.

8. John M. McFaul, *The Politics of Jacksonian Finance* (Ithaca and London: Cornell University Press, 1972), 172–175; Jenks, *Migration of British Capital*, 100; Governor William F. Johnston, "Annual Message," 6 Jan 1849, P.A. VII, 307.

9. See McGrane, *Foreign Bondholders*, 265ff; T.H. Worthington, "Historical Sketch of the Finances of Pennsylvania," Publications of the American Economic Association, II, No. 2., May 1887.

10. ab*The First Annual Report of the Acting Committee of the Society for the Promotion of Internal Improvement in the Commonwealth of Pennsylvania* (Philadelphia: Joseph R.A. Skerrett, 1826), 4.

11. Alvard L. Bishop, "The State Works of Pennsylvania," *Transactions of the Connecticut Academy of Arts and Sciences*, XIII (1907), 150–167; Robert E. Carlson, "The Pennsylvania Improvement Society and its Promotion of Canals and Railroads, 1824–1826," *Pennsylvania History* XXXI (1964), 295–310; Robert I. Shelling, "Philadelphia and the Agitation in 1825 for the Pennsylvania Canal," *Pennsylvania Magazine of History and Biography* LXII (1938), 175–204; Louis Hartz, *Economic Policy and Democratic Thought: Pennsylvania, 1776–1860* (Cambridge, Mass.: Harvard University Press, 1948), 82–89.

12. Hartz, *Economic Policy*, 125–142.

13. Worthington, "Historical Sketch," 24–26; McGrane, *Foreign Bondholders*, 66; Peter A. Wallner, "Politics and Public Works: Study of the Pennsylvania Canal System, 1825–1857," unpublished Ph.D. diss., The Pennsylvania State University, 235; Governor Francis R. Shunk, "Annual Message," Jan 1846, P.A. VII, 65.

14. James V. Longacre and James Herring, "George Wolf," in *The National Portrait Gallery of Distinguished Americans* (Philadelphia: Henry Perkins, 1835), 2; Governor John A. Shulze, "Annual Message," 4 Nov 1829, P.A. V, 844.

15. Governor George Wolf, "Inaugural Address," Dec 1829, P.A. VI, 868; Longacre and Herring, "George Wolf," 2–3.

16. Wolf, "Message," 1830, P.A. V, 918; id., "Message," 1831, P.A. V, 970–971, 982–983; id., "Message," 1832, P.A. VI, 42–44.

17. Wolf, "Message,"1832, P.A. VI.

18. Charles McC. Snyder, *The Jacksonian Heritage, Pennsylvania Politics, 1833–1848* (Harrisburg: Pennsylvania Historical and Museum Commission, 1958), 24–26; Longacre and Herring, "George Wolf," 3; Wolf, "Annual Message," 6 Dec 1832, P.A. VI, 53–54.

19. Wolf, "To the Assembly Concerning the Finances of the Commonwealth," 26 Feb 1834, P.A. VII, 166–170. *See also* Snyder, *Jacksonian Heritage*, 37–45.

20. Wolf, "Annual Message," 6 Dec 1832, P.A., 4th series, VI, 47–49.

21. Ibid. *See also* Snyder, *Jacksonian Heritage*, 65–67.

22. "No. 242, Report of the select committee relative to the management of the Canals and Railways of the commonwealth, together with the testimony taken in relation thereto," *House Journal*, 1836–1837, II, 801–965; "No. 178, Report of the committee appointed to investigate the conduct of the late board of Canal Commissioners," *House Journal*, 1839–1840, II, part 2, 1–14; "No. 133, Report of the Investigating Committee on the Columbia and Philadelphia Railroad—Accompanied with Testimony," *House Journal*, 1840–1841, II, 285– 419.

23. Governor Joseph Ritner, "Inaugural Address," Dec 1835, P.A. VI, 255.

24. Ritner, "To the Assembly Concerning the Report of the Canal Commissioners," 7 June 1836, P.A. VI, 268–269.

25. Ritner, "Inaugural Address," 15 Dec 1835, P.A., VI 254–257; id., "Annual Message," 6 Dec 1836, P.A. VI, 311–324, 327; Lyell, *Travels in North America*, I, 175–176.

26. The theme is developed in detail by Bray Hammond, *Banks and Politics in America from the Revolution to the Civil War* (Princeton: Princeton University Press, 1957). For a contrasting picture, consult Arthur M. Schlesinger, Jr., *The Age of Jackson* (Boston: Little, Brown and Company, 1945).

27. Albright G. Zimmerman, "The Columbia and Philadelphia Railroad: A Railroad with an Identity Problem," *Proceedings of the Canal History and Technology Symposium* III (1984), 53–92; id., "Iron for American Railroads, 1830–1860," *Proceedings* V (1986), 63–108.

28. Reginald C. McGrane, *The Panic of 1837, Some Financial Problems of the Jacksonian Era* (1924; reprint, New York: Russell Russell, 1965), 85–86. Biddle is reputed to have bragged of spending $130,000 in his campaign for the charter (Snyder, *Jacksonian Heritage*, 78).

29. Wallner, "Politics and Public Works," 142. The legislature was further pressured by rumors that New York, Maryland, and Washington, D.C., also sought to recharter the United States Bank. See *The Correspondence of Nicholas Biddle dealing with National Affairs, 1807–1844*, ed. Reginald C. McGrane, (Boston and New York: Houghton Mifflin Company, 1919), 248n, John Norris to Biddle, 16 Nov 1835, 256–257; Walter Buckingham Smith, *Economic Aspects of the Second Bank of the United States* (Cambridge, Mass.: Harvard University Press, 1956), 178–180.

30. McGrane, *Panic of 1837*, 70; Ritner, "To the Assembly Concerning the Proceedings of the Stockholders of the Bank of the United States," 22 Feb 1836, P.A., 4th series, VI, 266; McGrane, ed., *Correspondence of Nicholas Biddle*, Biddle to ———, 7 Jan 1835, 246–250.

31. "Act of 18th February, 1836—Pamphlet Laws, page 36," *Compilation of the Laws of Pennsylvania relative to the Internal Improvements together with the Canal and Railway Regulations as established by the Board of Canal Commissioners* (Harrisburg: Barrett and Parks, 1840), 146–148; Smith, *Economic Aspects*, 179–180; Henry R. Mueller, "The Whig Party in Pennsylvania," in *Columbia University Studies in History, Economics and Public Law*, vol. CI, No. 2, 1922 (reprinted by AMS Press, 1969), 25; McGrane, *Panic of 1837*, 70–90; McGrane, ed., *Correspondence of Nicholas Biddle*, 249, 256, 257n; Douglas E. Bowers, "From Logrolling to Corruption: the Development of Lobbying in Pennsylvania, 1815–1861," in *Journal of the Early Republic*, III (Spring 1983), 439–471, particularly 455.

32. Alexander Trotter, *Observations on the Financial Position and Credit of Such of the States of the North American Union as have Contracted Public Debt* (London: Longman, Orme, Brown, Green, and Longmans, 1839), 172n. *See also* "Art. IX—Enquiry into the Circumstances that have occasioned the present Embarrassments in the Trade between Great Britain and the United States of America, 8vo. London: 1837," *The Edinburgh Review*, LXV (1837), 221–238, especially 225–226.

33. Hammond, *Banks and Politics*, 501–518; Jenks, *Migration of British Capital*, 100; Shunk, "Annual Message," 20 Jan 1846, 65; Snyder, *Jacksonian Heritage*, 125–135, 153, 162; McGrane, *Foreign Bondholders*, 28–29.

34. Hartz, *Economic Policy*, 161–180; Governor David R. Porter, "To the Assembly Transmitting Certain Documents Concerning the Sale of Railroads and Canals Belonging to the Commonwealth," 4 Jan 1843, P.A. VI, 939–940.

35. See Hartz, *Economic Policy*, 42–53; Wallner, "Politics and Public Works," 108, 121ff.; Philip S. Klein, *Pennsylvania Politics, 1817–1832, A Game Without Rules* (Philadelphia: Historical Society of Pennsylvania, 1940), 337–339, 361–362; Mueller, "The Whig Party in Pennsylvania," 106, 110–114; Snyder, *Jacksonian Heritage*, 125–127.

36. Message of Governor David R. Porter, "To the Senate and House of Representatives of the Commonwealth of Pennsylvania," 1 April 1843, *Senate Journal*, 1843, 872–880.

37. The ferocity level of Pennsylvania Politics can be savoured in Snyder, *Jacksonian Heritage*, Klein, *Pennsylvania Politics, 1817–1832*, and Mueller, "The Whig Party in Pennsylvania."

38. See note 42.

39. Wallner, "Politics and Public Works," 214, 238, 252–253; Hartz, *Economic Policy*, 162; Shunk, "Annual Message," 7 Jan 1846, Reports of the Heads of Department, 1846, 7.

40. "Resolution of 19th Feb. 1839—Pamphlet Laws, page 640," *Compilation of Laws, (1840)*, 261–262; Ralph C.H. Catterall, *The Second Bank of the United States* (Chicago: University of Chicago Press, 1903), 339–40; Wallner, "Politics and Public Works," 158, 162–163, 178.

41. Trotter, *Observations*, 168–170.

42. Solomon W. Roberts, "Reminiscences of the First Railroad over the Allegheny Mountain," *Pennsylvania Magazine of History and Biography*, II (1878), 370–393, see 374 on Pennsylvania internal improvements; Richard Richardson, *Memoir of Josiah White* (Philadelphia: J.B. Lippincott Co., 1873), 80–85; Robert E. Carlson, *The Liverpool Manchester Railway Project, 1821–1831* (New York: Augustus M. Kelley, 1969), 206–215.

43. Zimmerman, "Columbia and Philadelphia Railroad."

44. Wallner, "Politics and Public Works," 217–219; *Compilation of Laws, (1840)*, 3, 33, 49, 145; "Canals and Railroads," in *Pardon's Digest* of the laws of Pennsylvania, eighth edition (Philadelphia: James Kay, Jun. Brother, 1853), 110–135, especially 111.

45. Ritner, "Annual Message," 6 Dec 1837, P.A., 4th series, VI, 376.

46. Wallner, "Politics and Public Works," 185; Bishop, "State Works," 229–261; id., "Corrupt Practices Connected with the Building and Operation of the State Works of Pennsylvania," in *Yale Review* XV (1907), 391–411. *See also* William Bender Wilson, *History of the Pennsylvania Railroad* (Philadelphia: H.T. Coates Co., 1899), 2 vols; W.H. Schotter, *The Growth and Develop-*

ment of the Pennsylvania Railroad (Philadelphia: Allen, Lane and Scott, 1927); George H. Burgess and Miles C. Kennedy, *Centennial History of the Pennsylvania Railroad Company* (Philadelphia: Pennsylvania Railroad, 1949); annual reports of the Pennsylvania Railroad.

47. Hansel Wilson, "Notes on the Columbia and Philadelphia Railroad," in *Journal of the Franklin Institute* XXIX, 333–341; Roberts "Reminiscences"; Governor William Bigler, "Annual Message," 4 Jan 1854, P.A. VII, 643.

48. See Thomas P. Govan, *Nicholas Biddle, Nationalist and Public Banker, 1786–1844* (Chicago: University of Chicago Press, 1959), 126–130.

49. Jenks, *Migration of British Capital*, 90–94; McGrane, *Foreign Bondholders*, 16–18; Govan, *Nicholas Biddle* 88–99; Ralph Hidy, "The Organization and Functions of Anglo-American Merchant Bankers, 1815–1860," in *The Tasks of Economic History*, Supplemental Issue of *The Journal of Economic History*, Dec 1941, 53–66; "Cushioning a Crisis in the London Money Market," in *Bulletin of the Business Historical Society* XX (1946), 131–145; Dorothy R. Adler, *British Investment in American Railways, 1834–1898* (Charlottesville: University of Virginia Press, 1970); Muriel E. Hidy, *George Peabody, Merchant and Financier, 1829–1854*, Ph.D. diss., Radcliffe, 1939 (reprint, Arno Press, 1938).

50. Marvin Meyers, *The Jacksonian Persuasion, Politics and Belief* (Stanford: Stanford University Press, 1957), 82–83.

51. *See* Hammond, *Banks and Politics*, Schlesinger, *Age of Jackson*, Govan, *Nicholas Biddle*.

52. Hartz, *Economic Policy,* 148–174; Wallner, "Politics and Public Works," 285–293.

53. Zimmerman, "Columbia and Philadelphia"; Trotter, *Observations*, 168–170.; Hartz, *Economic Policy*, 139.

54. Publius (pseud.), "Letter to the Members of the Pennsylvania Legislature on the Subject of the State Debt," 10 April 1844 (Philadelphia: King Baird, 1844), 6.

Notes to Chapter Five

1. Louis Hartz, *Economic Policy and Democratic Thought: Pennsylvania, 1776–1860* (Cambridge: Harvard Univ. Press, 1948), 162; Peter A. Wallner, "Politics and Public Works: Study of the Pennsylvania Canal System, 1825-1857," Ph.D. diss., Pennsylvania State University, 1973, 214, 238, 252-253.

2. "History of the Lehigh Coal & Navigation Co." (abridged), Hazard's *United States Commercial Statistical Register* III (August 1840), 81–85, 100–104; see also Minutes, Board of Canal Commissioners, 10 Sept 1827, hereafter, Minutes BCC.

3. Minutes BCC, 19 April 1833.

4. Minutes BCC, 26 April 1834.

5. Dusenbery to James Clark, 15 Jan 1835, Reel #7, item #182.

6. Senate Minutes, Friday 31 May 1839; Josiah White to James Clark, Pres. of Board of Canal Commissioners, 6 mo 3d, 1839, Delaware Division, reel #7(2), item #78.

7. White to Clark, 6 mo 3d, 1839, Delaware Division Reel #7(2), item #78.

8. *Ibid.*

9. *Ibid.*

10. "History of the Lehigh Coal & Navigation Company." There was already an extension of the Lehigh Canal north to Wright's Creek, 26 miles long with 34 high locks, with a 10- to 30-foot lift per lock. This was to be supplemented by a 19¾-mile railroad then being constructed from White Haven on the upper extension of the canal to connect at Wilkes-Barre with the North Branch Canal, which was still under construction. Lehigh Coal and Navigation Company officials anticipated traffic from southwestern and central New York and from north-central Pennsylvania would be attracted to this route as it would be the shortest one to New York City as well as to Philadelphia. See Albright Zimmerman, "First Years of the Delaware Division Canal," *Canal History and Technology Proceedings* VIII (1989), 161–213.

11. Josiah White to W.K. Huffnagle, 11th mo. 17th, 1841, appended to Huffnagle's annual report, "Delaware Division Pennsylvania Canal," Senate Journal, 1842, III, 53–55. In 1842, a report was presented to the canal commissioners concerning a petition of LC&N, which was asking permission to enlarge the basin at Morrisville, and to connect to it by means of a lateral railroad, which would actually be an inclined plane to connect with the Philadelphia and Trenton railroad. Minutes BCC, 26 July 1842.

12. J. Miller to David Wagener, Harrisburg, 11 Nov 1844, Reel #8 (2), Item #124.

13. Hazard to James Clark, September 2, 1844, Reel #8(2), item #191.

14. Hazard to Clark, 4 Nov 1844, Reel #8(2), item #191.

15. Josiah White to Clark, Phila., 1 mo. 31, 1845, Reel #8(3), item #38.

16. Van Horn to Foster, Bristol, 31 Dec 1845, Reel #8(3), item #201.

17. *Ibid.*, item #38.

18. "Communication from the Canal Commissioners relative to the construction of an Out-let Lock," 3 Feb 1846, Senate Journal II, Doc. No. 34, 256–259.

19. *Ibid.*

20. *Ibid.*

21. *Ibid.*

22. "Canal Commissioners Journal," 7 Jan 1854, 13–14; found in *Report of the Heads of Departments*, 1854.

23. Hazard to Canal Commissioners, Phila., 29 July 1846. See also 7 Nov 1846, Reel #8(3), Item #154, #157; Minutes BCC, 9 June, 14 Dec 1846.

24. Matheys Report to the Canal Commissioners, 30 Nov 1846, Reel #26, item #72.

25. *Ibid.*

26. Minutes BCC, 9 June, 14 Dec 1846.

27. Hazard to Canal Commissioners, Phila., 29 July 1846.

28. "Annual Report of the Board of Canal Commissioners," 31 Dec 1846, Reports of the Heads of Departments, 1847, 10.

29. Huffnagle to Commissioners, n.d. 1847, Reel 9(1), item #30.

30. Minutes BCC, 15 May, 21, 22 June 1847.

31. Minutes BCC, 31 Aug 1847.

32. Minutes BCC, 20 Nov 1847, 11 Jan 1848; Huffnagle to Commissioners, n.d. [1847], Reel #9(1), item #91; "Final Estimate—Outlet Lock at Well's Falls. Del Div. Pa Canal," from Huffnagle, n.d. [1848], Reel #9(1), item #91.

33. Huffnagle to Commissioners, April 30, 1848, Reel #9(1), item #87.

34. Samuel D. Ingham to Commissioners, 23 Sept 1848, Reel #9(1), item #92.

35. Report of Wm. B. Foster, 8 March 1951, House Journal 1851, II, Doc. No. 70, 608–609.

36. "Report of the Canal Commissioners," 21 Dec 1838, House Journal, 1838, Appendix volume, item #17, 4–5.

37. "Report of John P. Bailey, engineer, relative to Enlarging Delaware Division," 18 Nov 1837, House Journal, 1837, Appendix volume, 50–51.

38. Ibid.; Minutes BCC, 18 Oct, 9 Nov 1837.

39. House minutes, March 15, 1841, House Journal, 1841, I:429.

40. A simple surveillance of the indices reveals dozens of petitions and resolutions calling for widening of the canal, the construction or opposition to construction of the outlet lock, etc. See the minutes of the House of Representatives and of the Senate in the respective volume of the annual volumes.

41. Huffnagle's Report, 20 Jan 1841, House Journal 1841, No. 64, II, 116–123, particularly 120–121.

42. Ibid.

43. "Canal Commissioners's Report," 1 Jan 1841, House Journal 1841, Appendix volume, 13.

44. "Annual Report of the Canal Commissioners, Dec 30, 1845," Reports of the Heads of Departments, 1846, 10.

45. Report of John Matheys, 30 Nov 1846, Reel #26, item #72.

46. Ibid.

47. Ibid.

48. Ibid.

49. Ibid.

50. Senate Minutes, 21 Jan, 3 April 1848.

51. Huffnagle to Commissioners, 15 July 1847, Reel #9(1), item #2.

52. Huffnagle to Commissioners, 19 Feb 1848, reel #9(1), item #95.

53. Ibid.

54. Ibid.

55. Hazard to Commissioners, 1 March 1847, Reel #9(1), item #23.

56. John Matheys to Foster, Hartshorne & Burns (Board of Canal Commissioners), 6 May 1846, Reel #8(3), item #171.

57. Huffnagle to Commissioners, 30 April 1848, Reel #9(1), item #87.

58. Minutes BCC, 29 Jan 1852.

59. Minutes BCC, 2 March 1854.

60. Minutes BCC, Tuesday, 27 April 1847.

61. W.R. Burton to Commissioners, 14 Aug 1848, Reel #9(1), item #88.

62. John Ecky to A. Gamble, 26 July 1850, Reel #9(1), item #136.

63. Ibid.

64. Lewis S. Coryell to Commissioners, 16 Dec 1850, Reel #9(1), item #126.

65. Edward Gay to Commissioners, 15 Dec 1851, Reel #29, Item #56.

66. James Cox to Edward F. Gay, 13 Dec 1851, Reel #29, item #57;

67. Ibid.

68. Minutes BCC, 6 Nov 1851.

69. Minutes BCC, 25 Aug 1852.

70. Closson to Commissioners, 14 Feb 1851, Reel #29, item #38.

71. Minutes BCC, 13 Dec 1852.

72. Minutes BCC, 16 Dec 1852.

73. "Report of the Canal Commissioners," 29 Dec 1855, 14–16, Reports of the Heads of Departments, 1856.

74. Gay to Thos Forsythe, Esq., Canal Commissioner, 20 Dec 1855, reel #27, item #72.

75. Ibid.

76. Ibid.

77. "Report of Edward Gay, State Engineer," 25 Dec 1856, Reel #28, item #77.

78. Ibid.

79. Ibid.

80. Ibid.

81. Gay to Commissioners, 2 April 1857, Reel #26, item #5.

82. "Report of the State Engineer," [Dec 18, 1857], Reel #28, item #27.

83. *Ibid.*

84. Senate minutes, 4 Jan 1843, Senate Journal, 1843, I:24–25.

85. *Ibid.*; Governor Porter, "To the Assembly Transmitting Certain Documents Concerning the Sale of Railroads and Canals Belonging to the Commonwealth," Pennsylvania Archives, Papers of the Governors, 4th series, VI:939–940.

86. Senate minutes 1843: 10 Feb, 339; 15 Feb, 369; 27 Feb, 482; 5 April, 929; 6 April, 938; April 8, 965; 12 April, 1011; 13 April, 1041.

87. Minutes BCC, 14 Sept 1843; Patricia J. Marchwinski, "Following History Through the Erie Extension Canal," *Journal of Erie Studies* XII (Fall 1983), 8–9, 14.

88. F. Charles Petrillo, *Anthracite and Slackwater: The North Branch Canal 1828–1901* (Easton, Pa: Center For Canal History and Technology, 1986), 97, 118–121.

89. "North Branch Canal," *American Railroad Journal* XVIII, 10 July 1845, 435; Louise Welles Murray, *A History of Old Tioga Point and Early Athens, Pennsylvania* (Athens, PA: author, 1908), 531–536; Petrillo, *Anthracite and Slackwater*, 110–118.

90. Minutes BCC, 9 Jan 1844.

91. Annual Message of Governor Porter, 8 Jan 8, 1845, *Reports of the Heads of Departments* 1845, 10.

92. "Communication from the Secretary of the Commonwealth, relative to the sale of the Delaware Division, Pennsylvania canal," Evans to Charles M'Clure, Secretary of the Commonwealth, 18 Dec 1844, *House Journal*, 1845, II, Doc No. 10, 102–103.

93. "Report of the Committee of Ways and Means, relative to the sale of the Main Line," 17 March 1845, House Journal 1845, II, Doc. No. 85, 514–515

94. *Ibid.*

95. *Ibid.*

96. "Main Line of State Works of Pennsylvania," *Hunt's Merchants Magazine* XIII (1845), 138.

97. House Minutes 1847: 13 Jan; 6, 27 Feb; 12 March.

98. Governor Francis R. Shunk, "Annual Message," 5 Jan 1848, House Journal II, Doc. No. 1, 10.

99. Annual message of Governor Johnson, 7 Jan 1851, *House Journal* 1851, II, Doc. 1, 9.

100. Governor William Bigler, "Annual Message," 3 Jan 1855, *Report of the Heads of Departments*, 1855, 3–25, particularly, 4–5, 8–9.

101. *Ibid.*

102. *Ibid.*

103. House minutes, 10, 12 Jan 1855, House Journal, 1855; Senate minutes, 8 Feb; 21, 30 April; 2, 3, 7, 8 May 1855, Senate Journal, 1855.

104. Governor James Pollock, "Annual Message," 1 Jan 1856, *Reports of the Heads of Departments*, 1856, 3ff. For the slightly different figures for the Delaware division for 1855, see "Report of the Canal Commissioners," Reports of the Heads of Departments, 14–15.

105. House Minutes, 3 April 1856; Minutes BCC, Thurs 3 April, Wed 9 April 1856.

106. House Minutes, 3 April 1856.

107. *Ibid.*, 8 April 1856.

108. House Minutes, 3 March 1857, 406–412.

109. *Ibid.*

110. Minutes BCC, Wed 10 June 1857; "Sunbury and Erie Railroad," 149.

111. "Annual Report of the Board of Canal Commissioners," 4–10, *Reports of the Heads of Departments* 1857; "Sunbury and Erie Railroad," 149.

112. Governor James Pollock, "Annual Message," 6 Jan 1588, *Reports of the Heads of Departments* 1857, 9; see also Pennsylvania Archives, Ser 4, VII, 930ff.

113. *Ibid.*

114. Minutes BCC, 23 Apr 1858.

115. Annual Report of the Board of Canal Commissioners, 1858; *Reports of the Heads of Departments* 1856, 5–13; Alvard L. Bishop, "The State Works of Pennsylvania," *Transactions of the Connecticut Academy of Arts and Sciences* XIII, Nov 1907, 149–297, see 259.

116. Wallner, "Politics and Public Works," 272; Henry V. Poor, *History of the Railroads and Canals of the United States of America* (New York: John H. Schultz Co., 1860), I:544–545; C.P. "Bill" Yoder, *Delaware Canal Journal* (Bethlehem, Pa: Canal Press Inc., 1972), 227.

117. Minutes BCC, 21 Oct 1858.

118. Minutes BCC, Tues 25 Jan 1859; penciled notes of Hubertis M. Cummings in manuscript canal commissioners' minutes.

Notes to Chapter Six

1. LC&N Annual Report, 1853, 5, 10–11.

2. LC&N Annual Report, 1854, 12–13.

3. LC&N Annual Report, 1856, 12.

4. LC&N Annual Report, 1857, 11.

5 *Intelligencer*, 25 Aug 1857.

6.   *Ibid.*, 29 Sept 1857.

7.   *Ibid.*, 30 March 1858.

8.   *Ibid.*, 27 April 1858

9.   See *Intelligencer*, 20 April, 27 April, 11 March 1858.

10. Deed, Commonwealth of Pennsylvania to Sunbury & Erie RailRoad Company, 19 May 1858, recorded 2 Oct 1882, Deed Book No 203, p 100, Doylestown, Pa.

11. Typescript, Articles, 7 July 1858; Deputy Secretary's endorsement, 14 July 1858, H.S. McGraw's endorsement, 13 Sept 1858, PHMC; Deed, Sunbury & Erie RailRoad to Delaware Division Canal Company, 10 July 1858, recorded 31 May 1902, Deed Book No 305, p 457, Doylestown, Pa; Henry V. Poor, *History of the Railroads and Canals of the United States of America* (New York: John H. Schultz & Co., 1860) I:545–546.

12. *Intelligencer*, 18 May 1858.

13. *Ibid.*, 8 June 1858.

14. *Ibid.*, 7 July 1858.

15. *Intelligencer*, 7 July 1858; Earl J. Heydinger, "Jay Cooke and the 1858 Canal Sales," citing U.S. RR and Mining Register of 26 Feb 1859 in *Canal Currents*, No. 67 (Summer 1984), 6, 13.

16. Quoted in the *Intelligencer*, 20 July 1858.

17. See Chapter V, Problems of a State-Owned Delaware Division Canal.

18. *Intelligencer*, 27 July 1858.

19. Morris Canal and Banking Company minutes, 21 May 1858, quoted in Barbara N. Kalata, *A Hundred Years A Hundred Miles, New Jersey's Morris Canal* (Morristown, N.J.: Morris County Historical Society, 1983), 442.

20. *Ibid.*

21. MCBCo minutes, 29 Sept 1858; Kalata, *Hundred Years,* 442.

22. John N. Hoffman, *Anthracite in the Lehigh Region of Pennsylvania, 1820–1843* (Washington, D.C.: Smithsonian Institution Press, 1968); Anthony J. Brzyski, "The Lehigh Canal and its Effect on the Economic Development of the Region Through Which It Passed, 1818–1874" (unpublished Ph.D. diss., New York University, 1957), 280–288, NCM library/archives.

23. *Intelligencer*, 30 Nov 1858.

24. *Intelligencer*, 27 July 1858.

25. MCBCo. Report to the Stockholders, 1859, 8–9, quoted in Kalata, *Hundred Years,* 443.

26. *Intelligencer*, 8 Feb 1859.

27. *Intelligencer* Feb 22 1859.

28   *Intelligencer*, 1 March 1859.

29. *Intelligencer*, undated clipping [1860–1861], BCHS.

30. *Intelligencer*, 17 Dec, 24 Dec 1861.

31. Various LC&N Annual Reports; quote from LC&N Annual Report, 1865, 7; "Lehigh Coal and Navigation Company," *American Railroad Journal* XL (1867), 149. *American Railroad Journal* hereafter *ARJ.*

32. *ARJ*, 1865, 16.

33. *Ibid.*

34. LC&N Annual Report, 1866, 18; 1867, 11; see also *ARJ* XXXIX (1866), 342, 363, 797.

35. LC&N Annual Report, 1865, 16; Lance E. Metz, "A Brief History of the Lehigh and Susquehanna Railroad" (unpublished paper, 1999), 8–9, NCM library/archives.

36. LC&N Annual Report, 1866, 11.

37. *Ibid.*

38. LC&N Annual Report, 1867, 5, 21–22, 44.

39. LC&N Annual Report, 1868, 5, 24.

40. LC&N Annual Report, 1869, 26–27.

41. *Ibid.*

42. LC&N Annual Report, 1869, 14–15.

43. *Ibid.*

44. LC&N Annual Report, 1868, 11–12.

45. E.W. Clark, LC&N pres., to John Brown, Canal Manager, Philadelphia, 24 Sept 1870.

46. Brown to Clark, Easton, 23 Nov 1870, and estimate, same date.

47. Jules I. Bogen, *The Anthracite Railroads: A Study in American Railroad Enterprise* (New York: The Ronald Press, 1927), 158; Elaine Anderson, *The Central Railroad of New Jersey's First 100 Years, 1849–1949: A Historical Survey*, ed. James Lee and Lance E. Metz (Easton, PA: Center for Canal History and Technology, 1984), 44–45. The $143,692 figure given by Anderson as the payments obligated to the mortgage holders and stockholders of the Delaware Division Canal Company are shown in the 1872 Annual Report of the Auditor General of the State of Pennsylvania as $188,701.40 and in the report for 1874 as 178,668.00. Neither the report of the Delaware Division Canal Company nor of the Lehigh Coal and Navigation Company gives any indication of the arrangements with the Central Railroad of New Jersey.

48. Minutes, LC&N Board of Managers, 1 March, 21 March, 1871. Hereafter LC&N minutes.

49. "Articles of Agreement between The Lehigh Coal and Navigation Company and The Central Railroad Company of New Jersey," 30 May 1871, copies at NCM; Annual Report of the LC&N, 1871, 33–34; Bogen, *Anthracite Railroads*, 158–163; Anderson, *Central Railroad of New Jersey*, 44–45; "Central Railroad of New Jersey," *ARJ* XLVII (1874), 483–485.

50. LC&N minutes, Minute Book N, 19 Dec 1873, 72–73, 76–77; 30 Dec 1873, 77.

51. "Articles of Agreement;" Annual Report of LC&N, 1871, 33–34; Bogen, *Anthracite Railroads*; Anderson, *Central Railroad of New Jersey*, 44; for additional detail on corporate arrangements see "Lehigh and Wilkes-Barre Coal Company," *ARJ* XLVII (1874), 197.

52. "Central Railroad of New Jersey," *ARJ* XLVII (1874), 483–5.6.

53. "Central Railroad of New Yersey," *ARJ* XLVIII (1875), 290–292; "Central Railroad of New Jersey," *ARJ* XLIX (1876), 450–452; "Lehigh Coal and Navigation Co.," *ARJ* L (1877), 523–525.

54. Minute Book O, 26 June 1877.

55. *Ibid.*

56. LC&N minutes, Minute Book N, 3 March, 22 May, 9 June, 15 June, 1877, 246, 251, 253–254, 256; Minute Book O, 26 June, 30 June 1877, 1, 2. See also for details of the bankruptcy and receivership, "Lehigh Coal and Navigation Co.," *ARJ* XLIX (1876), 1264; "Central Railroad of New Jersey," *ARJ* L (1877), 265, 710; *ARJ* LI (1878), 48; "Lehigh Coal and Navigation Co.," *ARJ* LI (1878), 255, 316.

57. LC&N Annual Report, 1878, 8.

58. Compiled from various annual reports.

59. LC&N Annual Report, 1878, 8–9.

60. E.W. Clark, LC&N pres., to J.W. Woolstom, Pres. Del. Div. Canal Co., 1 May 1878, PHMC.

61. *Ibid.*

62. E.W. Clark, LC&N pres., to J.W. Woolstom, Pres. Del. Div. Canal Co., 1 May 1878, PHMC; LC&N Annual Report, 1878, 10.

63. "Memorandum of Agreement Between the Delaware Division Canal Company and the Lehigh Coal and Navigation Company," 1 Feb 1879, in LC&N Annual Report, 1878, 11–12; Clark to Woolston, 20 April 1878, PHMC; LC&N minutes, Minute Book O, 25 June 1878, 39–40; "Delaware Division Canal," *ARJ* LII (1879), 169; "Lehigh Coal and Navigation Company," *ARJ* LII (1879), 250.

64. Printed notice from Henry Giles, treasurer, Del. Div. Canal Co., 10 March 1884, [volume], NCM; LC&N Annual Report, 1885, 8–9.

65. "Agreement Modifying the Lease of the Delaware Division Canal made August 20th, 1866, and the Modification thereof dated February 1st, 1879," 2 Feb 1886, included in LC&N Annual Report, 1885, 14–15.

66. "From Minutes, Board of Directors Delaware Division Canal Co. June 20, 1898," including a letter from Lewis A. Riley, LC&N pres., dated 20 June 1898; Auditor's copy, "Agreements to create Delaware Division Canal Company and to purchase canal from Sunbury & Erie Railroad," n.d., 1858; State Treasurer H.S. Magraw's endorsement on mortgage of Sunbury & Erie Railroad, 19 May 1858; document from Governor approving delivery of Delaware Division by S & E Railroad to new Delaware Division Canal Company, 14 July 1858.

67. Printed announcements of Del. Div. Canal Co. and LC&N, each signed by Lewis A. Riley, President, and dated 7 June 1898, PHMC.

68. LC&N Annual Report, 1898, 9.

69. "Report of Superintendent of Canals," 1 Jan 1879 in LC&N Annual Report, 1878, 28.

70. Various LC&N annual reports, 1883, 1884, 1887, 1888, 1892, 1893.

71. LC&N Annual Report, 1893, 50.

72. *Ibid.*, 1893, 47.

73. *Ibid.*, 1893, 50.

74. *Ibid.*, 1894, 47.

75. *Ibid.*

76. *Ibid.*, 1896, 54–55.

77. *Ibid.*, 1894, 44; 1925, 90; 1929, 104.

78. *Ibid.*, 1897, 47.

79. *Ibid.*, 1896, 52–53.

80. *Ibid.*, 1897, 52.

81. *Ibid.*, 1890, 7; 1891, 8.

82. *Ibid.*, 1897, 52. NOTE: "kelson" or alternate "keelson" is defined in 1966 edition of The Random House Dictionary of the English Language as "any of various fore- and-aft structural members lying above or parallel to the keel in the bottom of a hull." "Coaming" is defined as "1. a raised border around an opening in a deck, roof, or floor, designed to prevent water from running below, 2. Ship-building, a. any of four raised members forming such a border around a deck opening, esp. either of the fore-and-aft members. ... b. either of the thickened uppermost and lowermost strakes of plating used to strengthen a metal bulkhead or deckhouse."

83. LC&N Annual Report, 1899, 52.

84. *Ibid.*, 1900, 51.

85. *Ibid.*, 1901, 61–62.

86. Carbon of memorandum of Delaware Division Canal Company, 24 Feb 1937, to Mr. S.D. Matlack, Re. Water Power at Raubsville, NCM library/archives.

87. LC&N Annual Report, 1903, 59.

88. *Ibid.*, 1904, 9–10.

89. *Ibid.*, 1901, 10.

90. *Ibid.*, 1902, 44.

91. *Ibid.*, 1903, 10, 50, 58.

92. *Ibid.*, 1904, 10.

93. LC&N Annual Report, 1904, 10.

94. *Canal Currents* 63, Summer 1982, 16.

95. *Ibid.*, 1906, 15–16.

96. *Ibid.*, 1907, 11.

97. *Ibid.*, 1909, 8; 1910, 10.

98. *Ibid.*, 1909, 8; 1910, 10.

99. Letter, Randolph L. Kulp, Editor, Lehigh Valley Chapter, National Railway Historical Society, Inc., to Harry L. Rinker, Historic Bethlehem, Inc., 15 May 1967, quoting a not specifically identified Allentown newspaper, in Delaware Canal folder, NCM, probably *The Morning Call*, see Yoder, 32; "Trolly Boats," 27 Sept 1906, and "Trolly Boats Successful," 29 Sept 1906, *Allentown Chronicle & News*; Raymond I. Stover, *My Golden Memories & History of Kintnersville Pennsylvania 1976* (self-published, 1976), pamphlet, in Delaware Canal folder, NCM library/archives.

100. Chester Lear oral history tape in possession of Yardley Historical Association, 3/19/81. In 1907 LC&N conducted major experiments in mechanical traction along the upper section of the Lehigh Canal. See Ann Bartholomew and Lance Metz, *Delaware and Lehigh Canals* (Easton: Center for Canal History and Technology, 1989), 150–155.

101. LC&N Annual Report, 1918, 8, 72.

102. *Ibid.*, 1919, 84.

103. *Ibid.*, 1918, 73.

104. LC&N Annual Report, 1927.

105. Various LC&N annual reports, 1920 to 1930, particularly 1922, 94.

106. See list, page 7; LC&N Annual Report, 1927.

107. LC&N Annual Report, 1926, 94.

108. *Ibid.*, 1928, 95.

109. Letter, J.C. Lear, supervisor, New Hope, Pa., 3 Aug 1927, to I.M. Church, canal superintendent, Mauch Chunk, in Harry Warford group, microfilm at NCM library/ archives; see list, page 7.

110. Letter, J.C. Lear, supervisor, New Hope, Pa., 3 Aug 1927, to I.M. Church, canal superintendent, Mauch Chunk, in Harry Warford group, microfilm at NCM library/archives.

111. LC&N Annual Report, 1930, 6.

112. Annual Report, 1931, 6–7.

113. Sara Maynard Clark, "Last Days of the Canal," *Bucks County Traveller* VI (June 1955), 31.

114. Oral history interview, Lance Metz, National Canal Museum historian, with the late Carlton Leedom of Yardley. Audio tape in NCM library/archives.

Notes to Chapter Seven

1.   Simpson Torbert to Board of Canal Commissioners, 22 Jan 1833, reel #6, II, item #24.

2.   *Village Luminary* (Yardley), Thursday 11 July 1872.

3.   Chester Lear oral history tape at Yardley Historical Association.

4.   Oral history tape, Anna K. Shaudys interviewed 1997 by A.G. Zimmerman and Lance Metz, copy at National Canal Museum library/archives.

5.   Oral history tape, Edna May Reed interviewed by Annamae Bakun, 8 May 1992, Yardley Historical Assn.

6.   James Lee, *Tales the Boatmen Told* (Exton, Pa.: Canal Press, Inc, 1977), 221, 223.

7.   *Boatman's Horn*, video, Vincent N. Mondillo and Hugh Moore Park, 1992; Clifford Best oral history tape.

8.   Oral history tape, Yardley Historical Association.

9.   Lee, *Tales the Boatmen Told*, 104–106.

10. *Boatman's Horn*.

11. W.H. Gausler, "Reminiscences of the Lehigh and Delaware Canals from 1840 to 1856," *The Penn Germania* Vol XIII, No. 6, Old Series, June 1912, 452–456; quoted in C.P. Yoder, *Delaware Canal Journal*, 159–160.

12. *Ibid.*

13. Oral history tape, Madeline Free Rilleria, interviewed by Lance Metz and Wouter DeNie, 28 April 1993, NCM library/archives.

14. Oral history tape, Clifford Best, interviewed by Lance Metz, 16 August 1993, NCM library/archives.

15. Oral history tapes, Clifford Best and Madeline Free Rilleria.

16. John H. Williams to John R. Butler, Raubsville, 6 July 1843, reel #7(2), Item #85. Misspellings are as in the original.

17. Doylestown *Daily Intelligencer*, 2 Dec 1856.

18. *Ibid.*, 10 June 1857

19. Wm. K. Huffnagle to T.L. Wilson, Sect. of Board, 21 May 1847, reel #9(1), item #28.
20. Yoder, *Delaware Canal Journal*, 17, 194.
21. John Matheys to canal commissioners, 14 March 1846, reel #8(3), item #127.
22. *Ibid.*
23. David Connor's signed report dated 12 April 1842, reel #7(2), item #69.
24. Matheys to canal commissioners, 8 April 1846, reel #8(3), item #123.
25. *Ibid.*, 6 May 1846, reel #8(3), item #171.
26. David Connor to canal commissioners, 5 July 1841, reel #7(2), item #8.
27. Connor to Thomas L. Wilson, Sect. to Commission, 24 Oct 1843, reel #8(2), item #87.
28. "Titles Along Delaware Division Canal," several versions in blue tied bindings under title "The Delaware Division Canal Co. of Penns. Lock Level Canal Between Bristol and Easton...", starting in May of 1931 and containing maps, various lists of original property owners with citations to where they are recorded and also a similar typed carbon entitled "Properties and Rights Acquired by the Delaware Division Canal Company of Pennsylvania and the Lehigh Coal and Navigation Company after July 10, 1858...", dated 30 Sept 1936 and including summary of 1858 title transfer from Lewis S. Coryell to J.B. Morehead, pres. of Delaware Div. Canal Co., for property including lockhouse at lock #11 (recorded in Bucks County Deed Book 107, page 511, 28 Nov 1859) and a deed from Martin Coryell and Samuel Lilly, Lewis's executors, transferring additional land at the New Hope locks (recorded in Bucks County Deed Book 133, page 5, 16 April 1866). All now at NCM library/archives.
29. Marjorie E. Alliger, "Life Along the Delaware Canal," *Bucks County Panorama* V (5), May 1963, 10–12, 21.
30. Chester Lear oral history tape.
31. Alliger, "Life Along the Delaware Canal," 21.
32. Yoder, *Delaware Canal Journal*, 138–139.
33. Harry Warford oral history tapes, 1985, NCM library/archives.
34. Oral history tapes, Lewis Strohm, Clifford Best; *Boatman's Horn*.
35. Oral history tapes, Clifford Best, Madeline Free Rilleria.
36. Doylestown *Daily Intelligencer*, 20 June 1854.
37. *Ibid.*, 6 May 1856.
38. Oral history tapes, Lewis Strohm, Clifford Best.
39. Oral history tape, Madeline Free Rilleria; Richard Arner in *Boatman's Horn*.
40. Doylestown *Daily Intelligencer*, ca. 29 July 1856.
41. Howard Swope and Jim Brown in *Boatman's Horn*.
42. Oral history tape, Madeline Free Rilleria.
43. Doylestown *Daily Intelligencer*, 27 Sept 1853.
44. *Ibid.*, 2 Sept 1851.
45. *Ibid.*
46. *Ibid.*, 8 Sept 1859.
47. *Ibid.*, 3 July 1855.
48. *Ibid.*, 30 July 1861.
49. From *People's Beacon*, Doylestown *Daily Intelligencer*, 11 Nov 1856.
50. Doylestown *Daily Intelligencer,* 6 Oct 1851.
51. *Ibid.*, 14 June 1859.
52. *Ibid.*, 28 May 1861.
53. *Ibid.*, 3 Aug 1852.
54. *Bristol Courier,* 20 Oct 1930.
55. *Ibid.*, 30 Aug 1930.
56. Yoder, *Delaware Canal Journal*, 144.
57. Information furnished by Bucks County art authority Frank Bianco.
58. Oral history tape, Clifford Best.
59. Doylestown *Daily Intelligencer*, 28 Nov 1854.
60. R.J. Linder, Supt. Phila office, Pinkerton's National Detective Agency, to E. Hiss, General Coal Agent, L.C.& N. Co., Phila., Saturday, 24 Oct 1891, in Spruance Library, Bucks County Historical Society.
61. Oral history tape, Estella Everest, Yardley Historical Association.
62. *Ibid.*
63. Oral history tapes, Anna Shaudys, Marjorie C. Dinges; Alliger, "Life Along the Delaware Canal," 21.
64. Oral history tape, Anna Shaudys.
65. Oral history tape, Clifford Best.
66. Erin Einhorn, "By the canal, a tradition of fine art continues," Philadelphia *Inquirer,* North Neighbors, 7 Oct 1996.
67. Oral history tapes, Madeline Free Rilleria, Edna May Reed.
68 Need citation

69. Alliger, "Life Along the Delaware Canal," 21.
70. Jim Brown in *Boatman's Horn*; oral history tapes, Madeline Free Rilleria, Harry Warford.
71. *Intelligencer,* 9 July 1867.
72. Doylestown *Daily Intelligencer*, 25 Sept 1855.
73. Alliger, "Life Along the Delaware Canal," 21.
74. Sara Maynard Clark, "Country Crossroads: Yardley," *Bucks County Traveler*, VII(9), June 1956, 17.
75. Numerous oral history tapes, particularly Madeline Free Rilleria and Anna Shaudys; *Boatman's Horn.*
76. Oral history tapes, Clifford Best, Madeline Free Rilleria.
77. Mrs. Best, quoted in Yoder, *Delaware Canal Journal*, 165.
78. Oral history tape, Clifford Best.
79. Lewis Strohm in *Boatman's Horn*.
80. James E. Stanton, "For new supervisor, canal work is family affair," Doylestown *Intelligencer*, 8 April 1994.
81. Oral history tapes, Clifford Best and others.
82. Richard Arner in *Boatman's Horn*; oral history tapes, Clifford Best and others.
83. Pinkerton's Linder to E. Hill, 27 Oct 1891.
84. Doylestown *Daily Intelligencer*, 15 Aug 1854.
85. Undated clipping from a Yardley newspaper.

PART TWO

Unless otherwise noted, all documents listed as PHMC are in MG–311, Records of the Lehigh Coal and Navigation Company, in the Division of Archives and Manuscripts, Pennsylvania Historical and Museum Commission, Harrisburg, Pennsylvania. Most items are file copies, not the signed originals.

All documents listed as NCM are in the collections at the National Canal Museum's Library/Archives, Easton, Pennsylvania. The manuscript minutes of the Board of Managers of the Lehigh Coal and Navigation Company are available on microfilm there; the archives also contain the most recent papers for the Delaware Valley Protective Association.

Bucks County or Doylestown *Intelligencer* items are from clipping collections or the microfilm runs in the Spruance Library of the Bucks County Historical society (BCHS) in Doylestown, Pennsylvania; the society also houses 14 cartons containing the Hal and Sara Maynard Clark collections (call number MSC299).

Delaware Canal State Park Office (DCSP), Lodi, contains clipping files, extensive correspondence, and some reports, maps and charts.

The Betty Orlemann collection in the Friends of the Delaware Canal headquarters in the lockhouse at Lock No. 20 contains an extensive newspaper clipping collection, 1979 to 1992, and some Friends of the Delaware Canal correspondence.

Notes to Chapter Eight

1.. Various conversations, author and Lance Metz with the late Carleton Leedom, Yardley PA.
2. LC&N Annual Report, 1931, 6–7; The Lehigh Coal and Navigation Company, October 1, 1931, Agreement, Typescript, PMHB.
3. "State Takes Over Old Lehigh Canal," Philadelphia *Public Ledger*, 18 Oct 1931; "Men and Things," Philadelphia *Evening Bulletin*, 15 Oct 1931; "Pennsylvania Canal Given to State for Park Purposes; To Preserve Beauty Spot," *Bristol Courier*, 19 Oct 1931; "State Takes Over Canal; 'Camel Backs' to Stay," *Intelligencer*, 23 Oct 1931.
4. *Bristol Courier*, 19 Oct 1931.
5. Paul R. Wueller, Assoc. Dir. in Charge of Research and Statistics to Representative Marvin V. Keller, 10 Sept 1958, MSC 299, Box 10, Folder 11: 99: 12; *Report of a Proposed Recreational Development Roosevelt Park A Pennsylvania State Park*, by James R. McConaghie, Landscape Architect, Harrisburg, June 1932. "Back to the future," *Canal News* (Friends of the Delaware Canal), Spring, 1993.
6. Sara Maynard Clark, "The Day the Aqueduct Collapsed," *Bucks County Traveler*, Fifth Year, Number 2 (Oct) 1953: 15–16, 25.
7. LC&N Annual Report, 1931, 6–7.
8. The Lehigh Coal and Navigation Company, October 1, 1931, Agreement, Typescript, PMHC.
9. Henry H. Pearse, VP and sect, LC&N, to Trust Department, The Real Estate-Land Title Trust Company, July 21, 1931, PHMC; questions posed on behalf of Charles P. Perot estate.
10. Henry H. Pease, Memorandum re Capital Stock of The Delaware Division Canal Company of Pennsylvania, 24 July 1931; The Pennsylvania Company etc. Investment Dept. to S.D. Warriner, President LC&N, 22 July 1931, PHMC.
11. Minutes of the LC&N Board of Managers, 23 Sept 1931.
12. "To Fill Canal Basin with Sand Dredged from River Channel; Expect to Start Work Today," *Bristol Courier*, 13 Oct 1931.
13. "Description in lease from The Delaware Division Canal Company of Pennsylvania to Lehigh Navigation Coal Company, April 1, 1932…, carbon copy in NCM Library/Archives. In 1961, the "covered sections" of the canal were "re-excavated" by the State Department of Forests and Waters. A tiny portion of the rail and its concrete base still survive under the Union Street Bridge in Morrisville. Tom Roler and Frederick Smith, *Morrisville Comprehensive Plan* (1966).

14. LC&N Annual Report 1932, 9.

15 . Clark, "The Day."

16. "Aqueduct Repairs Asked," Philadelphia *Bulletin*, 2 Nov 1934; "Rebuild Aqueduct by Spring," *Intelligencer*, 31 Oct 1934.

17. Clark, "The Day," 25. For further information, see "Form of Letter to Prominent Valley Residents (record) Modify first paragraph to send members of Delaware Valley Protective Association," n.d., PHMC.

18. Minutes of the DVPA, 4 Nov 1933, in Hal Clark collection, BCHS; *Towpath* IV No. 1 (July 1951); letter, Clark to David E. Seymour, Esq., 19 Feb 1975, MSC299, Box No. 1, series 1, Folder 3; Martha Onuferko, "45 Year Fight Won To Save Canal," *The News* (Frenchtown), 6 Jan 1977; Marty Van Atta, "Harold (Hal) Clark: nature's good friend," *New Hope Gazette*, 19 June 1980.

19. "Says the State Does Not Now Own the Canal," *Intelligencer*, 4 Oct 1935.

20. "Secretary Bashore Visits Park," 25 Feb 1935; "Meeting to Protect Canal," *Intelligencer*, 14 March 1935.

21. "Speakers Deplore Delay in Development of Delaware Valley's Scenic Beauties," *Intelligencer*, 22 March 1935.

22. "State Washes Hands of Canal," *Intelligencer*, 19 March 1936.

23. "Canal Company Will Make No Repairs," *Intelligencer*, 20 May 1936.

24. LC&N Annual Report 1936, 7–8.

25. Await Canal Company Action," *Intelligencer*, 28 May 1936.

26. For more information on Cooke see Jean Christie, *Morris Llewellyn Cooke: Progressive Engineer* (New York: Garland Publishing Company, 1983).

27. Morris L. Cooke to LC&N, June 2, 1936, PHMC.

28. "Report on Maintenance of Repairs on the Portion of the Delaware Division Canal Between Raubsville and Yardley, Pennsylvania," by Corporate Engineer of Delaware Division Canal Company, 16 Sept 1936, PHMC.

29. *Ibid.*

30. "Canal Dickering to Date," *Intelligencer*, 6 Aug 1936, contains letters, Thomas Ross to William Taylor, DVPA, 27 July; Ross to Grover C. Ladner, Deputy Attorney General, Commonwealth of Pennsylvania, n.d., from which quotation is taken, and Ladner to Taylor, 29 July 1936.

31. L.C. Conant, Corporate Engineer, Delaware Division Canal Company, to Wm. Jay Turner, General Counsel, 17 March 1936, PHMC.

32. Henry H. Pease, VP and Sect., Delaware Division Canal Company to Wm. Jay Turner, General Counsel, DDCC, 15 March 1937; appended, Turner to Pease, 16 March 1937, PHMC.

33. "Canal Company Promises Action," *Intelligencer*, 11 Sept 1936.

34. "Canal Company Willing to Return It to State," *Intelligencer*, 4 Feb 1937.

35. "Canal Company Springs Surprise," *Intelligencer*, 25 March 1937.

36. "Reported New Use to Which Canal May Come," *Intelligencer*, 14 July 1938.

37. LC&N Annual Report 1936, 8; 1937, 7.

38. LC&N Annual Report 1938, 6–7; "Canal Situation May Be Cleared Up," *Intelligencer*, 19 Oct 1938.

39. F.M. Fisher, Comptroller, to Robert V. White, President, LC&N, 12 Sept 1940, PHMC; LC&N Annual Report, 1936, 8.

40. LC&N Annual Report, 1939, 6–7.

41. "Delaware Val. Parkway Soon to be Certainty," *Intelligencer*, 22 April 1940.

42. "Certificate" true copy of resolutions, etc. adopted by Board of Managers, 24 Oct 1940, certification, Henry H. Pease, Sect., 28 Oct 1940.

43. Memorandum for Mr. Robert V. White, President, from H.H. Pease, 8 Aug 1940; Memo. Re Sale of Stock of The Delaware Division Canal of Pennsylvania (unsigned), dated 25 July 1940, PHMC.

44. Luther C. Conant to Provident Trust Company, Trustee, 12 Oct 1940, PHMC.

45. Typescript copy, President LC&N to The Pa Co. etc., 28 Oct 1940; (typescript form) Proxy for Special Meeting of Stockholders of The Delaware Division Canal Company (date not filled in), PHMC.

46. Typescript letter, Thomas Ross to William F. Taylor, 22 Nov 1940, PHMC.

47. *Intelligencer*: "Hope to Have Governor at Canal Acceptance," 16 May 1940; Canal Deed Being Studied By The State," 25 July 1940; "Delaware Valley Parkway Is Now Property of the State," 19 Dec 1940.

48. LC&N Annual Report 1940, 7.

49. "A Letter to the Delaware Valley Protective Association," *Towpath* I (June 1940), 3.

50. *Towpath* 1940.

51. "Memorandum of conference with Mr. G. Albert Stewart, Secretary of Forests and Waters, Harrisburg, Pa. December 30, 1940," attached to letter, L.S. Conant to LC&N V. Pres. and Secy., Philadelphia, 3 Jan 1941, PMHC.

52. "The Delaware Division Canal, Report Upon Its Present Condition and Its Relation to the Control of Floods in the Delaware River," Pennsylvania Water and Power Resources Board, 1942.

53. Mrs. Hogue to Pennsylvania Department of Forests and Waters, 5 Nov 1945, DCSP.

54. Brouse to Hogue, 16 Nov 1945, DCSP.

55. Brouse to Hogue, 6 Dec 1945, DCSP.

56. "D.V.P.A. Elects Officers," *Intelligencer*, 16 Sept 1947.

57. "Water Soon for the Canal," *Intelligencer*, 3 June 1948.

58. "The Canal idea was Penn's," *New Hope Gazette*, 29 June 1979; *Report for Improvements to the Delaware Division of the Pennsylvania Canal From Mile Post 24 to Post 60 Pennsylvania*, submitted by Damon and Foster, Consulting Engineers, 1950; C.P. "Bill" Yoder, *Delaware Canal Journal* (Bethlehem: Canal Press, Inc., 1972), 62.

59. Damon and Foster report, 4.

60. *Ibid*; Paul R. Wueller to Representative Marvin W. Keller, 10 Sept 1958, MSC 299, Box 12, Folder 11: 99: 12.

61. W. Wilson McNeary to members and friends of DVPA in *Towpath* IV No. 1 (July 1951); the reconstructed Durham Aqueduct was a steel chute that carried canal water until 1992 when it was replaced by a steel-and-concrete aqueduct.

62. *Towpath*, 1952.

63. *Towpath* IV No. 1 (July 1951).

64. *Towpath* V No. 6 (Jan 1952).

65. *Towpath* V No. 10 (May-June 1952).

66. *Towpath* V No. 6 (Jan 1952).

67. "Forests and Waters," *Towpath* VIII No. 2 (Oct 1956).

68. M. Nelson McGeary, *Pennsylvania Government In Action: Governor Leader's Administration (1955–59)* (State College, Pennsylvania: Penns Valley Publishers, 1972), 130–135; "Goddard Confirmation Vote: Both Overdue and Premature," "Goddard Controversy," both in *Philadelphia Inquirer*, 6 Nov 1971; Bob Reinhardt, "Goddard Gets Arbor Award," *The Tecumseh Chieftain*, 26 April 1979.

69. "Democratic Senator Wants Canal Made Into Useful Road," Quakertown *Free Press*, 7 Sept 1955; "Senator Yesko Would Fill It In, Effort Being Made In Pa. Legislature To Destroy the Canal Beginning at Easton," *Lambertville Beacon*, undated clipping, both MSC 299, Box 9, Folder 11:2; typed MSS, MSC 299, Box 4, Folder 2;7.4.

70. C.P. Yoder, Curator, Pennsylvania Canal Society, "Opposition to the Installation of a Culvert and Fill for a Road Crossing of the Delaware Canal at Morrisville," n.d., ca 1976, typescript in NCM library/archives.

71. "Policy Delaware Canal, Roosevelt State Park," submitted 30 Dec 1957, B.D. Murphy, chief engineer.

72. "The Gossiper," *Intelligencer*, 6 June 1948.

73. "State Plans Draining Water Of Bucks historic Canal," *Courier Times*, 28 May 1957; "Delaware Canal Drainage Receives Reprieve From state Till Monday," *Courier Times*, 29 May 1957; "Thousands Protest Drainage of Canal: Telegrams Flood capital," *Intelligencer*, 29 May 1957; Editorial, "A Foolish Threat," *Courier Times*, May 31, 1957; "State To Close Canal June 1st," *New Hope Gazette*, 30 May 1957.

74. Pat Greene, "How to Keep A Canal," *Bucks County Traveler*, VIII:9 (Aug 1957), 24–25, 66–67.

75. Rep. Kooker to Hal Clark, June 1957.

76. DVPA news release, 26 Oct 1966.

77. Theodore Elonis to Editor, *Courier Times*, 2 July 1965.

78. Fred Selby, "Farms, Industries, Threatened, Drought Imperils Fish In Delaware Canal," *Philadelphia Bulletin*, 27 June 1965; George Ingram, "Dying Fish In Canal Pose Many Problems For Yardley," *Sunday Times Advertiser*, 18 July 1965.

79. "That Canal Water's Dirty," *Bucks County Gazette*, 7 Aug 1986.

80. Letter, Richard L. Holland to Hal Clark, 2 Oct 1973; Florence Schaffhausen, "Delaware Canal Being Repaired Following Rains," *Intelligencer*, 26 July 1973.

81. Schaffhausen, *ibid*.

82. Engineer's report, 1950, 169.

83. "Deaths and Property Damage Have Occurred At the Entrance to New Hope, Pa. The D.V.P.A. Is Suggesting a Simple Remedy. Diagram and Story Inside," *Towpath* V No. 13 (Nov-Dec 1952); Schaffhausen, "Delaware Canal Being Repaired."

84. "New Hope Problem," *Towpath* IX No. 1 (Feb 1958); manuscript addressed to John R. Regolla Jr., Chief Counsel Penna. Dept. of Highways; typescript headed "Sequence of Events," both in MSC 299, Box 4, folder 2:7.4; typescript headed "Hal Clark—Del. Valley Protective Assoc—Doylestown, Pa.", MSC 299, Box 4, Folder 2:7.5; undated typescript memo from DVPA titled "Reasons for Redrawing Plans for New Hope Project," NCM library/archives.

85. Clark to Henry D. Harrah, Secretary Pa. Dept. of Highways, Harrisburg, Copies to Governor Scranton, n.d., MSC 299, Box 9, Folder 11:15:5f; Clark to Lewis M. Stevens, Secretary Pa. Dept. of Highways, 22 Sept 1958.

86. "About Retaining Wall Work, Road Dept. Briefs Rt. 32 'Watchdogs'," *Intelligencer*, 27 April 1967; "DVPA Supports $300,000 River Road Project," *Easton Express*, 29 April 1967; "Work Snagged On River Road By High Bids," *Philadelphia Inquirer*, 30 April 1967.

87. "Group Opposes Proposed Site of Shopping Center," *Philadelphia Inquirer*, 3 June 1961.

88. "DVPA To Attend Hearing On Delaware Canal Fill," *Intelligencer*, 1 May 1961; "Route 1 Plan threatens Part of Historic Canal," *Philadelphia Inquirer*, 1 May 1961.

89. Handwritten biographical material on Hal Clark, dated 4-27-76. Clark collection, Spruance Library.

90. Clark to Harrah, n.d.

91. Clark to Harrah, n.d.; Clark to Congressman Alan D. Williams, Jr., 30 March 1962; DVPA news release, 16 April 1962.

92. Clark to Williams.

93. Clark to Harrah, n.d.

94. W. Lester Trauch, "A Trunk Through A Transom," *Intelligencer*, 11 Nov 1967.

95. DVPA news release, signed Hal H. Clark, President, (n.d., but Aug or Sept 1966), MSC 299, Box 4, Folder 2:7.1.

96. "Goddard Believes In Saving Scenery In Interchange For Route 202 Bridge," *Sunday Times Advertiser*, 9 Feb 1964; "DVPA President Warns, River Road Link May KO Toll-Free Bridge," *Intelligencer*, 16 Dec 1966; Stephen R. Sandler, "Bridge Com-

mission Denies DVPA Charges On Site of New Hope Interchange," *Easton Express*, 16 Dec 1966; La Barbara Bowman, "At Meeting With State Officials, Residents hit New Hope Road Plan," *Sunday Times Advertiser*, 12 Jan 1969.

97. Ethel Davenport, "An Old Pennsylvania Canal Is Stirred by Summer Plans, *The New York Times*, 31 May 1942.

98. Bernard Ikeler, "Canal Barge Ride," *The New York Times*, 10 July 1955.

99. Obituary, John F. Winters, *Bucks County Gazette*, 8 March 1962.

100. Fred Selby, "Mules (Not Too Tall) Pull Tourists In Barges Along Canal In New Hope," *The Sunday Bulletin* (Suburban North & Northeast Section), 16 Aug 1964; DVPA News Release, 22 Sept 1961.

101. *New Hope News and Bucks County Eagle*, 2 May 1968.

102. "Dry Canal Ruins barge Business in New Hope," *Beacon/News*, 2 Aug 1973.

103. "Canal Boatman Balked At Every Turn," *Philadelphia Inquirer* (Northern and Northeast Edition), 8 June 1969.

104. "Barge Company celebrates 10 years this weekend," *New Hope Gazette*, 21 July 1988.

105. *Intelligencer*, 25 Sept 1994.

106. Walter F. Naedele, "Senators reflect, as namesakes plod forth," *Philadelphia Inquirer*, 9 March 1990.

107. Lease Agreement, 7 Dec 1954, between Commonwealth of Pennsylvania and Borough of Bristol.

108. "Subject: Ownership of Delaware Canal in Bristol Roosevelt State Park," William W. Shakely, Director, DER Bureau of Legal Services, 9 Aug 1988.

109. Oral interview, Carl and Hubert Nelson by Lance Metz and A.G. Zimmerman, 20 Sept 1996.

110. Eloise DeHaan, "Partnership to put new life into center," *Courier Times*, 15 March 1990.

111. Department of Forests and Waters press release, 10 May 1961.

112. Quoted from Doylestown *Intelligencer*, *Towpath*, April 1962.

113. James Lawrence, "Lower End of Canal In Jeopardy; Penna. Warns," *Trenton Evening Times* (Bucks County Today section), 28 May 1964.

114. Goddard to John Rogers, president of Bristol Borough Council, 6 Dec 1965, MSC 299 BCHS.

115. Fred Bender, "Wright Says He'll Give Canal Petition to Shafer," *Courier Times*, 28 March 1967.

116. Patricia Kaye, "Delaware Canal's Future Rests With Local Officials," *Sunday Times Advertiser* (Bucks County Section), 13 April 1969.

117. Mimi Reimel, "Boy Scouts to clean-up Part of Delaware Canal," *Courier Times*, 4 April 1969; "Response Comes from All Over," *Courier Times*, 13 April 1969; "250 To Help Clean canal, Wear Gloves and Bring Rakes Sunday," *Courier Times*, 26 June 1969; Mimi Reimel, "200 Pitch In To Help Clean Canal Out," *Courier Times*, 30 June 1969.

118. "'Patching Up' Canal", *Courier Times*, 12 Nov 1969; Goddard to Emilio Cardull, Bristol, 17 April 1969, NCM library/archives.

119. Fred Fiske, "Champion digs in to save the fading Delaware Canal," *Courier Times*, 6 Oct 1974.

120. *Ibid*.

121. Letter, Justice Douglas to Naomi Tomlinson, 26 Jan 1968; letter, Justice Douglas to Charles McClelland, Jr., 26 Jan 1968; letter, Tomlinson to Justice Douglas, 6 Feb 1968; Ric Sabatini, "U.S. Justice To Walk Canal: Douglas promises trip soon," *Courier Times*, 28 Feb 1968; Sabatini, "Douglas, Wife To Stroll canal," *Courier Times*, 29 March 1968.

122. Richard. V. Sabatini, "Storm Damage to Canal to Cost State $92,000," *Philadelphia Inquirer*, 25 Nov 1971. *See also* Barbara Murphy, "Justice Douglas Plans Hike to Aid Plea for Canal," *Evening Bulletin: Suburban Northeast*, 23 May 1968; "Sunday along the canal," *Delaware Valley Advance*, 6 June 1968; Carol Meyer, "Delaware Canal holds part of Bristol's early heritage," *Bristol Pilot*, 22 March 1990.

123. Address by Goddard at the annual meeting of the DVPA, 16 Nov 1971, MSC 299, Box 11, Folder 11:47 Goddard.

124. Helen B. Lodge to Goddard, 30 July 1964, MSC 299: Box 9: Folder 11:15:5b; DVPA news release (n.d. but 1960s) in Delaware Canal files, NCM library/archives.

125. Delaware River Basin Commission news release, Wednesday PM 24 Feb 1965; "Work On Wing dams Will Start Next Year," *Intelligencer*, 26 June 1965.

126. Howlett to Clark, 19 April 1967.

127. Marty Van Atta, "Harold (Hal) Clark: nature's good friend," *New Hope Gazette*, 19 June 1980.

128. "Wing Dams Cost $50,574 Less Than Appropriated," unidentified newspaper clipping, 2 April 1970, NCM library/archives.

129. *Towpath*, 1963.

130. Dexter Hutchins, "Historic Canal Is Preserved," *Philadelphia Inquirer*, undated clipping, DCSP.

131. Holland to Hal Clark, 2 Oct 1973, MSC 299, Box 9, folder 11:15:5c.

132. "Work Planned On Worn Locks Of Delaware Canal," *The News*, 8 May 1975.

133. Mary Amidon, "Bucks County Man Replaces Wargo," Erie, Pennsylvania, *Times-News*, 8 July 1979; "Giza To Leave Canal Park To Head Busiest Pa. Park," *Delaware Valley News*, 26 July 1979; "Giza is transferred from U. Bucks parks," *Intelligencer*, 27 July 1979; "Hal Clark bids farewell to Roosevelt Park chief," *New Hope Gazette*, 9 Aug 1979.

134. Mary Lennon, "Milford engineer to direct 2 state parks in county," *Intelligencer*, 7 Sept 1979. Betty Orlemann, "Engineer Likely to Oversee Parks," *The News* (Frenchtown) 12 Sept 1979.

135. Betty Orlemann, "State Selects New Canal Park Chief," *Delaware Valley News*, 23 Oct 1980.

136. James M. Denery, "Hoehn leaving canal park post," *Intelligencer*, 7 Aug 1989; Michele Passman, "Canal Superintendent Leaving After 9 Years," *Delaware Valley News*, 24 Aug 1989; "Delaware Canal State Park Superintendent Report to The Delaware Canal State Park Advisory Committee," 12 Sept 1989.

137. DVPA news release, 21 Sept 1961.

138. DVPA news release, 3 Aug 1964; Leonard MacBain, "Irish Visitors Taken For A Ride With Bucks Mule-Drawn Navy," *Intelligencer*, 10 Aug 1964.

139. Hal Clark to John F. Laudadio, chairman, Task Forces on Quarries and Strip Mining, Joint State Government Commission, Harrisburg, Pennsylvania, copy in NCM library/archives.

140. Letter is included in undated DVPA news release, MCS 299, Box 11, Folder 11:54:2, in yellow binder.

141. Fred Selby, "Canal Residents Will Get Better Police Protection," Philadelphia *Bulletin*, 26 Dec 1968; Charles F. McGurk, "Bucks Commissioners hear Canal Property Dispute," *Intelligencer*, 26 Sept 1968.

142. R. Bentley Carson, "Plumstead Canal Land Dispute Seeks Attention From State," *Intelligencer*, 31 Dec 1968; Curt Yeske, "Bucks Backs Down on Canal as State Takes Hard Line," *The Morning Call*, 22 Jan 1969; "The Old Canal Means Work," *Intelligencer*, 22 Jan 1969; "Protective Association Joins Canal Hassle," *Trenton Times*, 22 Jan 1969; "DVPA Expresses Concern On Delaware Canal Issue," *Easton Express*, 22 Jan 1969; "State May Drop Maintenance Along Canal," *Bulletin*, 23 Jan 1969; telegram, J.H.O. Canby, chairman of Bucks County Commissioners to Pennsylvania Dept. of Forests and Waters, 7 Jan 1969, MSC 299, box 10: Ser 11:27; telegram, Carl R. Mapel, Jr., to Donald R. Price, Esquire, MSC 299, Box 10: ser 11:27.

143. Editorial, The Delaware Valley Publishing Co., *The Beacon and Lambertville Record* and the *New Hope News—Bucks County Bugle*, 20 March 1969.

144. "Canal Property Owners Association, Position Paper," May 1979, MSC299, Box 10: Ser 11: 27.

145. "Centre Bridge Inn Destroyed," *The Bucks County Gazette*, 9 Feb 1961; "Holes drilled for water supply, Fireman get problems from frozen Delaware," *Intelligencer*, 26 Jan 1977.

146. "'Sabotage' Suspected in Dynamiting of Tree," *New Hope Gazette*, 20 June 1963.

147. "Reward Set For Vandals At Parks," unidentified newspaper clipping, 16 July 1963, MSC 299, Box 9, Folder 11: 2.

148. DVPA news release, 29 March 1966.

149. "Waterless Delaware Canal Yields Curious Junk," *Intelligencer*, 2 Dec 1966.

150. "From the pen of EMERY NEMETHY," signed by Emery Nemethy, 24 July 1976, NCM Library/archives.

151. Clark to Governor Shafer, 4 April 1967.

152. Goddard to Clark, 6 June 1967.

153. "Abandoned Gravel Pits," *Intelligencer*, 10 June 1967; "Gravel Quarries Seen Threatening Scenic River Road, Delaware Canal," *The Morning Call*, 13 June 1967; "Bucks Quarry Dispute Raises Dust," *Sunday Bulletin*, 7 April 1968.

154. Edward A. Scotch to Director of Pa Dept of Forests and Waters, 28 Jan 1968; C.E. McConnell to Scotch, 31 Jan 1968.

155. Quoted by Fred Bender, "Residents Blamed On Canal Misuse," *Courier Times* 2 Feb 1967.

156. Bender, "Wright Says He'll Give Canal Petition to Shafer," *Courier Times*, 28 March 1967.

Notes to Chapter Nine

1. Clark to David E. Milhous, DER Sanitary Engineer, 11 June 1974. For detail on Bethlehem Steel pollution, see news release, DVPA, 19 Feb 1962; typescript excerpt from DVPA news release, n.d. MSC 299, Box 4, Folder 2:7.1.

2. Marty Van Atta, "Harold (Hal) Clark: nature's good friend," *New Hope Gazette*, 19 June 1980.

3. Florence Schaffhausen, "Neglect, lack of water threaten historic Delaware Canal," *Intelligencer*, 20 Sept 1982.

4. Mary Blakinger, "Last ditch efforts, Pennsylvanians aim to restore canal," *Preservation News*, Jan 1988; "And it all began a dark and rainy night in October," *Canal News* (Friends of the Delaware Canal), Fall 1992; Bill Allison, "Friends of Canal formed," *New Hope Gazette*, 30 Sept 1982; "Canal Needs Friends: Woman In Tinicum To Begin Society," *Trenton Times*, 28 Sept 1982.

5. Steven F. Smith, "50 Friends of the Delaware Canal say they will clean it up themselves," *Intelligencer*, 7 March 1983.

6. "Heavy Rainfall Causes Minor Flooding," *Easton Express*, 14 July 1975; "Flooding Causes Dispute On Canal Storm Operation," *Delaware Valley News*, 17 July 1975; "Praise and Problem," *Delaware Valley News*, 24 Aug 1975; legend under photograph, "Already Rain-battered," *Delaware Valley News,* 24 July 1975; "Flooding Inquiry Continues But No Negligence Proven," *Delaware Valley News,* 31 July 1975; Bruce Kaleita, "Workers repair canal washout after rescue of 4,500 fish," *Intelligencer*, 7 Aug 1975.

7. Eugene V. Giza to Editor, *Intelligencer*, 14 Sept 1978.

8. Chris Newkumet, "Canal Stays Dry Through Winter," *Delaware Valley News* 24 Aug 1978; legend under illustration, "Housekeeping," *Intelligencer*, 12 Sept 1978; "County Separates Canal From Creek At Erwinna, Creek Broke Through Canal Bank in '77," *Delaware Valley News*, 14 Sept 1978.

9. Ann Schultes, "Delaware Canal is dry after culvert collapse," *Intelligencer*, 17 Aug 1978.

10. Jack Shadle, "Canal water gushes into Kenwood," *Courier Times*, 28 July 1980.

11. Betty Orlemann, "Dry Canal May Continue Locally Into Next Spring," *Delaware Valley News*, 19 Nov 1981.

12. Orlemann to State Rep. James Greenwood, 8 Aug 1982, NCM library/archives.

13. John Hilferty, "Savitch accident speeds up canal renovation," *Philadelphia Inquirer*, 18 April 1984.

14. Betty Orlemann to Forrey, 10 May 1986; Betty Barr, Pres., Friends of Delaware Canal, to Forrey, 8 May 1986; Forrey to Orlemann, 10 May 1986, Orlemann Collection, Flood Damage, 3/16/86 in Friends HQ, New Hope.

15. Betty Orlemann, "Muskrats Saboteurs Along Delaware Canal," *Delaware Valley News*, 6 Sept 1979; W. Lester Trauch, "Canal bids good riddance to muskrats," *Intelligencer*, 26 Nov 1979.

16. Legend under photograph, "In an Effort," *Delaware Valley News*, 2 Sept 1976.

17. Carol Meyer, "Delaware Canal holds part of Bristol's early heritage, Group says Lower Bucks on short end of stick for restoration funds," *Bristol Pilot*, 22 March 1990; Betty Orlemann to William C. Forrey, 8 July 1988, Orlemann Collection, Folder, Correspondence, W. Forrey; conversations and statements observed by author at DCSP Advisory Committee meetings.

18. Agenda of Briefing and Discussion Meeting regarding Roosevelt State Park, DER Office of Resources Management Bureau of State Parks, 26 Jan 1984, NCM library/archives.

19. "Hoehn leaving," *Intelligencer*, 7 Aug 1989.

20. Yoder to Bruce Singer, V. Pres. DVPA, 16 Jan 1968.

21. Quoted in Yoder to Singer, 16 Jan 1968.

22. C.H. McConnell to Hal Clark, 1 March 1968.

23. "Parkway Commission, State Coordinate Improvements," *Easton Express*, 20 Aug 1968.

24. Legend under photograph, "Locks In Delaware Canal Nearly Restored," *Easton Express*, 30 Jan 1971.

25. Ambrose P. Murray, "Delaware Canal Gets New Lease on Life," *Easton Express*, Dec 11, 1974.

26. Illustration, "Winter Installation," *Easton Express*, n.d., in file of DCST, clipping service date, 24 Jan 1975.

27. Maurice Carroll, "Exploring the Banks of Pennsylvania Delaware Canal," *New York Times*, 29 April 1979.

28. Anne Schultes, "Ground Hog Lock: a lesson about the Delaware Canal," *Intelligencer*, 8 May 1978.

29. Conversation with George F. "Sparky" Corkran, 15 Dec 1992.

30. "Canal Park Access For Handicapped," *Delaware Valley News*, 9 April 1981; Rick Epstein, "Canal Park To Build Headquarters," *Delaware Valley News*, 16 April 1981; "Office for Canal," *Delaware Valley News*, 19 Nov 1981; "New $150,000 Headquarters For Canal Park Depends On Zoning Variance From Tinicum," *Delaware Valley News*, 25 Feb 1982; "Park Reduces Plans For New Office," *Delaware Valley News*, 29 Aug 1982.

31. Virginia Forrest to Wilson Oberdorfer, 2 Aug 1982, NCM library/archives.

32. F.P. Schaffhausen, "Historic registry listing can help preserve Delaware Canal," *Intelligencer*, 18 April 1974; Elmer Smith, "Historic Bucks canal Needs Funds," *Evening Bulletin*, 24 Feb 1975; "Seek to Preserve Canal For Register," *Beacon*, 25 April 1974; Schaffhausen, "Delaware Canal is listed as historical," *Intelligencer*, 30 Oct 1974; "Delaware Canal on National Register," *Bucks County Gazette*, 28 Nov 1974; "Delaware Canal Wins Landmark Designation," *Philadelphia Inquirer*, 5 Dec 1974.

33. F.P. Schaffhausen, "Historic trail planned along Delaware Canal," *Intelligencer*, 29 June 1974; Schaffhausen, "Guidebook encourages biking, hiking and canoeing the canal," *Intelligencer*, 1 Nov 1975.

34. Smith, "Historic Bucks Canal."

35. F.P. Shaffhausen, "Canal is granted U.S. landmark status," *Intelligencer*, 21 Dec 1976; Marty Van Atta, "National Landmark Certification Will Aid Canal Preservation," *Bethlehem Globe-Times*, 21 Dec 1976.

36. Marty Van Atta, "Canal Dedicated in New Hope as National Landmark," *New Hope Gazette*, 22 June 1978.

37. Anne Shultes, "Who owns the canal? State claims the prize," *Intelligencer*, 30 July 1977; Shultes, "Residents join efforts to keep land by canal," *Intelligencer*, 19 Dec 1977.

38. Encelewski to Gov. Milton Shapp, 17 Sept 1978, copy in NCM library/archives.

39. Ireen E. Kudra, "Canal property owners join forces to fight state," *Intelligencer*, 16 March 1978

40. Letter, Giza to Editor, *Intelligencer*, 14 Sept 1978; Anne Shultes, "Delaware Canal draining draws citizen protest," *Intelligencer*, 1 Sept 1978.

41. "Towpath Parking And Little Trees Fuel State Versus Neighbor Feud," *Delaware Valley News*, 9 Aug 1979; "Park Chief Giza Says English Baits State," *Delaware Valley News*, 16 Aug 1979; "Canal Group Quits Fight, Aims To Work With State," *Delaware Valley News*, 27 Sept 1979; "Letters, English Says Canal Group Has Gone Off Its Course," *Delaware Valley News*, 27 Sept 1979; "Canal Group Quits Fight, Aims To work With State," *Delaware Valley News*, 27 Sept 1979.

42. "Linda" was probably Linda Quaste who succeeded English as president of the CPO.

43. Canal meeting at Conti's, 4 Oct 1979, transcript in NCM library/archives.

44. Lacy McCrary, "Canal hasn't worn the years well," *Philadelphia Inquirer*, 26 Nov 1985.

45. Kathy Canavan, "DER top brass responsible for culvert," *Courier Times*, 6 March 1973; Brigitta Nyholm, "Morrisville apartments … A 10 Million Question, *Sunday Times Advertiser*, 20 May 1973; letter, Adm. Asst. to Dept. Sect., Legislation and Boards, to Hutton Recycling Circle of Pennsylvania, c/o Virginia and Lefferts Hutton, 4 June 1974, NCM library/archives; "Statement of Mrs. Lefferts (Virginia) Hutton, Chairman, Environmental Council, Bucks County Conservation Alliance for the subcommittee of the Pennsylvania Senate committee on Environmental Resources Hearing on H.B. 1231 at 9:15 AM, August 11, 1976, Morrisville Borough Hall"; Glenn Kranzley, "Weidner Pushes Bridge Bill At Urging of Bucks GOP," Bethlehem *Globe Times*, 31 July 1975.

46. "Hearings needed on Morrisville canal case," *Courier Times*, 29 June 1976; Marty Van Atta, "Weidner pushed bill at GOP leader's request, Payoffs questioned in canal development," *New Hope Gazette*, 19 Aug 1976.

47. House Bill No. 1231, Session of 1975, The General Assembly of Pennsylvania, Printer's No. 1322, "referred to Committee on transportation, May 7, 1975; Kranzley, "Weidner Pushes."

48. Susan Silkwood, "Conservation groups rallying, Fires stoked for canal bridge fight," *Courier Times*, 21 July 1976; F.P. Shaffhausen, "Bucks unit challenges DER integrity in canal bridge," *Intelligencer*, 22 July 1976.

49. Agenda of Briefing and Discussion Meeting regarding Roosevelt State Park, DER Office of Resources Management Bureau of State Parks, 26 Jan 1984, NCM library/archives.

50. Ibid.

51. John S. Renninger to Mr. and Mrs. Lefferts Hutton, 14 June 1976.

52. Glenn Kranzley, "Political Maneuvers Push Bill Close To Passage," Bethlehem *Globe Times*, 15 June 1976.

53. Ibid.

54. Susan Silkwood, "Lewis' canal-bill stand draws Senate fire," *Courier Times*, 23 June 1976.

55. Letters to the Editor, Thomas J. Cowen, Supervisor, Lower Makefield Township, *Courier Times*, 29 June 1976.

56. "Bridge meeting on with Howard," *Evening Times*, 24 June 1976; Susan Silkwood, "Developer: 'Not a dime' offered to get permit for canal bridge," *Intelligencer*, 12 Aug 1976.

57. Birgitta Nyholm, "Canal bridge hearing draws quite a throng," *Evening Times*, 11 Aug 1976; Silkwood, "'Not a dime'"; Marty Van Atta, "Payoffs questioned in canal development," *New Hope Gazette*, 19 Aug 1976.

58. Susan Silkwood, "Borough councilmen irked by strangers on their turf," *Intelligencer*, 12 Aug 1976.

59. "Our Opinion," *Intelligencer* editorial, 20 Sept 1976.

60. David J. Hladick, "Morrisville gives tentative OK to build Ferry Arms complex," *Trenton Times*, 17 Jan 1978; Hladick, "Morrisville stalls Ferry Arms OK," *Trenton Times*, 11 Oct 1978.

61. Betty Orlemann, "Canal Backers Worried," *The Trentonian*, 26 Oct 1986; Orlemann, "14-Story Apartment Building, M'ville Councilman Blasts 'Towpath Towers'," *Trentonian*, 8 March 1987.

62. Michael Frome, "For the Love of Rivers," *National Parks*, Nov/Dec 1983, 17–19.

63. Bourquard to Nuss, 22 Aug 1974; Nuss to Bourquard, 9 Sept 1974.

64. Printed text of agreed specifications, n.d.

65. "'History' seen ploy for canal," *Evening Times*, 30 June 1976.

66. Forrest to Oberdorfer, 2 Aug 1982; Oberdorfer to Forrest, 9 Sept 1981.

67. "RE: Permit Application No. NAPOP-R-80-0534-3, NAPOP-R-80-0813-3, Statement of Neshaminy Water Resources Authority to be Presented at Army Corps of Engineers Public Hearing of September 15, 1981, copy in NCM library/archives.

68. Hal Marcovitz, "Point Pleasant slated for third environmental study," *Courier Times*, 20 April 1982; Peter Zernite, "Pump Builder Fined For Draining Canal," *Delaware Valley News*, 20 Oct 1983; Morris Kennedy, "NWRA, state feud over Pump," *Intelligencer*, 3 July 1984; "DER Blocks Mergentime Exit; Alleges Canal Needs Fixing," *Delaware Valley News*, 4 July 1984; Kennedy, "DER: Work not finished at Pump site," *Intelligencer*, 5 July 1984; Kennedy, "Canal dispute causes NWRA to postpone its Pump 'closing'," *Intelligencer*, 6 July 1984; Kennedy, "DER granted right to conduct canal work at Pump site," *Intelligencer*, 12 Aug 1984; Nicholas DiGiovanni, "Bucks County Gives Up Fight Against 'Pump'," *Delaware Valley News* 24 July 1986; Betty Orlemann, "NWRA Hires Manager, Engineer For Pump Project," *Delaware Valley News* 31 July 1986.

69. Edward Levenson, "Pump sale: $10M gain, but a resource is lost," *Courier Times* 3 Aug 1994.

70. "Locktender's shed fire called suspicious," *The Morning Call* (Allentown), 30 Oct 1979.

71. Patricia Wandling, "Living near towpath harrowing for family," *Courier Times*, 9 June 1980.

72. Forrest to Forrey, 13 Aug 1982.

73. "Canoeists Steal $50,000 In Jewelry Beside Canal," *Delaware Valley News*, 15 July 1982.

74. Anne Shultes, "NH policeman need permission to patrol canal," *Intelligencer*, 27 Jan 1977.

75. Virginia Hutton to John Carson, Delaware River Basin Commission, 20 April 1978, DCSP.

76. "Pa. May Give Canal To U.S.," *Delaware Valley News*, 25 Oct 1979.

77. Maryann Bird, "48 less homes in U. Makefield, Developer revises his plan," *Courier Times*, 26 April 1973; "110 new homes, U. Makefield approves development," *Courier Times*, 2 June 1973.

78. Letter, Garry L. Kunnas to Hal Clark, 8 Aug 1975, NCM library/archives; letter, Forrey to Finkel, 22 July 1975, NCM library/archives; News release, Bucks County Conservation Alliance, 22 Sept 1975; Betty Burke, "Supervisors discuss drainage problems at Shires crossing," *New Hope Gazette*, 25 Sept 1975.

79. Betty Burke, "Plans reviewed in U. Makefield," *New Hope Gazette*, 3 Dec 1981; "Virginia Forrest asks assurances on canal crossing," *New Hope Gazette*, 17 Dec 1981; "Letters to the Gazette," signed Virginia Forrest, *New Hope Gazette*, undated clipping, NCM library/archives.

80. "Letters to the editor," signed Nathan B. Golub, *Courier Times*, 23 Feb 1982. For further details, see letter, Larry E. Tise, executive director PA Historical and Museum Commission, to Golub, 16 Nov 1981, NCM library/archives; Betty Burke, "Will sewer line cross at Crossing park?" *The Advance of Bucks County*, 25 Feb 1982.

81. Letter, Mrs. Walter C. Hahn, Chairman, Bucks County Conservation Alliance, to Larry Tise, 18 March 1962, NCM library/archives; Virginia Forrest to Wilson Oberdorfer, 28 April 1982, NCM library/archives; Forrest to Tise, 5 June 1982, NCM library/archives; Beatrice Johnson, "Penn Oaks sewage system unsettled," *Courier Times*, 6 June 1982; C.T. Beechwood, P.E., to Forrest, 11 June 1982.

82. "Canal victim's widow files suit," *New Hope Gazette*, 23 March 1978; Dennis O'Brien, "Chez Odette canal death trial heard by county jury," *Intelligencer*, 9 March 1982; Ann W. O'Neill, "Bucks jury awards family $1.05 million in man's drowning," *Philadelphia Inquirer*, 17 March 1982; Patrick Jardel, "Barricade is installed at site of drownings," *New Hope Gazette*, 3 Nov 1983; James Hilferty, "Savitch accident speeds up canal renovation," *Philadelphia Inquirer*, 18 April 1984; conversations, author with Superintendent Hoehn.

83. Debra Cassens Moss, "Savitch Settlement," *ABA Journal*, 1 June 1988; "New barrier where Savitch died leaves most of canal unguarded," *Lehigh Valley Business Digest*, Oct 1984; conversations, author with Superintendent Hoehn.

84. Donald E. Wolf, "Commonwealth Court says state to blame for canal death," *Intelligencer/ Montgomery County Record*, 9 Sept 1984.

85. "New Barrier"; Peter J. Leffler, "A year later, Barrier guards site where Ms. Savitch drowned," *Intelligencer*, 23 Oct 1984; "Barriers are up," *New Hope Gazette*, 25 Oct 1984; conversations, author with Superintendent Hoehn.

86. Legend under photograph, "Early Morning Plunge," Easton *Express*, 16 Feb 1976.

87. Bruce Kaleita, "Workers repair canal washout after rescue of 4,500 fish," *Intelligencer*, 7 Aug 1975.

88. Legend partially torn in clipping file, Easton *Express* 10 May 1977.

89. "Horse saved from burial in canal," series of 10 photos, *New Hope Gazette*, 3 Aug 1978.

90. "Car hits bridge, lands in canal," *Intelligencer*, 29 Aug 1979.

91. Peg Rhodin, "Easton canal death ruled homicide," *The Morning Call*, 23 Oct 1979; "Murder victim was assigned to NADC," 24 Oct 1979; Peg Rhodin and Rick Heidorn, Jr., "Easton victim was California resident," *The Morning Call*, 24 Oct 1979; "Two are held in murder of engineer visiting NADC," *Intelligencer*, 8 Nov 1979; Emily Lounsberry, "Engineer was alive in trunk before death," *Intelligencer*, 20 Nov 1979; Lounsberry, "Two men plead guilty to beating engineer to death in Warrington," *Intelligencer*, 25 March 1980.

92. Janet E. Pinkerton, "Driver killed in canal plunge," *Intelligencer*, 2 Feb 1990; Donna M. Amici, "Man in canal was drowning victim," *Intelligencer*, 4 Feb 1990; Harold Shelly, "Erwinna man dies when car careens into canal," *Delaware Valley News*, 8 Feb 1990.

93. Hank Walther, "Dogged pursuit saves canine from icy death," *The Times*, 28 Feb 1993.

94. "Driver pulled from canal," *Courier Times*, 13 June 1995.

Notes to Chapter Ten

1. Julia McDonnell, "The canal's new boss, Meet Ken Lewis, new Delaware Canal State Park superintendent," *New Hope Gazette*, 24 May 1990.

2. Announced at DCSP Advisory Committee meeting, 17 Sept 1992.

3. "Smooth sailing," *New Hope Gazette,* Nov 1990; minutes, Advisory Committee, 11 Sept 1991.

4. James E. Stanton, "Wilderness corridor urged for canal, river," *Courier Times*, 16 June 1995; Edward Levenson, "State parks hot spots in Bucks," *Courier Times*, 13 Aug 1996.

5. Lease Agreement, 7 Dec 1954, between Commonwealth of Pennsylvania and the Borough of Bristol.

6. "Subject: Ownership of Delaware Canal in Bristol Roosevelt State Park,... From William W. Shakely, Director, Bureau of Legal Services (DER)...," 9 Aug 1988.

7. Citizen group seeking total restoration of piped-in canal," *Bristol Pilot*, 4 May 1989; James E. Stanton, "Advocate wants Delaware Canal navigable," *Intelligencer/Record*, 15 June 1989; Stanton, "Plan under fire, Advocate wants canal navigable," *Courier Times*, 14 June 1989; "PUBLIC FORUM," Advisory Committee minutes, 13 June 1989.

8. Carol Meyer, "Delaware Canal holds part of Bristol's early heritage: Group says Lower Bucks on short end of stick for restoration funds," *Bristol Pilot*, March 22, 1990; James E. Stanton, "Getting canal funds to flow south," *Courier-Times*, 9 July 1990; Stanton, "Officials seek ideas for canal," *Courier Times*, 19 Nov 1990; Stanton, "Delaware Canal may get benefit of historic status," *Courier Times*, 12 June 1992; Stanton, "Museum site opposed by L. Bucks officials," *Courier Times*, 15 Aug 1992; "L. Bucks seeks more canal representation," *Intelligencer*, 8 July 1990; John Worthington, "Protest highlights Canal woes: Activist says lower end is being ignored," *Bristol Pilot*, 12 July 1990; your author has been a member and on occasions a board member of both organizations during most of their existence and is well aware of the efforts made and how little was received from governmental sources by these organizations.

9. William Pezza to Willis Rivinus, Chairman, National Heritage Corridor Commission, 27 Nov 1990; "Local History Projects Proposal," on stationary of Association for the Restoration and Preservation of the Delaware Canal, Contact person listed, Elaine Beck; Marc Freeman, "Channeling an old canal's economic power," *Philadelphia Inquirer*, 11 July 1991; Erin Einhorn, "Along canal, renovation and disarray," *Philadelphia Inquirer*, North Neighbors section, 21 Oct 1996; "Congratulations to Joe Sagolla...," *Canal News*, summer 1991.

10. For the Black Bass hotel and the lawsuit, see David J. Gilmartin, "Historic hotel threatened by canal wall, lawsuit says," *Intelligencer*, 11 April 1990; Lacy McCrary, "Innkeeper seeks to save a landmark," *Philadelphia Inquirer*, 20 April 1990; Robert Benincasa, "Red tape mires repairs to canal in stretch near Lumberville," *Intelligencer*, 29 Sept 1991; Mary Gagnier, "Waterway neighbor wants ditch filled in, beauty restored," *The Morning Call*, 16 Sept 1991; Gagnier, "Down in history, Canal swallowing restaurant, owner blames poor upkeep," *The Morning Call*, 16 Sept 1991.

11. John Worthington, "Activist seeks reason for low water in canal, Despite rain, some parts are dry," *Bristol Pilot*, 22 Aug 1991; Robert Benincasa, "Black Bass Hotel settles for $495,000," *Courier Times*, 12 Nov 1992.

12. Jennifer Lee Reed, "Firm rises to occasion at canal," *Courier Times*, 10 Sept 1992.

13. "Park Manager's Report," Advisory Committee minutes, 1 Dec 1994.

14. James E. Stanton, "Canal walkway to be extended," *Courier Times*, 27 Oct 1992; Jim Provance, "Canal towpath gets $304,000 to become walkway," *Courier Times*, 24 Jan 1993.

15. "New name proposed for River Road," *Intelligencer*, 17 June 1992; Dominic DeFino, "Protests greet plan to replace bridge, UBE residents oppose straightening road over canal," *Delaware Valley News*, 11 July 1991; "Canal bridge in Bridgeton reviewed," *Intelligencer*, 7 July 1992; "Delaware River Scenic Drive," *Canal News*, spring 1993; minutes, Delaware Canal State Park Advisory Committee, 4 June 1992; "Scenic Highway—Routes 32 and 611," "Upper Black Eddy Bridge," Advisory Committee minutes, 4 June 1992; "Delaware River Scenic Drive," *Canal News*, spring 1993.

16. Lacy McCrary, "Hopes for a long and winding road," *Inquirer* (Suburban/Metro, Bucks. Chester. Delaware. Montgomery Edition) 24 Sept 1992.

17. "River Road Endangered," *Canal News*, winter 1995.

18. Betty Orlemann, "DER Wins Bridge Lawsuit," *Canal News*, spring 1992.

19. Harold Shelly, "Trash truck dumps load into canal, *Delaware Valley News*, 14 Dec 1989; "Precarious perch," *Intelligencer*, 10 Dec 1989; James E. Stanton, "Dumping of liquid angers canal park superintendent," *Intelligencer*, 16 Sept 1990; Will Scheihing, "100,000 gallons of raw sewage spills into canal," *Easton Express*, 25 July 1990; Janet E. Pinkerton, "Driver killed in canal plunge," *Intelligencer*, 2 Feb 1990; Advisory Committee minutes, 19 Dec 1989.

20. Julie A. Knipe, "Rodents are becoming regulars at some local eateries by canal," *Courier Times*, 28 Oct 1992.

21. Minutes, DCST Advisory Committee, 19 Dec 1989, 13 March 1990; David Lang, Bureau Chief, Division of Park and Resource Planning to Richard Hassell, U.S. Army Corps of Engineers, Philadelphia District, nd, National Canal Museum library/archives.

22. Harold Shelly, "Heavy rains bring millions in damage to Bucks," *Doylestown Patriot*, 28 Sept 1989.

23. "Superintendents's Report," *Canal News*, fall 1992.

24. Minutes, DCSP Advisory Committee, 12 June 1990; "Dredge Progress," *Canal News,* fall 1992.

25. Kathleen Fratti, "State ordered to 'cease and desist' canal dredging," *Yardley News*, 23 June 1993.

26. "Park Manager's Report," *Canal News*, spring 1994.

27. Letter, Eugene J. Comoss, P.E., Chief, Division of Park Maintenance, to author, 24 July 1992.

28. Robert A. Farley, "The deteriorating Delaware Canal is a testament to red tape," *Courier Times,* 13 June 1994. The almost identical article is found as "Bureaucracy stems flow of Delaware Canal Work," in the *Intelligencer/Record*, 13 June 1994.

29. "Clean Out the Process, Canal isn't the only thing that needs dredging," *Canal News*, fall 1993.

30. Jennifer Lea Reed, "A little Dutch boy can't plug this leak," *Courier Times*, 9 Sept 1993; Advisory Committee minutes, 17 March 1994.

31. "Ken Lewis, "Park Manager's Report," *Canal News*, fall 1994; information furnished to Advisory Committee by Ken Lewis at meeting.

32. Don't Sleep Here, Red-Bellied Turtle!" an article prepared by Park Educator Bonnie Tobin, *Canal News,* winter 1997; Milt Krugman, "Turtle winning race against endangerment: The redbelly has been pumped up to the threatened species list," *Courier Times*, 5 May 1997; James E. Stanton, "Mandate to red-bellied turtles: Take a Walk," *Courier Times*, 19 Oct 1997; "Red-bellied turtle drives canal maintenance," *Yardley News*," 23 Oct 1997; Advisory Committee minutes, 15 Sept 1994.

33. Petra Chesner Schlatter, " 'legalese' holds up canal dredging, project may not begin until summer," *Yardley News,* 9 April 1998.

34. Advisory Committee minutes, 15 Sept 1994, 1 Dec 1994; James E. Stanton, "After swamp of red tape dredge returns to canal," *Courier Times*, 19 Oct 1994.

35. "Canal support formed," *New Hope Gazette*, 2 Dec 1982.

36. Kathleen Fratti, "Yardley Council leader named canal director," *Yardley News*, 25 April 1991; "Friends of the Canal hire a new executive director," *Intelligencer*, 10 May 1991; "And it all began on a dark and rainy night in October. . .," *Canal News*, fall 1992.

37. "Friends to Paint Canal bridges," *Delaware Valley News*, 19 May 1983; Florence Schaffhausen, "Canal Friends doing the job," *Intelligencer*, 28 June 1983.

38. For example, see "Canal Friends Slate Riegelsville Program," *Delaware Valley News*, 10 Aug 1989; "The Travelling Canal Show," *Canal News*, winter 1992–1993.

39. Lenoir W. Fawthrop, DVPA treasurer, to "Ted" Schneider, Friends' treasurer, in Orlemann Collections, DVPA Folder.

40. "And it all began on a dark and rainy night in October …," *Canal News*, fall 1992; Delaware Canal Master Plan: A Plan and Program To Preserve and Improve The Delaware Canal And Roosevelt State Park July 1987, produced by Friends of the Delaware Canal"; Proposal for a Master Plan for The Delaware Canal, Submitted by Graham Kinsman and Betty Orlemann by Request of State Representative James C. Greenwood," [1985].

41. Betty Orlemann, "Friends of the Canal Feted at White House," *The News* (Frenchtown), 27 July 1989; "Friends of Canal take 'Pride in PA' award," *New Hope Gazette*, 15 Dec 1988; James E. Stanton, "3rd time charmed for canal Friends," *Courier Times*, 5 Dec 1990; "The Friends 'Take Pride in Pennsylvania'," *Canal News*, winter 1991–92, spring 1992.

42. "Suggested Zoning Provisions to Protect and Enhance the Delaware Canal Corridor," (draft) from Urban Research and Development Corporation, dated 11 Nov 1989; Advisory Committee minutes, 19 Dec 1989; conversation with Susan Taylor, 23 April 2001.

43. Friends of the Delaware Canal, "Highlights of 1989," 19 Dec 1989, note McLean Foundation grant for $17,000; Advisory Committee minutes, 12 June 1990.

44. "Park Manager's Report," *Canal News*, winter 1992–1993.

45. "Watch for the Signs!" *Canal News*, winter 1995; conversation with Susan Taylor, 2001.

46. "$100,000 Raised—It's Time to Buy the Dredge," *Canal News*, winter 1991–92, spring 1992; "Presentation of Check," Advisory Committee minutes, 21 Nov 1991; "Dredge Progress," *Canal News*, fall 1992.

47. Betty Orlemann, "The Dredge has a Name—Zabel Belle: Here's Why," *Canal News*, spring 1993; Bridget Wingert, "Canal dredge dedicated in honor of Yardley resident," *Yardley News*, 17 Dec 1992.

48. James E. Stanton, "Canal panel gets New hope site," *Courier Times*, 13 June 1990; data prepared by Friends for legislator's meeting, 15 Sept 1994.

49. "Lockhouse Restoration Process to Begin," *Canal News*, summer 1993; "News at the Lockhouse," *Canal News*, winter 1993; "Director's Report," Advisory Committee minutes, 12 June 1990; Kay Lazar, "New dreams of renovation pursued for historical Locktender's House," *Philadelphia Inquirer*, Neighbors, Bucks County edition, 11 March 1993; "Restoration is underway at Locktender's House," *Yardley News*, 5 Jan 1994; James E. Stanton, "Locktender's home restored to its period," *Courier Times*, 12 Jan 1994.

50. James E. Stanton, "Picture-perfect canal: Murals tell history of 60-mile county waterway," *Courier Times*, 24 June 1992; "Murals brighten walls of fire scene," *Intelligencer*, 3 July 1992; "Out of the Ashes," *Canal News*, summer 1992.

51. "Lockhouse Restoration Process to Begin," *Canal News*, summer 1993; "Media Celebrities," *Canal News*, spring 1994; "The Carpenters and Plasterers Are Coming," *Canal News,* winter 1994–1995; "Paint That Trim, Mix That Plaster," *Canal News*, winter, 1994–1995; "Park Manager's Report," "Lockhouse Restoration Complete: 'Life at the Lock' Exhibit Installed," *Canal News*, fall 1995; "It's Official—The Lockhouse is Open," *Canal News*, winter 1995.

52. *Canal News,* summer 1999.

53. "Be a Canal Tender," *Canal News*, summer 1993; "Canal Tenders Start Duties," *Canal News*, fall 1993.

54. "Friends Receive Oral History Grant," *Canal News*, winter 1995.

55. "Bringing Back the Camelback," *Canal News*, summer 1994; additional details provided by Susan Taylor, Oct 2001.

56. James E. Stanton, "A walk through three centuries," *Courier Times*, 21 Sept 1997.

57. Insert announcement in *Canal News*, 1996; "Yardley summer camp explores historic Delaware Canal," *Yardley News*, 24 April 1997; "Canal Camp," *Canal News*, summer 1997; "Canal Camp," *Canal News*, summer 1998; "Yardley summer camp to explore the Canal," *Yardley News*, 30 April 1998.

58. Agenda of meeting and notes on meeting, furnished by Friends; Advisory Committee minutes, 1 Dec 1994; "Legislators Form Canal Caucus," *Canal News*, spring 1995: "Canal Caucus Mission," *Canal News*, fall 1995; information furnished by Betty Orlemann and Susan Taylor.

59. Mimi Reimel, "200 Pitch In To Help Clean Canal Out," *Courier Times*, 30 June 1969; "Delaware Canal to get a cleaning," *Courier Times*, 19 April 1990.

60. Karen Baldwin, "Mobilization begins for battle on canal," *Courier Times*, 31 March 1970; Milt Krugman, "Friends of canal plan a day of spring cleaning," *Courier Times*, 15 April 1994; "Canal Clean-up Day," *Canal News*, spring 1996; "Volunteers to clean-up along Delaware Canal," *Yardley News*, 18 April 1996.

61. Betty Orlemann, "Towpath looks more like a garbage dump," *Delaware Valley News*, 30 April 1992.

62. John Worthington, "Motorcycle group plans to help restore Canal," *Bristol Pilot,* 25 April 1991; Glenn Berkey, "Pitching in: Motorcyclists, others go to work by Delaware Canal," *Philadelphia Inquirer*, 6 June 1991; Worthington, "Bikers brave the heat to clear canal: Nearly 100 volunteers come out to work," *Bristol Pilot*, 6 June 1991; Worthington, "Motorcycle group returns to finish canal landscaping," *Bristol Pilot*, 7 Nov 1991.

63. James R. Grace, Dep. Sect. for Resources Management to Assemblyman James L. Wright, Jr., 24 Nov 1987.

64. Advisory Committee minutes, 29 March 1988, 19 Nov 1989, 11 Dec 1990; Mike Frassinelli, "Historian says corridor will 'leave a big footprint'," *The Morning Call*, 9 March 1996.

65. Advisory Committee minutes, 11 Sept 1991. Advisory Committee additional minutes provide documentation for this statement.

66. Advisory Committee minutes, 4 June 1992.

67. Advisory Committee minutes, 20 Sept 1988; Michelle Passman, "State Changes Name of Delaware Canal State Park," *The News* (Frenchtown), 1 April 1989; Barbara Birt, "Park to be renamed for Delaware Canal," *Intelligencer*, 2 April 1989; "The Canal Name Change is Official," *Canal News*, postmarked 15 May 1989.

68. Will Scheihing, "This land is my land: Not so fast, Pennsylvania says to canalside landowners," *Express-Times*, 10 March 1994; editorial, "Canal dispute presents a positive opportunity," also editorial "Hope already is flowing" and copy of letter, Smith to Dear Mr. and Mrs. X, *Bucks County Courier Times*, 2 Dec 1993.

69. Letter from Susan Taylor to Editor, *Bucks County Courier Times*, 5 Dec 1993.

70. Doug Donovan, "Canal issue is on path to amicable resolution," *Inquirer*, 7 April 1994, BC3.S; Jodi Spiegel Arthur, "Peace Center wades into canal conflict," *Courier Times*, 9 May 1994.

71. Advisory Committee minutes, 22 March 2001.

72. Advisory Committee minutes, 22 March 2001.

73. Congressional Record, Vol 134, No. 125, Sept 1988; 100th Congress, 2d Session HR 3957; In the Senate of the United States, September 14 (legislative day September 7), 1988, Received; read twice and referred to the Committee on Energy and Natural Resources.

74. Friends of the Delaware Canal, "Report to the Canal Advisory Committee, 12 June 1990; Michele Passman, "Canal becomes 'national trail'," *The News* (Frenchtown), 28 June 1990; James E. Stanton, "Designation sought for canal path," *Intelligencer*, 31 Jan 1990; Stanton, "Towpath on track for U.S. list," *Courier Times*, 31 Jan 1990; "Delaware Canal dedicated as a national Heritage Trail," *The Beacon*, 27 June 1990; "Canal towpath recognized as Heritage Trail," *New Hope Gazette*, 29 June 1990; legend under photograph, "Trail of success," *Courier Times*, 24 June 1990.

75. J. Steven Humphrey, Chair, Delaware Canal State Park Advisory Committee Board, to Congressman Kostmayer, Dec 1988; duplicate to Congressman Ritter, same text, same date, Advisory Committee minutes, 13 Dec 1988.

76. "Progress Report," Corridor Commission over the signature of Willis M. Rivinus, Chairman, 31 Dec 1990.

77. Delaware & Lehigh Canal National Heritage Corridor and State Heritage Park Management Action Plan, 57–70.

78. Broadside, "Delaware & Lehigh Navigation Canal National Heritage Corridor," nd.

79. Corridor Commission minutes, 19 April 1990.

80. Various issues of *The D & L Interpreter: A Monthly Newsletter About What's Happening Along the … Corridor.*

81. "Progress Report," Corridor Commission dated 31 Dec 1990; "The Master Action Plan is Completed," *Along the Corridor,* Feb 1994, 2; Stanton, "Hiking Through History," *Courier Times*, 13 June 1994.

82. Edward Levenson, "Canal to get $157.6 million to lure tourists," *Courier Times* 18 April 1993; "Have You Heard This One?" *Canal News*, fall 1993.

83. James E. Stanton, "Millions of dollars earmarked for canal improvements," *Courier Times*, 13 June 1994.

84. *Along the Corridor*, Feb 1994, 1.

85. M. Floyd Hall, "Study to plan for tourism in southern Bucks portion of canal heritage corridor," *The Morning Call*, 7 July 1994; Pennsylvania Historical and Museum Commission News Release, 57–94, "PHMC Announces Aggressive Heritage Tourism Program with National Trust."

86. Mike Frassinelli, "Historian says corridor will 'leave a big footprint'," *The Morning Call*, 9 March 1996; "Governor lauds Oliver as first DCNR Secretary is sworn in," Update, I (44), (Dec 1, 1995), 2.

87. *The D & L Trail Workbook,* prepared for the Delaware and Lehigh Navigation Canal National Heritage Corridor Commission by the Rivers, Trails and Conservation Assistance Program Chesapeake System Support Office, National Park Service; James E. Stanton, "Global river team floats trail link between Pa., N.J.," *Courier Times*, 17 Oct 1996. Stanton, "Townships are hot on the trail of historic canal," *Courier Times*, 4 June 1998.

88. Jeff Werner, "Morrisville, Heritage Trail idea explored," *Yardley News*, 21 Aug 1997; Werner, "Heritage Trail on the move in Morrisville," *Yardley News*, 25 Sept 1997.

89. "Look what seed money has grown into," guest editorial by W. Paul Ferguson in *Courier Times*, 31 March 1998.

90. James E. Stanton, "Specter pushes for $20 million in funds for heritage trail," *Courier Times*, 8 Aug 1997.

91. James E. Stanton, "Platform to give rivergazers a rise," *Courier Times*, 17 Nov 1997.

92. "Volunteer cooperation sought to maintain canal park," *Yardley News*, 7 June 1990; "$2 million in repairs planned," *Intelligencer*, 18 July 1990; letter, Betty Barr, President, to Members of the friends of the Delaware Canal, 14 Nov 1980.

93. Tata Watras, "Rebuilding a historic link to the past: Durham aqueduct gets $900G facelift," *Delaware Valley News*, 18 July 1991; Hal Marcovitz, "Tohickon Aqueduct: a leaky weak link in canal," *The Morning Call*, 26 May 1993; Advisory Committee minutes, 22 March 2001; conversation with Susan Taylor, 23 April 2001.

94. "State Parks 2000" questionnaire circulated 1988–1989; *Pennsylvania State Parks 2000: Directions for the Next Century*, published Feb 92, pp 30–32; "State Parks, 2000: Directions for the Next Century," *Canal News*, summer 1992.

95. "New State Department," in Park Manager's Report, *Canal News*, fall 1995.

96. Leo Shane, "$7M rehab brightens canal's future," *Courier Times*, 1 Aug 1997; Bridget Wingert, "Improvements ahead for historic Delaware Canal: State commits $7.6 million to major revitalization effort," *Yardley News*, 7 Aug 1997; Advisory Committee minutes, 31 July 1997.

97. Christopher Elser, "Delaware Canal to get master plan," *The Morning Call*, 7 April 1997; Madeleine Mathias, "State approves $7.6 million for Easton museum," *The Morning Call*, 8 Sept 1997; Beth W. Orenstein, "Delaware Canal restoration still a political hot potato," *Eastern Pennsylvania Business Journal*, 21–27 April 1997.

98. Delaware Canal State Park: Opportunities for the Future, July 1997, 4.

99. Delaware Canal State Park: Opportunities for the Future, July 1997, 3.

100. Delaware Canal State Park: Opportunities for the Future, July 1997, 4.

101. "Canal Friends who fought are not done yet," Letters to the Gazette, from Willis M. Rivinus, *New Hope Gazette*, 15 May 1997.

102. Delaware Canal State Park: Opportunities for the Future, July 1997, 5-6; "Delaware Canal State Park Overview," nd.

103. Beth E. Fand, "New Hope bargeman replaced," *Times* (Trenton), 2 March 1997; Bridget Wingert, "State awards barge concession to new operators: Managers promise enhanced experience at canal landmark," *Yardley News*; James E. Stanton, "Mule barge attraction gets new operator," *Courier Times*, 9 Dec 1997; Bill Yoder, "History or Gossip? A bit of whimsy," *Canal Currents*, No. 36, autumn 1976, 11; James E. Wilkerson, "Barge getting facelift," *Courier Times*, 26 Jan 1998; Elser, "Delaware Canal to get master plan"; announcements at Delaware Canal State Park Advisory Committee meeting, 26 March 1998.

104. Madeleine Mathias, "State approves $7.6 million for Easton Museum," *The Morning Call*, 8 Sept 1998; "National Canal Museum Opens June 14th," *Canal News*, summer 1996.

105. Advisory Committee minutes, 22 March 2001.

106. Anthony Stitt, "Canal dredging—Flood relief or impending disaster?" *Courier Times*, 12 Aug 1998; Amy Neff Roth, "Dig It," *Courier Times*, 26 Aug 1998; Roth, "Dredging of canal underway," *Courier Times*, 2 Sept 1998; George Robinson, "'The Big Dig' begins in Yardley," *Yardley News*, 10 Sept 1998.

107. Amy Neff Roth, "Bottom of solution," *Courier Times*, 2 Oct 1998; "Enhancement project begins along towpath," *Yardley News*, 2 Sept 1999; interview with Ken Lewis, 16 June 2000.

108. Amy Neff Roth, "Delaware River pump to keep canal watered," *Courier Times*, 3 Sept 1998; interview with Ken Lewis, 22 June 2000.

109. "Annual Report 1997," The Pennsylvania Department of Conservation and Natural Resources, 15; "Hendrick Island joins Delaware Canal State Park," *Yardley News*, 9 Jan 1997; "Delaware River islands eyed by state for protection," *Yardley News*, 8 Jan 1998; Christina Hall, "Frog, Rock, Laughly's add to Delaware Canal park," *Courier Times*, 26 June 1998.

110. "Delaware Canal State Park Private investment Plan," 9 Feb 1998; Advisory Committee minutes, 26 March 1998.

111. Advisory Committee minutes, 22 March 2001.

112. James E. Stanton, "Canal gates forced open; flood fears eased in area," *Courier Times*, 24 Jan 1996; Joel Bewley, "Flood damage to canal at $1.7 M," *Times* (Trenton), 27 Jan 1996; No lifeline for Bucks," *Courier Times*, 22 Jan 1996; Ken Lewis, "Park Manager's Report: Chronology of the Flood of '96," *Canal News*, winter 1995; Stanton, "Canal's flood damage tallies $14 million," *Courier Times*, 7 April 1996.

113. James E. Stanton,"New flood victim: Canal aqueduct," *Courier Times*, 20 June 1996; Dave Sommers, "Creek erosion creates gasoline tank threat," *Courier Times*, 20 June 1996; Jeff Werner, "Yardley shaken by deadly storm," *Yardley News*, 20 June 1996; Werner, "Greenwood surveys damage; counts the toll," *Yardley News*, 27 June 1996; Stanton, "Towns must attack flooding on regional basis," *Courier Times*, 30 Oct 1996; Ken Lewis, "Park Manager's Report," *Canal News*, autumn 1996.

114. Jolyn Resnick, "Heavy rains dam up repair plans along canal," *The Morning Call*, 28 Aug 1996.

115. James E. Stanton, "Canal repairs seen as crucial to flood control," *Courier Times*, 10 Jan 1997.

116. Walter F. Naedele, "Innkeepers cry foul over river road closure," *Inquirer*, North Neighbors edition, 27 March 1996.

117. Christina Hall, " 'Green slime' on canal is nothing to worry about," *Courier Times*, 7 Aug 1997; James E. Stanton, "Seniors complain about canal's condition," *Courier Times*, 21 Aug 1997; for duckweed, see Ken Lewis "Duckweed: A Reason to Rejoice or to Worry?" *Canal News*, winter 1991–1992.

118. George Mattaar, "Spill kills hundreds of fish," *Courier Times*, 14 Jan 1998; David Sommers, "Fishermen warned away from spill site," *Courier Times*, 15 Jan 1998; Sommers, "Fish kill total at 5,000 after second spill," *Courier Times*, 10 Feb 1998.

119. Conversation with Susan Taylor, 23 April 2001.

120. Thomas Zolper, "Residents say canal draining left fish high and dry," *Courier Times*, 26 Sept 1990; James E. Stanton, "Dead fish stinking up Delaware Canal," *Courier Times*, 4 Aug 1993; Milt Krugman, "It's another life on the line: Boys try to save fish in canal," *Courier Times*, 27 Oct 1994.

121. Milt Krugman, "Bringing a barge up from the deep," *Courier Times*, 19 April 1994; James E. Stanton, "Canal's barge 'graveyard' revealed," *Courier Times*, 16 May 1996; Stanton, "Unearthing treasures from the Delaware Canal," *Courier Times*, 22 May 1996; "Canal Boat Graveyard to Be Surveyed and Photographed," *Canal News*, summer 1996; Stanton, "Dredging? No planks," *Courier Times*, 19 Jan 1998; Stanton, "Canal barge wrecks can stay put," *Courier Times*, 29 Jan 1998; "Canal Boat Remains Recorded," *Canal News*, summer 1998.

122. Letter, Parthenia M. Carabelli to editor, *Yardley News*, 22 Jan 1998; "Meeting to air canal concerns," *Yardley News*, 30 April 1998; interview with Ken Lewis, 16 June 2000.

123. Mark E. Jolly, "Unhappy Trails," *Courier Times*, Bucks section, 28 March 2000.

124. Joan Hellyer, "Owners complain about flooding," *Courier Times*, 9 May 2000.

125. Rick Martinez, "Plan reconnects, reroutes severed canal," *Courier Times*, 4 April 2000.

126. Letter to Editor, Narman Emslie, *Yardley News*, 13 April 2000.

127. "1,400 obstructions along canal's path," *Courier Times*, 8 May 2001.

128. Frank E. Stanton, "For new supervisor, canal work is a family affair," *Intelligencer*, 8 April 1992; "Personality Profile— Frank Swope," *Canal News*, summer 1992; Walter F. Nardele, "He Helps restore life to family's livelihood," *Inquirer*, Suburban/Metro edition, 26 Nov 1994; Stanton, "Swope, one of last canal boatmen, dies," *Courier Times*, 15 Aug 1995.

129. "In Memoriam Virginia Forrest," *Canal News*, summer 1991; Ken Lewis, "Superintendent's Report," *Canal News*, winter 1991–1992.

130. Amy Neff Roth, "Strong wills keep the canal running," *Courier Times*, Bucks section, 18 Jan 2000; Kate Mulligan, *Canal Parks and Museums and Characters of the Mid-Atlantic* (Washington, DC: Wakefield Press, 1999), 24.

131. "At canal site, dream becomes reality," *Bristol Express*, 13 Nov 1997; "Look what seed money has grown into," guest editorial by W. Paul Ferguson in *Courier Times*, 31 March 1998; "Bristol Lagoon Project Celebrates Unprecedented Response," *Along the Corridor*, IV (spring 1998), 4.

132. Stanton, "Upstream leak empties Bristol new lagoon," *Courier Times*, 4 Dec 1997; letter, Edna Roth to *Courier Times*, 18 Dec 1997.

133. Stephanie A. Stanley, "Tribute has early friends of canal feeling like strangers," *Philadelphia Inquirer*, 31 Oct 1997; Edna Roth, "Guest opinion, Give credit—and respect—where due for canal project," *Courier Times*, 2 Dec 1997.

134. Ibid.

135. Dave Sommers, "Lagoon bans fishing, swimming," *Courier Times*, 3 June 1998; Sommers, "Residents divided over Grundy Lagoon Activities," *Courier Times*, 8 June 1998.

136. "Partnerships = Water," *Canal News*, spring 1998; "Rep. Conti Aids Uhlerstown Lock," *Canal News*, summer 1997.

137. Naomi L. Jenkins, "Kids learn in a science 'classroom' without walls," *Courier Times*, 2 April 1996; Jenkins, "Clogged canal aids students, *Courier Times*, 22 April 1996; Jenkins, "Kids plunge into canal project," *Courier Times*, 24 April 1996; Kathy Boccella, "A big college boost for 47 area high school students," *Philadelphia Inquirer*, North Neighbors edition, 7 May 1996; James E. Stanton, "Canal stressed to global river group," *Courier Times*, 29 Oct 1996.

138. Stanton, "Students launch canal project," *Courier Times*, 17 Jan 1997.

139. Stanton, "Groups get grants for river work," *Courier Times*, 19 May 1998.

140. Sonya Beard, "Canal Kids won't give up an inch in appealing road plan," *Courier Times*, 9 June 1998; Lynn S. Roccograndi to Editor, *Courier Times*, 16 June 1998.

141. "Time to roll up their sleeves," *Courier Times*, 14 April 1999.

142. Lisa Conrey, Guy Risko and the FDR Middle School Flood Kids 2000, "Flood Kids do their part for flood control, do you?" *Courier Times*, 24 Jan 2000; "DCNR salutes conservation volunteer leaders," *Resource* (publication of DCNR), IV (6), May 2000.

143. "Teen's prize is a 4-year $40,000 scholarship to Fisk University," *Courier Times*, 18 May 2001.

144. James E. Stanton, "Millions of dollars earmarked for canal improvement," *Courier Times*, 13 June 1994; Stanton, "Volunteers, not feds, do more for canal," *Courier Times*, 3 Aug 1997.

145. "Park Manager's Report," *Canal News*, autumn 1999; interview with Ken Lewis, 16 June 2000.

146. "Work Begins on Easton's Two Rivers Landing," *Along the Corridor*, I(2) April 1994, 7–8; "At canal site, dream becomes reality," *Bristol Express*, 13 Nov 1997; James E. Stanton, "Millions of dollars earmarked for canal improvement," *Courier Times*, 13 June 1994; Stanton, "Volunteers, not feds, do more for canal."

147. Advisory Committee minutes, 1 Dec 1994; James E. Stanton, "Caucus to push canal protection," *Courier Times*, 6 Feb 1995.

INDEX